REAGAN AND THE WORLD

REAGAN
AND THE WORLD

★ ★ ★ ★ ★ ★ ★ ★ ★ ★ ★ ★ ★ ★ ★

Imperial Policy in the New Cold War

★ ★ ★ ★ ★ ★ ★ ★ ★ ★ ★ ★ ★ ★ ★

Jeff McMahan

Monthly Review Press • New York

Library of Congress Cataloging in Publication Data
McMahan, Jeff.
Reagan and the world.
Includes index.
1. United States—Foreign relations—1981–
2. Reagan, Ronald. I. Title.
E876.M4 1985 327.73 85-5028
ISBN 0-85345-677-1
ISBN 0-85345-678-X (pbk.)

Monthly Review Press
155 West 23rd Street, New York, N.Y. 10011

Manufactured in the United States of America

10 9 8 7 6 5 4 3 2 1

Contents

Preface

This book is a revised and updated version of a book which originally appeared in Great Britain in August 1984. Some of the points I made in the first edition have since appeared in other publications in the United States. Where this has happened I have tried to refer in the endnotes to those works whose arguments have overlapped with mine.

Noam Chomsky and Edward S. Herman each read various chapters of the first draft of the first edition, and Dan Smith read the whole of that draft. All three generously provided many valuable comments, and the book was greatly improved as a result of their help. Karen Judd provided comments on the first edition which have helped me in revising the book for American publication. I alone, of course, remain responsible for the views expressed. I am, finally, deeply grateful to my wife, Sally, who has made numerous helpful comments on various drafts, and who, during the preparation of both editions, not only did most of the typing, but also did virtually everything else that needed doing in order to allow me to complete the writing.

J. M.
December 1984
Cambridge, England

★1★

The Quest for Global Control

Introduction

There are phonograph records purporting to contain "the wit and wisdom of Ronald Reagan" which, when played, are entirely silent. It might be suggested that a book on the Reagan administration's foreign policy should similarly consist only of blank pages. For the notion of a foreign *policy* implies, at a minimum, a clear conception of the ends one aims to achieve, as well as a careful calculation of the means best suited to the achievement of those ends; but the Reagan administration seems to many observers merely to lurch about impulsively at the prodding of its anticommunist instincts. Hence the familiar complaint that the Reagan administration really has no foreign policy.

But a book which suggested that the Reagan administration lacks a foreign policy would, unlike the phonograph record, be a serious distortion. The Reagan administration does have a foreign policy, in the sense that it has a number of complementary aims which are clearly discernible and which it has pursued, if not with intelligence, then at least with considerable consistency and vigor. It has been engaged in a systematic effort to shape the world in a certain way. Yet for the most part, and especially within the United States itself, the consistency and coherence of this effort have been little understood—as is witnessed by the prevalence of the view that the administration's conduct in foreign affairs has been rather chaotic and desultory. To some extent this is a result of the frequent disarray within the administration caused by factional squabbling over questions of means; but it is also a tribute to the effectiveness with which the administration has propagated the official lies about its aims and activities. For it is primarily the divergence between the administration's *stated* aims and its actual behavior which has given rise to the impression that it is confused, inconsistent, and ineffectual.

The administration's efforts to shape the world according to its own vision have been incompatible with the fundamental principles of international morality which most Americans believe their country represents, and have also caused a vast amount of misery in many parts of the world, at the same time setting the stage for future slaughter on an unprecedented scale. These facts appear, however, to be little appreciated in the United States, where, as both public opinion polls and the recent elections have shown, most people have accepted the Reagan administration's own highly distorted account of its various aims and accomplishments. This book is intended as a modest attempt to explode the claims about American purposes which the administration has fabricated for public consumption, to reveal the real aims underlying its policies, and to lay bare the ugly consequences—both actual and potential—of the workings of those policies throughout the world.

An account of the general aims and ideology of the Reagan administration is presented in the remainder of this chapter. Many of the views expressed are controversial, and may initially seem to be inadequately defended. This is because the evidence for them will be marshaled as the views themselves are developed and elaborated in subsequent chapters. The facts about the administration's conduct which will be detailed in later chapters will both substantiate and be explained by the views expressed in this initial chapter.*

The explanatory principles I shall put forward in this chapter are in general not novel. Indeed most have been thought to provide at least a partial explanation of the behavior of earlier administrations. Those familiar with the postwar history of the United States will, I think, be impressed by the remarkable continuity between the Reagan administration's foreign policy and that of previous administrations. This continuity will probably persist in the future beyond Reagan, assuming that there is one.

The Basic Aims of U.S. Imperial Policy

The Reagan administration came to power with the belief that the American Way of Life was under threat. The wealth and privilege of the people and the power and prestige of the government were being increasingly challenged both by the menace of International Communism and by nationalist movements in the third world (which of course Reagan identified simply as elements in the Communist Conspiracy). The administration's overriding aim has been to meet these threats by regaining the control over world affairs which the United States exercised during the fifteen or

*Factual details about the administration's policies have been drawn from a variety of publicly accessible sources, including the major British and American newspapers. In many cases it has not been possible to substantiate or verify the information contained in these sources, so I have therefore provided extensive references in the endnotes for those who wish to examine my sources. Others may ignore the notes, which contain no substantive material.

twenty years which followed World War II. In short, the comprehensive aim of U.S. policy under Reagan has been to restore the United States to a position of global dominance in the economic, military, political, and ideological spheres.

A primary obstacle to this effort has of course been the Soviet Union, whose expanded military capabilities have for some years made the assertion of U.S. control in various parts of the world increasingly risky. Yet, despite these risks, the Reagan administration has abandoned the attempt of its predecessors to manage the competition between the United States and the Soviet Union within the framework of détente, and has instead adopted a more aggressive and confrontational posture. Indeed, administration officials believe that it was precisely the willingness of the United States to compromise and exercise restraint during the era of détente that was largely responsible for the erosion of its preeminent position in the world. As Secretary of Defense Caspar Weinberger put it, "If movement from Cold War to détente was progress, then let me say that we can't afford more progress."[1]

The administration's reversion to a policy of Cold War combativeness is manifest, for example, in its evident determination to "win" the arms race and restore U.S. strategic superiority over the Soviet Union. Once what Reagan refers to as the "margin of safety" is restored, the United States will then be better able to "defend its interests" around the world—extending its own influence and "rolling back" that of the Soviet Union—with less risk of being seriously opposed by the Soviets. Surging ahead with the arms race is also an important element in the administration's strategy of economic warfare with the Soviet Union. Forcing the Soviets to divert even more resources to the production of arms will, it is hoped, help to cripple the less robust Soviet economy, ultimately bringing about the collapse of the Soviet system from within.

The Soviet Union is far from being the only obstacle to the reassertion of U.S. global dominance. In order for the United States to maintain and expand its position of economic hegemony, there must be order and cohesion within the international capitalist system, and the United States must be the agency which imposes the necessary regulation.[2] Thus the allies in the developed world must be compelled to line up at attention and salute as the United States reasserts itself as leader of the Free World. And they must also be made to accept a greater share of the economic burdens of maintaining the hegemonic system from which they benefit—in particular, by contributing more to the rearmament effort, and, in compliance with the strategy of economic warfare, by forgoing certain advantageous trade relations with Eastern countries. While the United States has been ominously successful in stimulating a revival of militarism in Japan, the analogous pressure which it has applied to the West European allies has met with some resistance. The need to frighten the European allies into submission constitutes part of the motivation behind the administration's efforts to aggravate Cold War tensions.

The Reagan administration's crusade against the Soviet Union, in the service of which the allies must be mobilized, is to a considerable extent perceived as a battle for control of the third world. The ability of the United States to impose its will on certain third world areas is considered vital to the flourishing of the American Way of Life. For example, the U.S. economy is at present dependent (though not to the extent routinely suggested by the administration) on supplies of oil from the Middle East, and thus the defense of the America Way of Life requires that the United States must have the ability to ensure its own continued access to those supplies. The U.S. economy also depends, though to a somewhat lesser extent, on continued supplies of other resources and raw materials—in particular certain minerals—from various third world areas.[3] These supplies must also be guaranteed.

Perhaps equally important are the need to open up new markets for U.S. products in third world countries and the need to ensure that those countries provide conditions favorable for investment by American businesses. The reason why successive governments have deemed these to be important goals of U.S. foreign policy derives from their belief that the flourishing of the economy and the power of the government are inseparable from the flourishing of business. The reasoning behind this belief is as follows. First, growth is considered to be the measure of a business's success, and therefore general economic growth in the United States is necessary for general prosperity and the maintenance and improvement of the American Way of Life. Increasingly, foreign expansion has been held to be the most lucrative and efficient means of growth. As former Secretary of State Dean Acheson put it, "We cannot expect domestic prosperity without a constantly expanded trade with other nations. . . . To keep prosperity, levels of employment, production and income . . . we shall have to find increasing markets for our production and increasing investment outlets for our capital."[4] This view was widely shared, and U.S. direct private investment abroad increased tenfold from 1946 to 1972.[5]

In order for businesses to expand into the developing world, however, it is important to ensure stability and an otherwise favorable climate of investment. This must be done by the government. If expansion is necessary for general prosperity, then governmental efforts to guarantee favorable conditions for U.S. investment in the third world will serve the national interest. Since the ranks of the government are in any case filled with members of the corporate elite, and since domestic prosperity boosts the power of the government, it has not been difficult to persuade successive U.S. governments to open up and protect marketing and investment opportunities in the third world. (It should be emphasized that the fact that government and business leaders have accepted this pattern of reasoning shows only that it has been influential—*not* that it is true. There are in fact good grounds for skepticism about whether unconstrained foreign expansion is necessary for or even conducive to domestic prosperity.[6])

A concern to protect U.S. business interests has therefore been a primary motivating force behind various instances of U.S. intervention in developing countries in recent years. For example, the interventions in Iran in 1953, in Guatemala in 1954, in Cuba in 1961, in the Dominican Republic in 1965, and in Chile both prior to and throughout the tenure of Salvador Allende can all be explained to a considerable extent in terms of the U.S. government's determination to protect or restore the privileged positions of U.S. businesses in those countries.

The cases of Guatemala and Chile are particularly instructive. In 1951, Jacobo Arbenz Guzmán became president of Guatemala through free and fair elections in which he won almost twice as many votes as all the other candidates combined. Arbenz's principal aim was to implement reforms which would help to remedy the unjust social conditions which were the legacy of earlier dictatorial governments. In 1953, in an effort at land reform, he expropriated some uncultivated lands belonging to United Fruit Company, an American company which was Guatemala's largest landowner, offering as compensation precisely what, for tax purposes, the company had fraudulently declared the lands were worth. The principal beneficiary of Arbenz's scheme was to have been the desperately poor Indian population indigenous to the area. But United Fruit, which had extensive ties to the U.S. government, complained to the Eisenhower administration, which responded by organizing a small force of exile mercenaries under the direction of the Central Intelligence Agency (CIA) for the purpose of overthrowing the Arbenz government. The mercenary force was trained on a United Fruit plantation in Honduras, and, according to a former official of the company, "United Fruit was involved at every level" in the planning and execution of the coup.[7] In June of 1954 the force entered Guatemala and, as U.S. pilots bombed Guatemala City, quickly seized power. A new and appropriately deferential president was selected by the United States and flown to Guatemala City in the American Embassy plane. The new president moved quickly to execute his opponents and crush the fledgling labor movement, "promptly returned United Fruit's expropriated lands, and abolished the tax on interest and dividends to foreign investors, a reform which saved United Fruit about eleven million dollars."[8]

Since the coup, Guatemala has been ruled by a series of military dictators, all of whom have been attentive to the needs of American investors. Writing in 1971, one commentator gave the following description of investment conditions in Guatemala:

> There are no transfer restrictions of any kind on foreign owned assets, dividends and interest. There is no fixed amount of profit which must be reinvested in industry. . . . Today new foreign industries are exempt for ten years from payment of duties on imports of construction materials, factory machinery and equipment, raw materials, and automotive vehicles for industrial use. These industries receive exemption from payment of taxes for the following five years.[9]

The U.S. intervention in Chile was remarkably similar in its motivation and outcome. In 1970, Salvador Allende, a socialist, ran for the presidency in Chile on a platform which, among other things, called for the nationalization of major industries. At that time, crucial sectors of the Chilean economy, including certain major industries, were dominated and controlled by U.S. corporations. The total U.S. direct private investment in the country was $1.1 billion. Hence the largest U.S. investors, such as International Telephone & Telegraph (ITT) and Anaconda Copper, were anxious to prevent Allende's election in order to protect their assets from the threat of nationalization. The CIA conducted a number of dirty and unscrupulous covert operations in an attempt to manipulate the elections, but Allende was elected despite their efforts. Now increasingly desperate, ITT conspired with the CIA (whose former director, John McCone, was then on the board of directors at ITT), the U.S. ambassador to Chile, and with members of the National Security Council and the State Department in an attempt to pressure members of the Chilean congress into preventing Allende's inauguration. When this scheme failed, the U.S. government, in conjunction with ITT, devised a coordinated strategy aimed at provoking a military coup. The strategy combined three elements. The first was to "make the [Chilean] economy scream" (to borrow Nixon's evocative phrase) in order to foment domestic discontent and social unrest. As an ITT memorandum noted at the time, the most "realistic hope among those who want to block Allende is that a swiftly deteriorating economy . . . will touch off a wave of violence resulting in a military coup." The second element in the strategy was to aggravate internal tensions further through various acts of subversion carried out by CIA covert operatives. The third element was to cultivate closer ties with the Chilean military and to strengthen the military's position within the country. This strategy was successful. Because so many sectors of the Chilean economy were controlled by American corporations, and also as a result of policies implemented by Allende's predecessors, the Chilean economy was highly vulnerable to the pressures brought upon it by the U.S. government acting in coordination with a wide range of U.S. businesses. Eventually the economy was brought to its knees and Allende was overthrown and assassinated by the military in 1973.[10]

In 1971, while the assault against the Chilean economy was being conducted, the U.S. secretary of state told executives from ITT and other U.S. corporations that "the Nixon Administration is a business Administration. Its mission is to protect American business."[11] If this was true of the Nixon administration, it is even more true of the Reagan administration. Reagan's ideological affinity with big business is greater than that of any of his recent predecessors, and he has stocked his administration with persons drawn from the highest echelons of the U.S. business community. (Of the top one hundred officials in the administration, about thirty are millionaires and at least twenty-two of these are multimillionaires.[12]) The cases of Guatemala and Chile clearly demonstrate that the protection and promotion of U.S. business interests in developing countries has been an overriding aim in recent U.S. foreign policy, and the Reagan administration has certainly shown no inclination to break with that tradition.

Among the conditions which make investment in developing countries especially lucrative for U.S. businesses, and which the U.S. government therefore aims to provide, are the following: the absence of labor unions (or at least of "politicized" unions—that is, unions which are not controlled by either the government or the management), thus guaranteeing an obedient and disciplined workforce; the absence of environmental protection laws; the absence of health regulations for the workplace; laws permitting the repatriation of profits; the existence of wage controls; the existence of special tax concessions to foreign investors; and the devotion of public money to the creation of an infrastructure suited to the needs of industry. While it is in the interests of foreign investors for these conditions to obtain, it is obviously very much against the interests of the great majority of the domestic population. This helps to explain why the United States maintains cosy relations with so many violently repressive and corrupt dictatorships. For repression is generally necessary in order to maintain conditions of systematic exploitation—or, as they say in Washington, to maintain stability. Thus it is easy to see why U.S. client states in the developing world are so often ruled by persons of the most vicious character: for only persons of this sort would be willing to open their own countries to the ravages of foreign exploitation in exchange for a share of the plunder and a pledge of U.S. support if their rule is threatened. The need to support corrupt and repressive regimes in the interests of "stability" explains why the show of concern for human rights that was maintained by the Carter administration has now been quietly dropped from the agenda.

The pursuit and protection of resources, markets, and investment opportunities are by no means the sole motivating forces behind U.S. efforts to control the third world. While there are other factors, some of which we will examine shortly, which grow indirectly out of these economic concerns, there are still others which are at best only distantly related to economic motivations. Among these latter is a concern for national security. U.S. control of certain third world areas denies control of those areas to the Soviet Union and thus, for various reasons, increases the global strength of the United States vis-à-vis that of its major enemy. Denial of certain areas to the Soviet Union deprives it of economic benefits which could enable it to increase its military strength. Moreover, certain third world resources, such as oil and strategic minerals, are necessary for military production, and therefore it enhances U.S. security to have guaranteed access to those resources and to deny them to the Soviet Union.

U.S. reasons for wanting to control the third world are to some extent circular. Thus third world resources are required in part to guarantee military production, and increased military production is required in part to maintain and expand U.S. control over third world resources. Moreover, in order to defend its interests in various remote third world areas against nationalist challenges or the encroachments of the Soviet Union, the United States must have the ability to "project" its military power into those areas. This requires, among other things, assured access to strategic waterways and the acquisition and maintenance of overseas bases. But these initially instrumental goals eventually come to be seen as ends in themselves. Initially the pursuit of overseas bases is justified by the need to maintain stability, defend friendly countries from communist aggression, and so on—in other words, to subjugate and control the third world; but eventually the need to establish and maintain overseas bases becomes one of the *reasons* for wanting to subjugate and control the third world.

Finally, American leaders have reasons for wanting to control the natural and human resources of the third world which are neither economic nor military in character. Some of these are diplomatic—for example, the desire to have as many nations as possible lined up with the United States against its major enemy. Most, however, are simply manifestations of common foibles in human nature: pride and a concern for national status, the desire for power itself, and sheer great power assertiveness.

The pursuit of U.S. hegemony in the third world imposes four general requirements. The first is of course to preserve those regimes which cater to important American interests. Among the most important of these regimes is the conservative royal family in Saudi Arabia, whom Reagan has pledged to maintain in power regardless of the wishes of the Saudi people: "We will not permit [Saudi Arabia] to be an Iran."[13] The second requirement is to turn out those regimes which are insufficiently deferential, and replace them with ones which have a more judicious appreciation of the importance of U.S. interests. As we have seen, this was the course which the United States followed in Guatemala and Chile, and it is the course which the Reagan administration has followed in Grenada and Nicaragua, though so far without success in the latter.

The third requirement is less obvious, and applies in cases in which there are doubts about whether an undesirable regime can be dislodged. It is to uphold the model of third world development favored by the United States (which emphasizes the importance of foreign investment, export oriented production, etc.) by ensuring that alternative models of economic development do not succeed. If the adoption of policies detrimental to U.S. interests were to prove economically successful, this would set an example which might be imitated elsewhere; therefore countries which adopt such policies must not be allowed to prosper. It is this consideration (along with a determination to revenge the affront to American pride) which has to a considerable extent motivated the policy of economic warfare against Cuba since 1959, and against Vietnam since the U.S. withdrawal. It also influenced the successful effort at the economic strangulation of Chile under Allende. Thus at the time of Allende's election Henry Kissinger expressed his fear that the "contagious example" of Allende's policies would "infect" other countries, both in Latin America and in southern Europe.[14] These countries would have greater immunity to the contagion if Allende's policies were to fail. More recently, the Reagan administration has applied various economic pressures on Nicaragua under the Sandinistas: it has cut economic aid, successfully blocked loans from the World Bank and the Inter-American Development Bank, suspended wheat flour shipments, deprived Nicaragua of the right to sell most of its sugar crop to the United States, and directed the counterrevolutionary forces which it sponsors to focus their energy on acts of economic sabotage. As in the case of Chile, the United States has more than one reason for wanting to cripple the Nicaraguan economy, but certainly one is to deliver a warning to other countries about the consequences of exiting from the Free World and experimenting with alternative modes of economic organization.

The fourth requirement is to support "friendly" regimes and turn out "unfriendly" ones even in countries where U.S. economic and strategic interests are marginal. This is necessary in order to enhance U.S. "credibility"—that is, to demonstrate the willingness and ability of the United States to enforce its will around the globe. This motive has been influential in numerous interventions in the recent past. Thus Richard Barnet has argued that the "primary interest" of American "National-Security Managers" during the war in Vietnam "was to contain China and maintain a worldwide reputation for the United States as a nation willing and able to put a stop to insurgent movements." He also contends that consideration of this exemplary effect was a primary factor in the decision to intervene in Greece in the aftermath of World War II and in the American invasion of Lebanon in 1958.[15]

By contrast with past administrations, however, the Reagan administration is morbidly, even pathologically, preoccupied with its own credibility. This is well illustrated in its policies toward Central America, an area which has become the primary target for U.S. intervention, even though the region is generally barren of important resources and American investments there are relatively insignificant. (Investment in the Caribbean is, however, considerably more extensive; hence Vice-President Bush's statement in December 1982 that "we want to maintain a favorable climate for foreign investment in the Caribbean region, not merely to protect the existing U.S. investment there, but to encourage new investment opportunities in stable, democratic, free-market-oriented countries close to our shores.[16]) El Salvador in particular is a country which, according to one analyst, is "of virtually no inherent strategic or economic importance to the United States."[17] Yet, speaking before a joint session of Congress, Reagan asserted that virtually everything hinges on the ability of the United States to get its way in Central America:

> If Central America were to fall, what would the consequences be for our position in Asia and Europe and for alliances such as NATO? If the United States cannot respond to a threat near our own borders, why should Europeans or Asians believe we are seriously concerned about threats to them? If the Soviets can assume that nothing short of

> an attack on the United States would provoke an American response, which ally, which friend will trust us then? . . . The national security of all the Americas is at stake in Central America. If we cannot defend ourselves [*sic*] there, we cannot expect to prevail elsewhere. Our credibility would collapse, our alliances would crumble and the safety of our homeland would be put at jeopardy.[18]

(It is interesting to compare these remarks with the statement made by Lyndon Johnson eighteen years earlier, in April 1965, that "around the globe from Berlin to Thailand are people whose well being rests in part on the belief that they can count on us if they are attacked. To leave Vietnam to its fate would shake the confidence of all these people in the value of an American commitment and in the value of America's word. The result would be an increased unrest and instability, and even wider war."[19]) Echoing Reagan's calculated hysteria about the global consequences of the "fall" of Central America, Henry Kissinger, chairman of the president's Commission on Central America, claimed, with typical imperial arrogance, that, "if we cannot manage Central America, it will be impossible to convince threatened nations in the Persian Gulf and in other places that we know how to manage the global equilibrium."[20] In effect, the civil war in El Salvador, which has so far taken a toll of 53,000 lives, most of them civilians, and which the Salvadoran government would have lost long ago were it not for large infusions of U.S. military aid, is being prolonged indefinitely in order that the United States can impress the ruling family in Saudi Arabia with its managerial talents.

Credibility is also at stake elsewhere. Thus Reagan defended his decision to keep the marines in Lebanon after the bombing of their quarters in Beirut on the ground that keeping them there "is central to our credibility on a global scale."[21] Those who died during the U.S. invasion of Grenada were also sacrificed in part for the sake of American credibility, as was recognized at the time with some exultation by the conservative columnist George F. Will:

> U.S. soldiers' boot prints on Grenada's soil have done more than the MX will do to make U.S. power credible. . . . If the U.S. were too paralyzed to prevent the planting next door, near vulnerable nations and crucial shipping lanes, of another Soviet outpost with ports and airstrips designed for military use, then nations such as Saudi Arabia would correctly conclude that the United States is irrelevant to their security.[22]

But it is not just the Saudis who should be reassured by this supposed disciplinary action against Cuba and the Soviet Union; for, Will continues, "if Cuba cannot be 'Finlandized' by the United States, Western Europe eventually will be by the Soviet Union."

The most important group needing reassurance about the credibility of U.S. power is, however, the American public. U.S. power will be credible to the Soviets and others only if the American people are seen to be willing to support the exercise of military power abroad; but since the end of the Vietnam war this willingness has been lacking. The reluctance on the part of the American public to support military interventions abroad is often referred to as the "Vietnam syndrome"—a phrase intended to suggest that this reluctance is a pathological condition of sorts. As the recent opposition to the deployment of U.S. troops in Central America has shown, the Vietnam syndrome has, perhaps surprisingly, survived both the Iranian hostage crisis and the Soviet invasion of Afghanistan, and has been a major obstacle to the implementation of the Reagan administration's foreign policy.

The Vietnam syndrome has persisted, not so much because the American people believe that it is generally wrong in principle to intervene militarily in the affairs of other countries (though of course there are people who hold that view), but rather because their experience of the war in Vietnam conditioned them to believe that military intervention is likely to be both prohibitively costly and counterproductive. Thus Robert W. Tucker, who served as an adviser to Reagan during the election campaign, wrote in 1980 that the "one indisputable lesson" to be drawn from the war in Vietnam "is that success is the great solvent of serious public disaffection over foreign policy, and particularly over military intervention. . . . Unless future interventions can find a justification in security interests that the public finds compelling, they will have to enjoy relatively quick and cheap success."[23] This being the case, Tucker might have added that the best way of restoring the American people's confidence in the idea that U.S. military power can be used both efficiently and effectively abroad would be to achieve a quick, decisive, and relatively bloodless military victory. As the Green Berets' director of training recently remarked, "We're a hell of a lot better than the record shows, but we'll never be able to come from under that till we have a victory. We desperately need a victory somewhere."[24] The confrontational policies which the Reagan administration adopted immediately upon entering office led many observers to conclude that it was intent on overcoming the Vietnam syndrome in precisely this way. In Grenada the administration seemed to have found what it was looking for. The invasion was performed primarily for the edification of a domestic audience.

The invasion of Grenada was only one episode in a sustained and unremitting campaign to purge the Vietnam syndrome from the body politic. The administration's propaganda offensive has focused to a considerable extent on the U.S. citizens' increasingly robust sense of their own collective or national self-interest. Hence administration officials have been candid in acknowledging their view that, in the words of Jeane Kirkpatrick, the U.S. ambassador to the United Nations, "the central goal of our foreign policy should be not the moral elevation of other nations, but the preservation of a civilized conception of our own national self-interest."[25] Indeed, in promoting this view, Kirkpatrick has indirectly confirmed one of the claims made earlier in this chapter—namely, that the Reagan administration is guided in its foreign policy by a solicitous concern for the interests of U.S. businesses. For she pours scorn on the belief, which she absurdly attributes to the Carter administration, that "power was to be used to advance moral goals, not strategic or economic ones. Thus sanctions could be employed to punish human-rights violations, but not to aid American business; power could be used 'to the full extent permitted by law' to prevent terrorist actions against Cuba, but not to protect U.S. corporations against expropriation."[26] The implication here is of course that aiding U.S. business and protecting corporate assets are primary goals in the service of which American power should be exercised.

Usually, however, the appeal to the American public has been based on a more judicious mixture of self-interested and moral considerations. Consider, for example, Reagan's widely publicized address to Congress on the subject of Central America. He begins his speech with an ominous account of the threat to U.S. security posed by the problems in the region, noting, for example, the terrifying proximity of Central America to the United States ("El Salvador is nearer to Texas than Texas is to Massachusetts"), and the fact that it borders on the Caribbean, "our lifeline to the outside world."[27] But suddenly the emphasis shifts, and Reagan's audience is treated to some inspiring rhetoric about the U.S. "defense of freedom in the Caribbean Basin" and the growth of democracy in El Salvador. This focus on a careful blend of self-interested and benevolently paternalistic concerns is a recurrent feature of government propaganda.

As always, the ultimate source of the threat to U.S. interests is identified as the Soviet Union. The vision conjured up in government propaganda is one of International Communism, directed by the Soviet Union, creeping closer to American shores via such places as El Salvador and Grenada. In 1976 Reagan defended the war in Vietnam on the ground that it was intended "to counter the master plan of the communists for world conquest, and it's a lot easier and a lot safer to counter it 8,000 miles away than to wait until they land in Long Beach."[28] Later, in 1980, he invoked the same vision to explain events in Central America: "I think we are seeing the application of the domino theory . . . and I think that it's time the people of the United States realize . . . that we're the last domino."[29]

While the invocation of the Soviet threat is primarily useful for stimulating self-interested fears, it also serves to make U.S. military interventions morally more palatable by suggesting that they are simply defensive efforts to protect the weak against Soviet aggression.[30] In 1980 Reagan claimed that "the Soviet Union underlies all the unrest that is going on. If they weren't engaged in this game of dominoes, there wouldn't be any hot spots in the world."[31] For Reagan, a "hot spot" is, effectively, a place where U.S. interests are threatened. Thus his claim serves to legitimate in advance any U.S. intervention, however self-interestedly motivated, as a defense of another country against external aggression or subversion. Reagan has, in effect, resurrected the Johnson Doctrine, which holds, in Johnson's words, that, "in today's world, with enemies of freedom talking about 'wars of national liberation,' the old distinction between 'Civil War' and 'International War' has already lost much of its meaning."[32]

There is a further advantage to be derived from the attempt to portray every instance of domestic insurgency as a case of external communist subversion. The instances of domestic insurgency which the United States opposes constitute an ideological challenge to the United States in that they involve a rejection not only of American hegemony but also of certain American values. If it can be made to seem that this repudiation of the United States and its values is not voluntary, but is instead the result of external coercion, then the ideological challenge can simply be dismissed.[33]

When self-interested considerations have to be dressed up as moral concerns in order to be presentable to the American public, the usual claim is that the United States is concerned with the defense of democracy. Thus one of the principal considerations which is brought forward by the administration to justify its defense of the government in El Salvador against insurgents and its simultaneous support of guerrilla forces which threaten the government of Nicaragua is that the government of El Salvador is supposedly "freely elected," while the Sandinistas for years held power without elections and in the end had elections which the United States denounced as a sham. And one of the many confused rationales that was offered for the invasion of Grenada was that the United States was attempting to "restore democracy" there.

A glance at recent history, however, is sufficient to expose the mendacity of these claims; for the United States has provided repeated testimony to the depth of its commitment to democracy in the third world. In Guatemala, as we have seen, the United States overthrew the democratically elected Arbenz government and installed a military dictatorship in its place, thereby destroying the democratic institutions that had recently begun to develop there. The U.S. Government's respect for democracy was also displayed to advantage in Chile, where the United States was unwilling, as Kissinger remarked at the time, "to stand by and watch a country go Communist due to the irresponsibility of its own people."[34] Earlier, in Vietnam, the United States actively discouraged its client, Ngo Dinh Diem, from holding the elections to which he was committed by the Geneva accords. The reason was obvious; for, as one of Diem's American apologists wrote at the time, "if the elections were held today the overwhelming majority of Vietnamese would vote Communist."[35]

These, of course, were the acts of earlier administrations, but there is no reason whatsoever to believe that the nature of the Reagan administration's commitment to democracy is any different. While for years the administration persistently berated the Sandinistas in Nicaragua for failing to hold elections, it has been perfectly satisfied with the absence of elections in such countries as Chile, South Korea, and Pakistan, or with bogus elections such as those in Turkey, Guatemala, and the Philippines. The dictatorial regimes in countries such as these, which are "friendly to U.S. interests," are usually described by government propagandists as preparing for the transition to democratic rule. They are thus democratic *in principle.* Occasionally, if a country is sufficiently attentive to U.S. interests, it may even be granted honorary democratic status—hence Vice-President Bush's gushing tribute to the Marcos dictatorship in the Philippines: "We love your Government's adherence to democratic principles and to the democratic process."[36] This quotation exemplifies the tendency among administration officials to use the term "democracy" as Orwellian Newspeak for whatever arrangements are most conducive to the flourishing of U.S. interests. Another example was provided by Reagan in a recent speech concerning Central America in which he again stressed that "50 percent of everything we import comes through the Caribbean, the Panama Canal." Hence, he concluded, "it is vital *to us* that democracy be allowed to succeed in these countries."[37]

While genuine democracy in the third world is of little or no interest to the Reagan administration, and may even get in the way of U.S. policy, nevertheless a *show* of commitment to democracy by third world allies of the United States is of enormous importance in reassuring the American people about the legitimacy of the regimes which the administration is supporting. Thus, when conditions are such that an acceptable outcome can be guaranteed (as, for example, when the population is suitably terrorized and opposition candidates do not present themselves for fear of the consequences), the United States encourages its allies to hold elections.[38] The most cleverly managed of the recent U.S.–sponsored elections were those held in El Salvador in 1982 and 1984. These will be discussed in detail in Chapter 5. Elections have also been needed in Haiti in order to squeeze military and economic aid from the Congress. Thus in February 1984 the administration succeeded in pressuring President-for-Life Jean-Claude Duvalier into holding elections for the National Assembly. According to Duvalier, the elections were "free, honest, and democratic": opposition candidates who expressed an interest in running were either beaten and placed under house arrest or were denied reentry into the country after having been forced into exile, and the vote count was given in percentages rather than absolute figures in order to obscure the low level of voter turnout.[39] With an obvious eye on Congress, Duvalier announced that he was "democratizing" Haiti in order to combat "Russian expansionism."[40] The exceptionally crude handling of the elections may jeopardize their effectiveness in generating congressional support, but their purpose was clear enough.

The Reagan administration's claim to be a defender of freedom is rather more convincing than its pretensions as a champion of democracy. For there is a sense in which it does care about freedom. It cares about the freedom to get rich and stay rich. As Reagan recently affirmed, "What I want to see *above all else* is that this country remains a country where someone can always get rich. That's the thing we have that must be preserved."[41] That the administration is notably less concerned about other forms of freedom, even in the United States, is attested, for example, by Reagan's executive order removing restrictions imposed by the Carter administration on the CIA's ability to carry out surveillance on American citizens, and to infiltrate and "influence" domestic groups. Moreover, to the extent that individual freedom involves autonomy and self-determination, it is not something which this administration could plausibly be said to care about. For, as we shall see, the administration regularly treats the mass of American citizens as so many objects to be manipulated and lied to as readily and as often as is expedient. In the third world, any interest which the administration might have in the promotion of political liberties is eclipsed altogether by its concern for economic freedom—or, rather, the economic freedom of U.S. businesses. Indeed, Edward

Herman, professor of finance at the University of Pennsylvania, argues that, in government propaganda (as well as in much media commentary and academic analysis), " 'freedom' in its application to the Third World . . . *means* the ability of the larger economic interests to operate without constraint."[42] This is certainly consistent with the fact that one conspicuous consequence of the U.S. defense of "freedom" in third world countries is the gross and systematic suppression of the basic rights and liberties of ordinary people in those countries. As Uruguayan author Eduardo Galeano puts it: "Liberty for business, liberty for prices, liberty for trade: one throws the people in prison so that business will remain free."[43]

In attempting to provide a moral cover for its interventionist activities in Latin America, the administration often appeals, not just to the ideals of democracy and freedom, but also to the fact that Latin Americans are after all *Americans,* and thus have a special claim to be cared for and protected by the U.S. government. The moral responsibilities of the United States are therefore more extensive and more compelling in Latin America than elsewhere. These weighty responsibilities were solemnly acknowledged by Reagan in a recent speech: "Would America be America if, in their hour of need, we abandoned our nearest neighbors? From the tip of Tierra del Fuego to Alaska's Point Barrow, we are all Americans. We worship the same God and cherish the same freedoms."[44] The irony is that, when applied to the Reagan administration and the various Latin American dictatorships it supports, the last of these claims is true.

★2★

Nuclear Weapons as Instruments of Political Coercion

The Importance of Being Able to "Prevail" in a Nuclear War

Under the direction of Caspar Weinberger, the Pentagon has developed plans for the construction of 37,091 new nuclear warheads over the next ten or twelve years.[1] In most cases the new, more sophisticated warheads will replace older models, but the Pentagon's plans also project a considerable expansion of the U.S. nuclear arsenal. According to a Congressional Budget Office study, for example, the Reagan administration's plans envisage an increase in the number of strategic nuclear warheads (that is, warheads deployed in the United States or on U.S. submarines and capable of striking targets in the Soviet Union) from roughly 9,000 to 14,000—a net increase of almost 60 percent.[2] The administration's overall nuclear weapons program includes, among other things, the development and deployment of MX missiles, Midgetman missiles, B-1 bombers, "stealth" bombers, Pershing II missiles, Trident II missiles, the neutron bomb, and air-, sea-, and ground-launched cruise missiles, as well as the accelerated pursuit of other projects relevant to waging nuclear war, such as civil defense, the refinement of antisubmarine warfare (ASW) technology, the development of anti-ballistic missile (ABM) systems and antisatellite (ASAT) systems, and the expansion and protection of the American "command, control, communications, and intelligence" (C^3I) network.

The cost of these nuclear weapons projects is estimated at approximately $50 billion per year for the five years from 1983 to 1987, and in 1983 the administration proposed a level of spending on nuclear weapons which constituted a 40 percent increase over spending in 1981. Also in 1983 the Pentagon proposed a series of annual military budgets which projected a total military expenditure of $2,233 billion for the six years from 1984 to 1989. Yet, according to the London *Guardian*, the Pentagon is already receiving more money than it can spend, and hence has accumulated a stockpile of $128 billion in unspent funds, a stockpile which is projected to grow to $197 billion by 1985. Even in inflation-adjusted terms, the administration's proposed military budget for 1985 exceeds the annual U.S. defense expenditure during the height of the Vietnam war, when the United States had half a million troops in combat.[3] Meanwhile, in an unsuccessful effort to avoid the enormous budget deficits—the largest in U.S. history—occasioned in part by this unconstrained spending on "defense," the administration has slashed (among other things) child nutrition grants, welfare aid to the elderly poor, and educational aid for poor children and for poor students seeking to attend university.

What is the motivation behind this enormous buildup, with its disastrous side effects and opportunity costs? Administration officials of course claim that the buildup is necessary to maintain "credible deterrence" in the face of the relentless development and expansion of Soviet nuclear forces. It is necessary, moreover, not only to deter the Soviets from directly attacking the United States or its allies, but also to deter them from engaging in political coercion based on the threat of attack. This latter threat—the threat of "nuclear blackmail"—has indeed come to be regarded as a greater danger than the threat of direct attack. Thus Eugene Rostow, the first director of the Arms Control and Disarmament Agency (ACDA) under Reagan, has stated that "the greatest risk we face is not nuclear war but political coercion based on the credible threat of nuclear war implicit in overwhelming Soviet nuclear and conventional force superiority."[4] Similarly, General Bernard Rogers, the supreme allied commander in Europe, states that, while NATO aims "to deter both aggression and intimidation," it seeks, "*first and foremost,* to deter political intimidation against the nations of the Atlantic alliance and their vital interests."[5]

The need to deter nuclear blackmail has accordingly become the primary public justification for the various elements in the Reagan administration's rearmament program. For example, Rostow himself has argued for the deployment of cruise and Pershing II missiles in Europe on the ground that otherwise the Soviet Union would "retain its potential for nuclear blackmail."[6] Defense Secretary Caspar Weinberger has defended the Pentagon's 1982 Defense Guidance Plan, which contends that the United States must develop the ability to fight and "prevail" in a "protracted" nuclear war, by claiming that the provisions of the plan are necessary to prevent the Soviet Union from engaging in nuclear blackmail.[7] And both Secretary of State George Shultz and the Scowcroft Commission on Strategic Forces have argued that the MX missile is necessary to redress the currently unfavorable balance of forces which might tempt the Soviets to try to blackmail the United States.[8]

The fear—which, whether justified or not, nevertheless seems genuine—is that military and in particular nuclear superiority could enable the Soviets to push the United States around, and to pursue with impunity their aims and ambitions throughout the world. Of course, no one supposes that the Soviet Union would become emboldened to begin to exact concessions from the United States by threatening a nuclear attack as the penalty for noncompliance. The fear is rather more subtle. As Robert W. Tucker has explained, "The question is one of perceptions. If the perception persists that the Soviets are advantaged in some, we admit rather abstract, sense, in terms of strategic weapons, then it's going to have political consequences. These very, very minute probabilities nevertheless cast very long political shadows, given a crisis situation."[9]

The fear is thus that, if both the Soviet and the U.S. leaders were to share the perception that, if conflict were to break out, the Soviet Union would have the advantage, and would perhaps even be able to defeat the United States, this would inhibit the United States from defending its interests where doing so would entail an increased risk of confrontation with the Soviet Union.

The administration's position is therefore that the United States must act quickly and decisively to deprive the Soviet Union of what Reagan refers to as its "margin of superiority" before that superiority develops into a genuine coercive potential. The administration is not, however, content simply to deprive the Soviet Union of its alleged margin of superiority, but is also determined to establish a "margin of safety"—that is, superiority—for the United States. This was freely acknowledged by Reagan during the 1980 election campaign and during the early days of his tenure in office, when, in the United States, a Cold War consensus seemed to be shaping up to his satisfaction. In August of 1981, senior administration officials revealed that Weinberger had prepared for Reagan a proposal for the expansion of U.S. strategic nuclear forces which called for measures "intended to enable the United States to regain nuclear superiority over the Soviet Union within this decade."[10]

The aim of achieving superiority was also evident in the 1982 Defense Guidance Plan's insistance that, in a nuclear war, the United States "must prevail and be able to force the Soviet Union to seek earliest termination of hostilities on terms favorable to the United States"—that is, that the United States must have the ability to *win* a nuclear war.[11] The Defense Guidance Plan was not, however, made public (at least not voluntarily), for by that time many Americans were growing nervous about the possibility of nuclear war, and hence it had become necessary to deny that the administration sought strategic superiority, or the ability to win a nuclear war. Thus, in an astounding display of cynicism, Weinberger responded to the exposure of the plan by publicly denying what the planning document had explicitly asserted, noting that "we do not believe there could be any 'winners' in a nuclear war."[12] (Later, on television, Weinberger again asserted that "we don't believe a nuclear war can be won," though he went on to note that "we are planning to prevail if attacked."[13] The subtle distinction between winning and prevailing was never elucidated.)

It has not, however, been altogether possible for the administration's nuclear planners to disguise their aim of achieving the ability to "prevail" in a nuclear war with the Soviet Union. They must, after all, communicate among themselves and with other strategists otherwise than through private channels, and in any case the theories to which the administration subscribes were being debated in the professional literature long before Reagan ever came to office. If we consult the theoretical writings of administration members and advisers from the period before they entered office, we find a well-developed body of literature on the theory of nuclear war-fighting. Stated somewhat crudely, the core idea is that the United States must be able to threaten the Soviet Union not only with terrible *destruction* in the event of a war but also with *defeat.* Only then can the United States be confident of being able to deter the Soviet Union not only from directly attacking the United States or its allies but also from acting in other ways which would significantly increase the probability of confrontation with the United States. In particular, if the United States were to have the ability to defeat the Soviet Union in a nuclear war, then Soviet leaders would be unable to act in ways which would seriously threaten U.S. interests in the expectation that the United States would be too intimidated by the prospect of war to defend its interests—for both the Soviet and the U.S. leaders would be aware that the Soviet Union would stand to lose more from the outbreak of war than would the United States.

What would constitute defeat for the Soviet Union? The official view is that, in order to defeat the Soviet Union, the United States would have to ensure that while the United States would survive as a functioning political entity, the Soviet Union would not. The physical and political survival of the United States can, moreover, be guaranteed if the United States is able to destroy a significant percentage of the Soviet Union's strategic weapons before they can be used, and if it is also able to mitigate the effects of the remaining Soviet weapons through a combination of "active" and "passive" defenses (that is, a combination of anti–ballistic missile systems, air defense systems, and civil defense). To fulfill the other requirement—that is, to prevent the recovery of the Soviet state as a continuous and viable political system—it is necessary, above all, to destroy the leadership's instruments of political control. In an important and influential article written in 1980, Colin Gray and Keith Payne argued that

> the most frightening threat to the Soviet Union would be the destruction or serious impairment of its political system. Thus, the United States should be able to destroy key leadership cadres, their means of communication, and some of the instruments of domestic control. . . . Judicious U.S. targeting and weapon procurement policies might be able to deny the USSR the assurance of political survival.[14]

The importance to the administration of Gray's thinking on these matters (to which we shall return) was recognized when Reagan appointed him to the advisory board of the Arms Control and Disarmament Agency and established him as an adviser to the State Department. The argument which he and Payne presented in 1980, according to which what the Soviet leaders value most is not the lives of their citizens but their control over those lives, was later repeated by President Reagan's Commission on Strategic Forces, which was chaired by Lieutenant General Brent Scowcroft. In its report, the commission asserted that, in order to deter both a Soviet attack and Soviet nuclear blackmail, the United States

> must be able to put at risk those types of Soviet targets—including hardened ones such as military command bunkers and facilities, missile silos, nuclear weapons and other storage, and the rest—which the Soviet leaders have given every indication by their actions they value most, and which constitute their tools of control and power. We cannot afford the delusion that Soviet leaders—human though they are and cautious though we hope they will be—are going to be deterred by exactly the same concerns that would dissuade us.[15]

The foregoing points have become commonplaces of contemporary strategic thinking in the United States—especially in circles associated with the Reagan administration. As far as they go they seem to be an accurate reflection of the views of the administration itself. But they tell only part of the story. It does not require much imagination to see that, if nuclear superiority, or the ability to win a nuclear war, would enable the Soviet Union to intimidate and coerce the United States, then it would also, if it were the United States that had it, enable the United States to intimidate and coerce the Soviet Union. And indeed the United States has used the implicit or explicit threat of nuclear attack or nuclear war for purposes of coercion or intimidation on numerous occasions in the past—not just against the Soviet Union but against a variety of lesser powers as well. (Of course, it would be a manifestation of "extremism" to refer to the action of the United States on these occasions as nuclear blackmail. The polite phrase is "nuclear diplomacy.")

A brief review of some of the instances in which the United States has practiced nuclear diplomacy will suffice to show that the idea that nuclear weapons can be used for coercive purposes is by no means foreign or unfamiliar to U.S. leaders.

1. In March 1946 Soviet troops remained in Iran after the date on which the Soviet Union had agreed that they would be withdrawn. According to Truman's later accounts, the United States delivered an ultimatum to Stalin warning that, if the troops were not withdrawn, the United States would attack the Soviet Union with nuclear bombs.[16]

2. In November 1946, after a U.S. aircraft was shot down over Yugoslavia, the United States sent six B-29 strategic bombers to West Germany, making them highly visible to the Yugoslavs by flying them along the border.[17]

3. In February 1947 B-29s were dispatched to Uruguay in a show of force at the time of the inauguration of the president of that country.[18]

4. In 1948, during the Berlin blockade, B-29s were flown to bases in Britain and West Germany, and were several times sent aloft in order to send a signal to the Soviets.[19]

5. In 1950, after the outbreak of the Korean war, U.S. strategic bombers were again deployed in Europe. Later, after U.S. marines had been encircled by Communist Chinese forces at the Chosin Reservoir in Korea, Truman intimated at a press conference that the use of nuclear weapons was under active consideration. This sent British Prime Minister Attlee scurrying to Washington in an effort to ensure that nuclear weapons would not actually be used.[20]

6. In 1953, in an effort to achieve the armistice in Korea, Eisenhower and several of his emissaries "discreetly" warned the Soviet Union and China that, unless the war were ended, the United States would use nuclear weapons, not only in Korea, but against China as well. These threats were backed up by the deployment of nuclear weapons in Okinawa. The Eisenhower administration used similar threats to enforce the armistice. Evidence has recently come to light which shows that Eisenhower was quite prepared to fulfill these threats. According to a recently released report of a National Security Council meeting on December 3, 1953 (after the armistice): "The president expressed with great emphasis the opinion that if the Chinese Communists attacked us again, we should certainly respond by hitting them hard and wherever it would hurt most, including Peiping [i.e., Peking] itself. This, said

the president, would mean all-out war against Communist China."[21]

7. In 1954 U.S. strategic bombers were flown to Nicaragua as part of the background to the CIA's overthrow of the Arbenz government in Guatemala.[22]

8. In July 1958, 14,000 U.S. troops landed in Lebanon in response both to upheaval within that country and to the overthrow of the monarchy in Iraq. All accounts agree that U.S. forces brought "nuclear-capable" howitzers ashore with them, though there is controversy over whether nuclear shells were brought ashore as well. The Eisenhower administration judged that its intervention in the Lebanese crisis carried some risk of general war with the Soviet Union and thus, to signal U.S. "readiness and determination," the Strategic Air Command was ordered to increase its level of readiness.[23]

9. In 1958 the Eisenhower administration deployed strategic bombers in the Western Pacific and openly threatened the use of nuclear weapons in an effort to deter the Communist Chinese from invading the offshore island of Quemoy, which was occupied by Chiang Kai-shek's forces.[24]

10. In May 1959, during the Berlin crisis of 1958–59, the Eisenhower administration used various means, including the staging of naval exercises involving U.S. strategic strike forces, to emphasize to the Soviet Union both the strength and the determination of the United States.[25]

11. In 1962, during the Cuban missile crisis, the Kennedy administration deliberately manipulated the risk of nuclear war in order to coerce the Soviets into withdrawing their nuclear missiles from Cuba.[26]

12. During the period from 1969 to 1972 Nixon conveyed secret nuclear threats to the North Vietnamese via Henry Kissinger in an effort to end the Vietnam war on terms favorable to the United States and its South Vietnamese client.[27]

13. In 1973 the United States placed its nuclear forces on a worldwide alert, while Kissinger spoke gravely on television of the threat of nuclear war, in an effort to deter the Soviet Union from intervening in the Yom Kippur War to rescue the Egyptian Third Army, which, as a result of Israel's violation of the cease-fire agreement, had been surrounded by Israeli forces.[28]

14. In 1980 President Carter publicly threatened to use "any means necessary" to repel a Soviet attempt to occupy the Persian Gulf region. Government officials subsequently elaborated on Carter's remarks, indicating that, to stop a Soviet assault on the Gulf, the United States would probably have to resort to tactical nuclear weapons. This soon came to be known as the "Carter Doctrine."[29]

Blechman and Kaplan, on whose study much of this survey is based, also note that the United States made "an overt and explicit threat . . . directed at the USSR through global actions of U.S. strategic forces" during the Suez crisis of 1956, and that U.S. nuclear forces were also used for political purposes during both the 1961 Berlin crisis and the incident involving the *Pueblo* in 1968—though no details are given.[30] One conclusion they draw from their survey is that the use of nuclear threats by the United States "was more common in earlier years—when the U.S. strategic position vis-à-vis the Soviet Union was dominant—than more recently."[31] In short, U.S. decision-makers have thought that a favorable nuclear balance vis-à-vis the Soviet Union is important both in enabling the United States to threaten the Soviet Union with confidence and in reducing the risk of confrontation with the Soviet Union that goes with using nuclear weapons to threaten countries other than the Soviet Union.

Of course, another factor which has no doubt been partly responsible for the increasing restraint shown by the United States in making nuclear threats against third world countries is the increasing acceptance by the American public of the convention forbidding the first use of nuclear weapons, and especially the use of nuclear weapons against nonnuclear countries. Nixon himself conceded in his memoirs that the strength of the antiwar protests convinced him that he did not have the public support necessary for carrying out his threats against the North Vietnamese (and perhaps his threats were resisted precisely because the North Vietnamese knew this to be true). This was the last occasion, so far as we know, on which the United States issued a nuclear threat against a nonnuclear country. And, in spite of the fact that the American public felt a thrill of pride and pleasure when U.S. conventional forces recently were used to crush a defenseless microbe in the Caribbean, it is clear that they would not tolerate the use of nuclear weapons against a helpless nonnuclear country. Since a threat to use nuclear weapons against a nonnuclear country will therefore no longer be credible, the United States is very unlikely ever to make one.

Thus the Reagan administration's aims in seeking to restore U.S. nuclear superiority are, first, to be able once again to threaten and coerce the Soviet Union with relative impunity; and, second, to reduce the risk of confrontation with the Soviet Union attendant upon intervention in the third world by means of the threat or use of *conventional* force. (Of course, the aim is not for the United States to be in a position in which it can confidently make overt nuclear threats against the Soviet Union. Rather, the ideal is to have nuclear forces so evidently overwhelming in their superiority that the Soviet Union will be intimidated without the United States ever having to make an explicit threat. Blechman and Kaplan note that, "like Army ground troops deployed overseas, strategic nuclear forces serve vital political objectives on a continuous basis, perhaps thus obviating the need for discrete and explicit utilization."[32] If nuclear diplomacy could be carried out in this subtle fashion, there would then be a lesser risk of upsetting squeamish American voters who might be averse to risking nuclear war over control of some third world area.)

Over the years Reagan administration officials have made a great many statements which confirm both that they believe that nuclear superiority confers coercive power and that it is their desire for coercive power over the Soviet Union which to a considerable extent motivates their pursuit of nuclear superiority. Thus Paul Nitze, Reagan's chief negotiator in the abortive talks on Intermediate-Range Nuclear Forces (INF) in Geneva, has stated that "the nuclear balance is, of course, only one element in the overall power balance. But in the Soviet view, it is the fulcrum upon which all other levers of influence—military, economic, or political—rest. Can we be confident that there is not at least a measure of validity to that viewpoint?"[33]

Of course, Nitze and many others in the administration believe that there is more than just a measure of validity to this view. Richard Perle, the assistant secretary of defense for international security policy, has stated:

> I've always worried less about what would happen in an actual nuclear exchange than [about] the effect that the nuclear balance has on our willingness to take risks in local situations. It is not that I am worried about the Soviets attacking the United States with nuclear weapons confident that they will win that nuclear war. It is that I worry about an American president feeling he cannot afford to take action in a crisis because Soviet nuclear forces are such that, if escalation took place, they are better poised than we are to move up the escalation ladder.[34]

The clear implication here is that, if it were the United States rather than the Soviet Union which had superiority, then the U.S. president could feel comfortable taking risks in "local situations" (that is, he could feel comfortable intervening militarily around the world, a state of affairs which Perle obviously regards as desirable), because the Soviets would be paralyzed by the fear that the United States would be better poised than they would be "to move up the escalation ladder."

Nitze and Perle's concern that, without a favorable nuclear balance, the United States would be deterred by the prospect of confrontation with the Soviet Union from defending or aggressively pursuing its interests throughout the world has been echoed by other administration figures, past and present, including John Lehman, the secretary of the navy, and Eugene Rostow, formerly of the ACDA. Lehman has asserted that, until the United States is able to restore a favorable nuclear balance, "American decision makers must operate in an environment in which, if escalation is taken to the ultimate level, they know the United States would not prevail." Consequently, he argues, "much of the world, wherein lies [*sic*] the vital interests of the United States and its allies, is now for the first time outside of the nuclear umbrella."[35] Arguing along the same lines, Rostow asserted that if the United States were to accept the position of parity with the Soviet Union required by the second Strategic Arms Limitation Talks treaty (SALT II), "we would be in no position to use conventional or nuclear forces in defense of our interests in Europe, the Far East, the Middle East or elsewhere."[36] According to Rostow, "Our nuclear forces . . . must . . . provide a nuclear guarantee for our interests in many parts of the world and make it possible for us to defend those interests by diplomacy or by the use of theater military forces whenever such action becomes necessary."[37] Nuclear weapons make it possible for the United States to defend its global interests by holding the Soviet Union at bay, deterring it from challenging U.S. conventional operations around the globe. "The nuclear weapon" is thus "a persuasive influence in all aspects of diplomacy and of conventional war." Hence, Rostow argues, with a favorable balance of nuclear forces, "we could go forward in planning the use of our conventional forces with great freedom precisely because we knew that the Soviet Union could not escalate beyond the local level."[38] As General Edward Rowny, Reagan's Strategic Arms Reduction Talks (START) negotiator, has put it, "We could take certain slight risks without having those become big risks."[39]

The most forthright statement of the view that nuclear weapons are valuable for the purpose of political coercion comes from Colin Gray and his co-author Keith Payne. They write:

> The West needs to devise ways in which it can employ strategic nuclear forces coercively. . . . American strategic forces do not exist solely for the purpose of deterring a Soviet nuclear threat [i.e., nuclear blackmail] or attack against the United States itself. Instead, they are intended to support U.S. foreign policy . . . such a function requires American strategic forces that would enable a president to initiate strategic nuclear use for coercive, though politically defensive, purposes. . . . If American nuclear power is to support U.S. foreign policy objectives, the United States must possess the ability to wage nuclear war rationally.[40]

In this passage Gray and Payne go beyond the familiar idea that the value of nuclear superiority lies in the *psychological* advantage it bestows on its possessor. According to that view, nuclear superiority would enable the United States to impose its will on the Soviet Union without even incurring a substantially increased risk of war. Gray and Payne, however, seem fairly enthusiastic about the idea of actually *initiating* a nuclear war in order to put the Soviet Union in its place. Thus they conjecture that "nuclear war is unlikely to be an essentially meaningless terminal event. Instead it is likely to be waged to coerce the Soviet Union to give up some recent gain."[41]

It would be difficult to find a clearer statement than this of the view that nuclear war should simply be regarded, in Clausewitz's phrase, as a continuation of politics by other means. It is noteworthy that right-wing American ideologists routinely cite this view, which they claim is central to Soviet strategic thinking, as evidence of the chillingly insensitive and calculating attitude of the Soviets toward nuclear war.[42] It is worth recalling, moreover, that Gray was appointed to two advisory posts within the administration *after* he had published the article in which these views are articulated, which gives some indication of how his views were received.

The beliefs and assumptions which I have described, and which underlie current U.S. strategic doctrine, are seldom carefully defended. The claim that the Soviet leaders fear the loss of political control more than the annihilation of many millions of Soviet citizens is, for example, apparently not thought to require defense. It is simply asserted on the assumption, unfortunately correct, that hatred of the Soviet Union is so strong in the United States that the worst that can be said about the Soviet leadership will normally be accepted virtually without question. Few have bothered to ask, for example, how the Soviet leaders could hope to satisfy their desire to control the lives of Soviet citizens without also guaranteeing that there will be some Soviet citizens to be controlled.

The administration's views on the importance of nuclear superiority and the ability to prevail in a nuclear war are more difficult to assess. It is worth pausing at this point to examine these views more carefully. First, it is obvious that neither the ability to prevail nor even superiority is *necessary* to deter a nuclear attack or Soviet nuclear blackmail. (Note that there is a difference between nuclear superiority and the ability to prevail—or to defeat the Soviet Union—in a nuclear war: while the ability to prevail entails superiority, mere superiority does not entail the ability to prevail.) If the aim is only to deter a nuclear attack, this could be accomplished by a policy of "minimal deterrence." Such a policy would restrict the United States to the smallest possible nuclear arsenal compatible with maintaining the ability to inflict terrible destruction on the Soviet Union in a series of counterstrikes. (The ability to launch a *series* of counterstrikes is crucial; for, if it were expected that the United States would quickly exhaust its retaliatory capability in a war, so that it would then be without a means of deterring further Soviet strikes, this would weaken the credibility of its threat to retaliate in the first instance.) The size of the arsenal necessary for minimal deterrence would depend in part on the "survivability" of each of its components. If each component were largely invulnerable to preemptive attack, then the arsenal could be only a fraction of the size of those currently maintained by the United States and the Soviet Union. In other words, the United States could deter a nuclear attack even from a position of substantial nuclear inferiority. If, on the other hand, the aim is to deter both a nuclear attack and nuclear blackmail, then, even if one accepts the assumption (which I shall shortly challenge) that nuclear superiority confers the coercive power necessary for nuclear blackmail, this aim could be achieved by a policy of parity—that is, a policy which would deny superiority to the Soviet Union *and* to the United States.

What, then, can be said about the assumption that nuclear superiority, and *a fortiori* the ability to prevail, would provide the United States with the ability to intimidate and coerce the Soviet Union—or, to put it another way, that nuclear inferiority renders a country vulnerable to nuclear blackmail? The historical evidence seems to suggest that nuclear superiority has little bearing on the ability of one side successfully to coerce the other. Of course, as Blechman and Kaplan point out, U.S. leaders have seemed more inclined to make nuclear threats the greater the U.S. nuclear superiority over the Soviet Union. There are, however, several things to be said about this. One is that the same does not seem to be true of Soviet leaders. Soviet leaders, like their U.S. counterparts, appear to have become less rather than more disposed to make nuclear threats over the period in which they closed the strategic gap with the United States. While Khrushchev made various nuclear threats during the Berlin crises of 1958 and 1961, as well as during the Suez crisis of 1957, his successors appear to have been considerably more cautious. A second point is that the narrowing of the gap between the United States and the Soviet Union has coincided with both a growth in popular awareness, in the United States and in the world generally, of the potential consequences of nuclear war, and the development of a convention according to which nuclear weapons are to be used for deterrent rather than war-fighting purposes. Hence the operative factor in restraining U.S. leaders from making nuclear threats may have been the increase in domestic and international political constraints rather than the decline in U.S. nuclear superiority.

A third point is that, even if superiority *was* what emboldened U.S. leaders to make nuclear threats, this shows only that those leaders *believed* that the effectiveness of a threat depends on the state of the nuclear balance. It does not show that this belief is correct. Indeed, there is reason to think that, in many of the cases in which the United States made nuclear threats from a position of substantial nuclear superiority, the threats were not clearly successful—*even though* the United States succeeded in achieving its aims. For in many of these cases there were factors other than the nuclear threat which influenced the outcome. McGeorge Bundy has recently published a study in which he considers the cases of Iran in 1946, Korea in 1953, Quemoy in 1958, and Cuba in 1962—cases which are commonly regarded as ones in which an American nuclear threat, made against a background of American nuclear superiority, enabled the United States to achieve its aims. Bundy claims, on the contrary, that in each case other considerations suffice to explain the American success.

In the case of Iran, Bundy argues that Truman's claim to have forced the Soviets out was simply a bit of epic boasting, for the United States never in fact issued Stalin an ultimatum. The diplomatic notes the United States sent were all apparently rather tactful and polite. What moved the Soviets to withdraw, Bundy speculates, was simply the firmness of the Iranian government, the weakness of Stalin's supporters in Iran, and the pressure of world opinion.[43] In Korea, according to Bundy, Eisenhower's threats were made when there was considerable evidence that the Chinese had already shifted their position as a result of their perception that "there were . . . excellent reasons in 1953 for the Communist side to want to end the war: their own heavy losses, the absence of any prospect for further gains, and the continuing high cost of unsuccessful probes of United Nations forces on the ground."[44] In the case of Quemoy, Bundy suggests that "what actually held off the attacking Chinese forces . . . was not [Eisenhower's nuclear] threats but the effective use of local air and naval superiority," though he concedes that "the nuclear possibility may have contributed to Chinese unwillingness to raise the stakes."[45] Finally Bundy contends (as do Kennedy's other two senior advisers at the time, Dean Rusk and Robert McNamara) that the U.S. nuclear threat during the Cuban missile crisis was simply not credible, and that it was U.S. conventional superiority in the Atlantic and the Caribbean which enabled the Kennedy administration to compel the Soviets to withdraw their missiles.[46]

At a more general level, the historical evidence suggests that a background of nuclear superiority does not make success more likely when force or the threat of force is used in pursuit of foreign policy goals. Blechman and Kaplan conclude from their study of the instances during the postwar period in which the United States has used its military forces for political purposes that

> in general the data do not support propositions as to the importance of the strategic balance. It was not true that positive outcomes were proportionately less frequent, the less the U.S. advantage vis-à-vis the Soviet Union in the number of either nuclear warheads or delivery vehicles. . . . We did not find that the United States was less often successful as the Soviet Union closed the U.S. lead in strategic nuclear weapons that had been maintained for the first twenty or so years following the Second World War.[47]

This in fact understates their findings. The figures they cite show a consistent pattern: positive outcomes for the United States were proportionately less frequent the *greater* the U.S. nuclear advantage.[48]

During the late 1940s and throughout most of the 1950s the United States had the ability to prevail in a nuclear war against the Soviet Union. Even then, however, it did not have the coercive power over the Soviet Union which the Reagan administration wishes to acquire—contrary to the expectations of U.S. officials at the time, who clearly anticipated that during the period of U.S. monopoly or overwhelming superiority the United States would be in a position to dictate its own terms. Thus in the immediate postwar period Bernard Baruch claimed that "America can get what she wants if she insists on it. After all, we've got it—the Bomb—and they haven't and won't have it for a long time to come."[49] Yet, during the period of the U.S. nuclear monopoly, China was not prevented from becoming communist, and neither was the Soviet Union noticeably inhibited from pursuing its own "geopolitical" ambitions—for example, in Eastern Europe.

It might, however, be argued that, while the ability to prevail may not be *necessary* to deter a nuclear attack or nuclear blackmail, it would nevertheless enable the United States to threaten the Soviet Union more credibly, and would therefore not only strengthen deterrence, but would also, in spite of the historical evidence, give the United States enhanced coercive power vis-à-vis the Soviet Union. The argument for this claim is as follows. In order to strengthen deterrence against a nuclear attack or nuclear blackmail, the United States must alter things so that either it would be *less* reluctant to go to war or the Soviet Union would be *more* reluctant to do so. Either of these changes would, moreover, increase the ability of the United States to intimidate the Soviet Union, since in either case the Soviet Union would be more cautious about challenging U.S. interventionist policies around the world. To bring about one or the other of these changes, the United States must make it the case either that it would have *less* to lose than it does at present from going to war or that the Soviet Union would have *more* to lose, or both. Both of these further changes would result if the United States were to acquire the ability to defeat the Soviet Union in a nuclear war; for, as we have noted, the ability to defeat the Soviet Union implies both the ability of the United States to survive a nuclear war (which means that it would have less to lose) and the ability of the United States to destroy the Soviet leadership's instruments of political control (which means that they would supposedly have more to lose). Therefore the ability to defeat the Soviet Union in a nuclear war would strengthen deterrence against a nuclear attack and against nuclear blackmail, and would also allow the United States to pursue the goals of its foreign policy, and in particular to intervene throughout the world, with a substantially smaller risk of confrontation with the Soviet Union.

This reasoning, if correct, helps to show why mere nuclear superiority would not normally provide the advantages which the ability to prevail is supposed to provide. Nuclear superiority might reduce the damage the United States would suffer in a nuclear war (since it would enable the United States to destroy more of the Soviet Union's weapons before they could be used), and it might increase the amount of damage that the Soviet Union would suffer, but in neither case would the difference be likely to be sufficiently great to affect the political leadership's calculations about the rationality of going to war. In that case, mere superiority would neither increase deterrence nor confer enhanced coercive power. It would do so only if it were so decisive as to approach the ability to prevail.

This abstract argument for the claim that the ability to prevail would provide enhanced coercive power has, in Nitze's phrase, a measure of validity. While it is doubtful that the threat to destroy the Soviet leadership's levels of control would significantly affect their willingness to go to war, it seems undeniable that the ability of the United States to survive a nuclear war (in some fairly robust sense of that phrase) would substantially weaken U.S. inhibitions about going to war, while strengthening the inhibitions of the Soviet Union. (In general, the potential penalties which the United States or the Soviet Union would now suffer in a nuclear war are about as high as any penalties could be. Thus it is unlikely that either side will be able to improve its position vis-à-vis the other by increasing the penalties which the other would suffer. It can improve its relative position only by decreasing the penalties which it would itself suffer.) So the administration is not altogether deluded in its belief in the desirability, from its own point of view, of the ability to prevail.

Nevertheless, the administration's efforts to acquire the ability to prevail are unlikely to lead to anything but the most profoundly undesirable consequences. First, in the extremely unlikely event that the United States were to achieve the ability to prevail, so that it could then intervene militarily in various areas of the world with relative impunity, the consequences would be appalling—at least if future interventions are likely to resemble previous ones in their aims and methods. And, second, the effort to acquire the ability to prevail is itself dramatically increasing the risk of nuclear war—for example, by spurring the Soviets to seek an equivalent capability; by raising the prospect of nuclear blackmail or even of a first strike against the Soviet Union, thereby increasing the Soviets' incentive to launch a first strike against the United States before the United States can achieve the ability to disarm and defeat the Soviet Union; and, finally, by generally increasing fears and tensions on both sides. It will become clearer in the remainder of this chapter why the administration's nuclear programs are having these effects.

The MX: Missile in Search of a Rationale

What, specifically, would be necessary to give the United States the ability to prevail in a nuclear war? Paul Nitze has suggested the following force requirements:

1. A powerful counterforce capability—one sufficient to reduce the enemy's offensive and defensive capabilities significantly and progressively below one's own;
2. Forces sufficiently hardened, dispersed, mobile, or defended as to make a possible counterforce response [*sic*] by the other side disadvantageous—that is, such that a counterforce response would only serve to weaken the relative position of the responder . . . ;
3. Sufficient survivable reserve forces . . . ;
4. Active and passive defense measures, including civil defense and hardened and dispersed command and control facilities, sufficient to ensure survival and control;
5. The means and determination not to let the other side get in the first blow—i.e., to pre-empt if necessary.[50]

Nitze states these requirements in order to show that since the Soviets are "attempting to achieve capabilities consistent with fulfilling all five requirements," they must therefore accept the view that "a war involving nuclear missiles should and can be an extension of policy" (the view which Colin Gray, now Nitze's colleague at the Arms Control and Disarmament Agency, explicitly endorses).[51] Nitze then goes on to argue that the United States must make immediate and substantial improvements in its *own* capabilities where the first four requirements are concerned—though he is sufficiently adept at public relations to disclaim any aggressive designs: "The objective . . . would not be to give the United States a war-fighting capability; it would be to deny to the Soviet Union the possibility of a successful war-fighting capability."[52] This is a familiar pattern of argument. One first attributes evil designs to the Soviets. Next one reluctantly acknowledges that the only way to thwart those evil designs is by matching or surpassing the Soviets at their own game. One can then present one's own evil designs as purely reactive and defensive, regrettably necessitated by the unconquerable wickedness of the Soviets. (The Soviets have their own variant of this argument, in which the roles are of course reversed.)

Nitze's requirements in fact provide a reasonably accurate description of the goals of the Reagan administration's nuclear buildup. These goals include the development and deployment of a vast array of new counterforce weapons (requirement 1), and protection of U.S. nuclear forces by means of air defense and anti–ballistic missile systems (requirement 2), an overall increase in the number of U.S. nuclear weapons (requirement 3), the hardening and duplication of U.S. command and control facilities, and the protection of the American population by means of civil defense preparations and, ultimately, anti–ballistic missile systems capable of defending "area" targets as well as "point" targets (requirement 4)—all of which together would fulfill Nitze's fifth requirement: a first-strike capability.

Recall that the ability to prevail, or to defeat the Soviet Union in a nuclear war, has two dimensions: first, the ability to inflict "unacceptable" damage on the Soviet Union and, in the words of the Pentagon's Defense Guidance Plan, to "render ineffective the total Soviet (and Soviet-allied) military and political power structure";[53] and, second, the ability to ensure the survival of the political structures of the American nation as well as of the bulk of the American population. Of the various goals cited above, those which would contribute to the U.S. ability to destroy the Soviet Union and its political structures are: increasing U.S. counterforce capability, protecting and expanding the size of the U.S. nuclear arsenal, and ensuring the "survivability" of the U.S. command and control facilities. Those which would contribute to the ability of the United States to survive a nuclear war are: again, increasing U.S. counterforce capability, implementing an expanded civil defense program, and developing and deploying a large-scale network of ballistic missile defenses. As Gray and Payne remark, "A combination of counterforce offensive targeting, civil defense, and ballistic missile and air defense should hold U.S. casualties down to a level compatible with national survival and recovery."[54]

The centerpiece of the administration's projected counterforce arsenal is the MX missile. The current plan is for the deployment of 100 MX missiles, each carrying 10 independently targetable warheads (MIRVs). The MX force will therefore be capable of attacking 1,000 different targets (and possibly considerably more, if the launchers prove to be reloadable; for the administration plans to build 223 MX missiles—100 for deployment, 123 allegedly for training, testing, and spares).[55] What makes the MX an ideal counterforce weapon is the fact that it can deliver high-yield nuclear warheads with great accuracy, and can therefore be relied upon for the destruction of "hardened" targets such as missile silos and underground command posts. Missile accuracy is calculated in terms of a measure known as "circular error probability," or CEP, which is the radius of a circle, centered on the target, within which the missile's warhead has a 50 percent chance of landing. At present the MX has a projected CEP of between 400 and 600 feet. With further improvements now being prepared, it is estimated that the CEP can be reduced to less than 100 feet.[56] The Union of Concerned Scientists in the United States has calculated that, with the ability to land a 350 kiloton warhead within 300 feet of its target, the MX will have a 99.5 percent probability of destroying a missile silo using only a single warhead.[57]

It is easy to see why, with these specifications, the MX is such an important element in the administration's scheme to acquire the ability to prevail in a nuclear war. As General Vessey, the chairman of the Joint Chiefs of Staff, has put it, "The accurate MX warheads will let the Soviets know that their missile silos, their leadership, and associated command and control are placed at risk."[58] This remark was made in support of the contention that the MX is necessary to deter Soviet nuclear blackmail; but, as we have seen, administration officials also believe that what they claim is necessary to deter Soviet nuclear blackmail would also be sufficient to enable the United States to engage in a bit of nuclear diplomacy of its own.

The argument that the MX is necessary to deter nuclear blackmail is one of the many arguments which the administration has produced in its efforts to secure congressional funding for this highly controversial weapon. Most of these arguments, however, have been designed for public consumption, and therefore cannot prudently acknowledge the aim of increasing U.S. coercive power over the Soviet Union. Given this constraint, the task of finding suitably presentable rationales has strained the resources of the administration's propagandists, and the official arguments have consequently ranged from the confused to the ridiculous.

In the latter category is the argument that administration officials were urging even before they entered office—namely, that the MX is needed to solve the "Minuteman vulnerability problem." The argument was that, as a result of improvements in the Soviet Union's counterforce capability, existing Minuteman missiles were becoming perilously vulnerable to a Soviet first strike. The MX was therefore needed to narrow the "window of vulnerability." In the days of the Carter administration this argument had some superficial plausibility, for at that time the controversy focused on the question of the appropriate basing mode for the new missile, and there the relevant criterion was the degree of invulnerability which a given basing mode would afford. Even then, however, the apparent plausibility of the argument was entirely specious, since no one could explain why a new *missile* was necessary to reduce the vulnerability of American forces to a first strike. The extent to which a missile is vulnerable to preemption is a function of the way it is based; the characteristics of the missile itself are irrelevant. Thus, if the concern had really been with vulnerability, the challenge would have been to find a new basing mode for the old missiles.

Liberal critics, instead of challenging the relevance of the window of vulnerability to the debate about MX, have instead challenged the plausibility of the first-strike scenario, pointing out the many obstacles and uncertainties which the Soviets would face in attempting to conduct a successful first strike.[59] Moreover, successive commissions charged with finding a "survivable" basing mode for the MX concluded that the alternatives are either impractical or too expensive. It is doubtful whether anyone considered whether an alternative and less vulnerable basing mode for the Minuteman missiles would be economically feasible if no money were to be spent on the MX. In any case, the window of vulnerability has now been discreetly dropped from the lexicon of presidential clichés, and, instead of a new basing mode for the old missiles, the American public is going to get new missiles in the old basing mode—for the MX missiles are now scheduled to be deployed in existing fixed-position silos. Still, while the vulnerability problem has been shelved, either because people have ceased to believe that such a problem exists or because they believe it is a problem with no solution, its relevance to the MX debate remains unquestioned. Thus the *New York Times* continues repeatedly to assert that "the reason for building MX was to counter the alleged vulnerability of the land-based Minuteman force."[60]

It was the report of the president's Commission on Strategic Forces—usually called the Scowcroft Commmission after its chairman—which finally banished the vulnerability argument from the body of orthodox arguments for the MX. The arguments which have replaced it were, however, definitively stated in the commission's report. Principal among these is that the United States must develop a counterforce capability comparable to that of the Soviet Union in order to be able to deter the Soviets from attempting "a limited use of nuclear weapons against military targets" in the United States.[61] The commission assumes that, if the Soviet Union believes itself to have a superior counterforce capability, it will then be entitled to assume that it would have the advantage in a "limited" nuclear war. And this might tempt the Soviet leaders to threaten a limited nuclear attack for coercive purposes, or even to conduct such an attack.

I have already suggested why I think it is implausible to suppose that mere superiority would in fact reduce the Soviet Union's reluctance to initiate a nuclear war, and why, therefore, it would not enhance the Soviet Union's coercive potential. But let us grant the commission's assumptions, in case the Soviets share the administration's delusions about the importance of superiority. We may also, for the sake of argument, grant the commission's dubious assumption that the Soviets currently possess a superior counterforce capability. Even if we accept these assumptions, we can still reject the commission's conclusion that the MX is necessary to deny the Soviets a superior counterforce capability. For there are two ways to deprive the Soviets of their alleged superiority. One is to build comparable forces, as the commission recommends. The other is to reduce the Soviets' counterforce capability by increasing the invulnerability of U.S. forces. This could be done, for example, by abandoning land-based missiles altogether and, if necessary, deploying more missiles on submarines.[62] As we shall see, this would be a considerably less dangerous way to deprive the Soviet Union of any alleged superiority in counterforce capability.

The strongest objection to the commission's argument is, however, that it is simply incoherent. According to the commission, the whole point of the MX as a counterforce weapon is to pose a threat to "Soviet military targets, hardened or otherwise." Because the Soviets will thus view the MX missiles as the most threatening weapons in the U.S. arsenal, the one hundred MX silos will therefore be precisely what the Soviets would most want to destroy in a "limited" nuclear strike against the United States. Recall, moreover, that the commission has abandoned the goal of providing the MX with an invulnerable basing mode. Since the MX will thus be highly vulnerable to preemptive attack, it cannot serve the purpose which the commission cites as its primary justification. For the United States cannot hope to deter a "limited" preemptive attack against the MX by threatening retaliation with the MX itself—unless, of course, the United States adopts a policy of launch-on-warning (that is, unless the United States threatens to launch the MX on receiving warning of a Soviet attack), a matter to which we shall return.

Together these objections seem decisive. But the commission is ready with a cluster of further considerations intended to bolster its case. One is based on the commission's acceptance of the claim that the Soviet Union's buildup of heavy missiles has rendered the U.S. force of MIRVed missiles in fixed-position silos vulnerable to preemption. (This is not equivalent to the claim that there is a window of vulnerability. There would be a window of vulnerability only if the Soviets were insufficiently deterred from exploiting the vulnerability of the land-based missiles by attacking them preemptively.) The particular vulnerability of the current land-based missiles has led the commission to recommend that the United States should begin to develop a force of small, mobile missiles (referred to endearingly as "Midgetman" missiles), each with a single warhead. These would be less attractive targets for a preemptive attack, since their mobility would make them harder to target, and the fact that each would have only one warhead would mean that, in attempting to destroy them preemptively, the Soviet Union would have to expend *more* warheads than it could hope to destroy—a disadvantageous trade-off. The idea behind the Midgetman missile has been received with great enthusiasm by American liberals. The fact that the impetus for this idea came from the threat from heavy Soviet missiles suggests another argument for the MX. According to liberal columnist Tom Wicker, "Just as big Russian missiles have forced the recommendation for an American switch to Midgetman, the Commission apparently reasoned, so MX deployment might cause the Russians to think about a similar change in their ICBM force."[63]

This argument is not much of an improvement over the previous one. Suppose that the deployment of the MX were to pressure the Soviets to imitate the United States in building a mobile, single-warhead missile. What would that accomplish? It is relevant here, in assessing the importance of the U.S. example, to note that the commission stresses that the Midgetman must be a counterforce weapon: "It should have sufficient accuracy and yield to put Soviet hardened military targets at risk." (It is estimated that the Midgetman will have an accuracy of 300 feet CEP.[64]) Moreover, the Midgetman is envisaged as a supplement to rather than a replacement for the MX.[65] Thus, if the Soviets follow the U.S. example, that will simply increase their counterforce capability (by giving them more counterforce weapons) and decrease that of the United States (by increasing the overall "survivability" of the Soviet forces)—hardly a satisfactory outcome, especially from the point of view of the commission. A further point is that, since the Midgetman will be a counterforce missile, and since the existing Minuteman III missiles are counterforce weapons, and since the administration has plans for the deployment of large numbers of other counterforce weapons such as cruise missiles and Trident II missiles, it is difficult to see why the MX should be thought necessary to pressure the Soviets toward constructing their own version of the Midgetman, even assuming that were somehow desirable.

Let us now turn to the commission's remaining three arguments, which can be dealt with briefly. The first of these is that the new missile is needed, in effect, to frighten the Soviets into negotiating an arms control agreement with the United States. As Reagan noted in a letter to Congressman Jack Kemp, "There is no question that a failure to fund *and deploy* the MX . . . would handcuff our negotiators and require a reassessment of our START proposals."[66] (The remark about handcuffing the negotiators contrasts interestingly with an incident that was reported in the press the day after Reagan's letter to Kemp was reported. When, in a set of private talks, Paul Nitze took the initiative to discuss the possibility of a compromise in the INF talks with the Soviet delegate, he was promptly reprimanded by Reagan. Later, at a luncheon, Nitze and his Soviet counterpart were reduced to sitting on either side of Senator Gary Hart, and relaying their comments to each other through him, so that Nitze could report to his superiors that he had had no conversation with the Soviet delegate. Reagan apparently prefers a straightjacket to handcuffs.[67])

It is important to notice that the argument that new weapons are necessary to frighten the Soviets into negotiating is one which, if taken seriously, would justify any or all of the most lunatic and threatening weapons the United States could produce. In one respect, then, it is fortunate that there is no reason to take it seriously. For it presupposes that the United States is *itself* willing to negotiate seriously on arms control issues; yet, as the evidence in the next chapter will show, the Reagan administration has no intention of signing any arms control treaty which would in any way constrain its rearmament program. Indeed, Reagan's attitude toward arms control is strikingly manifest in the quotation just cited, in which he is engaging in a subtle form of blackmail by holding the future of strategic arms control hostage in order to coerce the Congress to give him the MX.

While the implication of the argument in the commission's report is that the MX is needed as a "bargaining chip" in negotiations with the Soviets, it is evident in their informal remarks that commission members recognize that the administration has no intention of using the MX in that way. Leslie Gelb, a former official in the Carter administration, writes:

> The bargaining chip concept implies the Administration is prepared to trade the MX away in return for Soviet concessions. But Commission members and Administration officials made clear that this is not what they had in mind. Thomas C. Reed, a Commission member and still a key Reagan adviser despite his recent departure from the Administration, said: "A bargaining chip is what we'll do if the Soviets don't come to the bargaining table." That is, as Commission chairman Brent Scowcroft also intimated, the Administration intends to deploy the first 100 MX's and threaten the Soviets with more to come.[68]

In his letter to Congressman Kemp, Reagan himself suggested that, in exchange for Soviet *reductions,* he would be prepared only to *limit* the number of MX missiles deployed. That is hardly a recipe for successful arms control.

The commission's next argument is that deployment of the MX is necessary to influence the Soviets' "perception of our national will and cohesion." The MX has not, however, been notable for its beneficial effects on national cohesion, having instead been a source of endless divisive controversy, and this is unlikely to change in the future.

Finally, the commission argues that the current ICBMs are aging and will soon need replacement. But, even supposing that this is true, and assuming (what is doubtful) that the United States needs ICBMs, this argument does nothing to explain why it needs to build MX missiles rather than new Minuteman missiles, which would have the advantage of being less expensive to build.

The members of the Scowcroft Commission were hand-picked for their devotion to the MX. Their arguments are probably the best that the Establishment can do on behalf of the new missile. If so, then there is effectively nothing to be said in favor of it. There is, however, quite a lot to be said against it. Of the many objections which critics have urged against the MX, two deserve special mention. The first is that, far from providing an added deterrent to a "limited" counterforce strike, the MX will actually provide the Soviets with a special and very strong incentive to launch a preemptive strike. There are three reasons why this is so. The first is that, because the MX will, as we have seen, be a first-strike weapon par excellence, it will be regarded by the Soviets as particularly threatening. The second is that the MX force will constitute an especially "lucrative" target for a preemptive strike, since it will concentrate 1,000 warheads in only 100 silos. (The present Minuteman force spreads approximately 2,100 warheads over 1,000 silos.) Finally, the silos themselves are a particularly vulnerable basing mode, and will become increasingly vulnerable as the Soviets refine the accuracy and reliability of their missiles. These three factors combine to provide a virtual invitation to the Soviets to launch a first strike. (It is worth noting, incidentally, that the administration's Trident program seems to confirm that invitation. For here too there is the same tendency toward providing the Soviets with targets which are both more important and more concentrated. In comparison with the older submarine-based forces, the Trident program will concentrate a larger number of missiles, each with a larger number of more accurate and therefore more threatening warheads, on each submarine, while the number of submarines will be reduced.)

The second objection to the MX is an outgrowth of the first. Because the MX program will involve placing so significant an investment in so vulnerable a position, it will undoubtedly push the United States closer to a policy of launch-on-warning. There have already been suggestions by various senior officials that the administration is considering such a move—as, for example, when Weinberger and General Vessey both responded to congressional questioning about the vulnerability of the MX by arguing that it would be vulnerable only "if we ride out the attack" (that is, wait until attacking missiles have landed before retaliating).[69] On another occasion, Lieutenant Colonel John Politi, deputy director of the Air Force MX program, stated that U.S. strategy dictated that the MX should be launched "on attack" (another phrase for launch-on-warning).[70]

The MX will not only encourage the United States to adopt a policy of launch-on-warning, but will also, by posing a threat to a significant proportion of the Soviet Union's land-based missiles, encourage the Soviets to adopt such a policy as well. If either side adopts launch-on-warning, this will be extremely dangerous. For, by making it more likely that one side might launch its missiles in response to a false alarm (generated, for example, by a computer error), such a policy would greatly increase the probability of accidental nuclear war.[71] If both sides were to adopt such a policy, the risks would obviously be even greater.

Because the MX provides the Soviets with a special incentive to launch a preemptive attack during a time of crisis, and because it thus puts pressure on both countries to adopt a policy of launch-on-warning, its net effect will be only to increase the risk of nuclear war. It is tempting to suppose that the administration believes that this is an acceptable price to pay for the enhanced coercive power it is hoped that the MX will provide. But, as we have seen, if the MX could provide enhanced coercive power, then it would also provide enhanced deterrence. In reality it will do neither. It is one of the great tragedies of our time that the administration's strategists do not have the wit to perceive that the MX will not give them anything they really want.

Cruise and Pershing II Missiles: The Real Reasons for Their Deployment

It is perhaps equally tragic that the same cannot be said for the cruise and Pershing II missiles which the United States has begun to install in Western Europe. For the deployment of these weapons stands a good chance of enabling the administration to achieve certain of its aims. In order to see why this is a rather ominous prospect, we need to distinguish the administration's aims in insisting on the deployment of these weapons both from the original aims of the Carter administration and from the pretended aims which the Reagan administration has provided for public consumption.

The initial decision by the Carter administration to deploy 464 cruise and 108 Pershing II missiles in Europe was motivated primarily by a concern with the credibility of the U.S. commitment to use nuclear weapons against the Soviet Union in defense of Western Europe. For many years the doctrine of flexible response had been thought to guarantee the credibility of the U.S. commitment by creating the prospect of *gradual* escalation from conventional war in Europe to strategic nuclear war—the idea being that it would be easier to reach strategic war by a series of small steps than by a single leap. Thus flexible response called for a "ladder of escalation," with a number of intermediate stages. But during the 1970s some people, primarily Europeans, became worried that a crucial "rung" in the ladder of escalation was missing, for there were no land-based U.S. missiles in Europe capable of reaching the Soviet Union. (F-111 nuclear bombers based in Europe could in principle strike within the Soviet Union, but their age, along with advances in Soviet air defenses, had cast doubt on their effectiveness.) Hence it was argued that the credibility of the U.S. commitment required the deployment on European soil of new, longer-range missiles. The presence of these missiles would provide a visible symbol of the U.S. commitment, and would fill the gap in the ladder of escalation, thereby making it more likely that the United States would retaliate against the Soviet Union in the event of a Soviet attack on Western Europe. Deterrence would therefore be strengthened.

This reasoning is probably still influential to some extent within the Reagan administration. How plausible is it? It is important to notice that the argument is not even relevant unless it is granted that the nuclear guarantee is desirable, and this is a matter which is very much open to question. A great many Europeans, for example, have come to believe that they could better defend themselves by wholly nonnuclear means.[72] But suppose for the sake of argument that the U.S. guarantee is desirable. The crucial assumption behind the argument is that the United States would be less reluctant to strike the Soviet Union with nuclear weapons based in Europe than with nuclear weapons based in the United States. This, however, is a dubious assumption, for the probability of retaliation against the United States would be the same regardless of whether the United States had launched its attack from its own territory or from that of its allies. The only reason why European-based weapons might be more likely to be used in the course of a European war is that the United States might feel pressured to launch them if the invading forces were about to capture them.

This consideration is, however, of little relevance. First, if the deployment areas were in danger of being overrun by Warsaw Pact forces, it is doubtful whether the missiles *could* be fired before they were captured. For it would probably take at least twenty-four hours for the operators to receive the authorization to fire the missiles, and by then it might be too late.[73] A second and more important point is that, even if the missiles could be fired, they would not have to be fired at Soviet territory. They could instead strike targets in non-Soviet Eastern Europe.[74] And indeed the United States would have a strong incentive to strike Eastern Europe rather than the Soviet Union, since that would carry a lesser risk of retaliation. Finally, if the deployment areas were about to be overrun, the missiles would not need to be fired at all. They could instead by withdrawn or destroyed. So there appears to be no reason to suppose that European-based nuclear weapons would be more readily used, in particular against the Soviet Union, than weapons based in the United States. Thus it seems unlikely that the stationing of these missiles in Europe will increase deterrence in Europe any more than a comparable addition to the U.S. strategic arsenal would. In short, cruise and Pershing II missiles will not significantly strengthen deterrence in Europe.

The argument that cruise and Pershing II missiles are needed to strengthen the credibility of the U.S. nuclear guarantee is apparently regarded by the Reagan administration's public relations experts as too esoteric to present to the public, so two other rationales have been devised for use in public pronouncements. One is that the new missiles are necessary to counter the threat from the Soviet Union's new SS-20 intermediate-range missiles. The other is that the new missiles are needed as "bargaining chips" in arms control negotiations with the Soviets. As for the first of these arguments, there is no evidence that this primitive idea that deterrence requires the United States to "match" every new Soviet deployment is actually an operative consideration in the minds of U.S. strategic planners. Rather, focusing on the threat from the SS-20s is simply an expedient intended to frighten reluctant Europeans into acquiescing in the deployment of the new U.S. missiles, and to allow the administration to present their deployment as a purely defensive reaction to the aggressive escalation of the arms race by the Soviet Union.

The administration's claim that its new missile deployments are simply a response to Soviet aggression has generally been accepted by the media, who have then been able to charge the Soviets with responsibility for the NATO action. Thus the *Washington Post* writes that "the single reason why there is a Euromissile issue at all is that in the 1970s the Soviets could not resist trying to steal a march on NATO by unilaterally modernizing the intermediate-range forces whose political shadow falls most darkly on Western Europe."[75] (Presumably the editors believe that NATO, rather than "modernizing" unilaterally, always does the fair thing by waiting obligingly to modernize in tandem with the Soviets.) Similarly, Strobe Talbott, a liberal American journalist and writer whom Walter Mondale referred to as "the nation's most respected author" on arms control, has said that "the purpose of the Pershing IIs and Tomahawks [the land-based cruise missiles] was to protect the West Europeans by countering the threat posed by the SS-20 ballistic missiles."[76] Talbott argues that "it was the Soviets who upset the balance in nuclear weapons in Europe. . . . Therefore the US and its West European allies are justified in deploying the Pershing IIs and Tomahawks in the absence of a negotiated settlement in INF."[77] According to this extraordinary logic, the possibility that the cruise and Pershing II missiles will actually make the situation worse all round is irrelevant.

The administration's second argument—that the new missiles are needed as bargaining chips to extract concessions from the Soviets in arms control negotiations—is an obvious ruse, as I shall demonstrate in the next chapter. The new missiles did not secure any concessions from the Soviets, but instead provoked the Soviets to break off negotiations and begin deploying SS-22 missiles in East Germany and Czechoslovakia. Now Reagan, using the same discredited logic, is claiming that only the deployment of MX missiles will force the Soviets to reopen negotiations. The failure of the negotiations, however, had nothing to do with a shortage of bargaining chips. As the evidence in the next chapter will show, the administration never had any intention of using the cruise and Pershing missiles as bargaining chips.

While the Reagan administration's announced reasons for the deployment of cruise and Pershing II missiles in Europe are constructions for the beguilement of the public, its deeper reasons for wanting the new missiles are not difficult to discern. One important reason is political: the deployment of these missiles in opposition to the wishes of the majority of the people in Western Europe will symbolize the reassertion of U.S. dominance over the European allies. (The *Washington Post* refers to those in Europe opposed to the new missiles as "militant minorities," but repeated polls in Europe have shown majorities opposed to the missiles in every country in which they are to be deployed. A recent poll in Britain, for example, found 55 percent opposed to the deployment of cruise missiles, and only 31 percent in favor.[78]) The acceptance of the missiles will, moreover, cast the allies in the role of closer collaborators in the U.S. global strategy. Other reasons are strategic in character. Cruise and Pershing II missiles are both highly accurate counterforce weapons. Because they are intermediate-range weapons, they are not covered by the SALT II treaty, which is concerned with strategic forces. Thus they will enable the United States to augment its counterforce capability against the Soviet Union without violating the constraints of the treaty, which the administration has pledged to observe as long as the Soviets do, even though it has not been ratified by the United States.

The Pershing II missiles are of particular importance in the administration's overall counterforce strategy. Recall that one of the principal aims of that strategy is to be able to prevent the Soviet leadership from being able to exercise control over Soviet society. Thus the Pentagon's 1982 Defense Guidance Plan insists that the United States must be able to threaten the Soviet Union with "decapitation"—the destruction of the political and military leadership, their centers of command and control, and their lines of communication. The Pershing II missiles are ideally suited to this task. They are extremely accurate, and may be fitted with special earth-penetrating warheads which would enhance their ability to destroy hardened command bunkers buried deep underground. Equally important, they will be able to reach targets in the Soviet Union within six to eight minutes after having been launched from West Germany. Thus they could be used to destroy certain vital Soviet command and control centers before the Soviets would have time to give any orders about the firing of their missiles, thereby leaving the Soviet Union in a state of strategic paralysis.

Cruise missiles also have a special attraction for the Reagan administration. Paradoxically, that attraction stems from the fact that these missiles—both the ground-launched missiles now appearing in Europe and the many air- and sea-launched missiles scheduled for deployment in the coming years—are highly vulnerable to interception and destruction by Soviet air defenses. The Soviets have been investing heavily in new early-warning aircraft and in new fighter aircraft which together will provide what U.S. defense sources describe as an "extremely effective" defense against cruise missiles. How could this possibly be construed as advantageous to the United States? The answer lies in the fact that, according to Pentagon estimates, it will cost the Soviet Union between $50 and $100 billion to construct effective defenses against cruise missiles. That is considerably more than the cost of the cruise missiles themselves. Thus the cruise missile program has an important role in the administration's strategy of economic warfare against the Soviet Union. It satisfies the requirement, laid down in the Pentagon's Defense Guidance Plan, that the United States should develop and deploy weapons which "are difficult for the Soviets to counter, impose disproportionate costs, open up new areas of major military competition and obsolesce previous Soviet investment [*sic*]."[79] The obvious idea behind the plan is, in the words of one U.S. analyst, "that confrontation works to our benefit. If only we gear ourselves to the task, we will outrun them"—thereby winning the arms race, consigning the Soviet Union to a position of permanent inferiority, and possibly also bringing about the collapse of the Soviet economy and, as a further consequence, the Soviet state as well.[80] The reason the United States can be confident about outrunning the Soviets is that, as Reagan has explained, the Soviets "cannot vastly increase their military productivity because they've already got their people on a starvation diet of sawdust."[81]

The administration's efforts to cripple the Soviet economy are both absurd and morally irresponsible. They are absurd because it seems obvious that they are doomed to failure, and will only cause suffering and deprivation among the ordinary people living under

Soviet rule—people whose human rights the administration affects to care so much about. Samuel Pisar writes:

> Russia's gross national product may not be much more than half of America's but it is large enough to enable the Soviet Union to keep up in the nuclear arms race. The experience of the last three decades makes that clear. If it comes to a choice between defense and consumer needs, the masters of the Kremlin will not hesitate to sacrifice the consumer, and will not need to fear that, in consequence, their regime will explode from within. For people who suffered twenty million dead in the last war, privation for the sake of defense is not that difficult.[82]

Moreover, while the Soviet leaders can safely impose quite severe deprivations on their citizens for the sake of defense, U.S. leaders cannot. American citizens are accustomed to being pampered, and will vote a president (or the members of his party in Congress) out of office if his policies cause too precipitous a decline in the rate of economic growth.[83]

The administration's efforts are also irresponsible because, to quote Pisar again, "a Soviet system caught in the grip of Western economic sanctions and internal food shortfalls could generate enough tensions to blow the world apart."[84] While the Soviet leaders need not fear being voted out of office, they are not indifferent to popular domestic opinion, and they could easily feel compelled to adopt more bellicose and confrontational policies in order to justify in the eyes of the people the privations entailed by an increase in defense spending to yet more extreme levels. In these conditions of heightened tension and animosity, the risk of war would be frighteningly high.

The perils of the administration's "decapitation" strategy are equally evident. As critics have pointed out, the destruction of the Soviet political and military leadership and their means of communication might mean that the Soviet Union's remaining missiles would simply be fired blindly and spasmodically, either by isolated lower-ranking officials to whom the responsibility for fighting the war would pass, or, worse still, by computers. Critics have also noted that decapitation would eliminate the possibility of a Soviet surrender. Yet the same planning document which calls for the decapitation strategy also insists that the United States must "force the Soviet Union to seek earliest termination of hostilities on terms favorable to the United States." But, as a former official of the Arms Control and Disarmament Agency has put it, "if the Soviet leadership is 'decapitated,' who would be left to seek such an end to hostilities?"[85]

An even more important objection to the decapitation strategy is that it will put the Soviet leadership under great pressure to strike preemptively at the Pershing II missiles during times of tension. Many critics have argued that the Pershing II missiles will lead the Soviets to adopt a policy of launch-on-warning, and the Soviets themselves have suggested as much. But it is doubtful that the Pershing IIs would allow the Soviets enough time to even launch their missiles on warning: and in any case that would only give the Soviet leaders the grim satisfaction of knowing that, shortly after they would be annihilated, the United States would be too. Much better from their point of view would be to try to destroy the Pershing II missiles preemptively at the first indication that they were being readied for use. The Soviets might even feel that such an act would be insufficiently provocative to prompt U.S. retaliation against the Soviet Union, and thus that the danger that would be averted would be greater than that which would be risked by a preemptive strike.

A common response to this objection is that the new cruise and Pershing missiles will not be vulnerable to preemption, since they will be mounted on mobile launching platforms, and thus can be dispersed during times of international tension. Notice, however, that the possibility of dispersal provides protection against preemption only when there are indications that war is imminent. A *surprise* attack could easily destroy the missiles at their bases. Of course, as I suggested, it would be during times of tension that the Soviets would have the greatest incentive to strike, so the missiles could be dispersed during the time when the Soviets might be most tempted to attack them. On the other hand, however, there is an important reason for refraining from dispersing the missiles during times of tension. Dispersal would be detrimental to what is known as "crisis stability." The Soviets would be alerted (by satellite reconnaissance, spies, or the Western media) when the missiles were moved from their bases, and could easily interpret the dispersal as a sign that the United States was preparing for war. Thus the dispersal of the missiles would serve to heighten tensions and therefore to increase the likelihood of war. It was because the West was afraid of alarming the Soviet leaders in this way that civil defense contingency plans were not implemented in the United States or Britain during the Cuban missile crisis. If, as one hopes, U.S. leaders are equally cautious in the future, then the new missiles will remain at their bases in times of tension. But then, of course, they will be vulnerable to preemption.

Even if the missiles were dispersed, however, this would not guarantee them immunity from preemption. A recent government study concedes that the Soviets could know by means of "covert intelligence" the general locations of many of the dispersed missiles. Recently the Soviets themselves have indicated that they could use high-yield warheads for "pattern" or saturation bombardment of the missile deployment areas in order to destroy the missiles preemptively.[86] It would be foolish to dismiss this threat as idle bluster.

In addition to the various objections already mentioned, there is also the common objection to cruise missiles that, being small and easily concealed, they will complicate problems of verification, and will thus make it even less likely that significant arms control or disarmament agreements will be reached in the future. But, as the evidence in the next chapter will show, the fact that cruise missiles may undermine the prospects for negotiated arms control and disarmament is, in the eyes of the Reagan administration, just another of their many virtues. For the administration has no interest in limiting its competition with the Soviet Union; rather, it is willing, as we have seen, to run great risks in order to *win*—if possible by coercion, intimidation, subversion, and economic pressure, but by war if necessary. Before concluding this chapter we should briefly examine one other crucial component of the administration's strategy for victory which is opening up a vast new area of dangerous and unconstrained competition.

Ballistic Missile Defenses

By banning the development and deployment of any but the most limited system of ballistic missile defenses, the first Strategic Arms Limitation Talks (SALT I) treaty of 1972 codified the understanding that existed at that time that the deployment, or even the threatened deployment, of any large-scale anti–ballistic missile (ABM) system is incompatible with the maintenance of stable deterrence. For stable deterrence requires that each side should retain the ability to inflict "unacceptable" damage on the other in a retaliatory strike. But the deployment of ABM systems would threaten the stability and mutuality of deterrence by raising the prospect that one side might be able to defend itself against a nuclear attack. This assessment of ballistic missile defenses remained virtually unchallenged (at least within government circles) until Reagan assumed office in 1981. Suggestions then immediately began to emerge from government quarters that the question of ballistic missile defense was being reconsidered, and that the continued commitment of the United States to the treaty was in doubt. In March 1983 Reagan announced that he was initiating a "comprehensive and intensive" research-and-development program on ballistic missile defense, and by early February 1984 the administration was proposing that $5.5 billion be allocated for this program over the next two years. The idea of ballistic missile defense had come a long way during Reagan's first three years.

It is not difficult to understand the administration's attraction to the idea of ballistic missile defense. As the earlier quotations from Paul Nitze and Colin Gray confirm, the administration regards ballistic missile defense—along with civil defense planning, which has also been revived—as essential to U.S. survival in a nuclear war. It is, therefore, necessary for its ability to prevail, and hence for its ability to intimidate and coerce the Soviet Union. As Gray himself has pointed out, "one need not be a strategic logician to appreciate that a United States capable of limiting damage to itself, would be a United States that should be perceived by Soviet leaders as far more willing (than may be presumed to be the case today) to take extreme risks on behalf of allies"—or, of course, for other purposes.[87]

Work on a network of ballistic missile defenses would have the additional benefit of putting a further strain on the Soviet economy. For the prospect of an effective ABM system would, it is sometimes argued, force the Soviets to increase by a significant amount the number of their offensive missiles in order to be able to saturate the U.S. defenses. That, it is claimed, would help to bring down the Soviet economy, or at least to stimulate domestic dissent. Thus Edward Teller, the man who invented the hydrogen bomb and who is one of the leading advocates of ballistic missile defense among Reagan's advisers, has argued that, if work on an ABM system were to force the Soviets to increase their offensive forces, "we would have accomplished something."[88]

As with the Reagan administration's other ambitions, the pursuit of ballistic missile defenses is fraught with peril. First, as was suggested earlier, it is doubtful whether the world would become a safer or more pleasant place even if the United States were to acquire the ability to prevail in a nuclear war. There is, however, little prospect that the United States will be allowed to acquire that ability. In addition to other obstacles, there are serious doubts within the scientific community about the technical feasibility of ballistic missile defenses.[89] And even if these problems can eventually be overcome, enormous problems will remain; as we have seen, the Soviet Union could increase its offensive forces, perhaps cutting costs by making extensive use of decoys, in order to be able to saturate U.S. defenses; or it could increase its reliance on cruise missiles or submarine-launched missiles with depressed trajectories, which would not be vulnerable to defenses designed to intercept ballistic missiles; or it could develop other countermeasures—some of which, such as hardened booster rockets, would be passive and defensive in nature, though others would be intended to destroy U.S. ABM systems preemptively. One of the reasons why the prospect of an effective ABM system seems so remote is that not only the ABM network itself but also the systems defending it must work with unprecedented efficiency—for, to be of value, an ABM system must remain effective throughout the duration of a nuclear war.

The fact that the United States is unlikely ever to succeed in devising an effective ABM system is the least of the objections to the attempt. It is astonishing that anyone—least of all the cold warriors of the Reagan administration—should welcome the prospect of the Soviets vastly increasing their offensive capability in response to U.S. efforts to acquire an effective ABM system. Yet that is precisely what can be expected to happen. Any ABM system will be exhaustible. If the United States develops a system which can stop half the Soviet Union's missiles, the Soviet Union could then recover its initial position by simply doubling the number of its missiles. (Of course the Soviets would no doubt work on the basis of worst-case estimates of the effectiveness of the U.S. defenses, and so would more than double the number of their offensive forces.[90]) Since the cost to the Soviet Union of doubling the number of its missiles would almost certainly be considerably less than the cost to the United States of deploying an ABM network, the Soviet Union could emerge from this competition in a stronger position vis-à-vis the United States than that from which it started.

Since, moreover, the Soviet buildup of offensive arms would begin well in advance of the time that a U.S. ABM system might become operational, the United States would undoubtedly seek to keep pace with the Soviet buildup by expanding its own offensive capability as well. With both sides having such strong incentives to increase their offensive forces, the prospects for negotiated arms control would be nil. Colin Gray has noted this fact, but does not consider it an objection. He regards the arms control process as having been a failure (which, for the most part, it has been), and contemplates its demise with scarcely concealed satisfaction.[91] No doubt his is a view which is widely shared within the administration.

This offensive arms race is only one of three arms races which the administration's work on ballistic missile defenses will provoke. For the Soviets will certainly intensify their own research on missile defenses—which, incidentally, will then prompt the British, French, and Chinese to expand their arsenals in an attempt to ensure that their forces remain effective.[92] And there will be an intensified arms race in space, where each side will be anxious to install systems which will defend its own ABMs, as well as systems which will threaten the ABMs of the other side.

Reagan administration officials discount these objections on the ground that the Soviet Union, being economically and technologically inferior to the United States, will simply be unable to keep pace. Again, the United States will outrun them. Objections on grounds of potential ineffectiveness are also dismissed. Thus Robert S. Cooper, director of the Pentagon's Advanced Research Projects Agency, has argued that, "even if only 50 per cent of all incoming missiles were stopped, the Soviets could then have no confidence in the success of a first strike, and war would become more remote."[93] This last claim assumes that any war would be started by the Soviets. Even if we make this assumption, however, it does not follow that a 50 percent effective ABM system would make war less likely. For the Soviets may be pardoned for declining to accept Cooper's view that only they would ever be wicked enough to launch a first strike. On the contrary, they would undoubtedly believe that, if the United States possessed the ability to destroy a significant proportion of their forces preemptively, as well as the ability to defend itself with greater than 50 percent effectiveness against any retaliation by the Soviet Union's remaining forces, the United States would then be strongly tempted to launch a first strike against them. (An ABM system with 50 percent effectiveness against a first strike would be considerably more effective against a retaliatory strike, since the latter would involve fewer missiles.) As members of the Union of Concerned Scientists have pointed out, "A defense that could not fend off a full-scale strategic attack but might be quite effective against a weak retaliatory blow following an all-out pre-emptive strike would be particularly provocative."[94] Thus, if the Soviets were to suspect (whether reasonably or not) that the United States was on the verge of acquiring an effective ABM system, they might decide to strike first, before the system became operational. For they would feel that, once it had become operational, they would then be effectively deprived of their retaliatory capability, and hence of their deterrent, so that the United States could attack them with impunity.

The period during the development and deployment of U.S. defenses would therefore be a particularly dangerous one. But the dangers would persist even beyond the transitional period. Let us assume that the United States has already installed an ABM system of 50 percent effectiveness against a first strike. If the Soviets believe that an American first strike is likely or imminent, as they well might in the circumstances, then they might be willing to risk a first strike themselves. For, even though their position if they were to strike first would be far worse than their present position, it would be preferable to what their position would be if they were to allow the United States to strike first.[95] Furthermore, if the United States were to suspect that the Soviets were thinking this way, it would then have a strong incentive to strike first itself, regardless of whether it had previously had any reason or intention to do so.

Thus far I have considered only situations in which the United States alone deploys missile defenses. In an important article on the topic, Charles L. Glaser has argued convincingly that, even if both sides were to have effective (though not perfect) defenses, the situation would not be clearly preferable to that which obtains under the policy of deterrence based on mutual assured destruction (MAD).[96] Even if both sides have effective defenses, each will nevertheless retain offensive forces. This would be true even if each's defenses were perfect; for there could be no guarantee that they would remain perfect and each side would need to retain offensive forces for purposes of deterrence in the event that an advance by one side were to limit the effectiveness of the other's defenses. Given that each side will therefore retain offensive forces, each will be constantly searching for ways to make those forces more effective against the other's defenses. Given that the advantage in this area belongs to the offense, changes which would reduce the effectiveness of one or the other side's defenses are likely to occur. Since, with defenses, each side's vulnerability is low, even a small change in one side's vulnerability could dramatically threaten its security, giving the other side a significant advantage. (If one side can hit the other with 10,000 missiles, then a change which would enable it to hit the other side with 100 more missiles would be insignificant. But if one side can hit the other with only 2 missiles, then a change would enable it to hit the other side with 100 more missiles would be very significant.) Since changes in vulnerability are likely to occur, this situation in which both sides have effective defenses would be highly unstable. Glaser also argues that, in such a situation, the political climate would be poisoned by mutual fears and suspicions, and that each side would have a stronger incentive to launch a first strike than it would under a policy of deterrence based on MAD. Glaser concludes that, if both sides had effective defenses, the probability of nuclear war would be higher—though, since the damage which would be caused by war might be less, the situation in which both sides have defenses is not necessarily worse than that under MAD.

In summary, I have argued that the U.S. pursuit of missile defenses will both provoke an offensive arms race and give each side an increased incentive to launch a first strike. What Glaser's arguments show is that, even if we were ultimately to arrive at the best possible outcome (though not, of course, best from the point of view of the Reagan administration), the world would not obviously have been improved. Given that the best that could result is no more attractive than the status quo, and might be worse, and given the great risks and costs that the administration's project involves ($43 billion on ABM research and related projects for the five-year period from 1984 to 1989, and a projected total cost as high as $500 billion), it seems obvious that ballistic missile defense, while superficially rather appealing, is the most chimerical, dangerous, and utterly senseless of all the administration's military projects.[97]

It will be apposite to conclude this chapter with a remark about the relation between the administration's nuclear weapons programs and its ambitions in the third world. Noam Chomsky writes:

> It is not unlikely that there will be a major nuclear war within the next few decades. It will not break out in Europe, but in some region of the Third World. . . . If we are seriously concerned to prevent nuclear war, our primary attention should be directed to the role of the USA in maintaining or heightening conflict and oppression within the domains of its influence and power.[98]

There is considerable sense in this. The prevention of nuclear war requires that we should oppose U.S. ambitions in the third world, since those ambitions are a large part of the motivation behind the U.S. nuclear buildup, and are also what is most likely to lead the United States into confrontation with the Soviet Union. But the point can also be turned on its head, with equal plausibility. For, if we hope to stop the United States from intervening throughout the third world, then we must directly oppose its nuclear buildup; for the nuclear forces are regarded by the administration as the necessary backdrop against which the United States can carry out its interventions in the third world in comparative safety. Nuclear weapons are regarded as the instruments which make U.S. imperialist ventures possible.

★3★

Arms Control as an Exercise in Public Relations

The official line is that Reagan is, in his own words "totally committed" to arms control and disarmament.[1] As we have seen, this is held to be compatible with the administration's intensive expansion and modernization of the U.S. nuclear arsenal on the ground that the weapons systems now being developed and deployed are in fact necessary for arms control. The litany of official clichés is by now familiar: new weapons are necessary to give the Soviets an incentive to negotiate seriously, to enable the United States to negotiate from a position of strength, and so on. In this chapter we shall review the administration's behavior with regard to arms control, in order to see how the reality compares with the rhetoric.

Both prior to and for a considerable time after the 1980 election, Reagan and other prominent administration members displayed open contempt for arms control. Reagan himself has in one way or another opposed every nuclear arms control agreement that has been made. For example, in 1963 he fought against the Partial Test Ban Treaty, while in 1968 he openly opposed the Non-Proliferation Treaty. And during the early 1970s he also opposed both the SALT I treaty on offensive nuclear forces and the Anti–Ballistic Missile (ABM) Treaty.[2] His continued hostility to arms control was evident in the late 1970s and early 1980s in his open espousal during that period of the aim of achieving nuclear superiority over the Soviet Union; for it was not to be expected that the Soviet Union would sign a treaty which would relegate it to a position of permanent inferiority (unless, of course, the strategy of economic warfare were to force the Soviets to accept such a position, in which case an arms control agreement would simply be a way of ratifying the U.S. advantage).

Reagan also came to office advocating the doctrine of "linkage," according to which the willingness of the United States to engage in arms control negotiations should be contingent on the Soviet Union's general good behavior—for example, in the third world. Thus Reagan initially asserted that U.S. participation in arms control talks would be conditional upon the abandonment by the Soviets of their "invasion" of El Salvador, while Weinberger claimed that talks with the Soviets would be "meaningless" as long as the Soviet Union continued to threaten Poland.[3] As critics noted at the time, such a stance fails to take arms control seriously, and instead treats it as something which the United States can withhold in order to punish the Soviets without thereby suffering any ill effects itself. (Public pressure later forced the abandonment of linkage.) Finally, the administration's dismissive attitude toward arms control emerged quite explicitly in Reagan's remarks at the graduation ceremony at West Point during the spring of 1982:

> No nation that placed its faith in parchment or paper while at the same time it gave up its protective hardware ever lasted long enough to write many pages in history. . . . The argument, if there is any, will be over which weapons, and not whether we should forsake weaponry for treaties and agreements.[4]

Around the time of Reagan's speech at West Point, presidential counselor Edwin Meese remarked privately that arms control "will be lucky if we let it get away with benign neglect."[5] Certainly no one could claim that arms control was an urgent or conspicuous item on the new administration's agenda. The administration delayed almost a year before entering discussions on theater nuclear weapons in Europe, to which it was already committed by a prior NATO decision; and it delayed almost a year and a half before opening negotiations with the Soviet Union on strategic nuclear weapons. The negotiations which many specialists on arms control considered most important—those concerning a comprehensive ban on nuclear testing—were suspended. The pretext for suspending the Comprehensive Test Ban (CTB) negotiations was that there was a more important matter which required tending to first: namely, the renegotiation of the verification clauses in two older treaties—the Threshold Test Ban Treaty of 1974 and the Peaceful Nuclear Explosions Treaty of 1976, neither of which had been ratified by the United States.[6] It is interesting that these two treaties provided for the most liberal and intrusive verification measures the Soviets ever accepted. In them the Soviet Union had agreed to accept limited on-site inspection (that is, direct examination of Soviet facilities by American inspectors) for the first time.[7] It is also noteworthy that a CTB treaty would have rendered both of these previous treaties superfluous. For the earlier treaties simply banned underground nuclear explosions of more than 150 kilotons, and "group explosions" with an aggregate yield of over 1.5 megatons; so everything which they ban would also be banned by a CTB treaty. But, in spite of these rather inconvenient facts, this particular pretext had irresistible advantages, for the predictable refusal by the Soviets to reopen negotiations on the earlier treaties allowed the administration to shift onto them the responsibility for the absence of negotiations on a CTB treaty.

It is ironic that, to the extent that there has been any candor about this matter, it has had to come from the U.S. Arms Control and Disarmament Agency (ACDA). Eugene Rostow testified before the Senate Foreign Relations Committee that "there is a feeling in many parts of the Government that given the uncertainties of the nuclear situation and the need for new weapon modernizations, we are going to need testing, and perhaps even testing above the 150 kiloton limit."[8] (The fact that, as Rostow suggests, the United States might need to violate the two earlier treaties is another reason why insisting on their renegotiation was such an attractive ploy.) Later, in a reply to questions from the House Appropriations Committee, the agency stated that "nuclear tests are specifically required for the development, modernization, and certification of warheads, the maintenance of stockpile reliability, and the evaluation of nuclear weapon effects."[9] This is of course the real point: a CTB treaty would prevent rearmament, and the achievement of superiority. While it is surprising that this is acknowledged at all, it is even more surprising that it should be defended by the ACDA.

The administration's hostility to arms control is not confined to negotiations and potential treaties; it embraces existing treaties as well. The treaties to which the United States is bound have received occasional lip service, but for the most part their existence has simply been ignored. The fact that they prohibit significant elements in the administration's rearmament program is regarded as a potentially embarrassing but nevertheless manageable problem of public relations. So far its actual treaty violations, or at least those which are publicly ascertainable, have been relatively minor. For example, Admiral Eugene Carroll of the Center for Defense Information contends that the administration's refusal to engage in CTB negotiations "constituted a clear violation of the Limited Test Ban Treaty of 1963, in which the US pledged to continue negotiations leading to an end to nuclear testing."[10] And I think the evidence which will be presented in the remainder of this chapter will be sufficient to show that the administration is also in violation of its obligation under Article VI of the Non-Proliferation Treaty "to pursue negotiations in good faith on effective measures relating to the cessation of the nuclear arms race at an early date and to nuclear disarmament under strict and effective international control."

The *potential* conflicts between the administration's rearmament program and the treaties to which the United States is bound are rather more significant. Beginning with the least serious charge, several of the administration's projects either would have violated or will violate the Strategic Arms Limitation Talks treaty of 1979 (SALT II), which Reagan has pledged to observe even though the

United States is not legally bound by it. For example, the administration's proposed "dense pack" formation for the deployment of MX missiles, had it been approved by Congress, would have violated the prohibition in SALT II on the construction of additional fixed ICBM launchers and the relocation of existing launchers. SALT II also forbids the United States to test more than one new strategic missile. Yet in accepting the recommendation of his Commission on Strategic Forces, Reagan has undertaken to build (and therefore to test) *two* new missiles—the MX and the Midgetman. Finally, the State Department has recently acknowledged that U.S. plans for the deployment of Trident missiles would give the United States more multiwarhead missiles than are allowed under SALT II.[11]

Turning now to treaties to which the United States is legally bound, fifty members of Congress (among others) have alleged that the Pentagon's plan to develop and deploy space-based weapons will involve the violation of various international treaties, presumably including the Outer Space Treaty of 1967, which prohibits the placement of weapons of mass destruction in space.[12] The most serious threat to earlier arms control achievements comes, however, from the administration's work on ballistic missile defenses. The aim of developing an effective ABM system clearly indicates a conditional intention to violate or abrogate the ABM treaty of 1972 (which is part of SALT I), which has arguably done more to reduce the risk of war than any other achievement of arms control during the nuclear age. Administration officials, of course, have denied that there is any intention to violate the treaty (though, while he denies that the treaty will be violated, Weinberger has suggested that it might have to be "amended" when the new systems are ready for deployment—an uncharacteristic bit of humor, perhaps).[13] Reagan dismissed the suggestion that his plans might require violation of the treaty by asserting that "the ABM Treaty has to do with deployment. There is nothing in it that prohibits research, which is what we're calling for."[14] Yet the treaty in fact prohibits the development, testing, and deployment of ABM systems, and on the same day that he made this denial Reagan also issued an executive order which explicitly called for a program for the *development* of an ABM system. And in any case it is not difficult to see that the administration's investment of many billions of dollars in intensive research on ballistic missile defenses is motivated by more than mere scientific curiosity.

As well as providing a clear indication of the administration's real attitude toward arms control, these facts shed an interesting light on its repeated allegations (some of which seem to have some substance) that the Soviets have been cheating on various treaties, as well as on its insistence on the importance of verification, implying as it does that the Soviets cannot be trusted to keep their agreements.[15] The aim of making these accusations public, rather than simply dealing with them through the Standing Consultative Commission, the body established for reviewing questions of treaty compliance, is to undermine public support for arms control generally.

The depth of the administration's devotion to arms control is also revealed in its evident efforts to emasculate and subvert the U.S. Arms Control and Disarmament Agency. The ACDA was founded in part to serve as a counterweight to the departments of Defense and State within the federal bureaucracy. The cause of arms control was to have its own representative, whose influence would help to offset the inherent bias of the Pentagon against the limitation of armaments. Yet, on entering office, Reagan immediately filled the senior positions in the agency with men (Eugene Rostow, Paul Nitze, and General Edward Rowny) who were not only among the fiercest opponents of SALT II, but were also notorious for their long-standing hardline views on the necessity of rearmament. Next Reagan began systematically depriving the agency of its resources—a result, no doubt, of his impartial application of the doctrine of fiscal austerity. Columnist James Reston has reported that

> there have been significant cuts in funding for the key activities of the agency. Also, its main computer was removed, and it must share a computer with another Government agency, meaning the disarmament agency must now rely on the Pentagon for classified research it used to be able to do itself. The number of permanent employees has been cut back 25 per cent, and half its library has been given to George Washington University.[16]

The effort to sabotage the agency reached a new high point with the appointment of Kenneth Adelman, one of Jeane Kirkpatrick's protégés, as its director (Eugene Rostow having proved to be too liberal). Adelman's devotion to arms control, as well as his expertise in these matters, are both well known. In 1981 he was quoted as saying that the real value of arms negotiations lies in their usefulness in managing public opinion. "My policy would be to do it for political reasons," he said. "I think it's a sham." He also told reporters that there was no point in seeking agreements with the Soviets because they had violated the 1925 treaty prohibiting chemical warfare—a reference, presumably, to the "yellow rain," chemical weapons which Soviet or Soviet-sponsored forces are alleged to have used in Afghanistan and Southeast Asia and samples of which a Harvard biochemist has recently suggested may be just bee excrement. Adelman's knowledge of matters relating to arms control was displayed to advantage in his Senate confirmation hearings, in which he stated that he did not know enough about the subject to be able to judge whether the United States could survive a nuclear war, and in which he confessed that he had never really thought about such issues as the possibility of limited nuclear war.[17] With Adelman at the helm, the ACDA has completed the transformation from counterbalance to the Pentagon to collaborator.

Despite its evident hostility to all forms of arms control, the Reagan administration was eventually forced by public pressure and in particular by the emergence of the peace movements in both Europe and the United States to open negotiations with the Soviets on the control of both strategic and theater nuclear weapons. In both cases the administration's strategy has been to play to the world audience, cultivating the image of a government deeply committed to the reduction of nuclear arms, while at the same time assiduously avoiding an agreement with the Soviets. In the next two sections we shall examine in detail the administration's behavior in these two sets of negotiations: the Strategic Arms Reduction Talks (START) on strategic nuclear weapons, and the Intermediate-Range Nuclear Forces (INF) negotiations on theater nuclear weapons.

The START Negotiations

The Reagan administration had been in office for seventeen months before it unveiled its initial START proposals before an admiring world. The proposals were cleverly crafted for public presentation, calling for two types of reduction, which would occur in stages. The first stage, it was said, would involve a reduction in the number of strategic warheads by one-third from present levels on both sides, down to equal levels. There would be a limit of 5,000 strategic warheads for each side. No more than half of these warheads could be land-based. Each side would be allowed 850 missiles. The second stage in the process would involve a reduction in total missile "throw weight" on each side to below the U.S. level at that time. (Missile throw weight is the weight of the package above the missile's final booster stage—in other words, the maximum weight which the missile can lift and carry.)

These proposals were generally greeted with great enthusiasm, even among liberals. Former President Carter referred to the overall plan as "an excellent proposal," and an editorial in the *New*

Republic called it "reasonable, serious, and ambitious."[18] The virtues of the plan, according to liberal commentators, were that it would "strengthen second-strike capacity by encouraging both sides to move their missiles out to sea where they are harder to detect, and where, at least at present, they lack the accuracy to launch at first strike."[19] A closer examination of the proposals however, suggests a rather different evaluation—and, incidentally, provides some evidence for the principle that if people are kept waiting long enough, and are uncertain whether they will get anything at all, they will be grateful for almost anything they get.

Notice first that the plan called for a one-third reduction in the number of warheads from present levels down to equal levels. That is possible only if present levels are equal. U.S. officials claimed at the time that each side had 7,500 strategic warheads. This was curious, since official sources had previously cited a figure of 9,000 strategic warheads for the United States and between 7,000 and 8,000 for the Soviet Union. The explanation behind this discrepancy is that the administration's proposal, and therefore its figure for the total number of warheads, covered only ballistic missile warheads, and excluded warheads carried by strategic bombers—though echoing official pronouncements, the press often reported that the proposal called for reductions in "strategic warheads." The fact that the proposal simply ignored warheads carried by strategic bombers is significant: for that is an area in which the United States enjoys a large advantage over the Soviet Union—one which is increasing and which will continue to increase as the United States equips more of its B-52s with cruise missiles, and begins to deploy B-1 and stealth bombers also armed with cruise missiles.

In an editorial expressing support for the Reagan administration's proposals, the *Times* of London argued that they were "reasonably fair in that the Americans would have to dispose of more warheads than the Soviets while the Soviets would have to dispose of more launching vehicles [i.e., missiles]."[20] The point about the required Soviet sacrifice is true though understated: since the Soviets have fewer MIRVs, and thus have their warheads spread over a larger number of missiles, they would have been required to give up almost twice as many missiles as the United States. The proposals therefore penalize the Soviets for a feature of their arsenal which strategists now agree is conducive to strategic stability—namely, the fact that their missiles have fewer MIRVs. The *Times*'s claim that the United States would have to give up more warheads is, however, false. Presumably the editors reasoned that, since the proposal calls for *equal* ceilings on warheads, and since the United States has more strategic warheads than the Soviet Union, it follows that the United States would have to give up more. But this reasoning either misses or suppresses the fact that the U.S. proposal covers not strategic warheads generally, but only strategic ballistic missile warheads.

It is interesting to recall, in this context, the Scowcroft Commission's argument that one benefit of the MX is that it will supposedly encourage the Soviets to develop single-warhead missiles, thus spreading their warheads out rather than concentrating them in clusters of MIRVs. Yet not only are the Soviet Union's warheads *already* in general less concentrated than those of the United States (while the latter will become even more concentrated with the advent of the MX), but also the effect of Reagan's START proposals, with their requirement that the Soviets give up a large number of missiles, would be to encourage the Soviets to *increase* their reliance on MIRVs and thus to increase the concentration of their warheads. At the time the proposal was made, U.S. officials estimated that the Russians had roughly 2,400 strategic ballistic missiles carrying a total of a little more than 7,000 warheads—an average of three warheads per missile. But under Reagan's proposal, they would be allowed 850 missiles and 5,000 warheads—an average of six warheads per missile. Thus Reagan's START proposals would have pushed the Soviet Union in exactly the opposite direction from that said to be desirable by the Scowcroft Commission. Revealingly, by forcing the Soviets to concentrate their warheads in a smaller number of targets, the U.S. proposals would in that respect have rendered Soviet forces more vulnerable to a first strike.

Of the warheads which the U.S. proposals would allow each side to keep, no more than 2,500 could be land-based, and at least 2,500 would be submarine-based. But, as many commentators noted at the time, approximately 72 percent of the Soviet warheads were then land-based, while only about 22 percent of the U.S. warheads were. That is, while the majority of the Soviet strategic warheads were (and still are) land-based, the majority of the U.S. warheads were (and are) submarine-based—though the U.S. warheads were more evenly distributed between the two basing modes, with a significant proportion of the total also being deployed on strategic bombers. A mutual reduction to equal numbers of land- and submarine-based warheads (which is the best that the Soviet Union could hope for under the U.S. proposal) would therefore have very different consequences for Soviet and U.S. forces. The United States would be able to implement its plan of increasing the number of its land-based warheads (the proposal would allow for an increase of 350), and would have to give up less than half of its submarine-based warheads (which it could do by phasing out a number of older Poseidon warheads, as it already has plans to do). The Soviet Union, by contrast, would have to give up well over half of its land-based warheads, and would have to increase the number of its submarine-based warheads by 600 or 700 in order to reach its ceiling.

It is important to understand the implications of these differential requirements. First, recall the *New Republic*'s claim that the U.S. proposal encourages "*both sides* to move their missiles out to sea where they are harder to detect, and where, at least at present, they lack the accuracy to launch a first strike."[21] This is obviously false. The proposal requires the United States to *cut back* its forces at sea, and allows it to increase its land-based forces, which are both vulnerable and sufficiently accurate to pose a first-strike threat to the Soviet Union. Nor is it true that the Trident missiles which the United States is beginning to deploy on its submarines lack the accuracy necessary in a first-strike weapon. Second, the requirement that the Soviet Union dismantle more than half of its land-based forces and seek compensation by increasing its submarine-based forces would put it at a profound disadvantage vis-à-vis the United States. The Soviets have invested disproportionately in land-based forces as a result of technological and geographical constraints. Their submarine-launched missiles are fairly primitive compared with those of the United States, being mostly liquid-fueled and relatively inaccurate, and their submarines themselves are noisy and relatively slow and are therefore much easier to detect and track than those of the United States. The United States is, moreover, considerably more advanced in antisubmarine warfare technology, so that Soviet submarines are significantly more vulnerable to preemptive attack than are their U.S. counterparts. Finally, the Soviets have access to fewer ports, and have no warm water ports, and they are thus unable to keep as many submarines at sea as the United States, even though their fleet is actually larger. At any given moment, therefore, a significantly greater proportion of the Soviet fleet will be resting vulnerably in port. In the light of these facts it is not difficult to see that, for the Soviets, the acceptance of the U.S. requirement that they reverse their priorities and invest heavily where they suffer from so many important disadvantages would be a complete catastrophe.

While the U.S. proposal would require the Soviets to dismantle more than half of their land-based missiles, thereby greatly weakening their counterforce capability, it would hardly constrain the U.S. counterforce capability at all. Within the constraints of the proposal, the United States would be free to deploy the MX missile, the Trident II missile, and B-1 and stealth bombers laden with highly accurate cruise missiles. The proposal also excludes sea-launched cruise missiles from consideration though the United States intends to deploy several thousand of these over the next few years. (After the Scowcroft Commission delivered its report, the administration revised its proposed ceiling on missile numbers from 850 to 1,200 in order to allow for the incorporation of the Midgetman into the American arsenal.[22]) The *New Republic* editorial quoted earlier comments that "we are not disturbed by the lack of restrictions on these nuclear modernizations," thereby providing some insight into what passes for liberalism in the United States.[23]

Next consider the second stage of the proposed reduction process. Here both sides would be required to reduce the total throw weight of their missiles to an equal level below the level of the U.S. forces at that time. (Again, since the throw-weight measure applies only to ballistic missiles, the proposals for the second stage also exclude nuclear weapons—including cruise missiles—carried by strategic bombers, as well as ground- and sea-launched cruise missiles.) Since the Soviet Union has roughly a three-to-one advantage in total throw weight, it would be required to make a vastly disproportionate sacrifice. U.S. officials tended to dismiss this objection on the grounds that it is not the fault of the United States that the Soviets have achieved superiority in this important respect. This, however, was a piece of conscious deception, for, as critics have pointed out, the United States had earlier made a deliberate decision to reduce its missiles' throw weight (and therefore their explosive yield) in order to increase their accuracy. (Weight detracts from accuracy, and, where counterforce targeting is concerned, accuracy is far more important than the explosive yield of the warhead.) The Soviets would perhaps have made the same decision had not the state of their technology at the time ruled out the possibility of achieving a comparable degree of accuracy. Thus, as in the case of the requirement to cut their land-based missiles, the Soviets were being penalized for their technological inferiority. Moreover, since the cuts in missile throw weight would not affect either side's bomber or cruise missile forces, they would leave the United States with another significant advantage.

Finally, since the U.S. proposals focused on counting warheads rather than missiles or launchers (in itself a reasonable proposal), it was clear that extensive on-site inspection would be required for verification. For, while satellites can detect how many launchers each side has, they cannot detect with any confidence how many warheads a particular missile contains. So any agreement based on the U.S. proposals would probably require the Soviets to open up their missiles to U.S. inspectors, something which the Soviets' (unjustifiable) obsession with secrecy has always made them loath to do.

In all respects, then, the Reagan proposal was designed to maximize the probability of its being rejected: it excluded strategic bombers and cruise missiles, where the United States has a growing advantage; it required the Soviets to give up nearly twice as many missiles; it required the Soviets to scale back their counterforce capability while allowing the Americans to increase theirs, and, because it also encouraged the Soviets to concentrate their forces, it would therefore have greatly increased their vulnerability to a first strike; it ignored the question of accuracy but required the Soviets to make disproportionate reductions in missile throw weight, thereby further weakening their counterforce capability; and, finally, it required intrusive verification techniques which the Soviets were bound to regard with suspicion and hostility. The Soviets would have to have been insane to accept it—a fact of which the Reagan administration was of course aware. At the same time, however, the proposal had a specious appearance of fairness since (if bombers could be kept out of sight) it called for equal levels on both sides. It also called for *reductions* on both sides, something which no arms control agreement had ever before achieved. Thus it had some superficial attractions even for the peace movement. The proposal appeased a wide section of domestic liberal opinion, and provided West European governments with ammunition for use against their own troublesome peace movements. The administration was not, however, giving anything away, either to the Soviets or to the peace movement. Since its proposal was bound to be rejected, and since its rearmament program would be safe even if, miraculously, the Soviets were to accept its proposal, it stood almost no chance of losing anything it really valued. The initial proposals were a highly successful exercise in the management of public opinion.

While the initial proposals served for some time, the inevitable calls for "flexibility" eventually began to be heard. Reagan then worked out a "compromise" with Congress. If Congress would give him the MX missile, he would give them a promise of greater flexibility in the U.S. negotiating position in the START talks. A sufficient number of Democrats agreed, and funding for the MX was granted. In October 1983 Reagan responded by revealing a new package of START proposals. In fact the proposals were essentially the same except that they contained an offer to establish a joint working group which would study the possibility of a negotiated "build-down"—an idea championed by several influential members of Congress. The details of the build-down idea as conceived by the administration were hazy, since no precise figures were given in the public announcement. But the basic concept of build-down is simple: as each side deploys new warheads, it would be required to retire a greater number of older warheads. At the same time both sides would be required to reduce the number of their strategic warheads by 5 percent each year for a certain number of years, regardless of whether the required reductions would be accompanied by the permitted modernizations. The administration's new proposals were also said to be more "flexible" on the question of strategic bombers and cruise missiles, which were now to be at least in principle negotiable. While again no precise details were given, administration officials suggested that the United States was proposing to limit its deployment of new bombers and cruise missiles in exchange for reductions in the Soviet Union's arsenal of land-based missiles.

The lack of details about the new proposals make them difficult to evaluate, though a few brief comments are possible. While the proposals would serve to reduce overall numbers, they would serve not only to legitimize modernization but actually to encourage it. If there were no requirement to make reductions in the absence of modernization, each side would then have an incentive to forgo modernization; but the new proposals encourage each side to modernize in order to keep pace with the required reductions. Because of this, the arms race would become a competition in improving the technological sophistication of the weapons systems which would survive the reductions—a competition in which the United States would have a clear and perhaps decisive advantage. An arms race focusing exclusively on technology rather than numbers would also be far more dangerous and potentially "destabilizing."

The new proposals retained most of the features of the old proposals to which the Soviet Union has most reason to object: they fail to constrain the U.S. counterforce capability; they retain the requirement that the Soviet Union should restructure its forces, shifting from a reliance on land-based missiles to a reliance on submarine-based missiles; they still require the Soviets to make a disproportionate reduction in missile throw weight; and they would still necessitate on-site inspection. While they make bombers and cruise missiles in principle negotiable, it would appear merely that they offer U.S. *restraint* in the deployment of new bombers and cruise missiles while requiring in return an actual *reduction* in the number of existing Soviet missiles. (In this respect the new proposals are similar to Reagan's "zero option," which will be discussed in the next section.) Finally, the proposals would have to be implemented for a number of years before significant results would be achieved. The build-down idea might, however, have one new and attractive feature, which is that it would provide both sides with an incentive to shift away from MIRVed missiles to single-warhead missiles (by requiring greater reductions for the modernization of MIRVed systems than for the modernization of single-warhead systems), but press reports were unclear about whether this was actually a feature of the idea of the build-down as it was presented to the Soviets.[24]

It would seem that, all things considered, the administration's new proposals do not mark much of an advance over the earlier ones. Both were designed to ensure their rejection by the Soviets, whose intransigence could then be cited as the reason why Reagan was unable to achieve an arms control agreement during his first four years in office. Shortly after the new START proposals were unveiled, the negotiations were adjourned without the Soviets agreeing to a date for their resumption. This was primarily in protest against the arrival of U.S. cruise and Pershing II missiles in Europe. But the Soviets clearly left wondering whether there was any point in trying to reach an agreement with the Reagan administration. The negotiations have remained adjourned for more than a year.

The INF Negotiations

As we have seen, the Reagan administration came to office committed to pursue negotiations with the Soviets about theater nuclear weapons in Europe. The commitment derived from a decision taken by NATO in December 1979 to pursue what was called a "two-track" program. One "track" called for the "modernization" of NATO's theater nuclear forces through the deployment of 464 cruise missiles and 108 Pershing II missiles in Europe. The other track called for negotiations with the Soviet Union. At the end of November 1981, almost two years after the NATO decision, negotiations opened in Geneva. (Naturally, the modernization track was implemented rather more expeditiously.) The negotiations were initially referred to as the "TNF negotiations"—that is, negotiations about theater nuclear forces. Soon, however, the name was changed to "INF negotiations"—negotiations about intermediate-range nuclear forces. The change was made because the original title had the unfortunate effect of reminding people of the unpleasant fact that Europe is regarded as a "theater," or an area of local military operations where, among other things, a "limited" nuclear war might be held. Moreover, the revised title had the additional advantage of excluding more weapons from the negotiations by definition—in particular the many thousands of short-range tactical weapons which NATO deploys in Western Europe.

Shortly before the negotiations began, Reagan revealed what the U.S. negotiating position would be: the zero option. The zero option refers to the proposal that the United States would forgo the deployment of cruise and Pershing II missiles in Europe in exchange for the removal and dismantling of all of the Soviet Union's SS-4, SS-5, and SS-20 intermediate-range missiles. Like Reagan's START proposals, it had its attractions: if accepted, it would eliminate the entire class of land-based intermediate-range missiles. Yet, also like the START proposals, it was proposed in the confident expectation that it would be rejected. That there was this expectation is shown by the fact that the zero option is incompatible with the administration's reasons for wanting to deploy cruise and Pershing II missiles in Europe, and also with NATO military doctrine.

The zero option was made to seem a rational option for the United States by the fact that the military rationale for the new missiles which was presented to the public was that they were necessary to counter the Soviet SS-20s. It follows from this that, if the Soviets were to give up their SS-20s, there would then be no need for the new cruise and Pershing II missiles. But, as we saw earlier, the threat from the SS-20s was never part of the real motivation behind the new missiles. Where NATO as a whole is concerned, the new missiles are considered necessary to fill a gap in the ladder of escalation, thereby reinforcing the credibility of the U.S. nuclear guarantee to Europe. And the Reagan administration has other reasons for wanting to deploy the new missiles: to reassert control over the European allies and bind them more closely to the U.S. global strategy, to augment the U.S. counterforce capability against the Soviet Union, and to fulfill the requirements of both the strategy of decapitation and the strategy of economic warfare. None of these reasons for deploying the new missiles would vanish with the disappearance of the SS-20s. In particular, even in the absence of the SS-20s, the perceived need to reinforce the credibility of the U.S. nuclear guarantee would remain. This is why the zero option is incompatible with NATO military doctrine, and why its proposal thus generated alarm among some members of the European establishment. France's former ambassador to NATO, for example, wrote in the *New York Times* that "what's troubling about the zero option is that it promotes the idea that our security would be better served if no medium-range missiles were deployed on either side—that we could do without the weapons that couple the United States to Europe and provide the cornerstone of deterrence."[25]

In fact there was never any cause for alarm. For the Reagan administration was fully justified in its anticipation that the zero option would be rejected. A glance at the proposal will reveal why this is so. According to U.S. estimates, the Soviets had 250 SS-20s and 350 SS-4s and SS-5s at the time that the zero option was put forward. Since each of the SS-20s carries three independently targetable warheads, that means that the Soviets were being asked to give up 1,100 warheads. In return, the United States would simply refrain from developing and deploying 572 missiles carrying one warhead each. That hardly looks like an equitable proposal from the Soviets' point of view. The Soviets also objected, and not without reason, that the proposal focused exclusively on one narrowly defined class of weapons in which the Soviet Union had the advantage, and ignored weapons in other categories; that it failed to allow the Soviet Union any compensation for the British and French arsenals; and that it would have required the Soviet Union to dismantle the SS-20s targeted on Asia, and thus ignored the threat which the Soviet Union faces from that direction.

This is not to say that the Soviet Union was right in rejecting the zero option. On the contrary, it is not unreasonable to believe that the Soviet Union (and indeed the United States) should begin to reduce its nuclear arsenal unilaterally—which is, in effect, what the zero option requires. Though there is no space to defend this view here, it can be argued that the Soviet Union ought to dismantle the SS-4s, SS-5s, and SS-20s regardless of what Western governments do. It was, however, entirely predictable that the Soviets would reject the zero option, even if they ought to have accepted it. And it is the crassest hypocrisy for the administration to pretend to believe that it would be reasonable for the Soviet Union to accept what it would never accept for the United States—namely, a "multilateral" proposal calling for significant unilateral reductions.

If the zero option is contrary to the requirements of NATO military doctrine, and if it was certain to be rejected, then it could have been proposed only in order to mobilize support for, or at least minimize opposition to, the deployment of the new U.S. missiles. Again, by putting forward a proposal with a certain specious plausibility (and undoubted appeal to much of the public in Western Europe), but which the Soviets would be certain to reject, the United States could hope to portray the Soviets as the villains whose military buildup, combined with an unwillingness to accept reasonable reductions, necessitated the deployment of the new missiles. The zero option was, as Simon Lunn has argued, "a political tactic for making the Soviet Union responsible for NATO reductions and deployments. Rather than acknowledging that NATO will modernize because of its own requirements the suggestion is that it will modernize only in the face of Soviet reluctance to make reductions."[26]

The Soviets responded to the zero option with a barrage of counterproposals. Their initial proposal was to limit each side (by which they meant NATO and the Warsaw Pact, and not just the United States and the Soviet Union) to 300 intermediate-range delivery vehicles—which included aircraft as well as missile launchers. Later they proposed their own zero option, which called for the elimination not only of land-based intermediate-range missiles but also of submarine-based and intermediate-range air-based theater nuclear weapons. Alternatively, they proposed to reduce their land-based intermediate-range missiles to the number of missiles in the British and French strategic arsenals—provided that NATO would not deploy the cruise and Pershing II missiles in Europe.[27]

All of these proposals were, of course, rejected by the West. The last of the three, which received the most attention in the press, was rejected primarily on two grounds. One was that the proposals made missiles rather than warheads the counting unit. Since the Soviet SS-20s carry three independently targetable warheads, the proposal would have allowed the Soviets to cover more targets than the combined arsenals of the British and French could. This was a reasonable objection within the conventional framework for thinking about arms control. The second objection was that the proposal insisted on counting the British and French arsenals, and this was unacceptable to the British and French, and hence to the United States. Notice, however, that the British and French were not being asked to disarm, or even to limit their arsenals. The Soviets were instead requiring only that they receive compensation for the weapons which the British and French have targeted against them.

The reasons which were offered for the exclusion of the British and French forces from the negotiations are rather interesting. Margaret Thatcher, for example, argued that Britain's Polaris missiles are *strategic* weapons, and must therefore be excluded "by definition" from talks on theater forces. She did not go on to explain why the British forces were kept out of the SALT negotiations on strategic forces, or why they were not covered in the U.S. START proposals. George Bush, however, offered the argument that the British and French forces "have no place in *bilateral* negotiations."[28] One would have thought that if Western leaders were really serious in wanting to achieve multilateral nuclear disarmament, as they say they are, then they would be sufficiently resourceful not to be thwarted by mere definitions.

The Soviets also made a number of other proposals in Geneva. They proposed that each side should pledge not to be the first to use nuclear weapons; they proposed a mutual nonaggression pact; and they called for a 310- or 370-mile-wide nuclear-free zone in Central Europe. All were rejected—the latter on the ground that a nuclear-free zone would require the withdrawal of NATO weapons but not of Soviet weapons, since the warheads for the Warsaw Pact's tactical nuclear weapons are stored in the Soviet Union, outside the proposed zone. In other words, it was claimed that the proposed zone was already nuclear-free on the Soviet side. Later, however, the Soviet Union threatened to deploy new nuclear missiles in Eastern Europe if the United States were to go ahead with the deployment of cruise and Pershing II missiles in Western Europe. Forgetting how useful it had been to tell people in the West that the Soviets kept their tactical nuclear weapons within their own borders, Weinberger responded by revealing that the Pentagon's intelligence sources had known for years that nuclear weapons are deployed with Soviet forces in Eastern Europe. This allowed him to dismiss the Soviet Union's threat as "nothing new" (an interesting departure from his usual hysteria about Soviet weapons deployments). But now a new lie will have to be invented if the Soviets ever revive the idea of a nuclear-free zone in Central Europe.[29]

The administration responded to this flood of Soviet proposals by seeing in how many different disguises it could serve up the zero option. About a month before the 1983 West German elections, Reagan offered, in "an open letter to the people of Europe," to meet Andropov at a summit meeting. But Reagan had already prepared the agenda for the summit, which was that the two leaders would agree to accept the zero option. Kohl, the West German chancellor, whose electoral prospects Reagan's offer was intended to boost, rapturously described the offer as "a breakthrough for peace." But the breakthrough failed to materialize, for Andropov unaccountably declined the offer. Later Reagan was asked whether there had been anything new in his proposal. His reply was: "No. Frankly, I was responding to this vast propaganda effort that would try to discount our legitimate proposals for arms reductions."[30] Despite its crudity, Reagan's ploy was probably a success on balance, for at least it gave the Western media an opportunity to condemn Andropov for refusing to meet with Reagan.

Later Vice-President Bush, for whom the zero option was "steeped in morality," produced his own rather novel contribution to the cause of arms control when he stated that "our challenge to the Soviet leadership is to come up with a plan to banish these [i.e., land-based intermediate-range] missiles."[31] In other words, Bush's ingenious idea was to invite the Soviets to propose the zero option themselves.

But no matter how cleverly it was packaged, the zero option was growing a bit stale. Western European leaders needed a new initiative with which to pacify their populations—something which, in the words of one French diplomat, would enable the Reagan administration "to appear sincere" in trying to reach an agreement.[32] Responding to this pressure, Reagan came forward with his "compromise proposal." Under this plan, the United States would install a certain number of intermediate-range missiles in Europe, while the Soviet Union would be allowed to retain as many missiles as would be necessary to give it the same number of warheads that the United States would have. The number of warheads each side would be allowed to deploy would be a matter for negotiation.

Western officials were unusually forthright in acknowledging the motivation behind the proposal. The *New York Times* reported:

> Reagan Administration officials and European diplomats acknowledged . . . that President Reagan's compromise offer on medium-range missiles would almost certainly be rejected by Moscow, but they felt it was nonetheless essential in the battle for the political support of Western Europeans. "That's what this negotiation" with the Soviet Union "is all about," a ranking State Department official said. "It all comes down to whether we or the Soviets are more convincing to the Europeans, and whether the Europeans will back new American missile deployments or will block them," the official said.[33]

In keeping with the spirit of the enterprise, the scheduled announcement of the new proposal was moved forward from the Thursday before Good Friday when officials learned that few newspapers are published in Western Europe on Good Friday. For it was considered vital that the proposal be publicized before the Easter demonstrations in Europe. Generally the Western media performed according to expectation, for, in spite of the transparency of his intentions in putting forward the compromise proposal, Reagan was ecstatically praised for this new "demonstration of flexibility."

Why was the new proposal almost certain to be rejected? The answer was forcefully stated by Edward Pessen in a letter to the *New York Times.*

> Simple arithmetic reveals that, however else it might be described, President Reagan's recent modification of his "zero option" proposal is not a compromise. Under [the] zero option, the Soviet Union would abandon its 600 SS-4, SS-5 and SS-20 intermediate-range missiles that are pointed at Western Europe. The effect on the total East-West balance of nuclear weapons would be a net gain of 600 for our side. Under the terms of the President's "compromise" proposal, we would install X number of Pershing 2 launchers and cruise missiles to match whatever number the Soviets reduce their intermediate missiles to.

The net gain for our side? 600. Since the Soviets know how to add and subtract, it is unlikely that they will find the modification of zero more attractive than zero.[34]

Professor Pessen's actual calculations are incorrect, since the "compromise" proposal makes warheads rather than missiles the counting unit. Around the time that the proposal was put forward, the Pentagon estimated that the Soviet Union had 150 SS-4s and SS-5s, and 351 SS-20s, 108 of which were targeted on Asia.[35] Since the SS-20s each carry three warheads, the total number of warheads on the Soviet side was 1,203. So the American "gain" under either proposal would not have been 600 missiles, but instead 1,203 warheads. Thus Pessen's basic point is sound, but understated. Since the compromise proposal satisfied none of the Soviets' objections to the zero option (for it too refused to compensate the Soviets for the British and French forces, ignored weapons in other categories, and insisted on global limits, thus ignoring the threat the Soviet Union faces from Asia), there was no danger of its being accepted. (This was not, however, apparent to Weinberger, who wanted to make the "compromise" yet another gilded zero option by offering it only on condition that the Soviets would agree ultimately to accept the zero option. But, as the *New York Times* observed, "Secretary of State George P. Shultz argued successfully that this would appear to Europeans as a disguised zero option, and therefore would not do the job."[36])

Seemingly the most reasonable proposal to emerge from the negotiations was Andropov's offer in 1983 to reduce the number of warheads on the Soviet intermediate-range missiles targeted on Europe to the number of warheads of the combined British and French strategic forces. Britain's 4 Polaris submarines carry a total of 192 warheads. France has 18 ground-launched missiles, each with one warhead, which are capable of striking Soviet territory, and its missile-carrying submarines are equipped with 98 warheads. The combined total is thus 290. So, while Andropov's proposal would not have required any reductions on the Western side, it would have required the Soviet Union to give up 588 warheads (all 150 SS-4 and SS-5 warheads, and 438 of the 729 SS-20 warheads which it was estimated that the Soviet Union had targeted on Western Europe at that time). This would have left the Soviets with only 97 SS-20 missiles.

Since this proposal would have prevented the deployment of any cruise or Pershing II missiles in Europe, it was of course rejected by the United States. Like all the other Soviet and American proposals, this one also had concealed biases. The 291 warheads on the remaining 97 SS-20s would be independently targetable, whereas

Britain's and France's multiple warheads are not. So the Soviet proposal would have enabled the Soviet Union to cover significantly more targets than Britain and France would have been able to cover. Moreover, the British and French missiles are almost entirely submarine-based, which means that only a certain percentage of these missiles are operational at any given time. A further problem was that Britain and France had (and still have) plans to "modernize" (i.e., expand) their strategic arsenals. The projected combined total of their warheads was expected to surpass the number of warheads which were deployed on the Soviet SS-4, SS-5, and SS-20 missiles. Thus, since the Soviet proposal would have allowed the Soviet Union compensation for the new British and French weapons, it might not have brought about any actual reduction in the number of Soviet intermediate-range missiles. The Soviets were clearly aware of this. On the other hand, if one accepts that the Soviet Union is entitled to compensation for the British and French arsenals, then the real problem lies, not in the Soviet proposal, but in the attitudes of the British and French governments to nuclear disarmament.

At only one point during the time that the INF talks were proceeding did the two sides come anywhere near to reaching an agreement. This was during the now famous "walk in the woods" when the American negotiator, Paul Nitze, and his Soviet counterpart, Yuli Kvitsinsky, privately explored and apparently agreed upon a compromise. Reports indicated that, under this compromise,

> the US would drop its demand for global INF parity and settle for a freeze on the SS-20s in Asia, cancel the deployment of the 108 Pershing IIs and deploy 75 cruise missile launchers with 300 single warhead missiles. In return, the USSR would drop its demands for inclusion of the British and French nuclear forces and cancellation of the NATO deployments, scrap the remaining SS-4s and SS-5s and reduce SS-20 launchers within range of Europe from 243 to 75.[37]

Despite the fact that, when the details of the compromise were leaked, the public reaction was one of great enthusiasm, it seems obvious that an agreement based on the compromise would have done exceedingly little to curb the arms race or to increase security in Europe. While such an agreement would have achieved modest reductions on the Soviet side, it would have permitted an expansion of the U.S. arsenal. Yet even this relatively favorable arrangement was totally unacceptable to the Reagan administration. Nitze was apparently reprimanded for even exploring the possibility of a compromise. Strobe Talbott has commented that, at the time,

"Brezhnev was still alive, but he was dying. As a result of Nitze's initiative, Brezhnev may have been tempted by the prospect of a breakthrough in INF and a last summit. We will never know, for the Reagan Administration rejected what the Soviets surely regarded as the key feature of the deal—the sacrifice of the Pershing II—and signaled its repudiation to Moscow before there was any Soviet response whatsoever."[38] With one notable exception, all other commentators have agreed with Talbott that the initial rejection of the compromise came from the United States (though the Soviets then repudiated it as well). The exception is Ronald Reagan, who asserted during his second debate with Walter Mondale that "it wasn't me that turned it down. The Soviet Union disavowed it."[39] It was not the first time that the president's assertions about his own past behavior have been at variance with what others regard as the public record.

When the new U.S. missiles began to arrive in Europe in late November 1983, two years after the talks had begun, the Soviets fulfilled their earlier threats by breaking off the negotiations and accelerating the deployment of new nuclear missiles in Eastern Europe. A couple of weeks later, both the Mutual and Balanced Force Reductions talks on conventional forces in Central Europe, which had been going on in Vienna for a decade, as well as the hitherto secret negotiations on measures to prevent accidental nuclear war, also collapsed, leaving East-West relations in a dreadfully deteriorated and dangerous state.

The Geneva INF negotiations were all along a diversion. They provided the occasion for a competition in statesmanlike gesturing which both sides were eager to exploit. It was an edifying spectacle, with militarists on both sides repeatedly capturing the headlines with impressive proposals and effusive professions of a deep yearning for peace. As an exercise in public relations, the negotiations were an enormous success. But there was never any intention, at least on the U.S. side, that they should succeed in producing a significant agreement. As Lawrence Freedman, an unusually candid figure in the British establishment, has recently remarked,

> Those responsible for the [NATO "two-track"] program hoped from the start that the addition of an arms-control offer to the force-modernization plans would be sufficient to deflect the opposition. It was never envisaged that arms control would lead to the abandonment of the plans for 572 cruise and Pershing missiles, but sufficient slack was built into the numbers to allow for substantial reductions in the name of arms control.[40]

Freedman's point has in fact been conceded by administration officials responsible for arms control policy. Before the INF negotiations began, General Rowny, Reagan's START negotiator, explained that

> in the interest of getting some ground-launched cruise missiles and some Pershing IIs into Europe, the Administration agreed, as had the past Administration, to a two-track approach. It is proper for us to live up to our commitment of getting modernized forces deployed in Europe. The Administration obviously considered it good for Alliance solidarity to open TNF negotiations at an early date.[41]

Around the same time, Richard Burt, the assistant secretary of state for European affairs, reportedly told his staff that "the purpose of this whole exercise is maximum political advantage. It's not arms control we're engaged in, it's alliance management."[42] Later, in November 1983, when the missiles were on their way to Europe and the negotiations were on the verge of collapse, Burt remarked that "if we had not entered into negotiations with the Russians, it would have been impossible to get the allies to deploy missiles on their territory. . . . So it was necessary to create the impression among our allies that we are seeking genuine progress on the limitation of nuclear armaments."[43]

More recently a new phase in the propaganda war was initiated, though this time the primary target of the administration's efforts was American rather than European public opinion. This new round of public posturing began in June 1984 when the Soviet Union proposed to open formal negotiations on space weapons in Vienna in September. There is some reason to think that, at least initially, the Soviets were genuinely interested in getting an agreement. At that point the Soviet Union was actually ahead of the United States in one crucial space-weapon technology—antisatellite systems. It had developed and successfully tested an antisatellite system capable of destroying satellites in low orbits. The United States, however, was in the process of developing a far more sophisticated and effective system capable of destroying satellites in both low and high orbits. Since the Soviet Union was in imminent danger of dropping farther and farther behind in this costly competition, it had a real incentive to try to reach an agreement which would freeze or ban the development of antisatellite weapons and space weapons generally. The Soviets may also have assumed that there was then a good chance of achieving progress toward an agreement, since Reagan was in the middle of an election campaign in which he needed to convey to concerned American voters the impression that he was devoted to arms control and eager to improve relations with the East. Certainly, in putting forward the proposal the Soviets were taking a serious risk of boosting Reagan's prospects in the forthcoming elections. This fact alone may be an indication of their seriousness.[44]

On the other hand they may have reasoned that Reagan would be unlikely to agree to negotiations and hence their offer would allow them to score a propaganda point at his expense. Certainly the Reagan administration had hitherto been adamant in its refusal to negotiate on these issues. Since coming to power the administration had declined to reopen the negotiations on banning antisatellite weapons which had been suspended by President Carter in the wake of the Soviet invasion of Afghanistan. It had also consistently ignored the draft treaty banning the orbiting of weapons in outer space which the Soviet Union had submitted to the United Nations in 1981. Predictably, the rationale the administration had offered to the public for refusing to engage in these negotiations was that a treaty would be unverifiable. (The irony here is that satellites are what make it possible for each side to monitor the testing and deployment of weapons by the other side, and thus to verify compliance with arms control and disarmament treaties. Continued work on antisatellite systems may therefore further complicate the problems associated with treaty verification which the administration claims to be so concerned about.) The real reason for the administration's intransigence was of course that this is an area in which the United States has a technological advantage which the administration is eager to exploit. Hence as recently as March 1984 Reagan had told the Congress that negotiations on space weapons would be inadvisable.[45]

Perhaps the most plausible account of the Soviets' motivation in proposing talks is that they assumed they would benefit regardless of whether Reagan accepted or rejected their offer. They were wrong, for Reagan had another option, which was to accept with alacrity while changing the agenda to one unacceptable to the Soviets. The initial U.S. reply welcomed the prospect of negotiations but spoke only of discussing "feasible negotiating approaches" to "limitations on antisatellite weapons."[46] The United States also made it clear that it regarded the proposed negotiations primarily as a forum for discussing the resumption of the START and INF negotiations—a suggestion which the Soviets described as "totally unacceptable."[47] There then followed a public squabble about whether the U.S. insistence on bringing up intermediate-range and strategic nuclear weapons constituted a "precondition," as the Soviets claimed, or a "unilateral declaration" of intent, as the United States claimed. In a later exchange, the Soviets suggested that the talks should aim at "preventing the militarization of outer space," while the United States responded that it was willing to discuss "mutual concerns relating to the militarization of outer space, antisatellite systems, and other systems relating to this matter"—omitting the word "preventing" and retaining the insistence on discussing "offensive" nuclear missiles.[48] The word "preventing" was omitted both because the United States would not allow negotiations to foreclose all its options in space and because the word implied that the problem to be addressed was the future deployment of space weapons rather than existing offensive missiles.

It was in this vein that the whole disgraceful business proceeded, with each side repeating the petty antics in which it had indulged in the START and INF contexts. While it was clear that the U.S. purpose in shifting the agenda was to prevent the talks from getting off the ground, while providing itself a pretext for blaming the failure on the Soviet Union, the Soviet Union was equally intransigent in its insistence that offensive missiles could not be discussed, and in its insistence that the talks could not proceed unless both sides first accepted a moratorium on the testing of space weapons. In the end September came and went, and neither side showed up in Vienna.

From the very beginning the administration's strategy was to avoid arms control issues and arms control negotiations if at all possible. Eventually, however, public pressures could no longer be ignored, and the administration was forced to confront the problem of arms control. Its strategy then became to use the arms control process as a tool in the new Cold War. Its efforts were not, however, directed primarily at the Soviet Union. The aim was instead the control of public opinion in the West. Arms control negotiations began to function as a propaganda forum which provided welcome opportunities for denouncing the wickedness of the Soviets, while the need for leverage in the negotiations provided a convenient and effective argument for the development and deployment of the various weapons considered necessary for rearmament. This strategy—starkly confirmed in the quotations from Rowny and Burt—reveals the sovereign contempt which the administration evidently feels for the mass of people in the Western democracies. From the point of view of Reagan and his image engineers, the masses are there to be manipulated, and can be managed well enough using an appropriate blend of Hollywood and Madison Avenue techniques. Judging from the general response to the administration's various arms control proposals, this brazenly cynical view is perhaps not without some justification.

★4★

Third World Interventionism

It is not only with regard to the control of nuclear arms that the Reagan administration has evinced a contempt for negotiations. Its relations with third world countries also reveal a determination to avoid compromise and instead to impose solutions by coercion and intimidation. Thus it ignored proposals made in 1982 by Mexico and Venezuela for negotiations on the problems in El Salvador and Nicaragua, and has also rejected offers of unconditional negotiations which have been made by the Salvadoran opposition itself. Until just recently it has either rejected or failed to respond to repeated offers by the Sandinista government in Nicaragua to open negotiations on the issues that divide the two countries, and it has consistently ignored various proposals by the Cuban government for negotiations on the problems of the Central American region, such as arms trafficking, which the administration claims to be so concerned about. While it has made the occasional public statement of support for the efforts of the Contadora group (Colombia, Mexico, Panama, and Venezuela) to achieve a peaceful settlement in Central America, it has worked behind the scenes either to bend the group to its will or, failing that, to undermine its work.[1] A secret National Security Council document on policy in Central America and the Caribbean which was leaked to the press in April 1983 recommends that the government "step up [its] efforts to co-opt [the] negotiations issue to avoid Congressionally mandated negotiations, which would work against our interests."[2] While the administration has clearly followed this advice, it nevertheless goes about in public with an injured air, complaining of the unwillingness of its enemies in Central America and the Caribbean to engage in constructive negotiations.

In place of negotiations, the Reagan administration has adopted a variety of means for imposing its will on third world countries. In the case of countries with which it has shared interests and a common ideology, it usually attempts to induce compliance with its wishes by providing incentives in the form of military assistance and arms sales. Regimes to which the administration is hostile are dealt with straightforwardly by means of coercion. This can take a variety of forms. Coercion can be indirect, as when "proxies" are used to apply force or the threat of force to ensure that U.S. demands are met. Proxies are normally rewarded for their services by further helpings of military aid and further arms sales on agreeable terms. Direct methods of coercion range from economic warfare to subversion by "covert action" or outright military invasion.

Arms Sales as a Source of Leverage

Under the Reagan administration, arms sales have assumed unprecedented importance as a source of leverage over third world allies and proxies. According to James Buckley, Reagan's under secretary of state for security assistance, "arms transfers should be viewed as an increasingly important component of our global security posture and a key instrument of our foreign policy."[3] Thus during his first three months in office Reagan offered to supply other governments with around $15 billion worth of weapons and other forms of military equipment. In 1982 the administration requested Congress to provide almost $7 billion in government credits to enable other countries to purchase the various weapons which the United States had on offer.[4] A recent study by the Congressional Research Service reveals that the United States now sells more arms to the third world than any other single country. In 1983 U.S. sales accounted for 38 percent of the worldwide total of official military sales, while Soviet sales accounted for only 17 percent. In 1982 the U.S. share was 31 percent, while the Soviet share was 27 percent. These figures do not include private commercial sales, where the United States also excels.[5]

The contrast with the Carter administration's policies is striking. Whereas the Carter policy emphasized restrictions on arms sales—to regimes notorious for human rights violations for example, or which seemed to be seeking a nuclear capability—the Reagan policy has been to remove all such restrictions, and to market U.S.-made weapons aggressively throughout the world. While Carter had forbidden the promotion of arms sales by U.S. diplomatic and military personnel abroad, the Reagan administration immediately issued a directive instructing embassies to assist U.S. arms manufacturers in marketing their wares.[6]

The administration's policy of selling arms to "friendly" countries on liberal terms and virtually without constraint is motivated by a number of considerations. In general, arms sales are viewed as a means of cultivating influence with other countries. They provide an inducement to wavering countries to side with the United States in its global struggle with the Soviet Union, and are used to reward client states for their attentiveness to U.S. interests. The buyers' subsequent reliance on the United States for spare parts and maintenance is also thought to place them in a desirable state of dependency, giving the United States continued leverage far beyond the time of the initial sale—though recent events in Iran have shown that this dependence does not always guarantee continued influence. Indeed, far from commanding allegiance to the United States, the fact that the United States provided a copious supply of arms to the Shah, which the Shah then turned upon his own people, is one of the primary reasons why the United States is almost universally despised in Iran today.

The case of Israel also casts doubts on the theory that arms sales serve to create dependent and therefore pliant allies. U.S. arms sales and military assistance have played a decisive role in transforming Israel into a regional superpower. (The International Institute for Strategic Studies estimates that Israel now commands the fourth most powerful military force in the world—after the United States, the Soviet Union, and China.[7]) Accordingly, Israel is now in a position in which it can do enormous damage to U.S. interests—for example, by provoking a conflict in the Middle East which would harm U.S. relations with the Arab oil-producing states, and which could conceivably lead to a clash with the Soviet Union. Some observers now fear that Israel may use the threat to act in ways which risk these consequences as a means of coercing or blackmailing the United States.[8]

A further benefit which arms sales sometimes provide is access to military bases abroad. In recent years, for example, various countries, including the Philippines, Oman, and Somalia, have stipulated that access to U.S.-made arms should be a condition of the establishment or maintenance of U.S. military facilities on their soil. Equally important, however, is the idea that arms transfers are useful for arming or rewarding proxies, whose services make the need for overseas bases less pressing. The idea that the United States could rely on indigenous forces for the policing of certain areas, thereby obviating the need for direct intervention, was developed in the period of retrenchment necessitated by the Vietnam war, and was grandly dubbed the "Nixon Doctrine." The basic idea, as described by one commentator, was that "by changing the color of the corpses . . . foreign wars could be made acceptable to the politicized American public."[9] This idea has lingered, for the surprising resilience of the Vietnam syndrome has made it necessary for the Reagan administration to continue to make extensive use of surrogate forces in protecting and promoting U.S. interests in certain areas.

The most notorious proxies on the Reagan payroll are of course the counterrevolutionary forces, known as the contras, which are attempting to overthrow the Sandinista government in Nicaragua. Their activities will be discussed in some detail in Chapter 6. It is worth noting, however, the extent to which Honduras, where the main contra groups are based, has become a willing instrument of U.S. policy in the region in exchange for military largesse. Honduras has not only provided bases for the contras, but has also assisted the United States in training and arming them and in directing their attacks on Nicaragua. It has also provided bases where U.S. "advisers" can train large numbers of Salvadoran soldiers. The aim of training Salvadoran soldiers in Honduras has been to evade the congressionally mandated restrictions on the number of U.S. advisers that can be stationed in El Salvador, while at the same time avoiding the expense of training the soldiers in the United States. Of course, training forces from another country on Honduran soil is illegal under the Honduran constitution, but the former commander of the armed forces, General Gustavo Álvarez Martínez, surmounted that little problem by informing the Honduran congress that the Salvadorans were to be regarded as "students." So far 4,000 Salvadoran troops have been trained by the United States in Honduras while another 3,400 were scheduled to receive training in 1984.[10]

Some 2,500 Honduran soldiers have also benefited from instruction in the art of counterinsurgency. Mainly, however, they have exercised these skills in the service of the government of El Salvador. Honduran troops have on more than one occasion obligingly collaborated with the Salvadoran army in massacring unarmed Salvadoran civilians—for example, during the 1980 Sumpúl River massacre (to which we will return), when Honduran troops stationed on their side of the border gunned down Salvadoran peasants who were attempting to flee from the slaughter being conducted by their own country's "security forces."[11] Later, in 1982, immediately following meetings between Reagan administration officials and the Salvadoran and Honduran ministers of defense, Honduran troops began to enter Salvadoran territory to participate in Salvadoran counterinsurgency campaigns, while Honduran aircraft bombed rebel-held villages in Salvadoran provinces on the Honduran border. In July 1982 approximately 3,000 Honduran troops participated in operations in the Salvadoran province of Morazán, and later in November another 1,000 Hondurans participated in fighting in the province of Chalatenango.[12]

Using virtually continuous joint military exercises with Honduras as a cover, the United States has been transforming the country into a forward base capable of supporting direct military intervention in Nicaragua or El Salvador. The United States has constructed four airstrips in Honduras, and is proceeding with a number of other major projects, including a munitions storage area at Palmerola, a radar station on the Pacific coast, and a $160 million naval complex at Puerto Castilla on the Caribbean coast.[13] At the same time, the United States has exercised substantial control over Honduras' domestic and foreign affairs. Between January 1982 and March 1984, while the nominal head of state was Roberto Suazo Córdova, the civilian president, real power lay in the hands of General Álvarez Martínez. A mere colonel at the time of Suazo's inauguration in 1982, Álvarez was immediately named chief of the Honduran armed forces (in violation of the Honduran army's rules of promotion) at the insistence of John Negroponte, the American ambassador. Álvarez subsequently worked in close collaboration with Negroponte in running the country.[14]

As payment for the services Honduras has rendered, and for those which it promises to render as the chief U.S. proxy in Central America, the United States has, in addition to training Honduran soldiers, provided a profusion of arms and a great increase in military aid. Military aid was trebled in 1982, ostensibly in order to prepare Honduras to defend itself against the terrible aggression of Nicaragua (to which we will return). In reality, while the administration likes to parade Honduras as a showpiece of Central American democracy, the increase in military assistance and arms transfers has been intended in part to reinforce the military's (and by implication U.S.) control over Honduran society.

One predictable consequence of the increasing militarization of Honduras under U.S. supervision is that a climate of terror has been established, with a dramatic increase in human rights violations by government forces. Immediately following Álvarez's rise to power in 1982, Honduras' first death squad made its appearance, suspected political dissidents began to be murdered, and "disappearances" began to be reported. By early 1983 around one hundred people were reported to have "disappeared," and clandestine graveyards were being discovered on the outskirts of Tegucigalpa, the nation's capital. According to Amnesty International, torture has also begun to be practiced on a widespread and systematic basis.[15] In short, Honduras is coming increasingly to resemble the two other main U.S. allies in the region, El Salvador and Guatemala.

The ubiquitous U.S. military presence, together with the visible intervention of U.S. officials in the governance of the state, has led to the perception within Honduras that the country has, in effect, surrendered its sovereignty to the United States. Ephrain Díaz, an American-educated Christian Democrat in the Honduran congress, argues that when the United States began to establish its military presence in the country, "Congress played no role at all. The country," he says, "has lost all autonomy in foreign affairs. This country has become an occupied country . . . a base of military operations for the US."[16] Recently, a young Honduran cleric announced at his ordination that "we live like foreigners in our own country."[17] Visitors to Honduras find that such sentiments abound, and recently there have been demonstrations in Tegucigalpa calling for the removal of foreign military forces.

Of course, it pleases the American public to think that U.S. troops are always welcome wherever they go, and it would interfere with the implementation of U.S. policy if the public were to discover that this is not the case. Hence *Time* magazine reports to its American readers that "most Hondurans . . . welcome the U.S. influx," citing as proof the statement of what *Time* presumably regards as a representative Honduran citizen—namely, "an influential banker in Tegucigalpa": "We need the U.S. Army. If we need defending from any outside threat, the U.S. will defend us. We want the American troops here." *Time* also quotes with approval another representative individual, a "Honduran businessman" who is enthusiastic about the expansion of the service sector of the Honduran economy caused by the presence of U.S. troops with money to spend. The article is illustrated with a photograph of a U.S. communications facility surrounded by tremendous rolls of barbed wire. The caption beneath the picture reads: "For the locals, a welcome sense of security."[18]

The article in *Time* was written in 1983. Since then even the Honduran military has grown somewhat restive under U.S. domination, and Honduras has made some efforts to salvage the tattered remnants of its own autonomy. A good many senior Honduran officers gradually came to feel that Álvarez was subordinating the interests not only of Honduras generally but also of the Honduran military to the interests of the United States. Specifically, they became increasingly worried by the fact that the United States was training far more Salvadoran soldiers than Honduran soldiers. Honduras fought (and lost) a war with El Salvador over a disputed border in 1969, and the Honduran officer corps do not discount the possibility of having to fight El Salvador again. Hence they are understandably reluctant for their own country to become the major training ground for their potential adversaries. In addition to worrying about the direction in which Álvarez was taking the country, many Honduran officers were alienated by his high-handed manner, and also resented his meteoric rise to power under U.S. sponsorship. In March 1983, therefore, a group of senior officers forced his resignation and sent him into permanent exile. He was replaced as chief of the armed forces by General Walter López Reyes, the chief of the Honduran Air Force, who has since told the Pentagon that he not only wants more Hondurans and fewer Salvadorans to receive training, but also wants the U.S. military exercises scaled down.

Of the various U.S. regional policemen, the most important is undoubtedly Israel. When the Reagan administration came to power, its Middle Eastern policy, such as it was, focused almost exclusively on the "security" of the Persian Gulf region—that is, it was largely concerned with ensuring continued Western access to the oil resources of the Gulf region in the face of perceived threats from the Soviet Union and from indigenous nationalist forces. Israel's role in maintaining the security of the Gulf had become particularly critical after the overthrow of the Shah in Iran. Thus in 1979 Reagan argued that "the fall of Iran [*sic*] increases Israel's importance as perhaps the only strategic asset in the area that the US can really rely on."[19] Reagan returned to this theme on numerous occasions. During the 1980 campaign he stated that "Israel is the only stable democracy we can rely on in a spot where Armageddon could come. . . . We must prevent the Soviet Union from penetrating the Mideast. . . . If Israel were not there, the United States would have to be there."[20] And again, shortly after his inauguration in 1981, he contended that "with a combat-ready and even a combat-experienced military, [Israel] is a force in the Middle East that is actually a benefit to us. If there were no Israel with that force, we'd have to supply that with our own, so this isn't just altruism on our part."[21] It was, perhaps, Reagan's repeated emphasis on the strategic importance of Israel which led former Israel Prime Minister Menachem Begin to proclaim in 1982 that Israel was more important to U.S. security than the United States was to the security of Israel.[22]

Israel does indeed perform a number of important services for the United States. It shares certain intelligence information and provides information on Soviet arms and military technology which it has acquired in its various wars with the Soviet Union's Arab allies. It maintains a highly developed infrastructure, including military bases, to which the United States could have access if it were to intervene directly in the Middle East. And most importantly, as Reagan has pointed out, Israel has developed a remarkably potent military machine which itself provides a formidable deterrent to Soviet aggression, and is also useful for keeping the Arabs in line.[23] In order to maintain Israel's regional military dominance, and in the hope of ensuring its obedience, the United States has provided Israel with the lion's share of its global dispensation of arms and military aid. During fiscal years 1978 through 1982, 48 percent of all American military aid worldwide went to Israel.[24] Most of the money Israel received was then used to buy U.S.-made arms. In 1984 the level of U.S. military and economic assistance to Israel exceeded all previous levels.

The uses to which Israel's military power has been put have not, however, always enhanced the U.S. position in the Middle East. Consider, for example, Israel's invasion of Lebanon and its subsequent bombardment and blockade of Beirut. The Reagan administration not only consented to this savage piece of aggression, but also provided the weapons with which it was executed.[25] During the first three months of 1982, while the invasion was being planned, there was a tremendous surge of U.S. military supplies to Israel. The value of these supplies was almost ten times that of the military supplies Israel received during the same period in 1980.[26] Moreover, both prior to and during the invasion, the United States deployed a huge naval force in the eastern Mediterranean, apparently to deter Soviet intervention.[27] The invasion was sold to the United States in terms the Reagan administration, the Congress, and the public all found intelligible: Yitzhak Shamir, who was then the Israeli Foreign Minister, told members of Congress that the upshot of the invasion and the seige of Beirut would be that "Soviet Russia and its agents—Syria and the PLO—will lose any influence in the region. That will have a tremendous impact on what will happen in the area. Everything will be different."[28] But, while Syria was initially humiliated, and U.S. generals were able to see their weapons tested in actual combat conditions, the longer term consequences of the invasion and occupation have hardly been gratifying for the United States. Syria was soon rearmed by the Soviets with weapons of greater sophistication, and Israel subsequently withdrew from Beirut, leaving the United States to fill the gap with a contingent of marines whose vulnerable presence eventually became a significant political liability for Reagan, and whose ignominious withdrawal certainly contributed rather little to U.S. global "credibility."

In addition to their usefulness in buying influence and bases, creating dependents, and arming and rewarding proxies, arms sales are also useful in helping friendly but domestically unpopular regimes to suppress internal dissent. They are, in short, a tool for sustaining in power various client regimes which would otherwise be turned out by their own people. Very often the unpopularity of these regimes is to a considerable extent a consequence of their repressiveness. Under the Carter administration, restrictions were imposed on the sale of arms to repressive regimes (though this policy was not impartially applied, and numerous exceptions were made on grounds of "national security"). But it is precisely the regimes which were affected by the Carter restrictions (or would have been had the restrictions been impartially enforced) that the Reagan administration intends to preserve in power, and with which it aims to cultivate more intimate relations. The Reagan administration has made various attempts, mostly successful, to remove congressionally mandated restrictions on arms sales to regimes notorious for the violation of human rights. As a White House document, "Conventional Arms Transfer Policy," stated: "We will deal with the world as it is rather than as we would like it to be."[29] Thus, now even more than in the past, the United States serves as the major supplier of weapons and other instruments of repression to many of the world's most brutal regimes.[30]

In 1981 the administration urged that Congress repeal the section in the Foreign Assistance Act which, citing the military government's record on human rights, prohibited military sales and assistance to Argentina; but the Falklands/Malvinas war soon intervened, making the restoration of military relations impossible. In 1982 the administration persuaded the Senate to revoke the similar ban on sales and assistance to the Pinochet dictatorship in Chile. And between 1981 and 1983, in direct violation of a mandatory United Nations embargo, the administration approved the sale of more than $28 million in military technology to South Africa, usually in the form of unassembled weapons components.[31]

The most interesting case, however, is that of Guatemala. It was clear from the moment Reagan entered office that he was eager to resume military sales and assistance to Guatemala, which had been banned in 1977. In 1981, however, the Guatemalan government was waging a grisly campaign of extermination against the indigenous Indian population, and was also engaged in the systematic torture and slaughter of vast numbers of people in other sectors of Guatemalan society; so it was equally clear that the administration would have a difficult time persuading Congress to lift the ban which had been imposed in response to lesser atrocities committed by an earlier government. So rather than trying to revoke the ban, the administration decided to evade it. During its first two years in office, for example, the administration turned a blind eye on the Bell Company's deliveries to Guatemala of civilian versions of military helicopters, which were converted for military use after delivery, thereby enabling the Guatemalan military to expand its fleet of counterinsurgency helicopters from eight to twenty-seven.[32] On another occasion Reagan managed to have certain essential counterinsurgency equipment such as military trucks, jeeps, and helicopters sent to Guatemala by simply deleting them from the catalog of military items covered by the embargo.[33] The administration was also able (as was the Carter administration) to rely on Israel as a surrogate merchant to help provide the military dictatorship with the necessary means for keeping the Guatemalan people in order.[34]

The administration evidently hoped that the Guatemalan elections in March of 1982 would provide sufficient grounds for the resumption of military sales and assistance, but this strategy suffered a setback when evidence of pervasive electoral fraud was exposed. Reagan's hopes were, however, immediately rescued when General Efraín Ríos Montt seized power in a virtually bloodless coup later that month. Ríos Montt's reputation as a pious born-again Christian and his pledge to respect human rights and to rein in the death squads provided the appropriate pretext, and approximately nine months after the coup the U.S. government lifted the ban on the transfer of military equipment to Guatemala, citing an increase in respect for human rights by way of justification. The Guatemalan government was immediately given permission to buy $6.3 million worth of supplies, consisting mainly of spare parts for U.S.-made counterinsurgency helicopters.

Shortly before the Reagan administration announced its satisfaction with the new military government's humanitarian reforms, several human rights groups, including Amnesty International, presented evidence to the United Nations in support of their claim that at least 2,186 people had been murdered in Guatemala in the first *nine weeks* after the coup that brought Ríos Montt to power. The Guatemalan Association of Democratic Journalists, a group of journalists living in exile, estimates that the true figure for that period is 4,000 killings. According to Amnesty International, the great majority of the victims were civilian noncombatants who had been killed by government forces.[35] Later the Council on Hemispheric Affairs reported that at least 5,000 and possibly as many as 10,000 people were killed by the Ríos Montt regime during the first nine months after it seized power, and hence that, at that time, more civilians had been killed since the coup than during any comparable period "under the universally condemned former regime of General Lucas García."[36] People living in the areas where most of the violence occurred claimed that 10,000 dead was a conservative estimate, and that the true figure was probably more than 15,000.[37]

Ríos Montt's counterinsurgency strategy has been accurately characterized as follows: "It shunned attempts to confront the guerrillas directly, and to a large extent did not even try to destroy their infrastructure in any systematic fashion. Instead, it focused upon eliminating the insurgents' popular base by massacring whole communities of suspected sympathizers, forcing those who did manage to escape the slaughter to become refugees."[38] Many villages were burned, and their entire populations slaughtered. Another device which the Ríos Montt regime employed was to force rural peasants to join civil defense patrols led by a small group of soldiers. The civilian members of these patrols were then forced by the threat of execution to participate in the torture and murder of other peasants—the idea being that they would then be coopted to the government side by complicity and guilt.[39]

Government killings were often characterized by their purposeless cruelty. A member of one of the civil defense patrols gave the following report of a man seized by a group of soldiers: "All his muscles were cut and gunpowder was placed in his navel and set on fire. The victim's eyes were put out and his skin was then peeled off. The soldiers joked that they were going to have a barbecue."[40] After Ríos Montt had been in power for over a year, the Americas Watch Committee issued a report based on interviews with Guatemalan refugees in Mexico which noted that "although civilian men of all ages have been shot in large numbers by the Guatemalan Army, women and children are particular victims; women are routinely raped before being killed; children are smashed against walls, choked, burned alive or murdered by machete or bayonet."[41]

Some of the refugees' accounts of the cruelty of the Guatemalan Army—accounts of little children, weeping with terror, being mutilated before their parents' eyes—are almost too painful to read.[42] While the essentials of the Americas Watch report have been confirmed by Amnesty International, one British apologist for the Ríos Montt regime has objected to the report on the ground that those who had interviewed the peasant refugees "had merely been sucking in communist propaganda, like pap." He particularly objects to the refugees' stories of children being thrown into the air and bayoneted, observing that "if you think about it, the feat would require quite a lot of practice. Even a child's body has a rib cage and a spine. The average Fascist beast would look pretty silly if he threw a child into the air and the little chap just bounced off his bayonet and fell to the ground. Or are they supposed to teach this trick in Guatemalan infantry school?"[43] With this neat piece of a priori reasoning, the accounts of eyewitnesses are decisively refuted, and the pristine image of the Ríos Montt regime is thereby restored.

Among the few people in the world willing to defend the record of General Ríos Montt was of course Ronald Reagan. At the end of his five-day tour of Latin America, during which he proposed his memorable toast "to President Figueiredo and the people of Bolivia" (Figueiredo being, unfortunately, the President of Brazil), Reagan stopped off in Guatemala to pay a visit to President Ríos Montt. Upon returning to Washington, Reagan declared Ríos Montt to be "a man of great personal integrity committed to restoring democracy" in Guatemala (which, it will be recalled, was crushed by the United States in 1954). Responding to the many and mutually confirming reports of atrocities committed by Ríos Montt's forces, Reagan stated: "He is totally dedicated to democracy in Guatemala. They have some very real problems . . . they brought a lot of information to us. Frankly, I'm inclined to believe that they've been given a bum rap."[44] Later, in July 1983, Reagan asked the Congress to provide the Ríos Montt regime with $10.25 million in military aid (which, it is worth pointing out, even at the risk of being maudlin, would have been devoted to the further mass extermination of little children) in addition to $66.5 million in economic assistance. The request was apparently initially approved but was then later rejected.[45]

In August 1983 Ríos Montt was ousted in a coup which brought to power the minister of defense, General Oscar Mejía Víctores. There is reason to believe that the United States collaborated in the coup. For despite his many virtues, Ríos Montt was concerned primarily with events in Guatemala, and had shown insufficient enthusiasm for the U.S. strategy for Central America as a whole. Two days before the coup, Mejía Víctores paid what was later described as a "courtesy call" to a U.S. aircraft carrier off the coast of Nicaragua, and the following day he conferred in Honduras with the defense ministers of Honduras and El Salvador, as well as with General Paul F. Gorman, the head of the U.S. Southern Command. The meetings hardly seemed coincidental, especially in the light of the fact that Major William Mercado, the U.S. deputy military attaché, was accidentally filmed by Guatemalan television cameras as he spoke into a walkie-talkie from the National Palace as the coup was taking place.[46] Certainly the United States was not unhappy with the coup, as was shown when the American ambassador presented himself to the new dictator the very next day, breaching diplomatic protocol, which requires that there should be a decent interval before a head of state who comes to power in a coup is recognized.

Since the coup the Reagan administration has been seeking closer relations with Guatemala, in spite of the fact that the Mejía Víctores regime has also been given a bum rap by various human rights organizations which have shown that, especially in the cities, government violence and repression have intensified even further.[47] The new regime has been responsive to Reagan's overtures, and soon after Mejía Víctores came to power the Central American Defense Council (Condeca), a military alliance between Guatemala, El Salvador, and Honduras, was enthusiastically resurrected. As we shall see in Chapter 6, Condeca has been assigned a central role in the U.S. plans against Nicaragua. As usual the administration has hoped to woo the Mejía Víctores regime with military sales and assistance, but so far it has met with considerable resistance from the House of Representatives, which is still dominated by the Democrats. Although the administration has been unable to gain congressional approval for its proposed sales and assistance to Guatemala (a problem which has led to a cooling of relations between the two countries), Guatemala has still been receiving supplies of U.S.-made arms. For, in a move which allowed the administration to kill two birds with one stone, Guatemala agreed to train Salvadoran troops in exchange for weapons and ammunition supplied to El Salvador by the United States.[48]

Human Rights in the New Cold War

Concern for human rights has not only ceased to function as a constraint on U.S. military sales and assistance; the protection of human rights has virtually ceased to be a goal of U.S. foreign policy. One of the primary aims of the Reagan administration is to establish closer relations with countries whose governments are willing to protect and promote U.S. economic and strategic interests. We have seen, however, that because the protection of U.S. interests in other countries normally requires the sacrifice of the interests of the domestic population, those regimes which are willing to cater to U.S. interests naturally meet with considerable domestic opposition, to which they usually respond with repression. Thus, not only would an outspoken commitment to the defense of human rights be an obstacle to the maintenance of friendly relations with these regimes, but also the repressive measures undertaken by these regimes may actually serve U.S. interests—if, that is, they are successful. For these reasons the Reagan administration has refused to utter a word of protest about the abuse of human rights in "friendly" countries. Since it is only with these countries that the United States has any real leverage (because they are the countries that depend on U.S. aid, arms sales, and so on), the administration's refusal to exercise that leverage on behalf of human rights indicates that the defense of human rights has effectively been abandoned as anything but the most subordinate aim of U.S. foreign policy.

The early signs of the Reagan administration's attitude to human rights were unmistakable. For example, in making his initial appointments, Reagan nominated for the position of assistant secretary of state for human rights and humanitarian affairs a man who in 1979 had stated in testimony before the Senate that "the United States should remove from the statute books all clauses that establish a human rights standard or condition that must be met by another sovereign government before our government transacts normal business with it."[49] Shortly after his election, Reagan himself said, "I don't think that you can turn away from some country because here and there they do not agree with our concept of human rights."[50]

The administration moved quickly to establish closer relations with a number of regimes notorious for their disagreement with "our" understanding of human rights. During his first few months in office Reagan began flirting with the government of South Africa, arguing that the United States could not abandon a country that "strategically is essential to the free world in its production of minerals that we all must have."[51] Around the same time, one of Secretary of State Haig's advisers noted that closer relations with South Africa would provide "an opportunity to counter the Soviet threat in Africa."[52] Thus the dominant view within the administration was that sentimental moralizing about the rights of the black majority in South Africa would have to be subordinated to a healthy sense of American self-interest, and the administration soon announced that its policy toward South Africa would be one of "constructive engagement" rather than "confrontation."[53] Shortly thereafter Jeane Kirkpatrick cast the sole vote against a United Nations Security Council resolution condemning South Africa's August 1981 invasion of Angola. Later she broke a long U.S. tradition of refusing contacts with the South African military by surreptitiously meeting with several South African intelligence officers. When the meeting was exposed, she affected innocence, audaciously claiming that she had not known who the men were with whom she had had secret discussions.

Before the restoration of democracy in Argentina in 1983, "the Reagan Administration made repeated good will gestures to the military rulers [there], despite their rapidly deteriorating standing with the Argentine people."[54] These gestures included, as we have seen, attempts to resume military sales and assistance. The United States even hesitated before finally giving its support to Britain in the Falklands/Malvinas war. Yet the military in Argentina had recently presided over the abduction, torture, and murder of between 15,000 and 20,000 Argentine civilians. When the military government was condemned for its actions by the U.N. Human

Rights Commission, the Reagan administration's delegate to the commission cast the sole dissenting vote.[55]

Another country with which the Reagan administration has established more intimate ties is South Korea. General Chun Doo Hwan, the president of South Korea, was the first foreign head of state to be received by Reagan at the White House. In toasting his visitor, Reagan admiringly announced that "in the short time you've had . . . you've done much to strengthen the tradition of 3,000 years' commitment to freedom."[56] Meanwhile the State Department delayed the release of its annual report on human rights in order to avoid embarrassing Reagan's exalted guest.[57] For in South Korea under Chun the jails are full of people either detained or convicted for political "offenses" (estimates of the number of political prisoners range from 400 to more than 1,000, some of whom have been in detention since 1971 for such grievous offenses as participating in student demonstrations); around 300 opposition politicians have been prohibited from engaging in political activity; trade unions have been virtually abolished; and the torture of political dissidents is routinely practiced both for purposes of intimidation and to extract confessions, which are often subsequently accepted as evidence in political trials.[58] Yet in 1981, in addition to selling the South Koreans a number of highly advanced weapons systems, including thirty-six F-16 aircraft, the Reagan administration licensed the transfer of more than $1 million worth of tear gas and police pistols to South Korea for the explicit purpose of "civilian control"—that is, to prevent the unruly masses from obstructing General Chun's efforts on behalf of the libertarian traditions to which he is devoted.[59] Later, in November 1983, Reagan visited South Korea, and, as political dissidents were being rounded up by the police (some for signing a letter which urged Reagan to pay attention to human rights), Reagan embraced General Chun, proclaiming that "America is your friend and we are with you."[60]

Another champion of freedom who was fêted and eulogized at the White House is President-for-life Ferdinand Marcos of the Philippines, who has recently decreed a new law which "makes life imprisonment or the death penalty mandatory for those convicted of sedition, inciting rebellion, illegal assembly, and anti-Government propaganda."[61] Although Amnesty International reports that, in the Philippines under Marcos, "human rights violations of the utmost gravity, including 'disappearances' and extrajudicial executions, were becoming increasingly common while torture remained prevalent," the question of human rights was never raised in the discussions between the two heads of state.[62] For Reagan is anxious not only that Marcos should remain on good terms with the United States, but also that he should remain in power, since, unlike some members of the opposition, Marcos is unlikely ever to deny the United States access to its two huge military bases in the Philippines. Thus, according to U.S. officials in Manila, Reagan is unwilling to cause "unnecessary friction" by bringing up for discussion the unpleasant subject of human rights—a good example of the administration's policy of "quiet diplomacy."[63]

No discussion of the administration's human rights policy would be complete without some mention of Reagan's ally in Haiti, President-for-life Jean-Claude Duvalier. In Duvalier's Haiti, whose people are the most impoverished in the hemisphere, political parties are not tolerated, and, as we noted earlier, opposition political figures have either been expelled or kept in detention or under house arrest, and have frequently been subject to beating and torture. Trade unions have been suppressed and most opposition lawyers, journalists, and intellectuals have either been imprisoned or forced into exile. "Disappearances" are becoming increasingly common, and torture appears to be widespread.[64] Yet in 1983 the Reagan administration pledged to thwart any attempts by any of the 500,000 Haitian exiles living in the United States to overthrow the Duvalier dictatorship. The administration proved as good as its word, and in 1984 a group of exiles were arrested in the United States as they prepared for an invasion of their country.[65] While large numbers of Haitians are eager to leave the country (and indeed often attempt to do so at great peril to their lives), the United States is refusing to grant them asylum, since to do so would be tantamount to acknowledging the repressiveness of the Duvalier dictatorship.[66]

As we have seen, Reagan has attempted to excuse his lack of interest in the violation of human rights by friendly governments on the ground that it would be unfair to punish a government just because it disputes some of the prevailing moral opinions in the United States. No doubt Reagan would find it repugnant to impose his own subjective values on Chun, Duvalier, Marcos, and Mejía Víctores, who also are no doubt firm in their conviction that the torture and murder of their political opponents is a solemn moral duty. But the operative consideration is that the activities of these gentlemen are thought to serve U.S. interests, and that is why Reagan does not intercede on behalf of the victims.

There are, of course, no comparable inhibitions about airing moral differences with the administration's proclaimed enemies, so human rights still have a role to play in U.S. foreign policy: complaints about human rights violations are still a useful bludgeon against communist, socialist, or anti-imperialist governments, and anti-imperialist insurgent movements. Thus the least evidence of human rights violations by, for example, the Soviet, Polish, Nicaraguan, or Vietnamese governments, or by the guerrillas in El Salvador, is sufficient to evoke a torrent of righteous denunciation from members of the administration. It is difficult, however, to reconcile the administration's noisy moralizing about the sins of its enemies with its conspicuous silence, or in some cases open apologetics, when some friendly regime engages in the violation of human rights. To maintain the appearance of consistency and impartiality, therefore, administration officials routinely assert that the peccadilloes of U.S. allies are barely noteworthy in comparison with the heinous atrocities of its enemies, and thus do not merit the same sort of public condemnation. (And in any case it is more effective to deal with the foibles of allies by means of quiet diplomacy—as in the case of the Philippines). Jeane Kirkpatrick, for example, has contrasted the "massive human rights violations by the Soviets and their satellites (Poland, Cuba, Vietnam, Ethopia)" with the "qualitatively and quantitively lesser violations committed by traditional non-Communist and anti-Communist autocracies in Latin America" (for example, the Pinochet regime in Chile, and the various military and military-civilian juntas in Argentina, Guatemala, and El Salvador).[67] Elsewhere she has claimed that the Sandinista government in Nicaragua has been more repressive than the previous Somoza dictatorship and, indeed, that the Sandinistas are the foremost violators of human rights in the world.[68]

One of course looks in vain for any evidence or argument for these preposterous allegations. If, however, one bothers to consult (for example) Amnesty International's various reports over the past few years, the most damaging charges one can find against the Sandinistas concern the forcible evacuation of Miskito Indians from border areas following violent U.S.-sponsored incursions from Honduras, and unconfirmed allegations that some detainees have been held in isolation and beaten. On the other hand, reports on Kirkpatrick's "traditional non-Communist and anti-Communist autocracies" are rife with grisly accounts of abduction, torture, mutilation, and murder on a vast scale by government forces—accounts with which she is well acquainted.

It is also instructive to note that the repressive policies of the Polish government, about which the administration has affected an almost frenzied concern, have been easily surpassed by those of, for instance, the military regime in Turkey, though the latter have failed to evoke even a murmur of protest. Since the military seized power and imposed martial law in 1980, 170,000 people have been arrested, and, according to official figures, there were still 21,046 political prisoners being held in military jails on June 30, 1983. Others put the figure as high as 33,000. Trade unions have been crushed, and prominent political figures, including two former prime ministers, have been barred from engaging in political activities for as long as ten years. Torture is practiced routinely and systematically, and Amnesty International has documented seventy cases in which prisoners have been tortured to death.[69]

Vast numbers of political prisoners are being tried before military courts. Fifty-two trade union leaders, for example, are being tried for alledgedly attempting to overthrow the constitution by force, and will face the death penalty if convicted. A large number of politicians, officials of religious philanthropic associations, and writers are also being tried—including fifty-six intellectuals who have been accused of violating martial law by signing a petition demanding greater democracy. The most notorious of Turkey's trials is, however, that of the leaders of the Turkish Peace Association (TPA), an organization which was devoted to campaigning for nuclear disarmament, publicizing the Helsinki Agreement, and promoting peace between Turkey and Greece. In November 1983 the twenty-three leaders of TPA, who were charged under a law derived from Mussolini which prohibits the formation of groups or the circulation of propaganda aimed at the "domination of a social class over other social classes," were given sentences of five or eight years' hard labor. Among those convicted are the former Turkish ambassador to India, who was nominated for the Nobel Peace Prize this year; the president of the Turkish Medical Association; the president of the Istanbul Bar Association, who is also a former member of the Turkish parliament; the former deputy head of the Istanbul Department of Education, the general secretary of the Turkish Writers Union, the dean of the Istanbul Academy of Political Sciences, and five members of the Turkish parliament.[70]

Conditions in Turkish military prisons are appalling, and virtually all political prisoners are tortured. In July and August of 1982 as many as 2,500 prisoners staged a hunger strike protesting prison conditions in a desperate though vain attempt to draw attention in the West to the plight of the victims of martial law. Several prisoners died. Hunger strikes continued in 1984 and relatives claim that twelve more strikers have died.[71]

Lesser abuses than these in Poland have provoked repeated displays of self-righteous moral outrage on the part of the administration, and even provided the occasion for an officially sponsored television extravaganza entitled "Let Poland Be Poland," which featured Frank Sinatra, Bob Hope, and other noted political and intellectual luminaries. (In a show of solidarity with the military regime, Reagan even allowed the Turkish head of state to put in an appearance—a lapse of good taste, perhaps.) In Turkey, by contrast, the military's efforts to "maintain stability" have been rewarded by an increase in military aid and a pledge from the U.S. secretary of defense "to be of as much assistance as we can be."[72] The joint report of several human rights groups notes that

> when a House of Representatives subcommittee held hearings in April 1983 on Turkey's human rights record, . . . the Assistant Secretary of State for Human Rights . . . testified that martial law censorship in Turkey is "something we can understand;" that purges at the universities are the Turkish government's effort to "insulate the universities from politics;" that those who criticize the powers exercised by Turkey's military President should recall that "our own Constitution certainly has been a great model of a strong executive;" and that, despite abuses such as torture, Turkey is in "transition to democracy."[73]

The reason for these grotesque apologetics is not difficult to discern. Turkey is a valued NATO ally which shares borders with the Soviet Union, Syria, Iraq, and Iran. With the largest land army in Europe, Turkey is therefore nicely situated to assist the United States with the defense of the Persian Gulf. Turkey houses 101 U.S. and NATO bases, is the largest purchaser of U.S.-made arms, and is the third largest recipient of U.S. aid. The administration has its priorities.[74]

In the face of these and a great many other equally damning facts, how can the administration continue to maintain the pretense that it is only in communist countries that human rights abuses are sufficiently serious to merit public condemnation? The administration's ideologists have developed two pieces of intellectual subterfuge designed to rescue the official position. One is the well-known distinction between "totalitarian" and "authoritarian" regimes. The essence of the distinction has been stated by Reagan's first secretary of state, General Alexander Haig, as follows: "The totalitarian model . . . draws upon the resources of modern technology to impose its will on all aspects of a citizen's behavior" while "the authoritarian regime . . . customarily reserves for itself absolute authority in only a few politically sensitive areas."[75] The distinction has been further elaborated by Kirkpatrick, who contends that

> traditional autocrats [i.e., authoritarians] leave in place existing allocations of wealth, power, status, and other resources which in most traditional societies favor an affluent few and maintain masses in poverty. But they . . . do not disturb the habitual rhythms of work and leisure, habitual places of residence, habitual patterns of family and

> personal relations. Because the miseries of traditional life are familiar, they are bearable to ordinary people, who growing up in the society, learn to cope. . . . Such societies create no refugees. Precisely the opposite is true of revolutionary Communist regimes [i.e., totalitarians]. They create refugees by the million because they claim jurisdiction over the whole life of the society and make demands for change that so violate internalized values and habits that inhabitants flee by the tens of thousands.[76]

The genius of introducing this distinction was that, since there were a couple of cases which fit the described categories tolerably well, the distinction had sufficient initial plausibility to gain considerable currency in Western political discourse. The administration was then provided with a widely accepted but conveniently morally loaded scheme of classification. If a regime attempted to alter the established distribution of wealth, or attempted to introduce a new or revolutionary ideology, it was then classified as a totalitarian regime, which by definition must be worse than the "traditional authoritarian" regimes supported by the United States.

But insofar as there is a distinction of any substance here, which draws a line where administration officials want one drawn (that is, between regimes such as those in El Salvador, Guatemala, Chile, South Korea, and the Philippines on the one hand, and those in the Soviet Union, Eastern Europe, Cuba, and Nicaragua on the other), the evidence which Kirkpatrick deliberately suppresses suggests that, in general, totalitarian regimes may actually be the lesser of the two evils, for reasons which are directly connected with her characterization of the two types of regime. A distinguishing feature of totalitarian as opposed to the authoritarian regimes is that they are concerned with the propagation of ideology. Related to this is a desire for legitimacy in the eyes of the population—for a base of popular support. No doubt it is to some extent a result of this that latter-day totalitarian regimes typically evince a concern for the welfare of their general populations (though this concern is usually supported by a variety of moral and ideological considerations as well). Thus in Kirkpatrick's paradigmatic totalitarian states, one does not find the same extremes of wealth and poverty, opulence and squalor, that she admits exist in her traditional authoritarian states. Nor does one find anything like the same levels of unemployment. In Cuba, her archetype of third world totalitarianism, malnutrition and preventable infectious diseases have been virtually eradicated, and the infant mortality rate has been lowered, while the literacy rate has been dramatically increased. The same process is occurring in Nicaragua. By contrast, in most of the authoritarian states in Latin America vast numbers of people remain illiterate and continue to be plagued by malnutrition and a host of preventable diseases, even though many of these countries have economies stronger than those of Cuba and Nicaragua.

The typical authoritarian regime regards the great mass of people simply as a workforce which exists to be exploited for the benefit of the few. It prefers a docile, apathetic, and apolitical population. The last thing it wants is an alert, ideologically motivated, and politically active populace. As Anastasio Somoza, Sr., the founder of the Somoza dynasty in Nicaragua and father of the recently deposed dictator, once remarked, "I don't want educated people. I want oxen."[77] Accordingly, authoritarian regimes do not ordinarily make much effort to mobilize popular support, but prefer to rule by force and intimidation, terrorizing the population by means of abduction, torture, and murder, often selecting their victims on a virtually random basis. Since the death of Stalin, these practices have hardly existed at all within the Soviet bloc, and certainly not on the same scale as in the typical authoritarian state in Latin America. It would be instructive to ask oneself where one would prefer to live as a member of the general population—or, more importantly perhaps, where one would prefer to be a political dissident: in Poland or El Salvador? Cuba or Guatemala? Nicaragua or the Philippines? Certainly one's life expectancy would be longer in one of the former.[78]

The irony is that, in its rather feeble efforts to clean up the images of some of its more barbaric third world allies, the United States is actually pushing them closer to the totalitarian model. This is particularly evident in the emphasis U.S. military advisers are giving to the "hearts and minds" aspect of the counterinsurgency campaign in El Salvador. Under U.S. guidance, the Salvadoran army is instituting a number of programs in rural areas aimed at convincing the civilian population that the military is "part of the solution and not the problem."[79] These programs will involve considerably more popular mobilization and more intervention by the state in the everyday lives and affairs of the people—both of which are primary characteristics of totalitarian societies.

The second device to which the administration has resorted in order to be able to focus its human rights policy on abuses in enemy (totalitarian) states consists in redefining human rights as "political rights." During Reagan's first year in office, Under Secretary of State Richard Kennedy became worried that public and congressional criticism of the administration's human rights policy might "disrupt important foreign-policy initiatives. . . . Human Rights has become one of the main avenues for domestic attack on the administration's foreign policy." In an "eyes only" memo to Secretary of

State Haig, Kennedy recommended that the administration take the initiative by redefining the human rights issue so that it would coincide with the administration's anti-Soviet crusade: "Human rights—meaning political rights and civil liberties—conveys what is ultimately at issue in our contest with the Soviet bloc." If, he pointed out, the administration were to "draw this distinction and . . . persuade others of it," then human rights could be made to appear "the core of our foreign policy," and critics could be effectively silenced.[80] As one observer has noted, the Kennedy memorandum became the guideline of a strategy "aimed at dissipating the humanitarian focus of U.S. legislation and substituting a more flexible standard keyed to political freedoms. . . . The strategy, in short, was to dehumanize human rights by substituting a manipulable political-science abstraction for widely accepted concern over security of the person."[81] In conformity with this strategy, Kirkpatrick, speaking before a Senate subcommittee on the question of human rights in Nicaragua, argued that "the list of human rights cannot be indefinitely lengthened like a shopping list in a global supermarket. I believe political and legal rights such as free speech, press, religion, freedom of assembly, freedom from arbitrary arrest, and the right to due process are the fundamental *rights:* they are the prerequisites to other social and economic goods."[82]

By implication, the right to life and the right against torture are simply luxury items on the shopping list. Kirkpatrick goes on, in an account liberally sprinkled with references to Nazism, to detail the frightful abuses of the foremost violators of human rights in the world (that is, the Sandinistas), including "banning a bishop from access to television," and criticizing and censoring the independent press.

It should be noted that the merit of the new definition is only that it allows the administration to express its fulminations against its enemies in the language of rights. It cannot be used to show that the administration's favorite authoritarian regimes are only minor violators of "human rights," for authoritarian regimes typically violate both nonpolitical human rights (such as rights against rape, torture, and murder) *and* the standard political rights. Admittedly, the exclusive focus on political rights does provide some grounds for differentiating between totalitarian and authoritarian regimes, though these grounds are relatively insignificant. For example, there is greater freedom of religion in most Latin American authoritarian states than there is in the Soviet Union—provided, of course, that it is understood that God is apolitical. (It is, however, significant that there is greater freedom of religion in Nicaragua as well.) Some authoritarian states, moreover, do not have elaborate provisions for press censorship. Censorship is not necessary, however, in countries in which it is customary for the publication of articles displeasing to the authorities to result in the disappearance of newspaper editors.

The only way in which the focus on political rights tends to distract discussion from abuses in authoritarian countries is that violations of political rights in these countries may seem hardly worth discussing in the midst of the wholesale massacre of large sectors of the population. In El Salvador, for example, complaints about the banning of a bishop from access to television might seem a bit of a bad joke in the light of the fact that the previous archbishop of San Salvador was gunned down by a death squad operating under government protection while he was saying mass.

To summarize, the administration's policy on human rights has been for the most part to ignore human rights violations by friendly regimes, while exploiting the rhetoric of human rights in denouncing its enemies. The consequences of this approach have been predictable. "Friendly" dictators in third world countries, who in many cases were made nervous by the Carter administration's policies, have heaved a sigh of relief, and returned to the repression of their people with renewed vigor. To be sure, Carter's human rights policy was implemented in a highly selective way: for example, in 1979 he tried unsuccessfully to persuade the Organization of American States (OAS) to intervene in order to save Somoza, and he also remained loyal to the Shah, expressing support for the embattled tyrant even as Iranian forces were machine-gunning civilians in the streets.[83] Nevertheless, his policies had some beneficial effects. As the Colombian novelist Gabriel García Márquez notes:

> During Carter's term of office, you had the Pentagon and the CIA telling the dictators not to worry. You also had the State Department, at the same time, telling them that they had to respect the human rights of their citizens. The double message made the dictators feel insecure. As a result, those of us who are involved in human-rights work were able to rescue many people. However, since Reagan's election, you have Jeane Kirkpatrick running off to Chile and telling Augusto Pinochet that his is the kind of "authoritarian democracy" Latin America needs. Since her visit, it's impossible to get *one prisoner* out of Pinochet's jails![84]

(García Márquez is referring to a visit Kirkpatrick made to Chile in August of 1982 during which she declared the administration's intention to "normalize completely relations with Chile in order to work together in a pleasant way." Two days after her visit Pinochet expelled four prominent political leaders, including the chairman of the Chilean Human Rights Commission, who had tried in vain to arrange a meeting with Kirkpatrick.[85])

Reagan's frequent and fierce denunciations of his enemies in the Eastern bloc have helped to bring about a collapse in East-West relations, with the predictable consequence that there has been a severe crackdown on dissidents and a general deterioration in respect for human rights as the authorities in the East have tightened their control over all aspects of their societies. For the more they feel threatened by the West, the more anxious they become to ensure domestic "stability." In the past the level of respect for human rights in the East has fluctuated with the climate of East-West relations, with intensified repression being correlated with periods of strained relations. For example, Jewish emigration from the Soviet Union increased during the high points of détente and declined during the times of tension. During the first year and a half of Reagan's tenure in office, emigration reached a new low.[86] None of this has, however, prevented the Reagan administration from continuing to aggravate Cold War tensions, for the simple reason that respect for human rights, even in the East, is not something about which the administration is concerned (except insofar as questions of human rights have implications for other matters of concern). Indeed, there is clearly a sense in which the administration is delighted by instances of repressions in the East, since they serve to vindicate its claims about the Eastern bloc in the eyes of the rest of the world. We will have occasion to return to this point in later chapters.

Nuclear Nonproliferation: Atoms for Friends

The Reagan administration's policy on nuclear nonproliferation has a great deal in common with its policies on arms sales and human rights. Just as the administration is unwilling to ruffle feathers among its allies by criticizing or penalizing them for their violations of human rights, so it is also unwilling to cause "unnecessary friction" by criticizing or impeding their efforts to acquire nuclear weapons. Rather, it is using the sale of nuclear technology in the same way that it uses arms sales—as a means of expanding U.S. power and influence. Therefore, rather than seeking to restrict the transfer of U.S. nuclear technology, it has been seeking to remove all such restrictions. Its policy is, of course, selective rather than promiscuous: as in the case of its arms sales and human rights policies, it draws a sharp distinction between its friends and its enemies. It is willing to allow or even to facilitate the proliferation of nuclear weapons among friendly countries, but, to the limited extent to which it is possible, it seeks to prevent the spread of nuclear weapons to enemy countries. Thus, just as Reagan's human rights policy has caused a deterioration in respect for human rights, so his nonproliferation policy has reduced the prospects for stopping or limiting the proliferation of nuclear weapons. His non-proliferation policy, like his policy on arms sales, has therefore made the world a considerably more dangerous place.

During the 1980 presidential campaign, Reagan was notable among the major candidates for studiously ignoring the problem of nuclear proliferation, except to remark that "I just don't think it's any of our business."[87] It was, in fact, only when the Israeli raid on the Iraqi nuclear reactor in the summer of 1981 made the problem of proliferation a matter of intense public controversy that Reagan was obliged to formulate a policy of sorts. This "policy" is in fact nothing more than a rationale for doing nothing, spiced with a bit of free-market ideology. Its primary aim is, in Reagan's words, to "re-establish this nation as a predictable and reliable partner for peaceful nuclear cooperation under adequate safeguards. . . . If we are not such a partner, other countries will tend to go their own ways and our influence will diminish. This would reduce our effectiveness in gaining the support we need to deal with proliferation problems."[88] Here the real aim of extending U.S. influence is acknowledged, though Reagan of course suggests that the United States would use its influence to discourage other countries from acquiring nuclear weapons.

The defects of this policy as a means of stopping nuclear proliferation are obvious (though it was not, of course, because of its effectiveness in this respect that the policy was adopted). Making it easier for countries to acquire nuclear technology, and thus to develop the potential for making bombs, does not guarantee that these countries will remain obligingly indebted to their patron. On the contrary, it may even work the other way around. For the development of nuclear weapons, or even the development of a nuclear potential, is regarded by those countries aspiring to possess nuclear weapons as an equalizer, giving *them* independence from and influence over other countires, including their nuclear suppliers.

Even if it were correct to assume that being a "reliable" supplier of nuclear materials and technology would give the United States influence over its customers, there can be no guarantee that those governments, or successor governments friendly to the United States, will be able to survive indefinitely. There are several instances in which one of the "superpowers" has provided a wealth of military technology and hardware to a friendly government, only to find that government overthrown and replaced by a regime hostile to its superpower patron. Iran is a good example. When the Shah was overthrown, not only did the United States lose all influence in the country, but all of the weapons it had supplied to the Shah fell into the hands of a hated enemy. This could just as easily happen in the case of nuclear weapons—though the fact that it could suggests a disturbing possibility. The acquisition of nuclear weapons by a friendly regime would raise the stakes considerably if that regime were then threatened by domestic opposition, and the possibility that the nuclear weapons would fall into enemy hands if the regime were to be overthrown would provide a powerful argument for intervention to preserve the regime. (For example, if the Shah had had nuclear weapons, would the United States have allowed him to fall?) It is perhaps implausible to suppose that Reagan's advisers are sufficiently cunning to recognize it, but the acquisition of nuclear weapons by friendly governments might actually be welcomed by the Reagan administration on the grounds that it would provide an argument which would be decisive in the United States for doing all that would be necessary to maintain those governments in power.

If, of course, what Reagan refers to as "adequate safeguards" were really sufficient to prevent other countries from acquiring nuclear weapons, and if it were clear that the administration would respect those safeguards, then the Reagan policy would have some plausibility. But neither of these conditions obtains. The safeguards on which Reagan's policy relies are those imposed by the International Atomic Energy Agency (IAEA). The IAEA is empowered by the terms of the Non-Proliferation Treaty (NPT) to inspect the nuclear energy facilities of those non-nuclear-weapon states which have ratified the treaty. In return for submitting to IAEA inspection, those states have received a pledge from the nuclear-weapon states which have ratified the treaty to cooperate with them in the development of their peaceful nuclear energy programs. All parties to the treaty are, however, forbidden to transfer nuclear materials or technology to states which refuse to accept IAEA inspection. The United States is a party to the NPT, and it is essentially the constraints embodied in the treaty—and in particular the system of IAEA inspection—to which Reagan was referring when he spoke of adequate safeguards.

Yet the system of IAEA inspection is notoriously unreliable, as was conceded even by a number of experts within the U.S. nuclear establishment shortly after Reagan's policy was announced.[89] Among the problems with IAEA inspection are the following. First, IAEA inspectors are responsible for tracing the paths of the radioactive materials that are processed through each country's nuclear installations in order to ensure that none of the material is diverted for the purpose of making bombs. But some radioactive material is inevitably lost, and there must be a margin of error built into the inspectors' accounting techniques to allow for this. It is, however, possible to divert small amounts of fissionable material within that margin of error, so that over time a significant total could be diverted within the limits of allowable "losses." For an ordinary nuclear reactor, it has been estimated that about eighteen pounds of plutonium—enough to make a bomb—could be diverted every year within the margin of error.[90] In the case of reprocessing plants, however, the Stockholm International Peace Research Institute (SIPRI) puts the figure much higher. It estimates that "a determined effort at systematic diversion could succeed in 'losing' enough material to make two bombs every month."[91] This is particularly disturbing given that one aspect of the Reagan administration's policy of being a reliable supplier has been to remove restrictions on cooperating with other countries in their efforts to develop reprocessing and breeder reactor facilities.

A second problem with the IAEA safeguards is that there is apparently ample scope for the deception of inspectors. For example, states can introduce undetectable distortions into the accounts they are required to submit. Moreover, inspectors must give advance notice of inspections, and this allows governments sufficient time to cover up evidence of clandestine activities. A third and more important problem is that the IAEA has no enforcement authority. If a country is discovered to be diverting fissionable material for the manufacture of nuclear weapons, all the IAEA can do is to notify other parties to the NPT in the hope that they will honor their commitment under the treaty to stop all cooperation in nuclear matters with the offending country. The IAEA has neither the ability nor the authority to impose sanctions. This brings us to the fourth problem, which is that, even if the diversion of fissionable material is detected, inspections are so infrequent that it is likely that significant amounts of material will already have been diverted by the time the deception is discovered. Even if other countries immediately cease to cooperate with the offender, it may by then be too late to prevent that country from being able to manufacture nuclear weapons. Finally, and perhaps most importantly, the NPT is not permanently binding; any party to the treaty can withdraw after having given three months' notice. Thus it is possible for countries to receive assistance in the development of their nuclear programs under IAEA safeguards and then withdraw from the treaty, leaving themselves free to use the technology they have acquired in any way they see fit.

Given these problems, it seems obvious that the safeguards on which Reagan's policy relies are grossly inadequate. But even if the IAEA safeguards were sufficient to prevent the diversion of fissionable material, that would not mean that the Reagan administration's policies would pose no proliferation risk. For, by transferring nuclear materials and technology to countries that have refused to submit to IAEA inspection, the administration has failed to respect even the existing safeguards. In 1982, for example, the administration approved the sale to Argentina of a computerized control system which "will become the 'brains' of a large heavy-water plant which, like uranium enrichment and plutonium reprocessing facilities, is classified as a 'sensitive' technology because it is the critical element in one route to the production of materials that could be used in nuclear bombs."[92] Later, in August 1983, the administration approved the sale from West Germany to Argentina of 143 tons of U.S.-made heavy water, which is necessary for the operation of Argentina's nuclear reactors. Argentina has refused to sign the NPT and, while it has allowed the IAEA to inspect some of its nuclear facilities, it has refused to allow all of them to be inspected and monitored. Most specialists believe that Argentina intends to produce nuclear weapons and that it is well on the way to being able to do so. After the Falklands/Malvinas war, Admiral Carlos Castro Madero, then chairman of Argentina's Atomic Energy Commission, stated that "Argentina . . . reserves the right for itself to undertake the development of euphemistically so-called non-proscribed military uses" of nuclear energy.[93] More recently, Argentina has claimed to have developed the ability to produce enriched uranium—a claim which appears to be true, and which means that Argentina is now very close to being able to produce nuclear weapons.[94]

The administration has also relaxed restrictions on the sale of nuclear-related materials to South Africa, another country which has refused to sign the NPT or to open its facilities to international inspection. The United States has, for example, sold South Africa an advanced computer designed for nuclear weapons research, and it has relaxed restrictions on the sale of materials which "will enable South Africa to acquire a small quantity of Helium 3, a substance which could theoretically be used to make Tritium, a form of hydrogen used in thermonuclear weapons."[95] South Africa has probably already acquired nuclear weapons, but has refrained from acknowledging the fact for fear of the international repercussions (for example, diplomatic or economic sanctions).[96] If it aspires to possess not just nuclear weapons but thermonuclear weapons as well, then it has every reason to be grateful to the United States for its assistance.

Other countries which have refused to sign the NPT or to submit their nuclear facilities to international inspection but which have nevertheless received U.S. assistance include Brazil and India. In 1981 the United States granted Brazil a "special-case exemption" from heavy penalties which it would otherwise have had to pay for buying enriched uranium for use in its new U.S.-built reactor. The administration was prevented by law from selling the uranium itself, but George Bush, addressing Brazilian leaders, expressed the hope that the United States would soon become "a reliable supplier."[97] While Brazil is generally agreed to be intent on acquiring nuclear weapons, India is known to have had the capability to amass a nuclear arsenal since it detonated a nuclear explosive in 1974. The Reagan administration has expressed its displeasure at the prospect of India's building up a nuclear arsenal by agreeing to resume supplies of spare parts for India's U.S.-built reactor at Tarapur. Supplies had previously been suspended when India refused to sign the NPT.

During a visit to China in April 1984, Reagan signed a nuclear cooperation agreement with China which would permit U.S. companies to sell civilian nuclear reactors in China. Negotiations with the Chinese were initially bogged down over the nonproliferation conditions which Congress imposes on all such agreements; but, given what the *New York Times* referred to as "Mr. Reagan's desire for something to sign on his visit, and the nuclear power vendors' thirst for customers," the administration threw its usual obsession with verification to the winds and agreed to accept mere verbal assurances from the Chinese.[98] The administration is required by law to submit all nuclear cooperation treaties to Congress for approval, but so far it has understandably failed to do so in this case. China has refused to sign the NPT, and is widely believed to be assisting Pakistan to produce nuclear weapons.[99]

Given its obligations under the NPT, as well as under the 1978 U.S. Nuclear Non-Proliferation Act, which also prohibits the export of nuclear materials and technology to countries that refuse to accept IAEA inspection, how has the Reagan administration managed to become such a reliable supplier to Argentina, South Africa, and India? In many cases it has exploited the same trick it used in allowing the Bell Company to sell helicopters to Guatemala: it has approved the sale of certain "dual-use, nuclear-related equipment" which, while ostensibly for use in civilian business endeavors or nonnuclear scientific research, has promptly been diverted for use by the recipient's nuclear industry.[100] In other cases it has conducted its transfers through intermediate agents. For example, the computer control system which it transferred to Argentina was actually sold to a Swiss company employed by Argentina which then passed it on to its employer.

One final point of interest about the Reagan administration's nonproliferation policy is that it has provided a useful rationale for selling conventional arms and providing military assistance to various third world dictatorships. The idea is that by providing these dictatorships with a liberal supply of conventional arms, one increases their sense of security, thereby decreasing their incentive to acquire nuclear weapons. There is a slight problem in the deployment of this argument, however, as was manifest in the case of Pakistan in 1983. The argument presupposed, correctly, that General Zia has aspirations to possess nuclear weapons, but the United States was barred by the 1976 Symington Amendment to the Foreign Assistance Act from providing military assistance to countries believed to be seeking a nuclear capability. At first the administration sought to have the amendment repealed, but later realized that the best solution to its problem would be to deny that Zia is seeking a nuclear capability. Thus a senior White House official stated that Zia affirmed during a meeting with President Reagan that he is "not interested in the manufacture or acquision of nuclear weapons." When asked whether Zia's assurance was accepted by President Reagan, the official replied with apparent indignation that "of course we accept that the President of Pakistan is telling us the truth."[101] If, however, one accepts that Zia is "not interested" in acquiring nuclear weapons, it then becomes nonsensical to argue that conventional military assistance will reduce his incentive to acquire nuclear weapons—though this did not deter the White House official from solemnly repeating that very argument. Naturally, the incoherence of the administration's position was politely overlooked, and the Senate voted in favor of Reagan's request for aid to Pakistan.

In this case, the administration's argument was not, however, merely incoherent. It was also—as one has come to expect from this administration—thoroughly dishonest. It is common knowledge that Zia has always hankered after a nuclear arsenal—a fact that has been acknowledged even by the U.S. Nuclear Regulatory Commission. For years Pakistan has been engaged in clandestine work on nuclear reprocessing and uranium enrichment, and during 1981 and 1982 there were numerous reports, based on Western intelligence data, that Pakistan was preparing for an underground nuclear test. At that time Zia's foreign minister openly argued that "we make a distinction between an explosion and weapons. We do not rule out the possibility of a detonation if it is necessary for our program."[102] Early in 1983, however, it emerged that, during the same meeting in which Reagan allegedly accepted Zia's assurances that Pakistan was uninterested in acquiring nuclear weapons, he actually persuaded Zia to postpone indefinitely his plans for a nuclear test on the ground that the adverse publicity generated by the test would jeopardize Reagan's own plans to provide $3.2 billion in military and economic assistance to Pakistan over the next few years.[103] Of course, this does not mean that the threat of a Pakistani bomb has now disappeared, for, as Reagan is well aware, Zia has continued with his research and development programs, leaving himself poised for the immediate construction of nuclear weapons if the need for them arises.[104]

The argument that conventional arms transfers can help to discourage nuclear proliferation is implausible for a number of reasons. One is that the strengthening of a country's conventional military capabilities has the effect of enhancing the power and prestige of the military establishment, which is then likely to use its influence to press even more insistently for the development of nuclear weapons, which it may want for a variety of reasons. More generally,

> the nuclear decision is likely to be made in many countries for reasons quite separate from a calculation of security requirements. These include factors of prestige, the desire to achieve regional dominance or to catch up with another state in the area, the interests of indigenous scientific and bureaucratic communities, or the pressures of domestic politics. . . . In none of these considerations would conventional arms be viewed as real alternatives to nuclear weapons.[105]

It should be obvious, however, that the Reagan administration is not particularly interested in the intellectual merits of the argument. It is interested in the argument as a tactical device; for, as we have seen, the administration is already committed to liberal arms transfers to friendly countries for other reasons—the same reasons why it is unwilling to prevent those countries from acquiring nuclear weapons.

Direct Intervention: The Rapid Deployment Force and the CIA

Before going on in subsequent chapters to examine in detail some recent instances of direct intervention by the United States in the third world, it may be helpful to conclude this chapter with a brief discussion of two of the administration's main instruments of intervention: the Rapid Deployment Force (RDF) and the Central Intelligence Agency (CIA).

The RDF was initially conceived by the Carter administration in 1977 as a light, highly mobile force whose function, according to the Pentagon, would be "waging 'brush-fire' wars in the Third World."[106] As the idea evolved, however, the RDF came to be conceived as a more substantial force whose primary mission would be the protection of U.S. access to oil supplies from the Persian Gulf region. While the original plan was for a force of about 100,000 men, the RDF had 220,000 troops at its disposal in January 1983, and Reagan has plans to double the current size of the force by 1988. By that time it is projected that "the rapid deployment package will include nine divisions, 36 tactical aircraft squadrons, at least two aircraft carriers, six amphibious ships, and 50 escort vessels."[107]

The RDF is intended to defend U.S. access to Middle Eastern oil against challenges both from the Soviets and from indigenous elements. Thoughtful observers have criticized the entire project on a variety of grounds, however. They have pointed out, for example, that the strategy for the deployment of the RDF in response to a Soviet threat to the oilfields involves the deliberate creation of risks much greater than the stakes in the Middle East would warrant.[108] The RDF's "preemptive strategy" calls for the immediate insertion of troops into the area at the first indication of Soviet mobilization in order to deter further possible moves by the Soviets. The appearance of U.S. troops in the area could, however, precipitate a major crisis, since the Soviets would be likely to interpret the U.S. move as the first phase in a U.S. operation to seize the oilfields (and not without reason, for sources close to the administration have for years been giving serious consideration to the possibility of seizing the oilfields).[109] Moreover, at present at least the administration does not anticipate that the RDF would be capable of actually preventing a Soviet thrust into the oil-producing regions. Rather, the RDF is envisaged more as a "trip-wire" whose presence would serve as a signal to the Soviets that an assault on the oilfields would lead to a military confrontation with the United States, with the significant likelihood of escalation to all-out war which that would entail. As the Pentagon's Defense Guidance Plan notes, "It is essential that the Soviet Union be confronted with the prospect of a major conflict should it seek to reach the oil resources of the Persian Gulf."[110]

What is more, there has been considerable discussion in planning circles about the possibility that an outnumbered RDF might have to resort to tactical nuclear weapons to defend itself.[111] Columnist Jack Anderson has reported government testimony which notes that there is a "contingency plan [which] calls for a nuclear strike to stop the Soviets from annihilating the force."[112] The use of tactical nuclear weapons would, of course, make escalation to all-out nuclear war even more likely. In short, the RDF is designed to convey and render credible U.S. willingness to fight a nuclear war for control of the energy resources of the Middle East.

Critics have also suggested that, in addition to being dangerous, the RDF may be a reaction to a largely imaginary problem. In 1980 the CIA was predicting that the Soviet Union's own energy resources would soon become insufficient to meet domestic needs, so that the Soviet leaders would have a strong temptation to try to gain control of the oilfields of the Middle East. These fears were heightened by the Soviet invasion of Afghanistan, which many saw as merely a step toward the ultimate goal of invading Iran. By 1981, however, the CIA had reassessed its earlier estimate of the Soviet Union's energy potential, and this time it concluded that the Soviets would be self-sufficient for the foreseeable future. By this time alarm about the Soviets' intentions in Afghanistan had also subsided, and military analysts had arrived at a more sober appreciation of the many obstacles the Soviets would have to face in launching an invasion of Iran, even from Afghanistan.[113]

Critics have argued that the "threat" from indigenous sources has also been exaggerated. As Michael Klare of the Institute for Policy Studies has noted, Western Europe and Japan are considerably more dependent on Middle Eastern oil than is the United States, yet they have not felt compelled to develop interventionist forces for use in the event of a cutoff. The reason, Klare argues, is that

> because OPEC countries *must sell oil* in order to gain the technology they seek, and because *only* the industrialized West can provide both the markets and the technology required by the oil producers, most European and Japanese strategists believe that the Gulf countries will take whatever steps are necessary to assure continued oil deliveries. . . . OPEC's prosperity has become far too dependent on Western economic stability to risk their own demise by shutting off oil.[114]

These are not, however, the most important arguments against the RDF. The strongest objection is simply that it compares unfavorably, both morally and prudentially, with the alternative of reducing or eliminating U.S. dependence on Middle Eastern oil.[115] This dependence could be reduced to some extent by seeking other suppliers: "Mexico is eager to sell what it can to save itself from bankruptcy, and China's offshore reserves are said to exceed those of Iran."[116] U.S. dependence could be further reduced by increased reliance on alternative energy sources, such as solar, wind, and geothermal sources, and by the development of synthetic fuels. Indeed, U.S. reliance on Middle Eastern oil could be decreased to a great extent simply by the adoption of more stringent conservation policies (though of course Reagan is ready with a devastating reply to this point: "Conservation means we will all have to be too hot in the summer or too cold in the winter").[117] The conversion to alternative energy programs would not be inexpensive, but neither is the RDF—nor, in particular, will be the expansion of the RDF to the proportions envisaged by the Reagan administration. A recent Bookings Institution study puts the total cost by 1988 at more than $500 billion, and that figure does not include the further costs that would be incurred if the RDF actually had to be used.[118] As Klare has pointed out:

> Any full-scale "energy war" in the Gulf area would probably cost several times the $250 billion spent on the Vietnam War (which was fought after all, with cheap, pre-OPEC gasoline). When we add the potential cost in human lives, and the risk of nuclear escalation, it is obvious that converting to non-Mideast energy sources would be the most economical and prudent solution by far.[119]

However decisive this argument may seem, it is unlikely to impress the Reagan administration, whose commitments to the RDF and to the maintenance of control over the flow of Middle Eastern oil are motivated as much by considerations of symbolism and ideology as they are by a concern to ensure an adequate U.S. energy supply. The abandonment of the RDF and the subsequent acceptance of the necessary retrenchment would be tantamount to a retreat from the administration's ideal of global dominance. For the oil resources of the Middle East are of great *strategic* importance: they are the largest and cheapest energy sources available, and thus whoever controls them will have a major role in controlling world affairs. (This explains why the United States sought to maintain control over Middle Eastern oil even during the period between World War II and the early 1970s when U.S. reliance on it was considerably less than it is at present.) The abandonment of the RDF would not only constitute the surrender of the divine right of the United States to the oil of the Middle East, but would also, as Reagan has so eloquently noted, compromise the American Way of Life by requiring Americans to make an effort to conserve resources. Worst of all, however, it would damage U.S. credibility. Parroting the administration's line, the Kissinger Commission on Central America has recently argued that the failure of the United States to save the government in El Salvador "would be read as a sign of U.S. impotence," and would thus erode "our power to influence events worldwide."[120] If members of the American Establishment can seriously imagine that this would be the consequence of a decision not to defend the Salvadoran government, then one can conceive of their horror at the thought of a decision not to defend U.S. access to the oil of the Gulf, which is vastly more important in terms of U.S. interests than the preservation of the status quo in El Salvador. The abandonment of the RDF and with it the ambition to "defend" the Gulf would thus be inimical to everything the administration stands for.

While the RDF is primarily intended for use in the Gulf area, that does not exclude the possibility of its being used elsewhere. As Caspar Weinberger has argued, "We must be able to defend ourselves [*sic*] in wars of any size and shape and in any region."[121] And indeed units assigned to the RDF were called into action in the invasion of Grenada, which will be discussed in detail in Chapter 7. Yet so far during the Reagan administration's tenure the principal instrument of direct overseas intervention has been the CIA. Because of the stubborn persistence of the Vietnam syndrome, the administration has considered it advisable to try to conceal most of its interventionist activities from the American public. It is partly for this reason that the administration has entrusted most of its dirty work abroad to the CIA's covert operations division.

The CIA has enjoyed a remarkable revival since Reagan entered office. It is at present undergoing the largest expansion it has ever experienced in peacetime, with its budget having risen at an average rate of 17 percent annually over Reagan's first three years in office—a proportional increase greater even than that which the Pentagon's budget has received. The CIA's budget for 1983 was estimated to be around $2 billion, roughly 25 percent greater than its budget for the previous year.[122] During the years of the Carter presidency the agency languished under a host of restrictions which Reagan has obligingly removed. In particular, whereas Carter had severely limited the range of permissible covert operations, and had cut back the number of covert operatives to around 200, the covert operations division is now flourishing, with over 1,000 operatives in the field. There are more than 200 working in Nicaragua alone.

Despite the administration's efforts to keep the public in the dark about its various interventionist and subversive activities abroad, a recent article in *Newsweek* has exposed a number of important facts about these activities.[123] In particular, the article reveals just how extensive the CIA's involvement in other countries is. The article reports, for example, that, while the administration denies providing material support for the rebels in Afghanistan, the CIA is in fact supplying them with about $100 million worth of arms and ammunition. It notes that the CIA (in collaboration with the Turkish military government) is supporting Iranian exiles in Turkey and in France who are working to overthrow the government of Ayatollah Khomeini, and that the agency is providing intelligence information, training, and other forms of aid to government forces in Chad. None of this is surprising. What is perhaps surprising is the revelation that in Kampuchea the CIA is supplying arms to Pol Pot—a figure who appears frequently in administration propaganda when it is necessary to demonstrate the wickedness and depravity of communists. (The supply of arms, together with diplomatic support—for example in the United Nations—are part of the continuing U.S. policy of "bleeding" Vietnam, against whose puppet regime in Kampchea Pol Pot is fighting.)

Where the CIA is having a real field day is of course in Nicaragua, where it is coordinating and directing operations to overthrow the Sandinista government. We will consider its not-so-covert activities there in detail in Chapter 6. What is less well known is that the CIA has also been unleashed in El Salvador. There it played a part in running the 1982 elections, and *Newsweek* reports that it has conducted "a 'propaganda and disinformation campaign' in the Salvadoran press aimed at 'convincing the civilian population that the guerrillas, not the Army, are the real bad guys,' according to one source." The glorious cause which the CIA is defending in El Salvador is discussed in the next chapter.

★5★

Some Notable Victims: (1) El Salvador

When the Reagan administration came to power, El Salvador was already in the throes of a bloody civil war. What was in effect a military government with token civilian elements was engaged in a savage though largely ineffective campaign to eradicate an armed insurgent movement which aimed to overthrow it. The Carter administration had provided considerable support for the military and military-civilian juntas which were in power during its tenure in office. Although "lethal" forms of military aid had been suspended in 1977 when the military goverment in El Salvador refused to accept congressionally imposed human rights conditions, and even though "nonlethal" forms of aid had also been suspended in 1980 when four North American churchwomen were raped and murdered by members of the armed forces, the Carter administration before leaving office resumed both forms of aid in response to an announcement by the guerrillas of a "final offensive." Nonlethal aid was suspended for only forty days.

By contrast with Carter's wavering and uneasy support, the Reagan administration committed itself to the preservation of the government in El Salvador with great determination and considerable fanfare. Military aid (of the lethal and nonlethal varieties) was increased by a factor of eight during Reagan's first year in office, reaching a total of $40 million. Economic aid was doubled, to $126.5 million.[1] The trend of increasing support continued in 1982, by which time El Salvador had become the fourth largest recipient of U.S. military and economic aid, surpassed only by Israel, Egypt, and Turkey.[2] By 1984 the Reagan administration had funneled nearly $1 billion into this tiny country. El Salvador had been elevated to a position of central importance in U.S. foreign policy.

The administration's position on El Salvador might be paraphrased in the following way. The United States is defending a moderate, reformist government—and later, after the elections in March 1982, and March and May 1984, a democratically elected government—against a "totalitarian minority" whose aim, in Reagan's words, is "to impose a Marxist-Leninist dictatorship on the people of El Salvador as part of a larger imperialistic plan."[3] While the government in El Salvador enjoys the support of the people, as the 1982 and 1984 elections demonstrated, the guerrillas do not, as they themselves have implicitly acknowledged by their refusal to participate in the elections. Instead of representing popular, nationalist ideals, the guerrillas of the various groups which in 1980 coalesced into the Farabundo Martí National Liberation Front (FMLN) are in fact the hirelings of an alien power, the Soviet Union, which regards a communist takeover in El Salvador as a stepping-stone toward its ultimate goal of conquering the United States. The Soviet Union's guiding hand is manifest, for example, in the fact that the guerrillas are armed by Cuba and Nicaragua, the Soviet Union's proxies in the region. In helping the government to suppress the insurgency, the United States is thus protecting a legitimate and popularly supported government against indirect external aggression.

Charges that the government is unworthy of U.S. support on account of its poor record of respect for human rights overlook, according to the administration, two vitally important facts. The first is that many of the violations of human rights that have occurred have been accidental and unintended. As Jeane Kirkpatrick has explained, "The insurgency has penetrated the population and attempts to hide itself within it—so that fighting violent insurgents spills over into the society."[4] Hence it is the guerrillas who are ultimately responsible for government violence against civilian noncombatants—just as, so it was claimed, the Palestine Liberation Organization (PLO) was ultimately responsible for Israel's killing many thousands of civilians in Beirut, where the PLO had tried to shield itself behind the civilian population.

The second fact is that much of the violence for which the government has been blamed is in fact attributable to various right-wing paramilitary groups—the death squads—over which the government has been unable to exert sufficient control. The death squads, operating independently of the government, are a reaction to the violence of the left-wing revolutionaries. As former President Alvaro Magaña's chief aide once remarked, the death squads "are people taking revenge. This is part of the moral chaos that the guerrillas have led us to."[5] In fact, the death squads are unwittingly serving the guerrillas' purposes. As Kirkpatrick has claimed, the guerrillas "have sought and invited reaction from the extreme right in the hope that it will ultimately lead a revolution from the extreme left, and have deliberately set off a chain of violence and counterviolence which imperils the freedom, security, and well-being of every El Salvadoran."[6] Indeed, the death squads are so effective in furthering the aims of the guerrillas that, according to Fred Iklé, the U.S. under secretary of defense for policy, "some of the more notorious elements in the death squad activities are in fact enjoying the practical protection of the Communist guerrillas."[7] Reagan has even suggested that some of the death squads are really guerrillas masquerading as right-wingers: "I wonder if all of this is right-wing, or if those guerrilla forces have not realized that by infiltrating into the city of San Salvador and places like that, that they can get away with these violent acts, helping to try and bring the government down, and the right-wing will be blamed for it."[8] In short, the situation in El Salvador is one in which, in Kirkpatrick's words, "murderous traditionalists confront murderous revolutionaries—with *only* the government working to end this mutual murder and attempting to pacify adversaries."[9]

The aim of U.S. policy in El Salvador, according to the administration, is to bring peace and stability to the country by helping the Salvadorans to defend themselves against externally directed communist subversion. The only way of resolving the conflict that is ultimately satisfactory is for all of the contending parties to submit to the test of the ballot box. Thus the administration continues to insist that the guerrillas must abandon their armed struggle and must instead seek power only through the democratic process.

That, in brief, is the official version of the events in El Salvador. The reality is utterly different. The Salvadoran civil war has its roots, not in the machinations of foreign communist powers, but in the fact that for almost a century the vast majority of the people in El Salvador have been ruthlessly and systematically exploited and oppressed by a group of wealthy oligarchs—the so-called fourteen families—acting in conjunction with the military. The oligarchs consolidated their alliance with the military in 1932, when the military crushed a peasant uprising which threatened to break the oligarchy's stranglehold on the economy. An estimated 30,000 peasants were murdered in the space of a month. The United States generously offered to help in suppressing the revolt, and even stationed gunboats off the coast, but, on that occasion at least, its services were not needed. Since the time of the *matanza* (massacre), the military has ruled the country on behalf of the oligarchy. While the oligarchs have lived in opulence, the overwhelming bulk of the population has lived in extreme poverty. A study conducted in 1979 showed that less than 1 percent of the landowners owned 77.8 percent of the land.[10] In 1982, some 2 percent of the population received almost half the country's income.[11] The general population in El Salvador is the worst nourished in Latin America, and 47 percent of those who die of natural causes in rural El Salvador are children under the age of five who die of starvation.[12]

The idea that the revolutionaries in El Salvador are acting on behalf of the Soviet Union is in any case self-evidently absurd.

Persons who join the antigovernment forces must leave their homes and families for a life of extreme hardship and deprivation; they run a daily risk of torture, reprisals against their families, and violent death. It is almost too obvious to require stating that one does not accept these conditions of existence simply in order to establish a "Marxist-Leninist dictatorship," or to hand one's country over to an alien power. Journalists who have spent time among the guerrillas have found that most are simply peasants, largely uneducated, who have themselves been victims, either directly or indirectly, of government violence and terror. For example, Clifford Krauss of the *Atlanta Constitution* reports that behind rebel lines he "met few people who had not lost at least one relative at the hands of the army, national guard or the paramilitary Orden force [a rural paramilitary organization which, though officially disbanded, still operates with the blessing of the government, and often in conjunction with the regular army]."[13] Contrary to Kirkpatrick's fatuous assertion that "revolutions in our times are caused not by social injustice," the guerrillas were driven to take up arms by the appalling cruelties, persecutions, and institutionalized injustices to which they, their families, and their compatriots have been subjected, and by the desperate conviction that change is possible only through armed insurrection.[14]

The Reagan administration does recognize the legitimacy of violent resistance to oppression, provided of course that it is directed against a communist power, as in Afghanistan. Moreover, in the case of Afghanistan at least, even Kirkpatrick seems capable of understanding that the decision to take up arms is not one to be taken lightly: "Resistance means putting your life on the line. It may mean death, torture, hunger, and all the other terrible prices freedom-fighters have to pay."[15] Yet she would have us believe that in El Salvador people are willing to take these terrible risks—and indeed "invite" violent reprisals against themselves and their families by the army and the death squads—just in order to oblige Fidel Castro and his superiors in the Kremlin.

Far from being a monolithic collection of Marxist-Leninist totalitarians, as the administration contends, the antigovernment forces in El Salvador comprise a broad coalition of diverse groups and individuals, including middle-class social democrats, disaffected Christian Democrats, trade unionists, students, teachers, priests, and peasants. According to an American expert on the Latin American left, who himself holds strong anti-Soviet views, the diverse groups which comprise the FMLN "all have anti-Soviet origins," and their members harbor "suspicions of the Soviet Union."[16] Many of the most prominent figures in the Democratic

Revolutionary Front (FDR), which is the opposition's political organization, come from center or center-left political parties, and attempted for many years to solve El Salvador's problems through democratic processes before joining the guerrillas. For example, the current president of the FDR, Guillermo Ungo, was a member of the first military-civilian junta before resigning in protest. Before that, in 1972, he was the vice-presidential running-mate of José Napoleón Duarte, the Christian Democrat who in 1980 became president of the junta and later, in 1984, president of the country.

In an effort to portray the opposition forces as tools of the Kremlin, administration officials routinely assert that the guerrillas are heavily armed by the Soviet Union and Cuba, which infiltrate their arms into El Salvador via Nicaragua. Kirkpatrick, for example, claimed in 1984 that "the amount of Soviet bloc arms funnelled into El Salvador is staggering."[17] Obviously the administration believes (with ample justification) that, if it repeats this claim often enough, people will accept it in spite of the fact that it has been decisively and publicly refuted. The only evidence which the administration has marshaled in support of its case was presented in a State Department White Paper released early in 1981, which was based on an analysis of captured guerrilla documents.[18] Some of these documents were later exposed as likely forgeries, while others were distorted through apparently deliberate mistranslation. In other cases inferences were drawn and claims were made which were clearly unsubstantiated by the evidence presented. Later the principal author of the White Paper conceded to the *Wall Street Journal* that it was "full of mistakes" and "guessing," and that parts of it were "misleading" and "overembellished." There was, moreover, nothing in the report which implicated the Soviet Union in the supply of arms to El Salvador, and some of the documents which the State Department did not release even suggest that the Nicaraguan government had on some occasions *obstructed* supplies of arms to the guerrillas.[19]

While undoubtedly the Cubans (and probably the Nicaraguans) have provided military assistance to the guerrillas in El Salvador, it has clearly been minimal. Although the United States has a large number of intelligence operatives in El Salvador and has for several years been backing a sizable counterrevolutionary force based in Honduras, one of whose tasks is said to be the interdiction of arms into El Salvador, no arms have ever been interdicted, either by the counterrevolutionary proxies or by the Salvadoran army. A British correspondent recounts a briefing held in 1984 in which a U.S. military adviser in El Salvador triumphantly displayed a single

North Korean cartridge—the sole visible evidence of the arsenal which so staggers Kirkpatrick.[20] Journalists who have lived behind guerrilla lines have consistently failed to find any evidence of the massive numbers of sophisticated weapons allegedly supplied by the Soviet Union and Cuba.[21]

Several mutually confirming accounts indicate that while Cuba did supply arms to the Salvadoran guerrillas prior to 1981, shipments were reduced shortly after Reagan's inauguration in January of that year and were halted altogether in April. This is the account which the Cubans themselves have given, and, according to Wayne Smith, senior U.S. diplomatic representative in Cuba from 1979 to 1982, there is no evidence to contradict the Cubans' claim.[22] Moreover, in a recent series of interviews with American news organizations, David MacMichael, who until his resignation in March 1983 was an intelligence analyst for the Central Intelligence Agency, has confirmed that evidence of an arms flow into El Salvador "just disappeared" after the spring of 1981: "If you have good solid information, you are going to intercept something. If you have air drops, planes crash. The planes we allegedly send into Nicaragua crash all the time. Stuff gets dropped in the wrong place, parachutes hang up in trees." No evidence of this sort has, however, been discovered. Hence, MacMichael concludes, "I do not believe that there is Nicaraguan government involvement or use of Nicaraguan territory in any significant way for the supply of arms or other war material."[23]

The response by El Salvador's President José Napoleón Duarte to MacMichael's reasoning is rather interesting. In a recent interview with Duarte published in *Playboy* magazine, the following exchange occurs:

> *Playboy:* Do you give any credibility to the statements made by former CIA agent David C. MacMichael, whose job it was to monitor the arms traffic from Nicaragua and who recently announced that there had been no such flow for more than three years? He got so disgusted with the Government line about the arms flow that he went off to pick cotton in Nicaragua.
> *Duarte:* Well, there you are. What kind of credibility could he have if he did that?
> *Playboy:* There are several ways to view his going to Nicaragua. It doesn't necessarily mean he is a liar.
> *Duarte:* Wrong. There is only one way to interpret this. The man is clearly a Marxist.[24]

These remarks occur in a context in which Duarte has expressed support for the counterrevolutionary forces, or contras, based in Honduras on the ground that they are helping "to stop the flow of arms from Nicaragua." Duarte's comments on the "flow of arms" are also illuminating:

> *Playboy:* The Reagan Administration also claims that Nicaragua is intervening here in El Salvador by supporting your enemies, the Salvadoran rebels. Yet it has never made public any proof of that accusation. Does your government have proof?
> *Duarte:* Look, it doesn't matter what I say or what proof I give you, you are always going to say it's not sufficient evidence.
> *Playboy:* That's not true. We are going to publish whatever you say.
> *Duarte:* No, it's normal that our side is ignored. The entire world does not want to accept any evidence that is offered by El Salvador or the US. In contrast, it accepts any evidence, even verbal evidence, that the *Sandinista* government offers as proof of US interference. Let the *Sandinistas* make any declaration about the US intervention and they have instant credibility. . . . Here in *Playboy,* you are not going to publish, "Duarte makes important declaration about Nicaraguan intervention." No, instead, you will say, "Duarte *alleges* some possibility without any proof of any kind." That's how the image of our country is distorted.[25]

Offered the opportunity to present his evidence of Nicaraguan intervention to the American public, Duarte declines to provide any support for his allegations, and then attempts to evade the issue by complaining that he will be misrepresented as having relied solely on unsupported allegations.

Whatever aid the guerrillas may have received from or through Cuba or Nicaragua has clearly been dwarfed by the massive infusion of money and arms the United States has provided for the government. (It is important to bear in mind, in assessing the extent of U.S. military assistance to El Salvador, that what is called "economic aid" enables the government to spend more on arms and on the prosecution of the war generally.) U.S. assistance has enabled the Salvadoran government army to acquire nearly fifty assault helicopters as well as a number of tanks and ground support jet aircraft. The guerrillas, of course, having nothing even remotely comparable to this. Indeed, it is precisely this asymmetry between the two sides' arsenals that explains the Reagan administration's refusal, mentioned earlier, to negotiate an end to arms shipments into Central America: for any fair and verifiable agreement would work to the disadvantage of the United States. Thus Edward Herman has noted that, where military aid (rather than sales) is concerned, "the United States has been the only serious supplier of arms to [any faction in El Salvador] over the past several decades."[26] (Where military *sales* are concerned, Israel has also been a major supplier to the Salvadoran government.)

Herman's observation is true in more than one sense, in that the United States has been the major supplier to *both* sides: "It is reliably estimated that 40 per cent (by value) of the US military equipment sent to the Salvadoran army in early 1983 passed to the guerrillas. Since the army outnumbers the rebels three to one, Washington may be doing a better job of equipping each guerrilla than of equipping each soldier."[27] In part it is their policy of treating their prisoners humanely and releasing them to the Red Cross that enables the guerrillas to capture such a high percentage of U.S.-supplied weapons. Many, if not most, of the Salvadoran soldiers are neither patriots nor ideologues but teenage peasants who were press-ganged into the army or enlisted in order to escape malnutrition. Because these soldiers know that if they surrender they will be treated well, they often surrender without a fight, turning over their arms in the process. In this way the guerrillas captured around 1,800 U.S.-supplied guns between October 1982 and May 1983, and another 1,000 in the closing months of 1983.[28] The guerrillas are also able to obtain U.S.-supplied weapons by purchasing them from Salvadoran army officers who are lining their pockets in preparation for the day when they will have to flee the country.[29]

The other major source of the guerrillas' weapons is the international black market, where often they buy from U.S. dealers, or dealers selling U.S. weapons. The guerrillas themselves admit that arms purchased on the black market are transferred to them through various Central American countries, including Nicaragua, but deny that the governments of these countries collaborate in the transfer of arms through their territory. The difference, they say, is that the governments of Honduras and Costa Rica attempt to interdict the shipments, while the government of Nicaragua simply looks the other way—hardly a form of aggressive intervention.[30]

Just as it is false that the guerrillas are the tools of an outside power, so it is equally false that they lack popular domestic support. The guerrillas are outnumbered by government forces by a ratio that is estimated to be between three to one and six to one.[31] Yet it is almost universally conceded (even by such persons as Henry Kissinger and Jeane Kirkpatrick) that without the enormous and continuing U.S. support, the government would be quickly defeated by the guerrillas. This has been the case for several years. Many U.S. military experts reckon that to win the war the government would need to deploy ten soldiers for every guerrilla. (The Reagan administration has recently begun to implement plans which will more than double the size of the Salvadoran army in order to provide it with something approximating a ten to one advantage.

In order to reach the administration's recruitment targets, the Salvadoran army has begun to impress large numbers of young men, often seizing them from busses or dragging them from their homes. In rural areas, young men leaving church or leaving football matches are often herded into trucks waiting nearby. Most of the victims are around sixteen or seventeen years old, and always come from the poorer Salvadoran communities. On occasion rebel fighters have been caught in the dragnet and hence have been able to receive U.S. training before deserting to rejoin the guerrillas.[32])
The fact that the army requires both overwhelming numbers and vastly superior hardware in order to avoid defeat at the hands of the guerrillas reveals a great deal about the guerrillas' popularity. Richard Barnet notes that "as all the standard textbooks on counterinsurgency insist, guerrillas cannot grow in numbers or strength unless the surrounding population is willing to protect them. . . . When foreign powers do not intervene militarily, the internal dynamics of revolution itself provide an important measure of the popularity of the contending forces."[33]

That the guerrillas in El Salvador enjoy the protection of the population is evident, for example, in Drew Middleton's report that the guerrillas have a "superb intelligence network," in that the peasants always alert them to the approach of the army in time to allow them to fade away.[34] It is also implicitly acknowledged by both the Salvadoran military, who have focused most of their efforts on terrorizing the civilian population in the hope of deterring support for the guerrillas, and by the United States, whose current strategy of "pacification" recognizes that, for the government to survive, the allegiance of the rural peasantry must be shifted away from the guerrillas and towards the government itself.

Former U.S. ambassador to El Salvador Robert White, who has been just as much concerned as the Reagan administration to prevent the Salvadoran guerrillas from seizing power, once estimated that the FDR was supported by more than 80 percent of the Salvadoran people.[35] Such an estimate must be treated with considerable skepticism since, in a climate of terror such as prevails in El Salvador today, it is extremely difficult to determine what people's preferences are. As in many other revolutionary situations, most people's greatest desire is probably that the violence should stop and that they should simply be left alone. Still, the recent Salvadoran elections notwithstanding, the evidence suggests that domestic support for the guerrilla opposition in El Salvador is considerable—probably greater than that for any other political group, the present government included.

While the Reagan administration has sought to portray the Salvadoran guerrillas as totalitarian pawns of Cuba and the Soviet Union, bent ultimately on subverting freedom and democracy throughout the whole of the western hemisphere, it has also consistently depicted the Salvadoran government as moderate, centrist, reformist, and above all, democratic. In fact, three different governments have held power (at least nominally) during Reagan's tenure in office, but the same labels have been applied to each. The reality, however, has been that, while some members of each government have had reformist and even democratic aspirations, they have been effectively powerless. In each case real power has remained with the army. And it would be difficult to find a more thoroughly corrupt, reactionary, antidemocratic, and utterly barbarous terrorist organization than the Salvadoran army.

When Reagan entered office in January 1981 the government in El Salvador consisted of a four-man military-civilian junta, the fourth in a succession of juntas which had ruled El Salvador since General Carlos Humberto Romero was overthrown in October 1979 in a coup led by younger officers, some of whom sought to enact serious democratic reforms. The first junta was the most genuinely pluralist and reform-minded of the four, but the efforts of several of its members to effect changes in the country and bring the military under civilian control were consistently thwarted by senior officers in the military. Having immediately regained control by outmaneuvering the junior officers who had supported the coup, the reactionary elements in the military openly defied the progressive members of the junta, launching a greatly intensified campaign of terror and repression against the civilian population. In less than three months the civilian members of the junta resigned in protest over the military's actions and in despair of their own impotence.

The second junta was formed when the two officers from the first junta were joined by three civilians, two of them members of the Christian Democratic party and one unaffiliated to any political party. Within two months, however, one of the Christian Democrats resigned on the ground that "we have not been able to stop the repression, and those committing acts of repression disrespectful of the authority of the Junta go unpunished."[36] No other parties were willing to lend legitimacy to the military by collaborating with them, but José Napoleón Duarte, a leading Christian Democrat, persuaded the delegates at the party's convention to allow him to join the junta—a decision which led a number of prominent Chrisitan Democrats to leave the party. The junta then remained unchanged until December 1980, a few weeks before Reagan's inauguration, when the one reformist officer was ousted and

Duarte was simultaneously elevated to the position of president of the junta.

With the creation of this fourth junta, over which Duarte nominally presided, the reactionaries in the military had firmly consolidated their power. Having progressively purged the junta of those civilians who insisted on sharing power and implementing reforms, the military had finally succeeded in putting together a junta in which the civilians were content to play a largely symbolic role, serving primarily to provide international legitimacy for the regime. The civilians were, in effect, decorations whose principle function was to guarantee continued support for the regime from the American people and the Congress.

More than six months after Duarte had first joined the junta, Ambassador White cabled to Washington that "the military have the power; no government can exist without their approval."[37] Subsequently Duarte has on several occasions acknowledged that as a member of the third and fourth juntas, he was effectively impotent, while real power rested with the military.[38] In short, Duarte had sold out.

While the Reagan administration persistently extolled the fourth Salvadoran junta as moderate and centrist, it was clearly nothing of the sort. During the junta's tenure, which lasted until March 1982, the government in El Salvador was, as it had been for decades, the military. During that period, operating behind the front provided by the civilians in the junta, and emboldened by the unambiguous and unconditional support of the Reagan administration, the military unleashed the bloodiest reign of terror that El Salvador has suffered since the *matanza* in 1932.

In the spring of 1981 the archbishop of San Salvador, Arturo Rivera y Damas, wrote to George Bush that "your views of the Junta as 'Centrist' do not concur with the reality and practice of the Junta, which is greatly influenced by the right wing of the military." He urged the administration to cut off military aid to the junta, arguing that "the provision of military assistance at this moment in our country's history simply strengthens the military."[39] Rivera y Damas's plea echoed that of his predecessor, Archbishop Oscar Arnulfo Romero, who had appealed to President Carter in February 1980 not to provide military aid to the second junta. Romero had written that "neither the junta nor the Christian Democrats govern the country. Political power is in the hands of the armed forces. They use their power unscrupulously. They know only how to repress the people and defend the interests of the Salvadoran oligarchy."[40] About a month later Romero was assassinated while saying mass by a government-sponsored death squad. Both churchmen's appeals were, of course, ignored. Rivera y Damas wrote to Bush that "I am convinced that the Administration does not understand the composition and nature of the Junta."[41] Here he was wrong. It was not that the administration misunderstood the nature of the junta. The junta was designated as centrist for public relations purposes. That the label did not fit the reality was irrelevant.

The tenure of the fourth junta ended when elections for the Constituent Assembly were held in March 1982. While Duarte's Christian Democrats received a plurality of the votes, the various parties to the right of the Christian Democrats won a majority of seats and together elected Roberto D'Aubuisson of the extreme right-wing ARENA party as president of the Constituent Assembly. This was a considerable embarrassment for the United States, since it would be hard to think of anyone in El Salvador farther from the political center than D'Aubuisson, described by former ambassador White as a "pathological killer." Not only was D'Aubuisson known to have strong links to the death squads, but there was also compelling evidence that he had been involved in two of El Salvador's most widely publicized recent murders—that of Archbishop Romero and that of two American workers for the American Institute for Free Labor Development (AIFLD) and a Salvadoran colleague who in January 1981 were sprayed by machine-gun fire in the coffee shop of San Salvador's Sheraton Hotel. The Reagan administration recognized that because D'Aubuisson was internationally notorious as the champion of the fascist right in El Salvador, he was not a marketable proposition in the United States. Yet not only had the Constituent Assembly elected him as its president, but it was also on the verge of selecting him as the provisional president of the country as well. The administration therefore warned senior Salvadoran officers that, unless a figurehead who would be salable to the American public were installed in power, Reagan's ability to get congressional support for further military aid would be jeopardized. Again demonstrating that, elections or no elections, power in El Salvador lies ultimately with the military, these senior officers first informed both D'Aubuisson and Duarte that neither was to be president, and then let it be known that they expected the Constituent Assembly to select the former president of the National Mortgage Bank, Álavaro Alfredo Magaña, as the country's next president.

Always willing to oblige, the Constituent Assembly duly appoined Magaña. Although he had intimate links with the military and the oligarchy (so intimate, in fact, that the junior officers who staged the 1979 coup had arrested him, seeking—unsuccessfully—

to bring him to trial for corruption on the ground that he had for years been giving illegal loans to senior officers), he at least had the virtue of being a civilian (D'Aubuisson being a cashiered major), with no apparent connection with the death squads.[42] Hence his "election" allowed the Reagan administration to paper over D'Aubuisson's ascendancy and again portray the Salvadoran government as civilian-controlled, centrist, and, above all, democratic. The only real change, however, was that the various right-wing political parties, in particular D'Aubuisson's ARENA party, had significantly increased their strength. The military remained firmly in control. Some eight months after the election a classified State Department report noted, in direct contast to what the administration was telling the American people, that "the military exerts a pervasive influence over the nation and . . . has sought to shield from justice even those who commit the most atrocious crimes."[43] Several months later Magaña himself confessed to a visiting congressional delegation that "I have no power, no authority."[44] The fierce repression of the Salvadoran people continued throughout his tenure in office.

The next change of government came in May 1984 when national elections for the office of president were held. Initial elections had been held that March but no candidate had emerged with a majority. The two candidates with the most votes were Duarte and D'Aubuisson, who faced each other in a runoff in May from which Duarte emerged victorious. The elections (to which we will return later in this chapter) were a tremendous propaganda coup for the Reagan administration. Duarte's victory was everywhere hailed as a triumph for the forces of moderation and democracy. Prominent U.S. liberals were effusive in their praise of Duarte's character. House Speaker Thomas P. O'Neill stated that "there is no doubt in my mind that Duarte is a very impressive man with great courage and bravery," while Democratic Majority Leader Jim Wright described him as "a man whom everybody recognizes to be a man of honor and a man of courage."[45] Despite Duarte's complaint, cited earlier, that the American media are biased against him, the liberal American press greeted his success with great enthusiasm. Invoking the standard formulas for describing Duarte's character, an opinion column in the *New York Times* written by a liberal opponent of the administration's policies in Central America proclaimed that "Mr. Duarte is an exemplary democrat and an astute leader of great courage and integrity," while the cover story of the *New York Times Magazine* portrayed him as "a champion of the democratic cause" whose "imperfect democratic center is the last chance for El Salvador to escape from the violent extremes."[46] The latter article was adorned with boldface captions at the bottom of certain pages which read like (and in effect were) advertisements for El Salvador's new president: "DUARTE SEEKS A DEMOCRATIC CENTER BETWEEN EXTREMES OF RIGHT AND LEFT," and "DUARTE HAS INITIATED MOVES HE HOPES WILL CURB HUMAN-RIGHTS ABUSES."[47]

While there have been some signs of liberalization in El Salvador since Duarte's election, and while Duarte has been granted more autonomy than he was allowed as a member of the third and fourth juntas, he still governs at the sufferance of the military. And it would be naïve to suppose that the military has overnight reformed itself, having suddenly been converted to "the democratic cause." The reforms which have been carried out have for the most part been token, or cosmetic, permitted by the military in order to ensure that the U.S. aid pipeline stays open. Shortly before the elections, which, given the Reagan administration's preferences, Duarte was fairly certain to win, the Salvadoran minister of defense, General Carlos Eugenio Vides Casanova, summed up the position of the military high command when he remarked that the army could "live with" Duarte. (The military's tolerance, he noted, was predicated on the assumption that Duarte would continue to perform as satisfactorily as he had when a member of the third and fourth juntas.[48]) But the limits of the military's tolerance were made clear in a letter which senior officers sent to Duarte prior to the election in which, according to the London *Guardian's* correspondent in San Salvador, they warned that "they were not prepared to accept civilian meddling in the affairs of what they always refer to as the 'institution of the armed forces' ".[49]

The new government which Duarte heads is still dominated by the same senior figures in the military who have been directly responsible for the orgiastic slaughter of civilian noncombatants in El Salvador over the past five years. For example, after the election, General Vides Casanova was reappointed minister of defense—nominally by Duarte. Though described by Duarte as a moderate, and given rave notices in the *New York Times* upon his initial appointment as defense minister in 1983, Vides Casanova is a notorious hard-liner within the military. He first achieved prominence after the coup in 1979 when the old guard in the military sought to seize power back from the reformist junior officers by installing reactionary officers in key positions. Vides Casanova was made head of the National Guard. He was then among the handful of officers whose intransigent opposition to reforms and evident determination to intensify the repression drove the civilian members of the junta to resign. In response to the civilians' argument that there would be a terrible bloodbath unless reforms were initiated, Vides Casanova noted that the country had survived the killing of 30,000 people in 1932, and that "today, the armed forces are prepared to kill 200,000–300,000, if that's what it takes to stop a Communist takeover."[50] It was he who made it clear to the civilians just how much influence they could expect to have if they remained in the government: "Colonel García [José Guillermo García, then the minister of defense] is the man from whom we take orders, not the junta. We have put you into the position where you are, and for the things that are needed here, we don't need you. We have been running this country for 50 years, and we are quite prepared to keep on running it."[51] (Compare the report of the *New York Times* in 1983 that it is one of Vides Casanova's merits that he "is considered able to keep the military out of politics."[52])

It was during Vides Casanova's time as head of the National Guard that guardsmen raped and brutally murdered four American churchwomen. (Later, as minister of defense, Vides Casanova was apparently involved in a cover-up aimed at shielding senior officers who were implicated in the murders.[53]) The murders of the two AIFLD officials and their Salvadoran colleague, all three of whom were involved in the implementation of land reforms, were also members of the guard. Among the guard's other notable achievements under the direction of Vides Casanova was the storming, ransacking, and closing of the National University in July 1980. At least fifty people were killed in the operation. The university was plundered and its assets sold off by officers of the guard. (Vides Casanova has "a reputation for honesty," the *New York Times* reported in 1983.[54]) The university remains closed today.

Another of Duarte's "appointees" is Jaime Abdul Gutiérrez (now a retired general), who has become the director of the state power commission. In 1979 Gutiérrez conspired to thwart the coup against General Romero but, seeing that his efforts were in vain, briskly sided with the rebel officers—only to betray them by then seizing power for himself and his reactionary associates. Without consulting the other members of the fledgling junta, he appointed as minister of defense his friend Colonel José Guillermo García, who immediately released the senior officers, including D'Aubuisson, whom the younger officers had arrested with the intention of trying them on charges of corruption, torture, and murder.[55] To the post of vice-minister of defense, Gutiérrez appointed Colonel Nicolás Carranza, the man who is widely believed to have headed and coordinated the death squads over the past five or so years (during which time he was also on the CIA payroll, drawing a salary of $90,000 a year).[56] Described as a "fascist" by Thomas

Pickering, the present U.S. ambassador to El Salvador, Carranza was later selected by Vides Casanova as head of the Treasury Police, the most dreaded of the country's "security forces."

Gutiérrez's attitude toward reform was vividly displayed in an incident which occurred in June 1981. When the minister of economy and foreign trade, Guillermo Salazar Díaz, proposed lifting the wage freeze, Gutiérrez responded by declaring the proposal "a grave threat to the nation"—a rather unsubtle death threat, given the source. Díaz immediately fled the country.[57]

Gutiérrez was the only officer to serve in all four juntas: he was one of two officers in the first three juntas, and the only officer in the fourth. In the fourth junta he, not Duarte, was commander-in-chief of the armed forces. He has therefore had a primary role in directing the vast slaughter that has occurred in El Salvador since 1979. Were it not for his manipulation of the 1979 coup, and his subversion of its guiding aims, the course of subsequent Salvadoran history would probably have been entirely different. He and Vides Casanova have played a decisive role in driving their country further to the right, transforming it in the process into a nightmarish inferno. They have consistently undermined every proposed reform and, while permitting some semblance of the outward forms of democracy, have made a mockery of the substance of genuine democratic institutions and processes. It is therefore difficult to understand how anyone could seriously suggest that a regime in which they continue to exert an overriding influence is "centrist," "moderate," "reformist," or "democratic."

Duarte himself, moreover, is a man whose credentials as a moderate and a reformist, as an embodiment of the political center, are not beyond question. Of course, he clearly does occupy the middle ground in Salvadoran politics, in that his position rejects and is rejected by the positions of both the left and the right. This, however, tells us only where Duarte's beliefs are located on the political spectrum in El Salvador. Still, even relative to international standards, Duarte has some claim to being a centrist: in many of his beliefs, for example, he is clearly to the left of Ronald Reagan and the Republican Party.

On the other hand, however, Duarte must be judged not only by his apparent beliefs, but also in terms of his actions. And, whatever his beliefs and aspirations, his actions in the past have clearly had the net effect of preserving and strengthening the position of the right wing of the Salvadoran military. It is instructive to recall that when the military took him on board in 1980, there was virtually no other civilian politician capable of serving as a front for the military regime and providing it with the appearance of legitimacy who was willing to do so. While the American media have lavished praise on Duarte for his supposedly high moral integrity, his behavior as a member of the third and fourth juntas seems very difficult to explain except in terms of opportunism and personal ambition. He was, of course, opposed to the continuous massacre of the civilian population that was carried out while he held office, but he is nevertheless guilty of complicity in the unspeakable crimes of the military during that period. How, one must ask, could any person with the least human decency, knowing what Duarte knew, consent to work in concert with the vile and barbarous mass murderers who commanded the Salvadoran military? How can Duarte continue to do so today?

Duarte's complicity in the slaughter of his fellow Salvadorans in any case has been fairly direct. It was he who facilitated the flow of aid from the U.S. Congress to the Salvadoran military, thereby providing the latter with the wherewithal to carry out its vicious war of extermination with greater efficiency. As Patricia Derian, then assistant secretary of state for human rights, observed during the final days of the Carter administration, Duarte's "standing with the military is a function of his general ability to obtain U.S. assistance."[58] This remains true today. Immediately after the 1984 elections—before he was even inaugurated as president—Duarte dashed off to Washington for some intensive lobbying of Congress in a successful effort to extract further pledges of military aid. He even urged that Congress should *not* attach human rights conditions to the provision of military aid, helping thereby to undermine what in principle might be the most effective means of enforcing some restraint on the Salvadoran military, since it is almost certain that the military could not now survive without substantial U.S. assistance. But, thanks to Duarte, the military continues to thrive. As two commentators on the recent elections have pointed out, "the paradoxical effect of the triumph of this 'reformer,' who has loosened congressional purse-strings and expedited the flow of bullets, may well be a higher rate of civilian deaths than would have prevailed with a less generously funded D'Aubuisson."[59]

While Duarte's strategy seems to be to try to reform the Salvadoran power structure from within (a strategy which has conveniently allowed him to enjoy the prestige and publicity that accompany the holding of a high office), he has often squandered valuable opportunities, and has had to make so many unilateral concessions to the far right that his position has often seemed indistinguishable from theirs. At the end of the summer in 1980, during the tenure of the third junta, sharp divisions arose within the military as Gutiérrez began depriving reformist officers of their command positions and sending them to posts abroad. The one reformist officer in the junta, Colonel Adolfo Arnaldo Majano, responded by setting up his own general staff in preparation for a showdown. There was thus at this point an opportunity for the reformists to seize control from the hard-liners. But while the two other civilians in the junta sided with Majano, Duarte supported Gutiérrez and even accompanied him on a tour of the barracks in an effort to forestall a coup. The confrontation never occurred and Majano lost all influence. A few months later he was forced out of the junta.[60]

Duarte's persistent capitulation to the far right has been evident in many aspects of his behavior, but it has perhaps been most strikingly manifest in his repeated efforts to cover up the many atrocities of the military. When, for example, in May of 1980 the armed forces massacred at least 600 peasants at the Sumpúl River, Duarte initially denied that the incident had occurred. Later, however, when the evidence of the massacre became so widely known that denial was no longer possible, Duarte conceded in an interview that "an action did take place in the area of Río Sumpúl" in which about 300 people were killed, all of whom, according to Duarte, were "Communist guerrillas."[61] Most of the victims were in reality women and children who were fleeing the indiscriminate violence of an army sweep through the countryside.

Later, when pressure from the U.S. Congress finally led to the arrest of six members of the National Guard for the murders of the four American churchwomen, Duarte refused to initiate an investigation of charges that there had been a high-level cover-up within the military. To this day he continues to reject the possibility of an investigation, claiming, literally, that he himself knows all there is to know about the case, and that there was no cover-up. But according to former deputy attorney general Harold Tyler, who was commissioned by the Reagan administration (under pressure from a Senate subcommittee) to investigate the murders, there was indeed a cover-up, in which it was "quite possible" that Vides Casanova participated.[62] (Though details of Tyler's report have been leaked, it remains classified by the State Department, which is anxious to spare the Salvadoran military any embarrassment.)

In 1981 the army carried out a well-documented massacre of civilians in the town of Armenia. Duarte publicly denied that the incident occurred. Later, when journalists discovered a dumping ground for the mutilated bodies of victims of army violence, Duarte denied that there were any bodies there and denounced the journalists' reports as "fabricated."[63] After again becoming president in 1984, Duarte told *Playboy* magazine that "in my first 30 days as president, I did not hear of one single complaint about a case of abuse of authority or actions that could be defined as military crimes. Not one." *Playboy* noted in brackets that "the legal-aid office of the Roman Catholic archdiocese of San Salvador reports that in the period to which President Duarte refers, there were 123 civilians killed by government forces and 11 more people killed by unidentified agents or death squads."[64] More recently, in August 1984, Duarte was asked whether there would be an investigation into the widely publicized massacre of sixty-eight peasants in the province of Cabañas by troops from the elite, U.S.-trained Atlacátl battalion. Although the massacre had occurred more than a month earlier, Duarte attempted to evade the issue by claiming that he had never heard of the incident. Two days later the military high command announced that it would conduct its own investigation (which, like all of the Salvadoran military's investigations of its own misconduct, will lead nowhere).[65]

Duarte, in short, has been a consistent and shameless apologist for the armed forces, repeatedly concealing and denying their crimes. He has attempted to portray their strategy of terrorizing the entire population while depopulating areas under guerrilla control as a "heroic battle" against what he calls "the subversives," and has even gone so far as to assert that "the army is giving us daily proof that it is striving to build democracy."[66] It is hardly surprising, therefore, that the army's wholesale slaughter of the rural population has continued unabated since Duarte reassumed the presidency.

The foregoing review of the various governments which the Reagan administration has sustained in power should be amply sufficient to expose the administration's claim to have all along been supporting moderate, centrist, and reformist governments as an obvious whitewash. Indeed it would not be an exaggeration to say that the administration has actively sought to undermine the formation of a genuine and influential political center in El Salvador. For example, in December 1980, before Reagan's inauguration, one of his advisers described the replacement of the Romero dictatorship by the series of military-civilian juntas in the following way: "A pro-US military government in El Salvador, which had been economically viable, has been replaced by a center-left government [which has] brought the country to near economic ruin by desperate and sweeping reforms."[67] In short, even the juntas were too far to the left for the Reagan team's taste. Around the same time, this adviser traveled to San Salvador to reassure members of the far right that public statements by the Reagan team that the new administration would not support a coup by the right were a regrettable political necessity and could be disregarded.[68]

As the quotation just cited shows, the Reagan administration has never been enthusiastic about reforms in El Salvador. Of the three reforms initiated in 1980—the program of land reform, the nationalization of the banks, and the nationalization of the export of coffee, cotton, and sugarcane—the administration firmly opposed both programs of nationalization, and also opposed the most significant aspects of the land reform.[69] Not only did the reforms run contrary to the administration's free-market ideology, but they also (or so some members of the administration thought) served to divert energy and resources away from the more important task of winning the war against the guerrillas. As Deputy Assistant Secretary of Defense Nestor Sanchez put it, "We believe that by acting as the guarantor of the political, economic, and social reforms, the High Command of the armed forces has been distracted from the principal task of fighting the guerrillas. In essence, the progress in implementing democratic reforms has been at the expense of active pursuit of the war."[70]

The administration's opposition to reforms is only one manifestation of a more general disposition to suppress any progressive or liberalizing tendencies within the Salvadoran government. When the struggle referred to earlier between reformist and reactionary officers broke out, and it seemed likely that there would be a coup attempt by the reformist faction, the United States, like Duarte, backed the reactionaries. And on those occasions when Duarte himself attempted to check the power of the right, he generally found himself without U.S. support. According to former ambassador White, the policies of the Reagan administration reduced Duarte's influence to nothing.[71] Like the Salvadoran military, the Reagan administration has needed Duarte to extract from Congress the funds necessary to keep the war going. In order to cash in on his reformist image, the administration has used its influence to keep Duarte (or some reasonable substitute, such as Magaña) in office, but it has rarely exploited its leverage to ensure that he would have any genuine control over the military, or the affairs of state.

The carefully nurtured fiction that the government in El Salvador occupies the political center serves the function in administration propaganda of dissociating the object of U.S. support from the violence in the country, which can conveniently be attributed to the "extremes" of left and right. The government, it is said, has been caught in the crossfire between the terrorist violence of the guerrillas and the reactive violence of the extreme right which, for some unexplained reason, the government has been unable to control. Unlike those who seek to impose their will by means of violence and terror, the members of the government are, as Kirkpatrick has put it, "the good guys in every sense of the word."[72]

According to the administration, most of the violence that is attributed to government forces is actually the responsibility of civilian "death squads" which operate independently of the government and the military. In fact, however, it is well established that the death squads are composed primarily of members of the army or the other "security forces," such as the National Guard and the Treasury Police, and that they operate with the consent and approval and, generally, at the command of the highest-ranking military officers. This has been demonstrated by Amnesty International and, to the Reagan administration's embarrassment, has even been conceded by Roberto D'Aubuisson, who "has stated publicly that soldiers carried out 'death squad' killings on orders from their superiors, and that these killings were not the work of fringe elements beyond the control of regular military and security forces."[73]

It is precisely because the death squads are not formally under the control of the military, and thus can be claimed to be "independent" and beyond control, that they are so valuable to the government and the military. In testimony before the Senate Committee on Foreign Relations, Amnesty International stated that "by consistently attributing the detentions, tortures and assassinations of alleged members of the opposition to groups beyond official control, the government of El Salvador is seeking a means of evading responsibility for the actions of its own security forces."[74]

While most of the death squad killings are ordered by the military, these killings are in fact responsible for only a relatively small proportion of the civilian deaths attributable to government forces. The Legal Aid Office of the Catholic Archdiocese of San Salvador, known as Tutela Legal, estimates that "an average of 76 percent of the civilians killed each month by government forces are killed by the army alone."[75]

When inconvenient facts such as these emerge, making it difficult to attribute the right-wing violence in El Salvador to the independent death squads, the Reagan administration and its supporters shift tactics and begin to lament that despite its valiant efforts, the government has been unable to control the deviant or renegade elements within the military. Thus when members of the Kissinger Commission "discovered," on visiting El Salvador, that the death squads consist of members of the armed forces, they were reportedly "aghast" that "the Government was unable to do anything about it."[76] One of the reasons why it has been important to the United States to have civilians in the government in El Salvador is to ensure that this sort of response should be available. Having civilians in the government is necessary to obscure the fact that, in the operative sense, the government *is* the military.

Government forces of one sort or another—the army, the death squads, the National Guard, the Treasury Police, or the National Police—have been responsible for virtually all of the violence against civilians in El Salvador over the past five years. In that time approximately 53,000 people—more than one out of every hundred—have been killed, most of them civilian noncombatants. Impartial investigators, including all the leading human rights organizations, agree that only a small fraction of these killings can be attributed to the guerrillas. For example, according to Tutela Legal, during the first six months of 1983 government forces or paramilitary forces operating under government protection killed 2,534 people and picked up 534 others, of whom 326 disappeared. During the same period, left-wing groups killed 43 civilians and kidnapped 22 others.[77] Of the 5,209 civilians killed in political violence during the whole of 1983, 3,883 (about 70 percent) were killed by government forces, 1,259 by death squads, and 67 by guerilla forces, according to Tutela Legal.[78]

Of course, the figures cited by Tutela Legal show that the guerrillas are not above killing civilians. But in general the guerrillas are discriminating in selecting their targets: the civilian victims of guerrilla violence are usually policemen, members of the paramilitary group ORDEN, members of the oligarchy, and so on. (Occasionally guerrilla groups have committed gratuitous acts of violence against civilians in no way engaged in the war effort, and, on other occasions, have, like the army, press-ganged teenagers into their ranks. Reports which I have seen, however, indicate that "credit" for these acts has been claimed by members of the Armed Forces of Liberation (FAL), the military arm of the Salvadoran Communist party, which, with only 500 persons under arms in 1983, is the smallest of the five groups under the umbrella of the FMLN.[79])

By contrast with the general practice of the guerrillas, the Salvadoran army has been particularly adept at carrying out indiscriminate massacres characterized by their mindless ferocity and gratuitous violence against women, children, the elderly, and the handicapped. Perhaps the most notorious of these massacres is that mentioned earlier which occurred along the Sumpúl River in May of 1980. It occurred as peasants fleeing the indiscriminate violence of an army sweep sought to gain refuge in Honduras by swimming across the Sumpúl River. As they did so they were fired upon by Honduran troops operating on the Honduran side of the river, by Salvadoran troops hovering overhead in U.S.-supplied helicopter gunships, and by members of the army, the National Guard, and ORDEN, who slaughtered any that returned to shore on the Salvadoran side. Amnesty International reported that

> peasants who survived the massacre later described to visiting foreign delegations of inquiry how Salvadorean soldiers and ORDEN members gathered children and babies together, threw them into the air and slashed them to death with machetes. Some infants were reportedly decapitated and their bodies slit into pieces and thrown to the dogs; other children were reported to have drowned after Salvadorian soldiers threw them into the water.[80]

Church sources reported that a Honduran fisherman later found the bodies of five small children caught in his fishtrap.[81]

Lieutenant Colonel Domingo Monterrosa, commander of the elite U.S.-trained Atlacátl battalion which participated in the massacre, remarked that "it is natural that in these subversive redoubts the armed men are not there alone. That is to say, they need their 'masses'—people, women, old people, or children, including the children who are messengers, or the wives, and they are all mixed up with the subversives themselves, with the armed ones. So, in the clashes . . . it's natural that there were a series of people killed, some without weapons, including some women, and I understand some children."[82] Monterrosa's recent death in a helicopter crash was much lamented by U.S. diplomats and military advisers in El Salvador, who considered him the army's most skillful commander.

A similar incident occurred less than a year later on the Lempa River when the Salvadoran Air Force bombed and strafed peasants attempting to cross the river into Honduras. At least 200 were later reported to be dead or missing. In November 1981 another massacre involving the Atlacátl battalion occurred in the province of Cabañas. An American graduate student from Stanford, Philippe Bourgois, who was in El Salvador doing field work, happened to be among the peasants under attack. He later reported his experiences:

> When the soldiers "apparently heard the wails of the babies that the mothers were carrying . . . they actually changed the direction of their fire, and started shooting directly at us. If you can imagine, in the darkness of the night, the government troops were firing into the sound of screaming babies." Bourgois found a little boy who had been hit by a grenade "staring up at me, writhing, with his hands on his hips, a gargling noise coming out of his throat. Then I looked more closely and saw there was nothing below his hips. His legs were blown away."[83]

Bourgois commented on the army's "scorched earth campaigns":

> The houses, crops and possessions of the local population are destroyed and all individuals are killed. . . . In the Cabañas invasion, as in most offensives launched by government forces in El Salvador, it is the less agile, the slower runners; i.e., the pregnant women, the elderly, the infirm, and the very young who constitute the bulk of the casualties.[84]

About two months later the Atlacátl battalion, led by Monterrosa, made a further sweep through the area around Mozote, in the province of Morazán. Again this "crack" battalion, regarded as the army's finest, simply rampaged through the countryside, killing everyone in sight. It is estimated that nearly 1,000 peasants—again primarily women, children, and the elderly—were killed. Of the 482 victims in the town of Mozote, 280 were children under the age of fourteen.[85]

The administration has often sought to justify its policy of training as many Salvadoran soldiers as possible by arguing that exposure to American values and counterinsurgency methods will instill in the trainees a healthy respect for human rights. It is interesting, therefore, to note that it is precisely those units—such as the Atlacátl and Ramón Belloso battalions—which have received the most U.S. training that are nearly always responsible for the worst atrocities commited by government forces. The Atlacátl battalion, in particular, has been on a nearly continuous killing spree since it first received this training: following the massacres at the Sumpúl River, in Cabañas, and at Mozote, the battalion conducted a great slaughter in the Guazapa Volcano area in the province of Cuscatlán in the spring of 1983, massacred hundreds more civilians in the provinces of Chalatenango and Cuscatlán in November of 1983, and, as noted earlier, killed some 68 peasants in Cabañas in July 1984.[86] After the massacres of November 1983, Monterrosa responded to charges that his men had killed children by noting that "once you have seen several 12-year-olds in action, you can no longer dismiss the possibility that any 12-year-old may be a guerrilla."[87] All peasant children were thereby declared to be legitimate targets. (Monterrosa himself was trained by the Green Berets.)

In April 1983 President Reagan declared before a joint session of Congress that "the Salvadoran battalions that have received U.S. training have been conducting themselves well on the battlefield and with the civilian population."[88] Readers may draw their own inferences.

The army's strategy in the countryside is similar in conception to the program of rural "pacification" adopted by the United States in Vietnam. The fundamental aim is to separate the guerrillas from the civilian population, depriving them of their infrastructure, of their network of support. A U.S. congressional delegation to El Salvador cites the remark of a Salvadoran military commander: "The subversives like to say that they are the fish and the people are the ocean. What we have done in the north is to dry up the ocean so we can catch the fish easily." The delegation comments that "the Salvadoran method of 'drying up the ocean' is to eliminate entire villages from the map, to isolate the guerrillas, and deny them any rural base off which they can feed." This method "involves, according to those who have fled from its violence, a combination of murder, torture, rape, the burning of crops in order to create starvation conditions, and a program of general terrorism and harassment."[89]

As the delegation indicates, murders committed by the army and other government forces are routinely preceded by the most savage and obscene forms of torture. Torture is used systematically, but not to extract information. A joint report of the Americas Watch Committee and the American Civil Liberties Union notes that

> of the many thousands of bodies which have appeared after detentions and abductions by security personnel, a very high proportion show signs of torture including dismemberment, beating, acid burns, flaying, scalping, castration, strangulation, sexual violation, and evisceration. . . . The victims' bodies are rarely given to relatives nor are they generally buried clandestinely, but are often displayed prominently, suggesting that the purpose of the mutilations and other tortures inflicted upon them are [*sic*] to intimidate and terrorize the population.[90]

It is perhaps worth mentioning that, according to a former agent of the Treasury Police who now lives in the United States, U.S. personnel have provided Salvadoran officers with "instruction in methods of physical and psychological torture."[91] A member of a death squad, when interviewed on television in Boston, was asked what types of tortures the death squads used. He replied: "Uh, well, the same thing you did in Vietnam. We learned from you. We learned from you the means, like blowtorches in the armpits, shots in the balls." In some cases, he said, "we have to pop their eyes out with a spoon. You have to film it to believe it, but boy, they sure sing."[92] There is perhaps a lesson here about the values which Salvadorans derive from exposure to U.S. counterinsurgency methods.

Another tactic which Jeane Kirkpatrick's "good guys" have used in their campaign to depopulate guerrilla-controlled areas is the systematic bombing of concentrations of civilians. Salvadoran pilots flying U.S.-supplied aircraft have, for example, regularly bombed

Red Cross feeding centers in the war zones as peasants were collected together to receive food. An American doctor who fought in the Vietnam war and who has recently spent a year behind guerrilla lines in El Salvador says that he has "incontrovertible" evidence that both napalm and phosphorus bombs have been dropped from the Salvadoran Air Force's U.S.-supplied aircraft.[93]

While it was hoped that these tactics would herd peasants into resettlement camps reminiscent of the "strategic hamlets" in Vietnam, well away from the possibility of any contact with the guerrillas, the effect has been to create a vast number of internal and external refugees. There is some irony in this, in that it is one of the administration's central arguments for supporting the government's war effort that, if the guerrillas were to win, and in particular if other Central American countries were then to "fall" like dominoes, the United States would then be swamped by refugees fleeing from communist oppression. Thus Reagan has argued that, if "the Soviet-Cuban-Nicaraguan axis [is allowed] to take over Central America, . . . the result could be a tidal wave of refugees—and this time they'll be 'feet people' and not 'boat people'—swarming into our country seeking a safe haven from Communist repression to our South."[94]

It is interesting, however, to compare the flow of refugees from Central American and Caribbean countries in which successful left-wing revolutions have occurred with that from El Salvador. Since 1979, 300,000 Salvadorans have illegally entered the United States, bringing the total number of Salvadoran refugees in the United States to 500,000.[95] Those who have entered in recent years have had to do so illegally because the Reagan administration has been following a policy of denying entry to Salvadoran refugees. The administration has sought to justify this policy on the ground that "most Salvadorans in the United States are not refugees fleeing persecution, but would-be immigrants who want to live here," having left El Salvador "to seek better jobs."[96] The real reason, of course, is that the administration refuses to do anything which would even implicitly acknowledge the fact that Salvadoran refugees are the victims of political persecution by their own government. In any case, the upshot of the administration's policy has been that many Salvadorans seeking asylum in the United States either have been sent back to El Salvador, where they have often been promptly murdered by government forces, or have managed to find refuge elsewhere. In 1982, there were some 220,000 to 272,000 Salvadorans in other Central American countries alone.[97]

By contrast with its treatment of Salvadoran refugees, the United States has welcomed Cuban refugees with open arms, since every new Cuban "defector" provides useful evidence for U.S. claims about communist oppression in Cuba. Thus there are now some 800,000 Cubans in the United States. Given that the population of Cuba is 10 million, while that of El Salvador is approximately 4.75 million, the number of Salvadorans in the United States is proportionally considerably greater than the number of Cubans—and this is so despite the fact that Cuba is much closer to the United States, despite the fact that Cubans are welcomed while Salvadorans are turned away, and despite the fact that Cubans opposed to the revolution have been migrating to the United States for a full twenty-five years.

On occasions when the administration is confronted with evidence that the extermination of civilians is actually at the heart of government policy in El Salvador, so that the administration is then unable plausibly to blame the violence on the extremes of left and right or on uncontrollable maverick elements in the military, it typically shrugs off governmental violence as what one must expect from a backward people: "Using force to settle political disputes is the way things have been in El Salvador," according to Elliot Abrams, assistant secretary of state for humanitarian affairs.[98] As former ambassador Deane Hinton put it, "It's in the culture."[99] This pose of innocent detachment—as if political violence in El Salvador were necessitated by factors beyond anyone's control—is hardly convincing. The U.S. government, and in particular the Reagan administration, bears a heavy burden of guilt for the tragic events which have occurred in that country. Evidence has recently emerged that many of the repressive institutions in El Salvador were originally the creation of the United States. A recent report by Allan Nairn in the *Progressive,* based on interviews with former Salvadoran officers and official American sources, has revealed that

> over the past twenty years, officials of the State Department, the Central Intelligence Agency, and the U.S. armed forces have:
>
> —conceived and organized ORDEN, the rural paramilitary and intelligence network described by Amnesty International as a movement designed "to use clandestine terror against government opponents." Out of ORDEN grew the notorious *Mano Blanco,* the White Hand, which a former U.S. ambassador to El Salvador, Raul H. Castro, has called "nothing less than the birth of the Death Squads";
>
> —conceived and organized ANSESAL, the elite presidential intelligence service that gathered files on Salvadoran dissidents and, in the words of one U.S. official, relied on Death Squads as "the operative arm of intelligence gathering"; . . .
>
> —supplied ANSESAL, the security forces, and the general staff with electronic, photographic, and personal surveillance of individu-

> als who were later assassinated by Death Squads. According to Colonel Nicolas Carranza, director of the Salvadoran Treasury Police, such intelligence sharing by U.S. agencies continues to this day.[100]

This is only a very partial listing of the article's findings. The article shows that U.S. collaboration in designing and running the various mechanisms of repression in El Salvador has been extensive.

It is, moreover, courtesy of the American taxpayer that repression continues in El Salvador today. As one research group recently put it, "U.S. assistance virtually feeds, clothes, equips and trains the Salvadoran armed forces."[101] It is, in short, the United States which maintains the military in power. As we have seen, even Reagan's closest advisers concede that the military and the governmental structures supported by it would not survive for long without U.S. assistance. That assistance now extends even to the running of the war. According to one official at the Salvadoran High Command, "nothing gets done without the Americans being consulted first."[102]

Because it is the United States which keeps the Salvadoran military in power, it could stop the killing if it wished to. The United States could threaten to withhold all forms of aid unless the death squads were immediately disbanded and all forms of violence against civilians ended. If the threat were to fail, then the United States could fulfill it, thereby allowing the army, whose morale would no doubt dissipate as quickly as its resources, to be defeated by the guerrillas. The choice would be stark: capitulate or collapse.

At the moment, however, such a threat from the Reagan administration would be utterly lacking in credibility, the administration having squandered its leverage by making it abundantly clear that the defeat of the army is not an outcome which it is prepared to accept. Salvadoran officers know from experience that the administration can be defied with relative impunity. On one occasion the administration was under considerable political pressure at home to get the Salvadorans to arrest and convict an officer known to have ordered the murders of the two American AIFLD workers. President Reagan himself made a personal phone call to President Magaña in an effort to have the officer punished, and the senior U.S. commander for Latin America met with senior Salvadoran officers to warn them that aid would be jeopardized if the officer were not satisfactorily dealt with. The Salvadorans, however, ignored the threats. Charges against the officer were dismissed and he was promoted to an important command position. Predictably, the United States imposed no sanctions. Instead, within days of his phone call to Magaña, Reagan increased the flow of military aid.

Another way in which the administration demonstrated that its demands could be safely ignored was in its treatment of what is known as the certification process. In 1981 Congress unanimously passed a bill which made the provision of military assistance to El Salvador and the stationing of military advisers there conditional upon certification by the president, every six months, that the Salvadoran government was making a concerted effort to respect human rights, was achieving control over the military, and was making progress in the implementation of social and economic reforms. Reagan provided the required certification on four different occasions, each time citing false or highly misleading claims by way of justification. (The first certification was issued in January 1982, two days after the December massacre in the area of Mozote was reported in the American press.) It was obvious to Salvadoran officers that certification would be forthcoming whatever they did.

By December 1983 the American public was becoming increasingly aware of the true character of the regime the United States was supporting. The administration was therefore obliged to make a public display of outrage over the activities of the death squads. During a visit to El Salvador, Vice-President Bush denounced the death squads and demanded action against some twenty-five persons, military and civilian, who were known to be involved with them, warning that aid would be terminated unless these demands were met. (Only a couple of months earlier, Ambassador Hinton had strongly criticized the death squads, feeling that their net effect was simply to increase domestic sympathy for the guerrillas; but he was afterwards reprimanded by his superiors and told to shut up.)

While the Salvadorans could write off Bush's threats as empty, they recognized that Congress was less predictable and might need to be appeased. (Reagan has frequently had to bypass Congress in providing military aid to El Salvador, and recently even attempted to blackmail the Congress by tacking a request for military aid onto legislation to send food supplies to starving Africans, thereby making it difficult for the Congress to reject the military aid without simultaneously cutting off food aid as well.) Had there been a strong threat from Congress, therefore, some business might have resulted. But Reagan had already taken care of the Congress. Shortly before Bush's trip, Reagan had vetoed the certification requirement, which, for obvious reasons, had been a bit of an embarrassment. The message that this act sent to the Salvadoran military was far more powerful than the contradictory one which Bush carried with him on his trip. The president was signaling, in effect, that he would keep the Congress in line, and that respect for human rights would not be a condition of military aid. In the end, of course, none of the officers named by Bush was punished, though a couple were sent to diplomatic posts abroad, and U.S. aid continued as before to pour into the military's coffers.

The reason why the administration has never seriously used the threat to withdraw support in order to force an end to the violence against civilians and to bring those responsible for it to justice is fairly obvious. If the climate of terror were lifted, so that people could freely express their opposition to the government, the weakness of the government's standing with its own people would soon be exposed, and opposition activities would become so widespread that the country might become ungovernable. Because of this, an end to the reign of terror would ultimately require some accommodation with the guerrillas. And this is something which the administration has made it clear that it will not tolerate. The same reasoning underlies the administration's unwillingness to press for the institution of the rule of law and the prosecution of the agents of state terror. As Christopher Dickey has written, "If the web of complicity tying the armed forces to death squad violence ever did unravel, . . . who would be left to fight the war?"[103] In short, the administration would prefer to collude with a "friendly" regime composed of active mass murderers and other assorted war criminals than to face the prospect of having to reach an accommodation with the Salvadoran left. Because they know this, the members of the Salvadoran military are virtually unconstrained in the pursuit of their U.S.-financed war of extermination. This is the primary reason why a large measure of responsibility for the continuing bloodshed in El Salvador must be laid at the doorstep of the White House.

Apologists for the administration's policy in El Salvador often point to the 1982 and 1984 elections, as well as to the program of land reform, as evidence that the administration's policy is in fact achieving the gradual liberalization and democratization of El Salvador. These accomplishments, it is claimed, demonstrate that the administration's policy is producing the results which its critics desire: greater social and economic justice, greater civilian control over the military, and the growth of democratic institutions. By briefly examining the elections and the land reform, we can see how much substance there is to these claims.

Let us begin with the land reform. The program of land reform, ritually described in the United States as "sweeping," was first introduced in March 1980, just before Duarte joined the junta. The program was divided into two phases. In Phase I, farms of over 500 hectares (1,235 acres) were expropriated and converted into peasant cooperatives. In Phase II, farms between 100 and 500 hectares (between 247 and 1,235 acres) were to be expropriated. Landowners affected by either phase were to be compensated by the government, which would be repaid over a thirty-year period by the newly created cooperatives. All landowners were to be allowed to retain between 100 and 180 hectares (between 247 and 445 acres) of their former estates. In April 1980 Phase III, known as the "Land to the Tiller" law, was added, giving tenants the right to purchase up to seven hectares (17 acres) of the land which previously they had rented or sharecropped. Landowners were again to be compensated, with tenants repaying the government over a thirty-year period.

Right from the beginning, however, each phase of the program was sabotaged in a variety of ways. Phase I, which, even if fully implemented, would have affected only 15 percent of the nation's farmland, was evaded by many landowners who quickly subdivided their estates into parcels of land of less than 500 hectares which they then distributed among family members.[104] Another factor in the subversion of Phase I was that many landowners, knowing that they would be immune from prosecution, simply called in the National Guard to murder or evict the peasants working on the new cooperatives.[105] Phase II, which was the most important and far-reaching of the reforms, was immediately aborted. It was strongly opposed by the oligarchy, since it would have had a significant impact on the nation's coffee plantations, and it also met with hostility from the Reagan administration. So in April Colonel Gutiérrez announced that it would be "postponed." Later, after the various right-wing parties gained control of the Constituent Assembly in the 1982 elections, Phase II was officially canceled. Phase III, quickly implemented in the wake of the stillborn Phase II, was evaded in many cases when landowners evicted tenants from rented lands before titles to the land could be issued.[106] It too was officially "suspended" by the Constituent Assembly after the 1982 elections and, according to José Antonio Morales Ehrlich, who had been a civilian member of the third and fourth juntas, within two months after the election 5,000 peasant families were evicted from land that they had acquired under the program.[107] Phase III was canceled by the Constituent Assembly in June 1984, soon after Duarte's election to the presidency.

In the end relatively few people benefited from the land reform (though many suffered from it, as the army and the National Guard systematically exterminated peasants who attempted to assert the rights to which the reforms had in principle entitled them). But then the purpose of the reform had never been to benefit the people. While the reform had many purposes, two stand out. One was to allow the government to cultivate a reformist image. The other was to bolster the government's campaign against the guerrillas. As Roy Prosterman, the American architect of Phase III, explained the matter to Salvadoran businessmen, "The left fears land reform. It deprives them of their most valuable weapon in implementing revolution because they can no longer appeal to the landless." Prosterman argued that "there is no one more conservative than a small farmer. We're going to be breeding capitalists like rabbits." Hence "the leftist onslaught will be effectively eliminated by the end of 1980."[108] In short, the land reform was simply part of the counterinsurgency effort.[109]

Let us turn now to the elections, which have been advertised as the crowning achievement of the administration's policy. The elections in March of 1982 were heralded in the United States as a triumph of democracy. According to the administration, they showed that the government and the military were committed to democracy, and that the new government that emerged victorious represented the will of an "unprecedented 80 percent of the electorate" who turned out to vote.[110] The failure of the guerrillas and their political representatives to participate showed, according to Kirkpatrick, "that they know they do not enjoy popular support, and [that] they do not in any case recognize popular sovereignty expressed through free elections as the legitimate basis of a legitimate government."[111]

Did the elections, however, really express the will of the people? The first point to note is that the administration's estimate of the percentage of those entitled to vote who actually voted appears to be inflated. Estimates of the number of people who voted range from 600,000 to 1.5 million (the latter being the official figure), while estimates of the number of eligible voters range from 1.3 million to 2.2 million.[112] Given those figures, the percentage of eligible voters who turned out could be anywhere from 37 percent to well over 100 percent. While circumstantial evidence of an inflated vote count and the absence of an electoral register make any estimate uncertain, it seems likely that the actual percentage was less than 80 percent.

A second and more important point is that in El Salvador voting is compulsory. Moreover, two weeks prior to the election the defense minister, General José Guillermo García, announced that the failure to vote would be considered "an act of treason."[113] Because the election officials recorded the identification card number of each person who voted, the military were able to determine who did and who did not vote. And because the failure to vote could be interpreted as an act of defiance expressing support for the guerrillas, and could thus be sufficient to earn a person a place on one of the death squads' hit lists, even a turnout of 80 percent may be considered surprisingly low.

Voters also had to be careful how they cast their votes. Ballots were numbered and ballot boxes were transparent, and so it was possible for the authorities to determine how each person had voted.[114] In any case voters were not presented with a very broad range of candidates. Voters had to choose between the candidates of a centrist party (the Christian Democrats) which had been collaborating with the military, and those of various right-wing parties which were either openly allied to the military or farther to the right than the military itself. The opposition was not represented at all. While Gutiérrez, then a member of the junta, declared that the FDR would not be allowed to participate, the FDR-FMLN refused to participate anyway on the ground that the safety of their candidates and supporters could not be guaranteed given the structure of power in the country at that time. Opposition leaders would have been perilously vulnerable to assassination had they attempted open campaigning (thus Ambassador Hinton thoughtfully suggested that they could campaign from outside the country), while attendance at an opposition rally would have been tantamount to openly declaring support for the guerrillas, a capital crime in El Salvador.

In November 1980, when high-ranking members of the FDR were meeting in San Salvador, five of their leaders were abducted by members of the "security forces." Their mutilated and disfigured corpses were dumped by a roadside some miles out of town. The new leaders of the FDR could scarcely have expected better treatment than their predecessors received had they reentered the country for campaigning in 1982. Indeed, Cynthia Arnson has pointed out that "just as election plans were getting underway, the army issued a 'hit list' of 138 'subversives' and 'traitors to the fatherland.' The list included church officials, human rights activists, and virtually all opposition leaders that the State Department wanted to return from exile to El Salvador to 'campaign freely'."[115] Yet it was the army that was charged with responsibility for keeping the peace and guaranteeing the impartiality of the elections. It had been proposed that an international peacekeeping force should be established to ensure the security of the opposition, but this was of course rejected by the military.

The results of elections in which the opposition are unable to participate do not provide a reliable indication of the preferences of the people. This is well illustrated by the case of Zimbabwe, to which several commentators on the Salvadoran elections have drawn attention.[116] In 1979 elections were held in Zimbabwe-

Rhodesia in which the guerrillas did not participate. Bishop Abel Muzorewa won approximately 67 percent of the vote. But during the next ten months international negotiations succeeded in bringing the guerrillas into the electoral process. New elections were then held in which the guerrillas' candidate, Robert Mugabe, won a majority, while Bishop Muzorewa's share of the total dropped to a mere 8 percent.

While there may have been less electoral fraud in 1982 than in previous elections in El Salvador, there was in this case no real reason to manipulate the elections. Since all the competing parties were closely tied to the military, and since many people felt compelled to vote for fear of the consequences of not doing so, a victory for the military was guaranteed in advance. (The most blatant manipulation came after the polling had ended when the Reagan administration indicated that D'Aubuisson would be an unsatisfactory president from a public relations point of view and thus had the military install a more marketable figure instead.) Yet the *New York Times* referred to the elections as "a huge vote for peace," while *Time* claimed that they conferred "indisputable legitimacy" on the resulting government.[117] Thus they achieved their primary purpose, which was to reassure American voters by providing a democratic façade for the antidemocratic military regime which the Reagan administration wished to support.

The 1984 elections differed rather little from those of 1982. Voting was still compulsory, and again occurred in a climate of terror and intimidation in which tens of thousands of civilians had been murdered by the government. The identity cards of the voters were stamped as they voted, and ballot boxes were still transparent; so potential voters were again keenly aware that the government could in principle know whether and, if so, how they had voted. The political spectrum represented was no broader than before. The vote count was apparently again inflated (70 percent according to the official U.S. delegation: "far better than we get in the United States").[118] The results were served up to the American public as one of the most astounding triumphs for freedom and democracy in recent history.

A more sober evaluation of the proceedings was provided by a British journalist, initially sympathetic to the Reagan administration's policy in Central America, who observed:

> This election, which I expected to be a redeeming showpiece of America policy in Central America, . . . was in fact, for me as for many of my colleagues, a sad and depressing occasion. It was depressing because the election campaign gave free rein to a movement (ARENA) which I have no hesitation in describing as fascist; and

> because this facist movement was sustained and largely run by the very Americanized business class that US policy has done so much to create. It was depressing . . . to watch so many illiterate people going quite uncomprehendingly through the mysterious ritual of voting—because they had to. But it was depressing, above all, because of the fantastical way in which the whole event was presented by the representatives of the United States.[119]

But the fantastical presentation was inevitable given the fact that the point of the whole spectacle was precisely to provide a "showpiece" for the benefit of the American public. (Of course, the Salvadoran political parties did not stage the affair just to reassure the American public, but then they did not pay for the election. According to one source, American financing for the election reached a total of $10 million.[120] The CIA, in an effort to ensure the defeat of D'Aubuisson, transferred $960,000 to the Christian Democrats and $437,000 to the National Conciliation Party, a total of $1.4 million.[121])

Admittedly, there have been signs of what might be considered progress since Duarte was elected president in the most recent elections. After three and a half years, five National Guardsmen were convicted for the murders of the American churchwomen. Carranza and a couple of other officers notorious for their involvement with the death squads are being sent to diplomatic posts abroad, and one particularly dreaded unit of the Treasury Police has been disbanded. One of the officers who ordered the shooting of the American AIFLD officials has been dismissed from the army. On the other hand, there has been no inquiry into the possibility of higher involvement in the murder of the churchwomen, and criminal charges against both officers who were involved in the killings of the AIFLD officials have been dropped. As the brother of one of the murdered officials has asked, "Since when is losing your job and pension considered appropriate punishment for a triple murder? . . . Let us acknowledge that the decision to fire this lieutenant has more to do with public relations than with justice."[122]

Talks have also opened between the government and the opposition. Until very recently Duarte was adamantly opposed to negotiations (as of course was the United States), while the FDR-FMLN have been advocating unconditional negotiations for the past three years. The American media have nevertheless consistently described the talks as *Duarte's* initiative, and have praised the boldness of his statesmanship in making this Sadat-like overture to his intransigent enemies. Two meetings have been held, but no progress has been made toward reaching a solution. Opposition leaders are proposing a negotiated settlement of the civil war based on what in the United States is called "power sharing." They are proposing the formation of a transitional government which would include members of the opposition as well as members of the present government, the reform of the country's year-old constitution, the reorganization of the armed forces, into which rebel forces would be integrated, and, finally, free elections once the country has been stabilized under the transitional government.[123] Duarte has rejected this proposal, as well as opposition proposals for a cease-fire, insisting that the only topic he is willing to discuss is the incorporation of the opposition into the Salvadoran political system as defined by the present constitution (which was drawn up by the Constituent Assembly elected in 1982). In short, Duarte is insisting that the guerrillas unilaterally lay down their arms and seek power only through the electoral process.

Durate's proposal is tantamount to inviting the guerrillas to surrender. And, as one writer has remarked, "it is all very well to argue that persons of good will ought to be able to find a peaceful solution peaceably. But if one side makes surrender a precondition of peace, then the alternatives are only to surrender or resist."[124] The author of these lines is Jeane Kirkpatrick. Her claim is that it is the opposition which is making surrender a precondition of peace. But in reality her argument applies more forcefully to the position of the government than it does to that of the opposition.

It should be obvious that, as long as the structure of power in El Salvador remains unchanged, it will be impossible for the opposition to participate in elections. Were the opposition to do so, they would simply be placing themselves at the mercy of the country's exceptionally ruthless and brutal armed forces, with whom they have been at war for five years. Moreover, even if the safety of the opposition could be guaranteed, El Salvador has an impressive history of electoral fraud, and attempts would doubtless be made to rig any elections involving participation by the left. Finally, even supposing that opposition leaders could somehow survive and win the elections, the military, backed no doubt by the United States, would surely attempt to thwart their accession to power, and the civil war would simply begin anew.

Before elections can become an expression of popular sovereignty in El Salvador, the structure of power there must be radically changed. But the changes necessary for genuine democracy to flourish are the ones which the United States is unwilling to permit. Instead, the goal is unconditional military victory for the forces of reaction. As Under Secretary of Defense Iklé put it, "We do not seek a military defeat for our friends. We do not seek a military stalemate. We seek victory for the forces of democracy," which, he points out, entails "defeating militarily those organized forces of violence that refuse to accept the democratic will of the people."[125] This aim is, however, in tension with the administration's disavowal of any intention to involve U.S. forces in the war. If anything short of defeating the guerrillas is unacceptable, then whether U.S. forces intervene presumably hinges entirely on the combat performance of the Salvadoran armed forces.

Direct U.S. involvement in the war is already steadily increasing. U.S. reconnaissance aircraft based in Panama and Honduras regularly overfly Salvadoran territory in order to monitor the movements of guerrilla forces and relay the information to army field commanders. U.S. helicopter gunships with U.S. crews are now permanently based in El Salvador. And during the summer of 1984 the White House instructed the Pentagon to draw up contingency plans for U.S. air strikes against guerrilla positions in the event of a threatening guerrilla offensive.[126]

What are the stakes in El Salvador which, in the administration's view, might warrant military intervention? The answer is perhaps surprising. In 1977, senior officials in the Ford administration acknowledged that the United States had no strategic interests, and certainly no vital interests, in El Salvador.[127] Nothing has really changed since then. During the 1980 election campaign, one of Reagan's advisers remarked that "El Salvador itself doesn't really matter. We have to establish credibility [there] because we're in very serious trouble [elsewhere]."[128] In short, what is at stake is American credibility: "It is not the safety of shipping lanes, or the prospects of a flood of refugees to this country, or the danger held out to the stability of Mexico that is ultimately at stake in Central America; it is the credibility of United States power."[129]

It may seem extraordinary that the Reagan administration's policies in El Salvador have as their deepest motivation a concern that the United States should enjoy a reputation as a country that does not hesitate to impose its will on other countries. And indeed this *is* extraordinary. It is also shocking. For the people of El Salvador have had to pay a very high price in suffering for these efforts to bolster U.S. credibility. By regarding El Salvador as a commodity to be "won" or "lost," and by siding with the forces of oppression and injustice, thereby prolonging the agony of the Salvadoran people, the United States is bringing upon itself the justified loathing and contempt of an entire people. Ironically, in making itself the enemy of the world's poor, and a symbol of oppression, the United States is defeating its own misconceived ambitions. For there is no number of nuclear weapons that will enable it to control a world by which it is despised.

★6★

Some Notable Victims: (2) Nicaragua

For the past few years Nicaragua has been the victim of an escalating series of guerrilla attacks. Operating primarily from bases inside Honduras, guerrilla bands have made forays into Nicaragua during which they have attacked buses and trucks, blown up bridges, attempted to capture towns, and assassinated local leaders and community activists. Their more recent attacks have concentrated on various forms of economic sabotage: disrupting harvests, threatening oil refineries and hydroelectric dams, and blowing up fuel storage depots. They have also bombed Managua's main airport and sabotaged an oil pipeline on Nicaragua's Atlantic coast. According to Nicaragua's Sandinista government, the guerrillas (known in Nicaragua as the *contras*) have assassinated 910 state officials, while the war has caused a total of 8,000 civilian deaths.[1] These figures may be exaggerated, but it is clear that the guerrilla attacks have taken a heavy toll in Nicaragua.

The ultimate source of these attacks is the United States. It was the United States, and in particular the CIA, which originally cobbled together the main contra army known as the Nicaraguan Democratic Force (FDN) out of a collection of diverse groups of Latin American exiles. It is also the United States which has supplied the FDN with their arms, including advanced aircraft—though Israel, under pressure from the United States, has also provided them with weapons captured from the PLO. (The Salvadorans have also done their bit: Salvadoran pilots, paid by the CIA, have regularly violated Nicaraguan airspace to resupply contra raiding parties at their bases inside the country.) The contras' uniforms and communications equipment, and even their salaries, have been provided by the United States. Many of the guerrillas have trained at camps in Florida, California, Texas, and several other states, while others have been trained by U.S. military advisers (assisted by a handful of Argentine advisers) in Honduras. In planning and coordinating their attacks on Nicaragua, the contras are advised and directed by U.S. personnel, who also provide them with intelligence assistance. At a higher level, the operation as a whole has been directed by the American ambassador to Honduras, John Negroponte, for a while in collusion with Honduran General Álvarez Martínez, until the latter was sent into exile.[2]

The most notorious form of assistance the United States has

provided the contras is a training manual drawn up by the CIA which advised the contras, among other things, to hire professional criminals to kill some of their own supporters at demonstrations in order to create martyrs for the cause, to blackmail Nicaraguan citizens in order to coerce them to work against the Sandinistas, and to assassinate selected government officials.[3] The exposure of the manual in the United States came shortly after the exposure of another piece of CIA handiwork, a comic book written in Spanish which recommended that Nicaraguans engage in various acts of petty sabotage, such as clogging toilets, leaving lights on, and pouring dirt in gas tanks, in order to help bring down the government.

According to Edgar Chamorro, until recently one of the directors of the FDN, the training manual was used extensively in training guerrilla leaders, who evidently followed much of its advice. As we have seen, the contras have assassinated Sandinista officials in large numbers. Indeed, this has been freely acknowledged by Chamorro, who stated that "frankly, I admit we have killed people in cold blood when we have found them guilty of crimes. We do believe in the assassination of tyrants. Some of the Sandinistas are tyrants in the small villages."[4] That the contras were conducting a series of assassinations was known within the Reagan administration, as is shown by the fact that a classified intelligence summary prepared in July 1982 by the Defense Intelligence Agency reported that "insurgent incidents" over the previous four months included "the assassination of minor government officials."[5] Nothing was done to stop the assassinations, even though Reagan had issued an executive order in 1981 which prohibited government personnel from conducting or assisting in assassinations. When challenged about the manual in his second debate with Mondale, Reagan claimed that a draft of the manual was reviewed by CIA officials and that the offending parts had in fact been edited out before the manual was printed, though twelve unedited copies somehow found their way to Nicaragua.[6] Even before the debate, however, Chamorro had denied similar White House claims, saying: "That is not true. There was only one draft."[7] This was later confirmed by the CIA, which acknowledges that all of the copies circulated contained the various offending passages.[8]

While the United States has been sponsoring the contras' raids against Nicaragua, it has itself, in conjunction with Honduras, been conducting a series of large-scale military exercises in Central America. The two most notable exercises in the series, code-named Big Pine I and Big Pine II, have been unusual both for their length and for the number of military personnel involved. While the Pentagon's joint exercises abroad seldom last for more than a few weeks, Big Pine II began in the summer of 1983 and continued until March 1984. Big Pine I involved 7,000 U.S. and Honduran troops, and by November 1983 there were nearly 13,000 U.S. military personnel in Honduras in connection with Big Pine II. At the same time, the American ambassador to Costa Rica announced that the United States would, in addition, be dispatching between 400 and 1,000 National Guardsmen to Costa Rica to work on certain unspecified civil engineering projects near the Nicaraguan border. The U.S. under secretary of defense for policy suggested that the National Guard might be accompanied by a further 1,000 "combat engineers." Barracks capable of housing up to 2,000 troops have been constructed near the Nicaraguan border. More recently, 100 paratroopers from the Army's 82nd Airborne Division, which participated in the invasion of Grenada, have arrived in Honduras, allegedly to help build roads at the U.S. base at Palmerola.

In addition to the deployment of large numbers of combat troops in Honduras, Big Pine II also involved extensive naval maneuvers, with an eight-vessel flotilla operating in waters off Nicaragua's Pacific coast, and another naval task force deployed off its Caribbean coast. The naval forces were instructed to practice tactics for a naval quarantine, and on one occasion a U.S. destroyer hailed a Soviet freighter heading for Nicaragua and demanded a list of the ship's cargo, as well as its destination. Ships from other countries were harassed in the same way. U.S. military officials openly acknowledged that the military exercises were intended in part as a "warning to Nicaragua."[9]

Later, beginning in late February 1984, the CIA began to lay mines in Nicaragua's harbors. A great many ships were struck by the mines, including a Soviet oil tanker, five of whose crew members were seriously injured. (It is interesting to speculate on what the Reagan administration's reaction would be if a U.S. ship were to be struck by a mine laid by the Soviets in the harbor of some country of whose government the Soviets disapproved.) The reaction of the Nicaraguans to the mining of their harbors was to take their case to the International Court of Justice, the judicial organ of the United Nations. Three days before the case was to be brought before the court, however, the United States announced that it would not recognize the court's jurisdiction in cases involving Central America for the following two years. Yet in 1945, when the court was established, the United States recognized the court's "compulsory jurisdiction," except with regard to cases involving "domestic" issues, and pledged to give six months' notice before withdrawing. In the past, moreover, the United States had appealed to the court itself—for example, in the case of the Iranian hostage crisis, when the justices voted unanimously to support the American position. It was clear that the administration was rejecting the court's authority in order to avoid the inevitable verdict that the U.S. action was in violation of international law. (On the same day that the administration announced its refusal to accept the court's jurisdiction, Reagan announced that May 1 was to be "Law Day USA," proclaiming that "without law, there can be no freedom, only chaos and disorder."[10])

Later, after the court voted unanimously to order the United States to stop the mining, the United States agreed to accept the ruling but argued, with obscure logic, that it "was not inconsistent with current U.S. policy towards Nicaragua."[11] The mining was stopped and the court's ruling accepted primarily because of congressional pressure. Less than a week after voting to provide the contras with $21 million, the Republican-controlled Senate had voted eighty-four to twelve to condemn the mining. Congressional outrage focused primarily on the administration's failure to consult the Congress before proceeding with the mining. The Congress was happy to finance a proxy war against Nicaragua as long as the proxies did the dirty work and the Congress itself was adequately briefed.

For what reason has the United States been conducting this extraordinary and multifaceted campaign of intimidation, provocation, and outright military aggression against Nicaragua? Again, let us first consider the administration's story. Despite the exposure in January 1983 of the fact that William Casey, the director of the CIA, had confirmed in testimony before the House and Senate intelligence committees that the CIA was backing the contras, and despite the publication of a secret National Security Council document in which it was acknowledged that "the Sandinistas are under increased pressure as a result of our covert efforts," the administration chose at first to feign innocence of any involvement with the contras, though it never explicitly denied its backing for them.[12] For the benefit of its domestic audience it even attempted to explain its refusal to deny being involved with the contras on the ground that this would keep the Sandinistas guessing and perhaps encourage them to stop their alleged arms supplies to the guerrillas in El Salvador.[13] Administration members did, however, *implicitly* repudiate the charge that they were backing the contras by, in effect, denying that the contras existed. For example, the *New York Times* reported that John Negroponte "dismissed Nicaragua's assertions that it was under attack as 'a diversionary tactic' . . . designed to shift attention away from what he called more important regional questions, like the presence of Cuban military advisers in Nicaragua and the buildup of Sandinist military forces."[14] And, months after the disclosure of Casey's testimony before the two congressional committees, and also after the release of the secret National Security Council document, Reagan asserted before both houses of Congress that "Nicaragua's dictatorial junta . . . like to *pretend* they are being attacked by forces based in Honduras. The fact is, it is Nicargua's Government that threatens Honduras, not the reverse."[15]

While in general the media politely allowed these audacious assertions to pass without comment, there are limits to the extent to which even the president can lie to the Congress and the country when the facts are freely accessible to anyone who cares to know them. So, while the administration never explicitly acknowledged its support for the contras, it had to provide some rationale for what everyone knew that it was doing. This rationale had to satisfy two constraints. First, it had to be acceptable to public opinion, and thus had to take account of the persistence of the Vietnam syndrome and the aversion of the American people to the prospect of becoming bogged down militarily in Nicaragua. And second, it had to be in conformity with U.S. law; but the Boland Amendment to the fiscal 1983 intelligence authorization states that

> none of the funds provided in this act may be used by the Central Intelligence Agency or the Department of Defense to furnish military equipment, military training or advice, or other support for military activities, to any group or individual, not part of a country's armed forces, for the purpose of overthrowing the Government of Nicaragua or provoking a military exchange between Nicaragua and Honduras.[16]

There were two reasons, therefore, why any rationale that the administration might provide for its support for the contras had to avoid the suggestion that the United States sought to overthrow the Sandinistas. Thus, while Reagan did not conceal his desire to see the Sandinistas toppled from power, he nevertheless put it forward as a necessary truth that the United States did not aim to overthrow them: "What I might personally wish, or what our Government might wish, still would not justify us in violating the law of the land." Hence "*anything* that we're doing in that area [Central America] is simply trying to interdict the supply lines which are supplying the guerrillas in El Salvador."[17]

This, then, became the official rationale for backing the contras: to block the alleged arms pipeline between Nicaragua and the guerrillas in El Salvador. This rationale was also cited by Secretary of State Shultz in justification for the U.S. decision to hold the Big Pine maneuvers in southwestern Honduras, provocatively near the

Nicaraguan border. For it was held that one of the aims of the exercises was to prepare the Honduran army to interdict arms transfers from Nicaragua to El Salvador and thus the maneuvers needed to be conducted over the relevant terrain.[18] We have seen, however, that the "flow" of arms from Nicaragua was at most a trickle, and in any case it is difficult to see how murdering teachers and doctors, burning villages, and the other assorted activities mentioned earlier in which the contras have been engaged could be construed as interdicting arms between Nicaragua and El Salvador. Furthermore, the administration was never able to explain convincingly how it was that it had the right to arm guerrillas fighting against the government of Nicaragua, while the government of Nicaragua did not have the corresponding right to supply arms to guerrillas fighting against the government of El Salvador. Thus a new rationale soon became necessary.

The next argument was that "covert" support for the contras was necessary to pressure the Sandinistas to stop their efforts to "export revolution" throughout the area.[19] The idea was said to be that the United States would continue "inconveniencing" the Sandinistas until they were willing to negotiate an end to their subversive activities aimed at their neighbors. Thus administration members and associates repeatedly called attention to the strengthening of Nicaragua's armed forces as evidence that the Sandinistas aimed to "destabilize" the entire region. And Henry Kissinger, as he was preparing his report on Central America, warned that "the pressure of a heavily armed Nicaragua, with Soviet, East German, Cuban, and other intelligence services operating there, can exercise at a minimum a great political and subversive pressure on all of the surrounding countries."[20]

In order to bolster its case that the Sandinistas pose a threat to all of Central America, and even to Mexico, the administration has regularly portrayed the Sandinistas as Soviet agents working to implement what Reagan calls "the master plan of the Communists for world conquest." According to the official view, moreover, the Sandinistas' Soviet-inspired designs on their neighbors are made yet more sinister and alarming by the fact, which Jeane Kirkpatrick has noted, that the Sandinistas are the worst violators of human rights in the world. Thus George Bush has accused them of "almost unprecedented brutality," while George Shultz has said that they are, in effect, "the same people who took over Kampuchea," implying that they are but a more recent instantiation of the same homogeneous global revolutionary force which in the 1970s manifested itself in the form of Pol Pot and his murderous Khmer Rouge.[21]

Like their ideological soul-mates in El Salvador (who, according to Shultz, were also cast in the same mold as Pol Pot), the Sandinistas are said to have little popular support, except among those whom they have succeeded in brainwashing. This is evident in the fact that for years they were afraid to hold elections, and in the end held only "sham" elections aimed at giving them the appearance of legitimacy. According to the administration, discontent with the Sandinistas is and has been broad-based and pervasive, and has found expression in the activities of the contras. Indeed the contras are themselves disaffected revolutionaries who, according to Reagan, "once fought beside the Sandinistas": they "are the other revolutionary factions totally ousted from any participation in the Government [who are] now fighting back on that."[22] Because the Sandinistas have failed to respect human rights, failed to move toward genuine democracy, and failed to honor their promise to allow political pluralism and a mixed economy in Nicaragua, they have betrayed the principles of the revolution and forfeited the support of the people. By contrast, the contras are, in Reagan's words, "freedom fighters" who are "asking [the government] to go back to its revolutionary promises and keep faith with the revolution that the people of Nicaragua supported."[23]

By this point there has been a conspicuous shift away from the idea that the United States is supporting the contras in order to prevent the spread of revolution. Reagan has now become the defender of the revolutionary faith, the true heir of Sandino: "Here was a revolution that took place that seemed to express all the things that we all believe in. . . . Isn't it time that all of us in the Americas worked together to hold [the Sandinistas] accountable for the promises made and broken four years ago?"[24]

The administration's characterization of events in Nicaragua is widely accepted in the United States, even among liberals. Thus Tom Wicker of the *New York Times* refers to Nicaragua under the Sandinistas as "an obstreperous nation," while the editors of that paper describe the Sandinistas as "an undesirable and offensive Managua regime," and go on to speak of "the condemnation [the Nicaraguan government] deserves . . . for its provocative ties with Cuba and the Soviet Union."[25] Congressman Robert Michel has claimed that the contras are "more compatible with our way of life" than the Sandinistas, while the American Veterans of Foreign Wars organized a collection in support of the FDN.[26] Morton Kondracke, executive editor of the liberal *New Republic,* has argued that the contras "would seem to deserve Reagan's characterization—'freedom fighters'—and to deserve congressional sympathy and American support."[27]

Some liberals, while accepting the desirability of turning out the

Sandinistas, nevertheless dispute the administration's choice of means. The *New York Times,* for example, argues that "instead of weakening the leftist regime in Managua, the blatant U.S. promotion of the rebels has allowed the Sandinists to mask their ugly repression with slogans of wartime nationalism." And a group of distinguished American liberals, many of whom (including Cyrus Vance and Edmund Muskie) held senior positions in the Carter administration, have argued that "sharp external confrontation with revolutionary regimes is more likely eventually to breed intensified nationalist and revolutionary sentiment than the more restrained approach we recommend."[28] The *New York Times* takes it as axiomatic that weakening the Sandinistas is a desirable goal, while the prominent liberals assume that it is uncontroversial that "intensified nationalist and revolutionary sentiment" in Central America would be an unwelcome occurrence. Most liberals also agree with the administration in taking it for granted that the United States has the right to impose its goals on the region. Thus the *New York Times* speaks for both liberals and conservatives alike when it writes that "our concern for who rules those backward nations arises naturally, from history and geography," and "Marxist-Leninists who would serve Soviet purposes are . . . unwelcome and worth resisting."[29]

That is an impressive consensus, even if there is widespread disagreement over the means for achieving the administration's goals. What is the source of this remarkable hostility to the Sandinistas, both within the administration and among the general population? We have seen that it cannot have much to do with the Sandinistas' support for the guerrillas in El Salvador, which is minimal at best. Nor is it likely to have to do with their other alleged efforts at "exporting revolution" in the region. As the earlier discussion of the Salvadoran revolution should have made clear, revolution is not something which can be "exported." Revolutions will not occur in Central America unless the people are provoked to revolt by intolerable domestic conditions. Where the requisite conditions are not present, no amount of pressure or proffered support from the Sandinistas could be sufficient to cause a revolution to erupt. Where such conditions are present, revolution is likely to occur eventually regardless of what the Sandinistas do. While the *example* of the Nicaraguan revolution may be a source of inspiration to revolutionaries in countries such as El Salvador and Guatemala (and, one might add, Honduras, where revolutionary violence will increase as the country is increasingly transformed into a garrison state under U.S. supervision), in each country the responsibility for the revolution lies with those responsible for the conditions which have brought it forth. (We will return to the importance of the example of the Nicaraguan revolution toward the end of the chapter.)

The administration, however, charges that Nicaragua has been engaged in an enormous military buildup which poses a direct threat to its neighbors, especially Honduras. As Alan Romberg, spokesman for the State Department, said recently, Nicaragua's armed forces "exceed anything that is justifiable in purely defensive terms."[30] (The administration regularly makes this same claim about the military forces of all its official enemies, including the Soviet Union and Grenada before the invasion.) Yet, while it is true that Nicaragua has strengthened its military forces in recent years, one does not have to look far to find defensive reasons for the buildup. The United States has invaded and occupied Nicaragua several times this century, and the threat of a repeat performance must be ever-present in the minds of the country's present leaders, especially in view of the Reagan administration's undisguised hostility to their program and its evident determination to reassert U.S. control in the region. To its immediate north, moreover, Nicaragua is faced with three hostile states, each effectively controlled by a right-wing military establishment, which recently formed a military alliance against Nicaragua (the Central American Defense Council, Condeca) under U.S. sponsorship. Since 1981 Nicaragua has been under more or less constant attack from guerrillas based in Honduras and Costa Rica, and has also suffered repeated violations of its airspace, territorial waters, and even its land territory by Honduran forces. Its many offers to discuss differences with Honduras, as well as its proposals for a mutual nonaggression pact and for the establishment of observer teams to patrol the joint border, have all been rebuffed.[31] In the light of these facts it can hardly come as a surprise that the Sandinistas have attempted to strengthen their defenses.

That the Sandinistas' military buildup is defensive in character is in any case evident from the nature of the weaponry that is being acquired. The CIA, for example, reported in 1983 that 80 percent of the arms being supplied by the Soviet Union were defensive in character.[32] While air support would be necessary for any large-scale ground invasion, Nicaragua effectively lacks an air force, and has instead concentrated on developing an air defense system to shield itself from the Honduran Air Force, which is the most formidable in the region. Nicaragua's heavy armored forces slightly outnumber those of Honduras, but Nicaragua's Soviet-built tanks are of inferior quality and could not in fact cope with the gradients they would be required to climb in order to reach Tegucigalpa.[33] In short, Nicaragua has not acquired the wherewithal to make a successful invasion of Honduras possible.

What about the charge that the Sandinistas are just puppets of the Kremlin? Nicaragua has of course developed closer relations with the Soviet Union since the revolution, but it is far from being a member of the Soviet bloc, or even a Soviet client. What is more, the extent of Nicaragua's relations with the Soviet Union is, as many observers have pointed out, to some degree a direct result of the policies of the Reagan administration. When the Sandinistas came to power in 1979, they inherited a country devastated by civil war, and an economy ravaged both by the war and by decades of corruption and mismanagement by the Somoza dynasty which they had overthrown. The war had caused more than $1 billion worth of damage to industrial and commercial facilities, and Somoza and his cronies had fled with most of the national wealth, leaving Nicaragua with a $1.64 billion national debt and only $3.5 million in the national treasury.[34] The Sandinistas required a vast inflow of capital to enable them to rebuild the country and revive the economy. Being a very heterogeneous group which was publicly committed to a nonaligned foreign policy, they had no ideological qualms about seeking assistance from and good relations with the United States. The Carter administration initially responded to their requests with relatively generous amounts of aid (which was eventually specified for the private sector), but when Reagan entered office aid was promptly cut off and pressure was successfully applied to the international lending agencies to deny credits to Nicaragua. This withdrawal of support, together with the combination of military and economic pressures which the Reagan administration began to exert, pushed the Sandinistas farther to the left, and increased their dependence on the Soviet Union.

While there is no doubt some ideological affinity between the Sandinistas and the Soviet Union, and while there are some members of the Sandinista directorate who advocate closer relations with the Soviet Union on ideological grounds, the relations between the two countries are nevertheless based for the most part on a marriage of convenience. Nicaragua has maintained its independence in all important respects. It has, for example, no military agreements with the Soviet Union, and has explicitly rejected the suggestion that it might accept the stationing of Soviet nuclear missiles on its soil. On the other hand, it is often said that the fact that Nicaragua votes with the Soviet Union in the U.N. General Assembly far more often than it votes with the United States demonstrates that it has become de facto aligned with the Soviet Union. But, given the ideological distance between the two governments and the fact that the United States is in effect making war against Nicaragua, it is hardly surprising that Nicaragua should usually vote against the United States, and therefore with the Soviet Union. And, in any case, there are other countries—for example, Peru—which are clearly nonaligned whose voting patterns show the same tilt against the United States in favor of the Soviet Union.[35] (On the other hand, the fact that Nicaragua did not vote to condemn the Soviet invasion of Afghanistan is both inexcusable and inconsistent.)

The extent to which the Sandinistas have allowed the Soviet Union and its allies to penetrate their country has also been consistently exaggerated. Reagan, for example, has claimed that there are 2,000 Cuban military advisers in Nicaragua, supplemented by "additional thousands of civilian advisers from Cuba, the Soviet Union, East Germany, Libya, and the P.L.O." Yet, according to the *New York Times,* "a well-placed diplomat said that United States Government sources had told him there were 'no more than a few hundred persons' from those countries [excluding, presumably, Cuba]."[36] Anthony Quainton, formerly Reagan's ambassador to Nicaragua, remarked while he was there that the "Soviet presence is quite small; there are 150 to 200 Russians including embassy personnel." He also noted that the total number of Cubans in Nicaragua was around 2,000.[37] Of these, most were teachers and doctors.

In matters of domestic organization as well the Sandinistas have eschewed the Soviet and Cuban models. Political pluralism is a reality in Nicaragua. As Richard Fagen, professor of Latin American Studies at Stanford University, has observed:

> A vast array of political, social, and cultural forces are at work in the country. Professional and business associations in deep disagreement with government policy meet openly and protest loudly. Opposition political parties, although not able to mobilize wide popular support, are nevertheless active and vocal. The opposition trade-union movement is small but vigorous. The Catholic Church, some of whose members are supportive of the Sandinista revolution and some of whom are in opposition, continues as a major cultural and political force. A multitude of Protestant sects flourish. Private schools, both religious and secular, remain open. Even in the state of emergency decreed in March 1982, as a result of multiple threats from the Reagan Administration and the constant incursions of former national guardsmen across the border from Honduras, the opposition newspaper *La Prensa* continues to publish—albeit under the censorship that is also applied to other publications. And certainly in the streets, markets, churches, bars, and buses of the country one hears plenty of openly voiced complaints and criticisms—hardly what one

> would expect in a "totalitarian" society. . . . Objectively and concretely, there is very clearly more political freedom, more political discussion, more personal liberty in Nicaragua today than at any other time in the last half century.[38]

In conformity with the pledge they made on coming to power, the Sandinistas have also maintained a mixed economy. The main targets for expropriation and nationalization have been estates and enterprises formerly owned by the Somoza dynasty, and it has generally been estimated that 59 percent of the nation's gross domestic product (GDP) is produced by the private sector. While there is evidence that the share of the GDP produced by the public sector has now increased beyond the generally accepted figure of 41 percent, the state's share in the economy is still less than that in most West European countries, and considerably less than that in the Scandinavian countries and the Netherlands.[39]

One could go on citing evidence of Nicaragua's independence from the Soviet Union, but it is unnecessary to labor this point further. Even if Nicaragua had extremely close ties to the Soviet Union, that would no more legitimize the U.S. campaign of harassment and intimidation than Britain's close ties to the United States (and indeed its acceptance of American nuclear bases on its soil) would justify the Soviet Union in sponsoring proxy attacks against it.

The charges concerning the violation of human rights are more serious. It would, however, be surprising if the Sandinistas were guilty of "almost unprecedented brutality" given the nature of their initial behavior upon assuming the reins of power. On their first day in office they issued the Estatuto Fundamental, which "dissolved the National Guard, the secret police and the military intelligence service. It also gave full recognition to the Universal Declaration of Human Rights. The death penalty was outlawed, and torture, and cruel, inhuman and degrading treatment forbidden."[40] The maximum penalty for any offense became thirty years' imprisonment. At the same time the Sandinistas freed some 2,500 of Somoza's National Guardsmen, giving them safe conduct into Honduras. Some National Guardsmen were executed by peasants in rural areas, but the new government moved quickly to stop the executions, and in doing so arrested several hundred of its own supporters.[41] There was, in short, no official retribution against those whom the Sandinistas had defeated. This moved West German novelist Günter Grass to comment:

> The French, the North American, and the Russian revolutions all resulted in vengeful violence, murder, and mass liquidation. Indeed,

> all known revolutions have wanted to appease their ideals and make people happy with theories soaked in blood. Yet in this tiny, sparsely populated, powerless land, where Christ's words are taken literally, the Sandinista revolution provides a different example.[42]

The question whether government forces engage in torture is controversial—which is itself rather remarkable given the practices of the previous Somoza regime and those of the governments of Nicaragua's neighbors. Many independent observers, including members of Nicaragua's independent Permanent Commission on Human Rights (which is critical of the Sandinistas and has consequently been subject to harassment by pro-Sandinista mobs), deny that the Sandinistas torture or physically abuse their prisoners.[43] Others, such as the American Embassy, claim that torture does occur. The disagreement here may be mainly over what counts as torture, for those who allege that torture occurs do not cite instances of severe torture, but instead cite cases in which prisoners are interrogated in the nude, subjected to psychological abuse, and, on occasion, beaten.[44] They also say that these alleged cases are isolated incidents rather than instances of government policy. Thus Amando López, a member of the National Commission for the Protection and Promotion of Human Rights who claims that "individual cases of torture" have occurred, nevertheless asserts that the Sandinista government "basically . . . respects human rights."[45]

Other prominent charges against the Sandinistas are that they have mistreated Nicaragua's Miskito Indian population, persecuted the Catholic Church, and muzzled the press. Let us consider these in turn.

The Miskito Indians form a community of about 70,000 people living primarily in the northeast region of Nicaragua's Atlantic coast. They are predominantly Moravian Christians who speak Miskito or English rather than Spanish, and have traditionally lived in isolation from Nicaragua's Latin majority. In the immediate aftermath of the revolution, the Miskitos suffered mistreatment at the hands of insensitive Sandinista officials who were sent out as representatives of the new government to the Atlantic coast region. Sandinista leaders now freely concede this. According to Tomás Borge Martínez, the interior minister, "we sent a group of *compañeros* into the region who didn't understand things the way they should have—they knew more about astronomy, some of them, than anthropology. They made terrible, alienating mistakes in dealing with the Miskitos."[46] Later, in late 1981 and early 1982, the contras began making almost daily raids into Nicaragua's northern Atlantic coast region where many of the Miskitos lived. The Sandinistas responded by forcibly relocating as many as 8,500 Miskitos to areas away from the fighting, claiming that this was necessary for the Indians' protection. The fact that some leaders within the Miskito community supported the relocation on the ground that it was necessary for the protection of the Indian community lends credibility to the idea that this was at least part of the Sandinistas' motivation.[47] But, insofar as the move was made to deny the contras a popular base among the already disaffected Indian population, the Sandinistas are to that extent deserving of the strongest condemnation. (At present the Sandinistas are in the midst of negotiations with Miskito leaders who have been fighting with the contras. The negotiations concern the possibility of the establishment of an "autonomous zone" in the northeastern part of the country which would be controlled by the indigenous inhabitants of the area.)

Many allegations against the Sandinistas have been clearly exaggerated. Allegations about the persecution of the Church in Nicaragua are in this category. We have already had occasion to remark Jeane Kirkpatrick's claim that a Nicaraguan bishop was denied access to television, and there have been other charges of a similar nature, many of them true. It is, however, a misrepresentation of the reality in Nicaragua to characterize the government's action in these cases as persecution of the Church. The conflict is not so much between the Church and the state as it is *within* the Church itself. The struggle within the Church is between those who defend the traditional conception of the role of the Church and the priesthood and those who accept the conception of the Church's role articulated in the new "theology of liberation." Since the latter believe that the Church and its representatives should be actively engaged in serving the poor and promoting social justice, the divisions between these two groups are profoundly manifest in their differing views as to the appropriate relation between the Church and the revolution. While the traditionalists (who also fear the liberationists' rejection of the authoritarian structures within the Church) believe that the Church should itself not be involved in revolutionary politics, the adherents of liberation theology have taken an active part in promoting the Sandinista revolution. The Nicaraguan foreign minister, the minister of education, the minister of culture, and the ambassador to the Organization of American States are all Roman Catholic priests—a fact which is itself sufficient to expose the absurdity of the charge that the Sandinista government persecutes "the Church."

For obvious reasons, the Sandinistas have sided with the liberation theologists. Hence they, and in particular their members who are themselves priests, have been attacked from the pulpit by the traditionalists, who have also used their influence in the Vatican to try to confront the priests serving in the government with the choice of resigning their posts or being unfrocked. (Very recently, in fact, the minister of education, Father Fernando Cardenal, was expelled from the Society of Jesus for his refusal to resign his post.) In short, the persecution has been entirely mutual, with the traditionalists making frequent and fierce denunciations of the government and, ironically, becoming increasingly involved in politics. (For example, the archbishop of Managua, Miguel Obando y Bravo, has recently been demanding that the Sandinistas open negotiations with the contras.)

The "oppression" which the traditionalists have suffered at the hands of the government has not been particularly severe. Jonathan Steele, the chief foreign correspondent for the London *Guardian,* recently returned from Nicaragua with the following report:

> I asked Bismark Carballo, the Archbishop's right-hand man [and press secretary] to discuss the persecution of the Church. After talking in generalities he could not mention one case of a closed church, a closed church school, or a murdered priest. He listed three priests who had been expelled from the country in the last four years—less than the number of foreign priests who have had to leave because the Archbishop withdrew their permission to stay.[48]

Later, in July 1984, ten more foreign priests were expelled after Archbishop Obando y Bravo led a protest march against the government.[49]

One of the most notorious instances of the "persecution of the Church" occurred in the fall of 1982, and involved Bismark Carballo himself. According to the American Embassy:

> One of the most visible attacks on the church involved a plot to entrap the head of the Catholic radio station [Carballo]. The priest, who was lunching with a female parishioner, was forced to disrobe by an intruder and then led off naked by the police who detained him for six hours. Pictures of the naked priest shown on Sandinista TV and published in pro-government newspapers deeply shocked the populace.[50]

This account is based on Carballo's own story. Other reports gave a quite different account:

> Monsignor Carballo was photographed running naked in the street by TV and print photographers in the Managua suburb of Las Colinas. The photographers were there to cover a demonstration when shots rang out and dashing past them and the demonstrators came a naked man—later identified as the monsignor—with a dressed man in pursuit. Police took both away. Press accounts later reported that

> Monsignor Carballo had been caught at the home of his mistress by her angry husband. Interviews with the woman indicated a lengthy romantic involvement with the monsignor.[51]

In the absence of further evidence, readers must themselves decide which account seems more plausible. One thing, however, is clear, and that is that if Carballo was framed in order to discredit the traditionalists, the scheme miserably backfired. For the United States and the conservative church hierarchy certainly stole the propaganda advantage: American diplomats throughout Central America publicly denounced the "Communist oppression of the Church in Nicaragua," and the State Department apparently urged religious leaders in the United States to make their protests heard.[52]

The advantage was pressed on the occasion of the Pope's visit to Central America in March 1983. In a mass held in Managua, which was attended by hundreds of thousands of people, the Pope lectured his audience on the authority of the Nicaraguan bishops, pointedly failing to give any recognition to the accomplishments of the revolution or express any compassion for the victims of the contra war—though elsewhere in the region he managed to speak in defense of social justice and on behalf of the victims of violence and persecution. After the mothers of youths recently killed by the contras vainly sought the Pope's blessing, members of the crowd began to chant "We want peace!" The Pope responded by angrily demanding "Silence!" The episode was widely reported as the Sandinistas' "insult" to the Pope.[53]

Let us turn now to the question of censorship. It is certainly true that all of the media in Nicaragua, including the opposition paper *La Prensa,* are subject to official censorship, and that *La Prensa* has on occasion been temporarily shut down. These facts must, however, be viewed in context. In an article drawn from a briefing paper prepared for Anthony Quainton, then Reagan's ambassador to Nicaragua, one expert on the Nicaraguan media has argued that

> the academic literature on comparative foreign journalism indicates that, via this selection process [called "editing" if done by the media or a political party, "censorship" if done by the government], all countries tend to limit the amount of criticism of the established order and to limit the range of new information and ideas during times of national crisis. For example, all countries regardless of political ideology control (usually by act of government) the dissemination of criticism and unsettling information during times of war, other external threats, or domestic economic instability. In addition, research indicates that the level of national development and the degree of institutional complexity affects the amount of criticism and dissident information carried in a nation's media. In short, only after the

> difficult and volatile process of modernization and national development and only during times of tranquility can a country tolerate a wide range of news and opinion. Considering that Nicaragua is an extremely poor country that has recently experienced a devastating revolutionary war and is currently confronted with a continuing power struggle, economic chaos, and real or perceived external threat, the fact that an opposition newspaper continues to publish and other government and non-government media discuss Nicaragua's political future and other unsettling topics is remarkable.[54]

When this article was written in 1982, the "covert" contra war was in its early stages. The fact that *La Prensa* has continued to publish throughout the widening and intensification of the war is all the more remarkable.

It is perhaps difficult for Americans to appreciate the full extent of the disruption and chaos caused by the U.S. proxy war in Nicaragua. In a situation of this sort, it is not unjustifiable that there should be a certain amount of censorship. The expert on the Nicaraguan media just cited, John Spicer Nichols, points out that in the United States during World War I, newspapers were prohibited from "publishing criticism of the federal government or advocating radical political or economic change," and that this was defended by Supreme Court Justice Oliver Wendell Holmes on the ground that "words may create a 'clear and present danger' to the public and may be legitimately suppressed by the government."[55] The case for censorship in Nicaragua is, if anything, more compelling given the nature of the media there. Nichols observes that

> because the Nicaraguan media have the same physical appearance as the media of North America, analysts usually assume that they also serve the same function for Nicaraguan society. Nothing could be further from the truth. . . . In the less complex society of Nicaragua, the mass media have always served as political tools of powerful combatants for national power. Rather than functioning as news media intended to carry balanced and dispassionate reporting of national affairs, all Nicaraguan media are close collaborators with specialized power contenders in society, primarily political factions.[56]

(An example of *La Prensa*'s petty partisanship was provided by its coverage of the recent Nicaraguan elections in which an estimated 75 to 82 percent of the electorate turned out for noncompulsory voting. *La Prensa* 's two main headlines read: "Great Apathy in the Voting," and "Eighteen Percent Abstention." The Sandinistas' victory was hardly mentioned.[57]) Nichols concludes that because "*La Prensa* is both pen and sword in a highly unstable political system," the "failure to curb [its] inaccurate or inflammatory reporting threatens the economic and political stability of the country."[58]

In spite of the censorship and occasional closures, *La Prensa* continues to circulate widely. In mid 1984 it had a circulation of approximately 50,000 while the two pro-government papers, *Barricada* and *Nuevo Diario,* had circulations of 90,000 and 40,000, respectively. (The editor of *La Prensa* is the brother of the editor of *Barricada,* and the editor of *Nuevo Diario* is their uncle.) Though *La Prensa* is of course subject to heavier censorhip than the other two papers, it is nevertheless permitted to display censored articles on a bulletin board outside its offices in Managua where the articles may be read by anyone sufficiently motivated to come read them. More importantly, it is allowed to send photocopies of censored material to the various international embassies in Managua, thereby guaranteeing an international outlet for material which the government considers too dangerous to be circulated at home.[59]

While there appears to be considerable justification for a certain amount of press censorship in Nicaragua, it does not follow that the Sandinistas have used censorship only in those ways which would be justifiable. While generally up to 85 percent of the items censored have dealt with military affairs (with the percentage rising to 100 in the months prior to the election), the Sandinistas have certainly abused the censorship to further their own political aims.[60]

The Sandinistas are clearly guilty of a variety of other abuses as well. While the injustices suffered by the Miskitos and the harassment suffered by traditionalists within the Nicaraguan Church have been exaggerated in the United States, it is difficult to deny that the Sandinistas have occasionally abused their authority in their treatment of these two groups. Robert S. Leiken, an American scholar whose field is Latin American studies, recently returned from ten days in Nicaragua bearing reports of economic mismanagement, high-level corruption, enforced popular mobilization, bullying and intimidation of the opposition by pro-Sandinista mobs, unscrupulous distortion in the pro-government press, and widespread popular discontent. Even though what he reports appears to be only part of the truth (for other reports give another side to the story), many of us who are strong sympathizers with the Sandinistas and their revolution have reason to be keenly disappointed.

The relevant question here, however, is whether the Sandinista abuses can reasonably be cited in justification of the Reagan administration's sponsorship of the guerrilla attacks against them. It is certainly the height of hypocrisy for the administration to suggest that they can. While in Nicaragua some sectors of the population have suffered mistreatment, in El Salvador whole communities have been exterminated by government forces. While in Nicaragua there are occasional reports of isolated instances of torture, in El Salvador tens of thousands of people have been subjected to the most hideous forms of torture on an official basis. While in Nicaragua certain priests may be subject to some slight harassment, priests in El Salvador have been singled out as a special target for the death squads, and many, including the previous archbishop of San Salvador, have been killed. In Nicaragua *La Prensa* has been subject to government censorship. Opposition newspapers in El Salvador were driven out of existence several years ago when the "security forces" repeatedly bombed and attacked their offices and mutilated and killed many of their editors and reporters.[61] In every conceivable respect, government violations of human and political rights in El Salvador are in an altogether different category from those in Nicaragua, and yet this has certainly not led the United States to sponsor attacks against El Salvador, or even to diminish the level of its support for the government.

Consideration of the government of El Salvador suggests that there may be governments whose violations of human rights are so grave and extensive, and whose merits are so few, that outside support for forces seeking to overthrow them would be justified. But even if the Sandinistas were guilty of all that has been charged against them, their overall record would still not be such as to put them in that category. Their positive achievements have been notable. After visiting Nicaragua, British journalist John Pilger reported that "polio has gone completely. Infant mortality has been cut by a third. Life expectancy has risen. Production and consumption of basic foods is up by as much as 100 percent. A literacy campaign, spectacular by any standards, has reduced the illiteracy rate from more than half the population to less than 10 percent."[62]

These observations have been corroborated by a variety of sources, including a representative of SANE, an American peace organization, who adds that "housing and other basic needs for the poorest of the poor are being slowly met, and people are being organized to participate in the political and economic decisions that affect their daily lives."[63] As Professor Richard Fagen has noted, "With all its faults and problems, the current government of Nicaragua is the first in the country's entire history that is genuinely attempting to improve the living and working conditions of the majority of citizens."[64]

More than anything else it is the fact that the Sandinistas enjoy substantial popular support which demonstrates the wrongness and illegitimacy of the U.S. attempts to undermine them. For the fact that the Sandinistas and their revolution in general have the support of the Nicaraguan people means that U.S. support for the contras is against the will of the people, and violates their right to national autonomy and self-determination. The Sandinistas' popular support is manifest in many ways. For example, in response to the escalating threat from the United States, the Sandinistas have organized militias and supplied arms to tens of thousands of civilians without any fear that the weapons will be turned against them, or turned over to the contras. But the most important expression of public support for the Sandinistas came in the Nicaraguan elections of November 1984.

For years the Reagan administration had cited the Sandinistas' failure to hold elections as proof not only of their totalitarian leanings but also of their lack of popular support. The administration, citing the Sandinistas' "contract to establish a true democracy" made with the OAS in 1979, claimed that their failure to hold elections constituted a major betrayal of the promises of the revolution.[65] (In fact the Sandinistas did tell the OAS that they planned to hold "free elections," but without stipulating a time when the elections would be held. In 1980 the Sandinistas gave a pledge to hold elections in 1985.) In reality the absence of elections was neither a betrayal of the revolution nor a betrayal of the people. Had the Sandinistas held elections soon after the triumph of the revolution, when virtually the whole of the population was united in support for them, they would rightly have been denounced as taking unfair advantage of the possibly transient popularity which their victory over Somoza had bestowed upon them. Both the people generally and even the major opposition political groups recognized that democratic political struggles would have to await the achievement of economic stability and national reconstruction.

This is not to say, however, that there was no democracy in Nicaragua. Democracy, in the sense of popular rule, is not necessarily identical with holding elections. The Sandinistas created a Council of State in which representatives of a broad range of groups were invited to participate, giving the people an influence over the formulation of policy through the various groups represented. Among those groups whose representatives participated in the Council of State were various political parties, trade unions, the peasant union, the women's movement, the teachers' union, the Sandinista youth movement, and various professional organizations.

When the Sandinistas announced that elections to choose a president, vice-president, and Constituent Assembly would be held in 1984 rather than 1985, the United States, which had all along clamored for elections, immediately changed tack by arguing that the elections would be illegitimate. Indeed, a secret briefing paper prepared for the National Security Council and recently leaked to the *Washington Post* reveals that the administration devised a plan well in advance of the elections to have them denounced as a sham by diplomatic personnel, American politicians, trade unionists, independent experts, and others.[66] The reason for the administration's hostility was of course that, if the elections, which the Sandinistas seemed almost certain to win, were regarded internationally as having been legitimate, then the political costs to the United States of continuing with its proxy war against the government could become prohibitively high.

In an effort to deprive the election of legitimacy, the United States did everything in its power to prevent the various right-wing Nicaraguan parties from participating. Clemente Guido, leader of the Democratic Conservative party, revealed before the election that an official from the American Embassy had offered to pay his party thousands of dollars if it would abstain.[67] Most pressure, however, was exerted on the main opposition grouping known as the Democratic Coordinating Committee (CDN), an alliance comprising several small conservative parties and the Superior Council of Private Enterprise (COSEP), an association of Nicaraguan business leaders. According to certain senior administration officials, the United States worked behind the scenes to ensure that the CDN's presidential candidate, Arturo José Cruz, would either refuse to enter the race or at least withdraw before election day. As one official remarked, "the Administration never contemplated letting Cruz stay in the race."[68] Without Cruz's knowledge, the CIA worked with a number of his associates, principally from COSEP, to ensure that they would object to and thereby block any agreement which he might reach with the Sandinistas concerning the CDN's participation in the elections. Thus a Western diplomat in Nicaragua has claimed that CDN leaders told him well in advance of the election that Cruz would go to Nicaragua to generate publicity but in the end would abstain from participating in the elections.[69]

Supported by the United States, the CDN insisted that the Sandinistas had to satisfy a number of conditions before it would participate in the elections. Among these conditions was a demand that the Sandinistas open negotiations with the contras. (The administration staunchly defended this demand, though it has never explained how this was compatible with its opposition to negotiations between the Salvadoran government and the FDR-FMLN, between the Israeli government and the Palestine Liberation Organization, and between the British government and the Irish Republican Army—though in each of these latter cases the opposition enjoys substantially more popular support than the contras do in Nicaragua.) The Sandinistas expressed a willingness to discuss with the CDN such matters as lifting the state of emergency, ending press censorship, and providing the opposition with greater access to television. But the CDN twice refused even to discuss these matters until the Sandinistas agreed to negotiate with the contras.[70]

In August the CDN dropped its demand for negotiations, not because it recognized that the demand was unreasonable as a condition for participating in an election, but because Adolpho Calero, a contra leader, announced that the contras would not talk to the Sandinistas. The CDN, however, maintained its insistence that the Sandinistas declare a general amnesty for the contra leaders (many of whom, as we shall see, were former officers of Somoza's National Guard).[71] Later, in September, CDN leaders held a joint press conference with Calero and other leaders of the FDN, as well with Edén Pastora, a former Sandinista commander who now leads a smaller contra group based in Costa Rica known as the Revolutionary Democratic Alliance (ARDE). At the conference CDN leaders threatened to take up arms with the contras, whose leaders were declared by Cruz to be "the best leaders in the country."[72]

The CDN's behavior made it clear that it was rapidly becoming the political arm of the contras. Yet the Sandinistas continued to try to entice the alliance to participate. In the end, however, their efforts failed and the CDN boycotted the election. One Western diplomat in Managua remarked: "Just as the Sandinistas start to create the conditions for a reasonably fair election, the Coordinadora [CDN] decides to pull out. One has to conclude they never wanted to run and that they merely want to embarrass the Sandinistas."[73]

Although the CDN boycotted, seven other parties, including the Sandinistas, chose to stand. This was the largest number of parties to run in one election in the whole of Nicaraguan history.[74] There were three parties to the right of the Sandinistas, and three to the left. Of the three right-wing parties, one, the Independent Liberal party, at the last moment decided to pull out of the election, but its campaign advertisements continued to appear in the papers and on television and its vice-presidential candidate, Constantine Pereira, issued a call to people to vote, saying he at any rate intended to stand. The other two parties to the right of the Sandinistas were the Democratic Conservative party and the Social Christian party. The Democratic Conservative party opposes state control of the economy as well as military conscription, and advocates religious instruction in schools. The Social Christians, while favoring conscription, advocate a stricter doctrine of mixed economy and criticize the Sandinistas' "disrespectful attitude" toward the Church hierarchy.[75] The three parties to the left of the Sandinistas were the Nicaraguan Socialist party, the Communist party, and the Marxist-Leninist Popular Action Movement, all of which argue that the Sandinistas have made too many concessions to the middle class and the United States. Each party received 9 million cordobas ($900,000 using the then official exchange rate of ten cordobas to the dollar) from the state to finance their campaigns.[76]

While there was some disorder and violence in the months preceding the polling, with pro-Sandinista groups attacking groups of CDN supporters and vice versa, the polling stations were calm and orderly on election day itself.[77] The only significant disruption was a series of loud blasts around the country which people assumed to be bombs exploding. The noises turned out to be caused by U.S. spy planes breaking the sound barrier in order to spread panic throughout the country.[78]

The elections appear to have been both free and fair. Restrictions on civil liberties, such as suspension of habeas corpus, which had been imposed under emergency legislation in 1982, were lifted some three months before election day, and censorship had been relaxed at the same time. Though neither the United States nor Britain sent official delegations to observe the elections, both countries were represented by unofficial delegations composed of members of the major political parties, including the Republican party and the British Conservative party. These groups agreed that the voting was secret and that there was no evidence of electoral fraud.[79] As mentioned earlier, voting was not compulsory. Lord Kennet, representing Britain's Social Democrat party, said he found the voting system "extremely well thought out and a little bit superior to what we do in Britain." A Conservative Member of Parliament reported that "there were no irregularities . . . in the conduct of the electoral process or the counting which I could see. I asked people if they considered the vote was secret, and the answer was in the affirmative. I asked if they felt free to vote for any party and the answer was yes."[80]

When the results were in, the turnout was estimated to have been between 75 and 82 percent of the electorate. The Sandinistas won by a large majority, taking sixty-one seats in the new Constituent Assembly. It is estimated that 47 percent of the eligible voters (*not* just of those who voted) voted for the Sandinistas. The three parties to the right of the Sandinistas won twenty-nine seats, while the three to the left won six.[81]

The Reagan administration predictably denounced the election as a farce, basing its judgment on the claim that there was no meaningful opposition.[82] Not only was this false, but it was also grotesquely hypocritical given that the United States had done its utmost to prevent the CDN from participating. It was also difficult to reconcile with its ecstatic endorsement of the Salvadoran elections half a year earlier. While the CDN boycotted the Nicaraguan elections on the ground that the Sandinistas had unfair institutional advantages over their opponents, the only genuine opposition in El Salvador was excluded from the elections there by the very real threat of extreme violence against their leaders and supporters.

Suppose for the sake of argument, however, that the administration were right that the election did not demonstrate that the Sandinistas enjoy considerable popular support. Even if that were true the *clear* lack of popular support for the contras still shows that U.S. backing for their attacks is contrary to the will of the Nicaraguan people and is therefore a form of intervention which violates the Nicaraguans' sovereign rights. The contras consist essentially of externally sustained commando armies which conduct periodic invasions of Nicaraguan territory.[83] The fact that unlike the Salvadoran guerrillas they control no territory and thus have to be based in Honduras and Costa Rica shows that they have no popular base in Nicaragua. A privately conducted poll in Nicaragua found that 90 percent of the people questioned were willing to have their sons and daughters serve in the militia, the group which at present is charged with defending the country against the contras' attacks.[84] It would appear, moreover, that the degree of popular aversion to the contras is proportional to the amount of exposure people have had to them. Thus in Jalapa, a town in an area near the Honduran border where the contras have been operating, the Sandinistas (whom the contras aim to overthrow) won 96 percent of the vote in the recent elections.[85]

That the contras lack popular support is unsurprising given their composition. The main group of contras, the FDN, far from being a collection of dissident revolutionaries, in fact consists largely of the remnants of Somoza's hated National Guard whom the Sandinistas allowed to seek asylum in Honduras after the revolution. Ex-guardsmen are said to comprise the whole of the FDN's officer corps.[86] (The reason why, despite repeated attempts, the United States has been unable to forge the FDN and the ARDE into a unified force is that Pastora, the leader of the ARDE, has consistently refused to collaborate with the Somocistas of the FDN.) Of those contras who are not ex-members of the guard, most are simply mercenaries. (Recall that, unlike most guerrilla fighters in recent history, these have been drawing handsome salaries, courtesy of the U.S. taxpayer. Honduran boys are recruited at the contras' offices in Honduras to fight in Nicaragua for a monthly wage of 200 lempiras—equal to $100.[87])

Somoza's National Guard was legendary for its brutality, and so far the contras have been true to their reputation. As mentioned earlier, their specialties include burning villages and crops and murdering doctors, teachers, and church officials; and they have also performed other feats of military valor such as kidnapping peasant children and attacking and destroying buses, ambulances, and hospitals. Whether their aim is to create a climate of terror or simply to revenge themselves on a population which rejected them, their methods have been every bit as gruesome as those of the other U.S.-backed forces in the region. A survivor of a contra attack on a state farm in the province of Jinotega described to British reporters the contras' treatment of the farm workers: "Rosa had her breasts cut off. Then they cut into her chest and took out her heart. The men had their arms broken, their testicles cut off, and their eyes poked out. They were killed by slitting their throats, and pulling the tongue out through the slit."[88] Similar accounts abound.[89] (*Time,* in one of its more egregious performances, wrote in an article vindicating the administration's support for the contras that "American covert methods are tame compared with those used by the Soviets, who have no qualms about using front organizations, disinformation [a commodity totally unfamiliar to readers of *Time*], and even terrorist groups."[90])

In short, the men whom Reagan has referred to as "heroes" and "freedom fighters," and whom the U.S. government reckons are more compatible with the American Way of Life than the Sandinistas, are themselves undoubtedly the worst violators of human rights in Nicaragua today. If they were to seize power, respect for human rights would undoubtedly deteriorate to the abysmal levels that were reached when these same "heroes" were unleashed on the Nicaraguan people by Somoza.

By now it should be clear that, as one would expect, none of the Reagan administration's public rationales for its sponsorship of the contras stands up to the least scrutiny. Nor is it likely that anyone has ever paid much serious attention to them, since the administration's real reasons have all along been perfectly transparent. If anyone needed to be told, the administration's real purpose emerged quite explicitly in the remarks of some senior administration officials around the end of the summer in 1983. Thus, Reagan's pose as keeper of the revolutionary faith notwithstanding, Jeane Kirkpatrick argued that the Sandinista revolution was not irreversible, and that she was persuaded (to her evident satisfaction) that the Nicaraguan people "have the will and determination to reverse it."[91] Later, in a speech to the Baltimore Council on Foreign Relations, Under Scretary of Defense Iklé declared that the United States "must prevent consolidation of a Sandinista regime in Nicaragua"; otherwise "we have to anticipate the partition of Central America," with the United States then having "to man a new military front-line in the East-West conflict right here on our continent"—an interesting prospect.[92] (One may wonder what has happened to the Boland Amendment. Around the same time that Kirkpatrick and Iklé were letting it be known that the United States sought to dispose of the Sandinistas, George Shultz was busy on television reassuring the American public that the administration was not trying to overthrow them, and thus was acting in conformity with the law. At the same time, however, he conceded that the contras' "goal is one that, given our opinion of that [Sandinista] government, we can hardly turn away from." The contras' openly avowed goal is the overthrow of the Sandinistas—as Shultz himself had earlier confirmed in emphatic terms in testimony before the Senate Foreign Relations Committee.[93] So much for the Boland Amendment.)

The administration's aim of throwing out the Sandinistas is not open to compromise, as is evident when one considers the record of U.S. responses to the many proposals which Nicaragua and various other countries have made for a negotiated solution to problems which are ostensibly the objects of American concern. As mentioned in Chapter 4, in 1982 the administration completely ignored a proposal from Mexico and Venezuela to mediate between Nicaragua and Honduras. During that same year Nicaragua proposed discussions with the United States covering such matters as the cutting of Nicaragua's ties to the insurgents in El Salvador and the reduction of its own armed forces. The United States rejected the proposal.[94] By August 1983 it was estimated that "Nicaragua's overtures were rejected at least eleven times by Reagan administration officials."[95]

In the autumn of 1983 Nicaragua presented draft treaties to the State Department indicating Nicaragua's willingness to open negotiations on matters about which the United States had voiced a concern, including the reduction of the Nicaraguan army, a prohibition on the establishment of foreign military bases in the Central American region, the prohibition of arms traffic between Central American countries, and the prohibition of actions aimed at overthrowing other governments, including support for groups attempting to overthrow other governments. The Sandinistas also expressed a willingness to discuss a regional freeze on arms purchases and the removal of all foreign military advisers from the nations in the region.[96] These proposals were accompanied by numerous concessions and conciliatory gestures intended to appease the wrath of the lowering superpower. The Sandinistas sent home over 1,000 Cubans, including many military advisers, had some Salvadoran rebel leaders leave the country in a "goodwill" gesture, and granted an amnesty to the contras (excluding only the leadership and certain specific individuals who had been condemned through judicial processes) which allowed them to "return to the country, form political parties, stand for election, recover confiscated property, and even receive gifts of land from the Ministry of Agriculture."[97] In spite of all this, the United States declined to enter negotiations, making a ritual display of anxiety and pessimism about the prospects of verification by way of justification. And just for good measure it denied the Nicaraguan interior minister a visa when he attempted to enter the United States in order to discuss the possibility of a reconciliation between the two countries.[98]

Nicaragua's various proposals have followed the outlines of those which have periodically been made by the countries of the Contadora group (Colombia, Mexico, Panama, and Venezuela.). While the United States has officially endorsed the efforts of the Contadora group, its behavior has hardly been what could be called supportive. In July 1983 the Contadora group put forward a number of detailed proposals which were welcomed by both Nicaragua and Cuba. The United States acknowledged them but then immediately dispatched naval task forces to patrol the waters off Nicaragua's Caribbean and Pacific coasts, thereby considerably heightening international tensions.[99] That may have been coincidental, but Mexican Foreign Minister Bernardo Sepúlveda Amor has since stated that the timing of certain acts by the contras, such as the "shelling of the City of Managua, the attack on Puerto Corinto, the attack on Puerto Sandino, [and] border incidents," had convinced the Contadora group "that there is a connection between our meetings and the desire to disrupt them with actions of this sort."[100]

In the autumn of 1984 the Contadora countries presented a draft treaty which called for the prohibition on the introduction of new weapons systems into the region, and an end to arms supplies to "persons, organizations, irregular forces, or armed bands who want to destabilize governments," the removal of foreign advisers from the region, and talks on the reduction of present arsenals.[101] To the administration's chagrin, Western European countries supported the plan and Nicaragua immediately announced that it was ready to sign the treaty. With evident embarrassment the United States rejected the treaty, attempting to save face by having its allies in the region reject it as well. Around the same time a secret National Security Council briefing paper was revealed in which the administration congratulated itself for having "effectively blocked" the Contadora process: "We have trumped the latest Nicaraguan/Mexican efforts to rush signature of an unsatisfactory Contadora agreement."[102]

The reason for the administration's behavior is of course that it is simply not interested in dialogue or mutual accommodation—though of course it had to pretend to be, and therefore it had to blame the absence of negotiations on the Sandinistas. Hence the claim of Thomas Enders, the former assistant secretary of state for inter-American affairs, that the Sandinistas have a "contempt for real negotiations," and Reagan's equally unsubstantiated assertion that they have "rejected our repeated peace efforts."[103] These "repeated peace efforts" consist of a couple of occasions on which the administration has simply stated a number of outrageous demands as conditions for calling off the contras. The first such set of demands was presented to Arturo José Cruz, then Nicaragua's ambassador to Washington, in December 1981. The United States demanded that Nicaragua freeze the acquisition of heavy weapons ("armed or unarmed helicopters and planes, armored personnel carriers, howitzers, and armed vehicles"), recrate and return all types of weapons not possessed by other countries in the region to the countries from which they were acquired, and reduce its army to between 15,000 and 17,000 soldiers, and eventually to 10,000.[104] (For the sake of comparison, one might note that the Salvadoran army now boasts some 42,000 men, and is rapidly expanding.) Cruz has since commented that "I was flabbergasted by the demands. . . . I told them this sounds like the conditions of a victorious power."[105] The "proposal" was withdrawn at Cruz's request.

In order to pacify public opinion in the United States, the administration agreed in June 1984 to a series of meetings between Harry Shlaudeman, U.S. special envoy to Central America, and Victor Hugo Tinoco, Nicaragua's deputy foreign minister. The administration's position in the talks is a development from its earlier "peace efforts." The United States is now demanding that the Sandinistas completely "sever" their ties with Cuba and the Soviet bloc, cut their armed forces "down to size," terminate all forms of support for the Salvadoran rebels, and "keep their promise and restore democratic rule" (a reference, presumably, to the happy days when democracy flourished under the Somozas).[106] According to

Nicaragua's new president, Daniel Ortega Saavedra, it is unclear what the United States is offering by way of reciprocation.[107] State Department officials assert that reciprocal U.S. actions would be roughly equivalent, but it is difficult to imagine that the United States would agree to sever ties with NATO and other allies, significantly reduce the size of its armed forces, stop its support for various rebel groups around the world (for example, in Afghanistan, Libya, and Iran), and completely overhaul its domestic political system. The talks, needless to say, are getting nowhere.

The administration's continued insistence on these various impossible conditions is completely unsurprising. As we noted earlier, mutual accommodation is the last thing the administration wants. It will not be content until the Sandinistas have been disposed of and Nicaragua has returned entirely to the fold, renouncing its ideological heresies and abandoning both its experiments with alternative modes of economic organization and its flirtations with Cuba and the Soviet Union. For the Nicaraguan revolution represents a direct challenge to the United States, its values, and its system of global control. To the administration, moreover, the revolution constitutes a continuing gesture of defiance, an insolent assertion of a tiny nation's sovereignty within a U.S. sphere of influence. Augusto César Sandino, the spiritual father of the revolution, is remembered for his efforts earlier this century to rid his country of the U.S. Marines. The appeal to his memory is *intended* to rub the nose of the United States in its ugly imperial past—which, incidentally, goes some way to explaining why even liberals in the United States have been so hostile to the Sandinistas: for their revolution is a standing rebuke to an aspect of the United States and its past of which liberals would prefer not to be reminded.

Once it is recognized that the United States is aiming for the overthrow of the Sandinistas and will settle for nothing less, its various acts of provocation and harassment become readily comprehensible. For example, the contras' repeated attacks have created a state of seige which in turn has given the Sandinistas a reason (most Americans would say an excuse) to enact repressive measures and to tighten their grip on the media, the churches, the free trade unions, and on the population generally. It is not that the administration has made a tactical mistake here, thinking that increasing the pressure on the Sandinistas will cause them to abandon their repressive policies when in fact it is having the reverse effect. Rather, it is one of the administration's primary aims in backing the contras to provoke the Sandinistas to become increasingly repressive, intolerant, and dictatorial. For the farther the Sandinistas go in that direction, the more the citizens, and especially the "moderates" and the middle classes, will become angry and alienated, and the more the internal opposition to the Sandinistas will grow—or so, at least, the administration reasons. There is some evidence which suggests that this strategy has to some extent backfired. Not only have the mass of people in Nicaragua seemed willing to endure (though not without some grumbling) the harsher policies implemented by the Sandinistas as long as these policies are seen to be necessary in defending the country from U.S. imperial aggression, but they also seem to have rallied behind the Sandinistas in order to present a united front to what they rightly perceive as an external enemy. Hence the complaint of the *New York Times* and others that the administration's support for the contras has actually served to bolster the position of the Sandinistas.

This understanding of the administration's aims sheds an interesting light on Jeane Kirkpatrick's many righteous denunciations of the Sandinistas' abuses. For her rhetorical performances become less than edifying when we realize that the policy of the government she serves is precisely to provoke those abuses. It is also interesting to note at this point some comments of Kirkpatrick on the supposed strategy of the guerrillas in El Salvador:

> The essence of their strategy is provocation: through persistent attacks which disrupt society and make ordinary life impossible, such revolutionaries challenge authority and force repressive countermeasures in the expectation that such repression will alienate parts of the population, polarize the society, undermine the legitimacy of the regime, and create the "objective" conditions needed to bring themselves to power.[108]

One could scarcely hope for a better description of the strategy behind the administration's support for the contras. It is worth remarking, moreover, that, while it makes sense to attribute this strategy to the United States, it does not make sense to attribute it to the guerrillas in El Salvador. Why should they want to provoke further repression? The mutilated corpses that are part of the landscape in El Salvador are there for everyone to see, and have been for many years. Indeed, repression in El Salvador predates the revolution, and was one of its causes. Furthermore, as we noted earlier, any repression which the guerrillas might provoke would be directed against members of their own class, perhaps their own families or friends. By contrast, neither Kirkpatrick nor anyone else in the administration has any personal reason to fear intensified repression in Nicaragua. (The contras might, but that is another matter: for it is the United States that is calling the shots.)

In another speech, Kirkpatrick responded to accusations by the Sandinistas that the United States was intervening illegitimately throughout Central America by arguing that "these charges—as extravagant as they are baseless—are an interesting example of projection, a psychological operation in which one's own feelings and intentions are simultaneously denied and attributed—that is projected—to someone else."[109] What seems clear, however, is that if anyone is guilty of projection, she is. If one could suppose that she really believes her own claims about the Salvadoran guerrillas, then her remarks would constitute a textbook case of the phenomenon she describes. Moreover, in then accusing the Sandinistas of projection, she would be guilty of what might be called "second-order projection": projecting onto someone else one's own tendency to engage in projection. These are amusing speculations, but it is doubtful that Kirkpatrick is really a victim of projection. What is more likely is that her remarks about the Salvadoran guerrillas, as well as her claim about the Sandinistas, are but further instances of the tendency among members of this administration to say whatever seems expedient, without regard for truth.

The aim of provoking repression in Nicaragua is only one of the administration's aims in backing the contras. One of the most important functions of the contras is to contribute to the strategy of economic warfare by conducting acts of economic sabotage. Among their most notable achievements, for example, were their attacks in the autumn of 1983 on three oil installations which left Nicaragua facing the prospect of being entirely without oil. In the first of these three ventures FDN speedboats blew up two fuel storage tanks at the Caribbean port of Benjamin Zeledón. Ten days later the contras attacked a fuel storage depot at the port of Corinto, causing more than 3.2 million gallons of gasoline and other liquid fuels to be consumed in flames while the town of 25,000 people was evacuated.[110] Three days later the FDN also inflicted severe damage on an oil pipeline at Puerto Sandino. These attacks were the three most significant of five different attacks the contras carried out against Nicaragua's oil installations in a space of less than two months. All three were planned by the CIA, and CIA commandos appear to have taken part at least in the Corinto attack.[111] Several months before the attack on Corinto, Honduran aircraft had overflown the port, "apparently," the London *Guardian* reported at the time, "to photograph the port installations."[112] After the attack, the Esso Oil Company announced that it would no longer permit its tankers to transport oil from Mexico to Nicaragua, thereby increasing the pressure on the already beleaguered Sandinistas. It was clear that the alleged danger to Esso's tankers was an excuse rather than a reason, since the U.S. government would never allow its proxies to attack the assets of so important a U.S. company.

In addition to the more spectacular raids on Nicaragua's port facilities, the contras have conducted numerous attacks on state farms and peasant cooperatives backed by the state. Grain silos, farm machinery, and irrigation projects have been particular targets, though roads, bridges, and other parts of the rural transportation network have also been destroyed. These attacks have been intended not only to reduce Nicaragua's agricultural exports, but also to deplete its domestic food supply.

The mining of Nicaragua's ports was also an integral part of the campaign of economic sabotage. It was intended to close Nicaragua's major ports, making it impossible for the Sandinistas to receive oil and other vital imports or to ship out export commodities on which Nicaragua's economy depends. According to the London *Guardian,* the mining was timed "to coincide with the height of the harvest in coffee, cotton, and sugar, which between them represent well over half the country's dollar export earnings. Corinto has no facilities for storing large quantities of these commodities."[113]

In addition to damaging the Nicaraguan economy directly through the destruction of economically important facilities, the contras' attacks have also had indirect economic effects. Of primary importance is the fact that the threat from the contras, in conjunction with the pressure stemming from the revival of Condeca and the joint American-Honduran military exercises on Nicaragua's border, has forced the Sandinistas to divert resources from development to defense. At present at least half the government's budget is being devoted to the military. This not only greatly weakens the Nicaraguan economy, but it has the additional advantage of allowing the administration to point to the strengthening of Nicaragua's defenses as evidence of the Sandinistas' aggressive designs on their neighbors. The various military pressures which the United States has applied have also led the Sandinistas to establish a network of civilian militias, which, in conjunction with the fact that a great many young people have been killed, has caused an acute labor shortage in the country. Thus nearly 40 percent of Nicaragua's coffee crop was expected to go to waste in 1984 for lack of anyone to harvest it—another triumph of Reagan's declared policy of providing "the people of that region a more free and prosperous future."[114]

As we noted in the first chapter, the activities of the CIA and the contras have been but one element in the administration's overall strategy of economic warfare. During its first year in office the

Reagan administration terminated all economic aid to Nicaragua and even stopped payments on loans that had previously been approved. This, in conjunction with an embargo on wheat exports, produced breadlines in Nicaraguan cities.[115] Later the administration reduced imports of Nicaraguan sugar by 90 percent, depriving the Sandinistas of about $15 million annually in foreign exchange. More importantly, U.S. pressure on such institutions as the World Bank, the Inter-American Development Bank, and the International Monetary Fund has successfully blocked loans that were crucial to the goal of postwar reconstruction.[116] (U.S. efforts to have Nicaragua excluded from European Economic Community [EEC] aid packages to Central America have been less successful.)

What is perhaps most extraordinary is that this fierce and multifaceted assault on the Nicaraguan economy often goes unmentioned when Nicaragua's economic woes are discussed in the United States. The problems are instead attributed entirely to economic mismanagement by the Sandinistas (of which there has also been plenty).[117]

The administration's strategy of economic warfare has two basic aims. In part it is intended, like the efforts to provoke repression, to increase popular disaffection with the Sandinistas, especially among the middle class. For the past few years, popular discontent in Nicaragua has been primarily focused, not on such abuses as censorship of the press or the harassment of antirevolutionary clergy, but on economic privations, including the rationing of gasoline, sugar, and flour. Thus, unlike the efforts to provoke repression, which, as we remarked earlier, are generally perceived as the work of a foreign hand, the administration's subtler economic pressures have enjoyed some measure of success.

As we noted in Chapter 1, the administration's other aim in its efforts to cripple the Nicaraguan economy is to ensure that the case of Nicaragua does not present an attractive example which other countries might be tempted to follow. With regard to El Salvador, Secretary of State Shultz has argued that "the existence of this guerrilla activity makes it difficult for economic development to take place, and it's obviously one of the reasons why you want to stop it."[118] In Nicaragua, however, that is one of the reasons why you want to promote it. If the Sandinistas were to succeed in promoting economic development where Somoza and other U.S. clients in the region have failed, that would encourage aspirations among people in other countries under U.S. domination to break free and instead follow an alternative path similar to that which Nicaragua has followed. The result would be the gradual erosion of the system of control which guarantees the United States its disproportionate share of the world's wealth. (This, incidentally, is the real "domino effect" feared in American elite circles. The caricature involving the Reds landing on Long Beach which Reagan has served up to the public is probably believed, in government circles, only by him.)

Nicaragua's economic development programs must therefore not be allowed to succeed. Obviously it is best if it can be made to appear that the Nicaraguan economy has collapsed because of the inherent defects in the Sandinistas' policies, but, failing that, it will suffice if the message that other countries get is that departures from the U.S.-dominated economic system will not be tolerated. The administration's strategy in Nicaragua is therefore similar to its strategy of "bleeding Vietnam," as well as to the strategy which, until public pressure recently intervened, it followed in Ethiopia. Officials of various international relief agencies, including the Reverent Dr. Charles Elliott of Christian Aid, have argued that the United States deliberately withheld food aid from Ethiopia in the hope that a disastrous famine would bring down the country's Marxist government—just as the famine in 1972–74 had brought down the Emperor Haile Selassie.[119]

Recognition of the administration's real purposes in Nicaragua also sheds considerable light on the Big Pine exercises and their successors in Honduras. In addition to fulfilling the general function of harassing and intimidating the Sandinistas, the Big Pine maneuvers were also designed both to serve as a shield for the contras and to provide an excuse for shipping arms into the region which could then be either distributed directly to the contras or left behind for them after the exercises were completed.[120] As we noted in Chapter 4, the exercises have also allowed the United States to establish a permanent military presence in the area through the construction of bases and other facilities in Honduras. Most importantly, however, the exercises have allowed the United States to be on hand for direct intervention in Nicaragua in the event a suitable occasion presents itself (an occasion that could be provided by the very presence of U.S. troops, in an incident analogous to the blowing up of the *Maine* or the attack on the U.S. destroyer in the Gulf of Tonkin). As one State Department official stated at the beginning of Big Pine II: "We wanted to persuade the bad guys in Nicaragua and Cuba that we are positioned to blockade, invade, interdict if they cross a particular threshold."[121] The London *Guardian*'s Washington correspondent comments that "the threshold is seen as the invasion of a pro-US country such as Honduras or [El Salvador]."[122] Some observers have in fact speculated that the administration's primary aim in backing the contras has been precisely to provoke the Sandinistas to violate Honduras' border. Thus Robert White, formerly Carter's ambassador to El Salvador, has argued that "the invasion [of Nicaragua by the contras] was part of a systematic plan to provoke the Sandinists to cross the Honduran border and attack the counter-revolutionaries' base camps. Honduran troops were poised to repel the invaders and enter Nicaragua in hot pursuit—creating a border war."[123] He might have added that as a result of the Big Pine exercises, the United States has also been poised to intervene on the side of Honduras, and to assist the Hondurans in the exercise of their right of self-defense by helping them to overthrow the Sandinistas.

Since Reagan's reelection the threat of a U.S. invasion of Nicaragua has become very real. A number of ominous indications point in that direction. The seemingly endless series of army exercises in Central America and naval maneuvers in the Caribbean is continuing. An American senator who has recently visited U.S. installations in Honduras claims that the new maneuvers "could go on as long as five years."[124] So the United States will continue indefinitely to be poised for intervention. Moreover, the Council on Hemispheric Affairs claims to have gained access through a source within the administration to contingency plans for an invasion of Nicaragua. The strategy for intervention follows very closely the pattern which critics have been suggesting the administration might adopt. The operation, code-named "Pegasus," would begin with an attack by the contras. Then, according to a report in the London *Guardian:*

> Once Nicaragua reacted, perhaps by attacking Honduran border positions, the US would have a legal pretext to move against the Sandinistas. . . . At that point, the Central American Defense Council (Condeca) would appeal for US intervention claiming that Honduras was under attack. . . . Pegasus called for US navy and air attacks on Nicaragua, but no American troops would be sent to the country to avoid a protracted war that might arouse public discontent.[125]

Thus an invasion is clearly under active consideration. As one administration official put it, "The day may come when we will be asked to help a country under the Río Treaty and to come in with military force."[126]

On the other hand, there is considerable opposition in the United States to an invasion of Nicaragua. Opinion polls show that the public is still reluctant to commit U.S. forces to Central America. For this very reason the Pentagon has also resisted the idea of an invasion. Recognizing that an invasion of Nicaragua, unlike the invasion of Grenada, would be an extremely costly venture, the Pentagon rightly fears that its inevitable unpopularity would damage the reputation of the military, thereby jeopardizing public support for its continuing arms buildup. Finally, even the Congress has come to have doubts about the viability of a military solution in Nicaragua. Recently it gave concrete expression to these doubts by voting to suspend assistance to the contras, who are now living off the fruits of previous congressional munificence, aid from private American sources coordinated by the Pentagon, and official and private aid from U.S. clients in Israel, Taiwan, Guatemala, and El Salvador.[127] (Except for the administration, the contras—or at least the FDN—seem to be the only group with any real enthusiasm for an invasion. Edgar Chamorro, until recently one of the leaders of the FDN, says he would be "very glad for direct intervention. I want to get the Americans involved. . . . Americans bring many things. Hershey candy bars, 3.2 beer. They bring good things to life. I think we could become a state, like Hawaii."[128])

Resistance in high circles to the administration's policies in Nicaragua is normally based on political calculation rather than moral principle. Thus Stansfield Turner, who was director of the CIA under Carter, has argued against supporting the contras on the ground that

> we are not likely to get away with toppling the Nicaraguan government by covert means. Even if we do, the other costs to us will be high. We are widely seen as sponsoring the return to Nicaragua of the supporters of the dictator Anastasio Somoza. This can only reduce our standing in the countries in this region where we have truly important interests: Mexico, Panama, Venezuela, and Brazil. Another cost that is very apparent in this case is the risk of the CIA being accused of improper performance.[129]

The implication here is of course that overthrowing the Sandinistas would be perfectly acceptable if the United States could get away with it. Turner's objections are based entirely on a concern for U.S. interests. He is worried about potential perceptions and accusations if the United States were to overthrow the Sandinistas; but questions about the substance or truth of these perceptions and accusations simply do not arise. (Compare the *New Republic*'s objections to the mining of Nicaraguan harbors: "The operations risked discovery, risked accusations that the United States was violating international law, risked arousing the indignation of countries whose shipping might be damaged."[130] Again, if the United States could have got away with it with its image untarnished, the mining would have been unobjectionable.) "What is required," Turner writes, "is a careful judgment as to when *our national interests* are so likely to be damaged that we should consider destabilizing a foreign government, taking into account whether a successor government would likely be better *from our point of view*."[131] Nicaragua, he concludes, fails this test.

Even though Turner's objections to the administration's policies occur within what would seem to be an acceptable framework for discussion, since they do not challenge the desirability of turning out the Sandinistas or the right of the United States to do so, they nevertheless fall within Henry Kissinger's category of dangerous and subversive views. When Kissinger was selected to chair Reagan's special Commission on Central America, he effectively defined the commission's function in terms of stifling or suppressing all meaningful debate on the issues. According to a report in the London *Guardian*, "Dr. Kissinger said that strident opposition to Vietnam policy was responsible for the US's failure. His aim was to create a national consensus to avoid a similar outcome in Central America. 'We weakened ourselves unbelievable by the Vietnam debate,' Dr. Kissinger said."[132] Turner's objections to U.S. intervention in Nicaragua have exactly the same form as the mainstream liberal objections to the war in Vietnam: "Success is not possible within the margins of acceptable cost." Views such as his are therefore precisely the ones which it is most important for Kissinger to suppress. If the United States allows itself to think out loud about what it is doing, it will lose credibility, and weaken itself unbelievable.

Objections like Turner's are the ones which it is most important to suppress because they are the ones most likely to be attended to and taken seriously by persons in positions of power. It is therefore good that these objections are pressed, even though they entirely miss the point, which is that the United States simply has no right to intervene in Nicaragua to remove the Sandinistas. The many and varied acts of subversion, sabotage, terrorism, and intimidation by the United States add up to nothing less than blatant, unprovoked aggression. Were it being done by the Soviet Union, this crude bullying of a tiny neighbor would be instantly recognizable for what it is, and Americans of every political stripe would be justifiably outraged. But, far from being indignant that this administration daily violates every principle the United States claims to cherish, Americans have instead joyously returned it to power.

★7★

Some Notable Victims: (3) Grenada

The U.S. invasion of Grenada differs in at least one important respect from the interventions in El Salvador and Nicaragua, in that the majority of Grenadians seemed to welcome the intervention when it occurred. It is not obvious, however, how much that tells us about the justifiability of the U.S. action. In this chapter we shall examine the circumstances of the invasion and the reasons behind it, in order to determine how it fits in with the administration's overall foreign policy, and in order to judge whether the invasion was justified. The chapter will follow the by now tedious but nevertheless unavoidable pattern of previous chapters in attempting first to cut through the thicket of official distortions in order to uncover the reality concealed beneath the propaganda.

The basic outlines of the story of the invasion are by now familiar. Internecine strife had broken out within the four-and-a-half-year-old People's Revolutionary Government (PRG) in Grenada. On October 14, 1983, the prime minister, Maurice Bishop, was interned by opponents within the regime led by his deputy, Bernard Coard, and General Hudson Austin, commander of the People's Revolutionary Army. Five days later Bishop and several of his ministers were executed, and a new Revolutionary Military Council (RMC) was established in place of the PRG. The new military government immediately imposed a four-day, twenty-four-hour curfew on the island, announcing that violators would be shot on sight. On October 22 the Pentagon revealed that a naval task force, consisting of two aircraft carriers and ten warships carrying around 1,900 marines, had been diverted from its course for Lebanon and was now heading for Grenada. The ostensible purposes were to deliver a dramatic warning to General Austin that the administration was "concerned for the safety of U.S. citizens" on the island, and to have forces on hand to evacuate those citizens if the necessity arose. At that time there were roughly 1,000 Americans in Grenada, including 800 medical students at St. George's University Medical School. On October 25, accompanied by 300 troops drawn from six Caribbean countries, U.S. forces invaded Grenada. Though reinforcements had to be brought in, the invading forces shortly overcame the resistance from members of the Grenadian army and from Cuban construction workers who had been involved in building an airport at Point Salines. The leaders of the coup against Bishop were arrested, and an interim government was established under the supervision of the British Commonwealth's Governor-General, Sir Paul Scoon.

That is but the briefest sketch. Details of the story will emerge as we examine the administration's various justifications for its action. Four justifications were offered. It was claimed (1) that the action was necessary to protect innocent people, and in particular the American citizens on the island, from the violence of the new military regime; (2) that it was also intended to "restore order and democracy" in Grenada; (3) that the United States was responding to a legitimate request for intervention from members of the Organization of Eastern Caribbean States (OECS); and (4) that the invasion rescued Grenada from the clutches of Cuba and the Soviet Union and thus prevented it from becoming "a major military bastion to export terror and undermine democracy."[1] Let us examine each of these claims in turn.

At a press conference announcing the invasion, Reagan asserted that the aim which was "of overriding importance" was "to protect innocent lives, including up to 1,000 Americans whose personal safety is, of course, my paramount concern."[2] Later, in Orwellian fashion, Reagan insisted that the invasion be referred to as a "rescue mission." But "Operation Urgent Fury" (the Pentagon's code name for the invasion) was a rescue mission in the same sense that Israel's "Operation Peace in Galilee," which involved bombarding, blockading, and occupying Beirut, was just an attempt to ensure the security of Israel's northern border region. Just as the protection of Israel's northern border area did not require the occupation of Beirut, so a simple rescue mission in Grenada would not have required the overthrow of the government, the occupation of the island, the expulsion of Cuban workers, and so on. While ensuring the safety of the Americans in Grenada was one aim of the invasion, it was by no means the *sole* aim. And, even if we grant that protecting the Americans in Grenada was one aim of the invasion, it clearly does not follow that that aim *justifies* the invasion. In fact there are decisive reasons why that aim does not provide even a partial justification for the invasion.

On Sunday, October 23, two days before the invasion, both a British diplomat and two American diplomats visited Grenada, and plans were made with the RMC for the orderly evacuation of those on the island who wanted to leave.[3] Returning home, the U.S. diplomats reported that in general the students did not wish to leave or be evacuated. One of the diplomats stated that "we have not recommended that they leave."[4] Also on Sunday the parents of more than 500 of the students met in New York where they received assurances both from their children and from the rulers in Grenada that their children were in no danger. They then sent a telegram to Reagan in which they passed on these assurances and urged him "not to move too quickly or to take any precipitous or provocative actions at this time."[5] That the students were not in danger was also the view of the medical school's chancellor and his deputy, the latter of whom was on the island at the time.[6]

On Monday, October 24, the day before the invasion, the curfew was lifted, people began to return to work, and classes resumed at the medical school. A member of the RMC visited the medical school where, according to an American student there, "he talked to us to reassure us of our safety. He said basically it was an internal conflict and, above all, the nation wanted to stay independent and we were not involved in the conflict."[7] The RMC also sent a note to the American Embassy in Barbados (there being, at the time, no American Embassy in Grenada) saying that the Americans on the island were in no danger and would be allowed to leave if they wished to go.[8] (Earlier, on October 22, Cuba had sent a message to the U.S. government saying that it was ready to cooperate with the United States in ensuring the safety of the Americans. This communication was not even acknowledged until after the invasion had begun.) In Britain, the foreign secretary, Sir Geoffrey Howe, told the House of Commons that foreigners in Grenada were not at risk, and that the RMC had given assurances that those who wished to leave were free to do so.

In accordance with its pledges to the U.S. and British governments, the RMC had reopened Grenada's airport on the morning of the twenty-fourth. Four chartered planes left the island with the small number of American medical students who wished to leave on board.[9] Nevertheless, at a press conference on the morning of the invasion, Reagan asserted that "several hundred" Americans had wanted to leave, "but the airports [*sic*] were closed. There was no way of leaving." Later *Newsweek* amplified the president's claim, stating that no Americans "had been allowed to leave since the coup."[10]

It is true that commercial flights from the island were obstructed, and that, as a consequence, some British and Canadian citizens who sought to leave the island were unable to do so. The obstacle, however, came not from the RMC but from the United States and its Caribbean allies. Ostensibly to "isolate" Grenada, the U.S. Caribbean allies banned the regional airline, LIAT, from landing in Grenada. The countries which imposed the ban were then collaborating closely with the United States in planning the invasion, and it seems clear in retrospect that the orderly evacuation of those who wanted to leave was deliberately obstructed in order to enable the United States to present its invasion as a "rescue mission."[11]

What these various facts clearly show is that there was no immediate danger to the Americans on the island, and that the administration was well aware of it. Moreover, even if the administration believed that there were *potential* dangers on the island, there were clearly various possibilities for the peaceful evacuation of American citizens. Yet none of these possibilities was tried, nor, apparently, even seriously considered.[12] Rather, the option of peaceful evacuation was *deliberately avoided.*

While the Americans were in no immediate danger prior to the invasion, it seems undeniable that they were endangered by the violence of the invasion. Even if there was no danger of their being taken hostage during the fighting, there was no guarantee that they could be shielded from the effects of the fighting itself. Being in the midst of armed conflict is never very safe. A U.S. congressman who later visited the island notes that "the advancing Marines did not secure the 255 students at the Grand Anse Medical School campus until after nearly two days of fierce fighting," and adds that "this fact sheds light on both the intent of the military operation and the unlikelihood of the students being taken hostage."[13] It also reminds us that the students were in a highly vulnerable and dangerous position for a considerable period. A Reuter dispatch published on November 1 reported that

> six Canadian aid workers just back from Grenada said in Ottowa yesterday that the US and Caribbean States invasion of the island led to disintegration of law and order and looting. Barbara Thomas, spokesman [*sic*] for the six flown home yesterday, said: "Our lives only became endangered . . . when the marines began landing in Grenada and when it became impossible for us to leave the island."[14]

The various facts cited above seem to confirm the Canadians' view that the danger they and other foreigners faced was largely the creation of the invasion.

Despite the complete lack of evidence that the safety of the students was threatened, the American public by and large accepted that Reagan's invasion had been a "rescue mission." They were helped in forming this perception by scenes shown on television in which students emotionally kissed the ground upon returning to the United States. *Time* capitalized on these scenes, arguing that they "testified to the dominant feeling among [the students] that the President's action had been justified"—the intended implication being that what the students believed must be true.[15] But the students' relief at being home in safety did not necessarily indicate a belief that the invasion was justified. In the case of many of the students their relief at being home was probably the result not so much of the fear they experienced *before* the invasion as that which they experienced *during* it. And, in any case, given their emotional condition and their presumed inability at the time to understand the larger implications of the U.S. action, the students were certainly not the best judges of whether the invasion was justified, or even of whether it was necessary to ensure their safety.

In summary, what the evidence suggests is that, since the Americans on the island were in no immediate danger, and since in any case there were options for a peaceful evacuation, and, finally, since it was the invasion itself which brought the Americans into immediate danger, the invasion cannot possibly be justified—even partially—in terms of the need to protect American lives. On the contrary, while Reagan was clearly concerned with the safety of the American citizens (at least in part for obvious political reasons), he knowingly put those citizens at *greater* risk in order to achieve other aims. He was, in short, gambling with American lives, exploiting the alleged threat to those lives as a pretext for an invasion which he hoped (with some justification, as it turned out) would provide a number of benefits, and also result in the safe evacuation of Americans.

It is important to note that, while the primary aim of the invasion, according to Reagan, was "to protect innocent lives," the invasion itself cost many people their lives. The fact that many of them had on uniforms, and were thus in some technical sense not innocent, hardly reduces the scope of the tragedy. The official U.S. estimate is that 18 Americans were killed and 116 wounded. The Cubans say that 24 Cubans and 16 Grenadians were killed, while 57 Cubans and 280 Grenadians were injured. In the end the State Department claimed that 45 Grenadians were killed and 337 were wounded. The actual figures are probably higher than either of these estimates.[16] For some time the United States refused to give casualty figures, and the same anxiety about domestic opinion that led to the initial suppression of this information may later have led officials to give doctored estimates—especially of the Grenadian casualties, where figures would be difficult to check. The U.S. officer who directed the invasion estimated that 160 Grenadian soldiers had been killed.[17] Certainly the Cuban figure of 16 Grenadians killed is too low, since almost twice that many were killed when U.S. planes by mistake bombed the Grenadian mental hospital. Later Grenadian and British witnesses of the invasion claimed that perhaps as many as 1,000 Grenadian civilians had been killed. The Grenadian high commissioner has stated that information he has received suggests that approximately 1,500 Grenadians were killed.[18] These latter estimates are almost certainly inflated, but the total number of casualties was clearly well in excess of 500.

By the standards of other recent slaughters (whether unilateral, as in the case of Israel's invasion of Lebanon, or mutual, as in the case of the war between Iran and Iraq), the affair in Grenada was comparatively tame. (In *relative* terms, the number of people killed when the Soviets shot down the Korean airliner is also rather small.) That should not, however, be allowed to obscure the significance of the absolute numbers. As we have seen, there is little reason to think that anywhere near this many people, or any people at all, would have been killed or injured had the invasion not taken place.

The administration's second justification for the invasion was that it was intended to restore order and "to help in the restoration of democratic institutions in Grenada."[19] Several points are relevant here. One is that "order" was already being restored by the RMC, which had announced that there would be a return to civilian government within twelve days, and which was already consulting prominent Grenadian citizens about the possibility of their joining the government.[20] A more important point is that, if the alleged aim of "exporting democracy" can justify the invasion of Grenada, then it could presumably justify the invasion of a fair number of other countries as well—including, significantly, Nicaragua. It seems uncontroversial, however, that the aim of restoring or creating democracy cannot by itself justify the invasion of a sovereign state. This becomes obvious in the case of Grenada once we understand what Reagan means by "democracy." When he spoke of "restoring" democracy, he meant to suggest that the former regime of Sir Eric Gairy, which Maurice Bishop's New Jewel Movement overthrew in 1979, had been democratic. (Reagan had earlier claimed that the revolution which ousted Gairy involved "the overturn of Westminster parliamentary democracy in Grenada."[21]) Judging from the other third world regimes which have evoked Reagan's admiration, the Gairy government was indeed a model of Reagan's favored form of democracy: it was corrupt, venal, ruthless, and conservative. As one commentator has put it, "As prime minister, Gairy transformed a nominal parliamentary democracy into a brutal dictatorship: he organized a secret police, rigged elections, seized opponents' properties, squandered public funds, and imprisoned, tortured, and murdered political adversaries."[22] Familiarity with the character of the Gairy regime may provide some insight into the nature of the democracy Reagan aimed to restore.

As we remarked in Chapter 1, the administration's justifications for its interventions normally appeal to a blend of moral and self-interested concerns. Certainly both types of concern were addressed in public pronouncements about Grenada. Thus Reagan proclaimed that "we are not somewhere else in the world protecting someone else's interests. We are there protecting our own."[23] It is not altogether clear, however, how Reagan proposed to reconcile this statement with his claim that the invasion was intended to restore democracy.

Democratic values were not always conspicuous in the way the invasion and occupation were conducted. For example, while a free press is vital to the functioning of democratic institutions—since without it the citizens cannot make well-informed judgments and choices—the press was excluded from the island during the invasion, and restrictions on coverage of the invasion were imposed. Reporters who sneaked onto the island were promptly removed. Others who attempted to reach the island were turned back by force or intimidation.[24] As one commentator has noted:

> By keeping the press off the island during the critical first few days of the invasion, the administration was able to insure that the right images of Grenada would take shape in the public consciousness. "If you get the news people into this you lose support of public opinion" is how one White House official relayed the views of top military brass, including the chair of the Joint Chiefs of Staff.[25]

The exclusion of the press (which seems to have been inspired in part by Britain's successful control of the media during the Falklands/Malvinas war) enabled the administration to suppress casualty figures, to play down the size of the invasion force, to inflate the number of Cubans on the island and distort their status, and, most important of all, to prevent images of violence from entering people's living rooms and influencing their reactions to the invasion. It is perhaps ironic that, while the invasion was in progress, the information that Cuban citizens were being presented by their state-controlled media was far more accurate than the carefully prepared stories and images Americans were receiving from their government through the shackled free press.[26]

While the administration initially based its exclusion of the press from the island on a pretense of concern about the safety of reporters, George Shultz later implied that the reason was that reporters were no longer on "our side." Shultz's remark was then elucidated by Reagan, who argued that "certainly" during the Vietnam war the media were not on "our side, militarily."[27] Implicit in these remarks is the idea that, in times of conflict, the role of the media is simply to contribute to the war effort. If the media cannot be trusted to fulfill that function, then the people have to be protected from the facts and the arguments by other means: censorship. Otherwise, as in Vietnam, the people are liable to indulge in awkward and unpatriotic controversies, thereby "weakening the U.S. unbelievable." (Of course, these considerations do not apply in the case of Nicaragua, where it is obviously appropriate if the media are not on the side of the Sandinistas.)

The invasion force's treatment of the islanders, and especially those associated with the Bishop government, is another area in which the administration's devotion to democratic values was less than obvious. The island's only newspaper was shut down, public meetings were banned, and around 1,260 Grenadians were detained without warrant. Members of Gairy's "Mongoose Gang," one of the paramilitary groups used to brutalize and intimidate the former regime's opponents, were released from prison in order to assist with roadblocks and house-to-house searches aimed at identifying suspects for interrogation. Many of those detained and interrogated were imprisoned in eight-by-eight-foot wooden packing crates. Among the first to be detained in this manner was Kendrick Radix, Grenada's former minister of justice and one of Bishop's closest allies. He was charged with "sowing discontent and ill will in public places" and, when released, was issued a card which instructed him to "refrain from participating in any anti-government activities." These hardly sound like "operations to restore democracy," to borrow Sir Geoffrey Howe's description of the invasion.[28]

Potential voters in newly democratic Grenada were provided with much useful pre-election information by the U.S. Army's Psychological Operations Unit. Shortly after the occupation began, posters began to appear all over the island. Some showed pictures of prominent members of the group that had killed Bishop, including Coard and Austin. Each photograph had an "X" over it, and a caption underneath it that read: "These criminals attempted to sell Grenada out to the Communists. Now they have surrendered. The Grenadian people will never again allow such characters to assume power and cause such hardship. Support democracy for Grenada."[29] The pictures showed Coard and Austin bound and blindfolded, with Coard wearing nothing but boxer shorts—raising questions about the invasion force's respect for the Geneva Convention.[30] Other posters showed photographs of Cuban arms, accompanied by the question: "Are these the tools that build airports?" Army jeeps roamed the island with loudspeakers urging the Grenadians to "help send the Cubans back to Havana where they belong."[31] A writer in the *New Republic* has commented that "the U.S. troops were assigned the formidable task of establishing democracy where repression had reigned for four years" (that is, under Maurice Bishop—apparently there was no repression during the halcyon years of Sir Eric Gairy's "democratic" rule).[32] With 1984 then imminent, the troops were pursuing their formidable task with admirable efficiency.

As we saw earlier, American citizens were also treated to a bit of Orwellian manipulation. Speaking to reporters, Reagan commented: "Incidentally, I know your frequent use of the word invasion; this was a rescue mission"—forgetting, perhaps, that he too had mistaken the mere rescue mission for an invasion when he first announced it.[33] Later in his talk with reporters he referred to the invasion as "the liberation of Grenada," failing to explain how the "liberation" of an entire country, involving the overthrow of a government and the detention of well over 1,000 persons, could simultaneously be merely a rescue operation.

It seems obvious that the administration's first two rationales for the invasion are not overly impressive. Let us move on to the third. This is that the action was requested by members of the Organization of Eastern Caribbean States. Reagan explained the matter in these terms:

> Last weekend [the weekend before the invasion], I was told that six members of the Organization of Eastern Caribbean States, joined by Jamaica and Barbados, had sent an urgent request that we join them in a military operation to restore order and democracy to Grenada. They were proposing this action under the terms of a treaty, a mutual assistance pact that existed among them. These small, peaceful nations needed our help. The legitimacy of their request, plus my own concern for our citizens, dictated my decision.[34]

Again, however, the facts are rather more complicated. For one thing, it is clear that an invasion was being planned by the United States for some time before the OECS request was received. How far in advance the invasion was planned is unclear. After the invasion had occurred, the assistant secretary of state for inter-American affairs disclosed in congressional testimony that the United States had been planning military action in Grenada for several days before it received the request from the OECS states—that is, about a week before the invasion took place. On the other hand, in an unguarded moment on French television, the American ambassador to France stated that planning began *two weeks* in advance of the invasion. That preparations had been in progress for more than a few days is further attested by the fact that the invading troops brought with them prepared tapes for propaganda broadcasts as well as various printed handbills and posters—materials which must have taken some time to prepare.[35]

There is even evidence which suggests that the invasion was being planned more than a month before it actually took place. One of the regiments which would later parachute onto Point Salines airport in Grenada and fight the Cuban construction workers there spent late September and early October rehearsing just such an operation at a small airport in rural Washington. There the soldiers practiced parachuting onto the runway, clearing it of construction materials, and securing the surrounding area so that transport planes carrying more troops were enabled to land. That the resemblance between these operations and those that eventually took place in Grenada was more than coincidental is suggested by the fact that efforts were made to prevent the practice operations from receiving any publicity.[36]

It has also emerged that the "request" from the OECS was itself requested by the United States. The request was apparently drafted in Washington and then sent by special emissaries to the Caribbean for approval, whereupon it was then returned to the United States with the relevant signatures.[37] This is in fact a well-established U.S. practice. The U.S. military intervention in Greece in 1947 on behalf of the monarchy was "requested" in much the same way. A high official at the State Department summoned the Greek chargé d'affaires to the State Department where the two of them drafted the request for military assistance. The State Department official later stated that the request "had been drafted with a view to the mentality of Congress [which had to approve the request]. . . . It would also serve to protect the U.S. Government against internal and external charges that it was taking the initiative of intervening in a foreign state. . . . The note would also serve as a basis for the cultivation of public opinion which was under study."[38] Eighteen years later, in 1965, when the United States was preparing to invade the Dominican Republic in support of General Wessin y Wessin's forces, a request for intervention was drawn up in the State Department and sent to the general for incorporation in his official appeal for help.[39] In Grenada, as in these earlier cases, it was not (as Reagan claimed) that the request dictated the U.S. decision; rather, it was that the United States dictated the request.

Another problem with this third justification is that the small, peaceful nations who were eager to invade one of their neighbors had no legal right whatsoever to do so or to request U.S. assistance. The treaty to which Reagan refers is the OECS Charter, Article 8 of which restricts the member states' competence in requesting outside intervention to cases involving "external aggression," and furthermore requires that such a request be unanimously agreed by the member states. Neither of these conditions was met in the present case: there was no external aggression against Grenada prior to the invasion, and only five of the eight member states supported the request.

While it is clear that the device of the request was intended to produce the impression that the invasion could be justified under international law, the invasion in fact placed the United States in breach of several treaties to which it is bound by domestic and international law. The invasion violated the U.N. Charter, which prohibits recourse to the use of force except in self-defense, as well as the Río Treaty, which states that "all members shall refrain in their international relations from the threat or use of force against the territorial integrity or political independence of any state or in any other manner inconsistent with the principles of the United Nations." The invasion was also in breach of the charter of the Organization of American States (OAS), which states that "no state or group of states has the right to intervene, directly or indirectly, for any reason whatever, in the internal or external affairs of any other state," and also declares that "the territory of a state is inviolable; it may not be the object, even temporarily, of military occupation or other measures of force taken by another state, directly or indirectly, on any grounds whatever."[40]

The administration's clear violation of various moral and legal principles governing international relations brought forth some plaintive cries from the American media. *Time,* for example, lamented that, "by invading Grenada, the U.S. risks tarnishing the high moral standard, based on respect for national sovereignty and self-determination, that distinguishes its conduct in the world from that of its Soviet adversary."[41] While we need not linger over the patriotic fiction that the United States had suddenly strayed from (or, rather, *risked* straying from) a previous deeply held commitment to nonintervention and self-determination, it was not unreasonable to expect that the administration had at least forfeited the ability to sound off about its lofty commitment to these sublime moral principles. But, as usual, Reagan dismissed the charge of hypocrisy with one of his cute "one-liners": "When we liberated Grenada from Communist thugs, we were being a good friend to our Caribbean neighbors. My opponent [Mondale] said we had eroded our moral authority to criticize the Soviet Union. *I* have never had any problem criticizing the Soviet Union."[42]

It may, however, facilitate understanding of the nature of official pronouncements in the United States if we pause to review some of the administration's righteous declarations from the period before the invasion. As usual, the primary source of the administration's rhetorical flights is Jeane Kirkpatrick. Some of her remarks now appear in an amusing light. For example, on one occasion at the

United Nations, she proclaimed that "the United States doesn't invade small countries on its borders"—obviously alluding to the Soviet invasion of Afghanistan.[43] (Of course, one explanation for the fact she cites might be that the United States does not have any small countries on its borders, but we know what she means. Incidentally, it is interesting in this connection to note that one of the acknowledged concerns of the officials who drafted Reagan's speech announcing the invasion was, as one official put it, "that this does not sound like what Brezhnev said when the Soviet Union went into Afghanistan."[44]) On another occasion she addressed the following remarks to the U.N. Security Council:

> I should like to begin by thanking the various members of the United Nations who have spoken today in support of the principles of national self-determination, national independence, strict respect for territorial integrity, the principles of nonintervention in the affairs of other states. Those are principles which are very dear to my country and which the United States in its foreign affairs does its very best to honor in a serious and consistent fashion. . . . We are profoundly committed to the principles of nonuse of force in international affairs and committed also to following and abiding by the principles of the Charter of the United Nations concerning the use and nonuse of force.[45]

Yet when the United States invaded Grenada in contravention of every principle cited here, she blandly defended the invasion by remarking that the United States had simply provided "support for the Eastern Caribbean forces as they assist the people of Grenada in restoring order and establishing functioning governmental institutions."[46] (The nature of this "support" calls for comment. At the height of the invasion the United States had 6,000 troops on the island as opposed to 300 from the Caribbean states. Even though the Americans outnumbered the Caribbean troops by twenty to one, and even though the United States never allowed the Caribbean troops to take part in the fighting, the U.S. troops were, according to Kirkpatrick, merely providing back-up support.)

It is perhaps worth citing one further example. In an interview which, unfortunately for her, was published five days before the invasion and was on the news stands when the marines hit the beaches, Kirkpatrick asserts that a basic U.S. value is "nonintervention in the internal affairs of others." She takes a firm stand on the view that "self-determination is superior to coercion . . . national sovereignty to foreign hegemony," and accuses the Soviet Union of acting "as if violence were an instrument of first resort in foreign affairs."[47] The contrast between these fine sentiments and the reality of U.S. action shows about how much credence should be given to expressions of the administration's official values.

Returning to our main line of argument, we should note that, when it became apparent that the request from members of the OECS was incapable of providing the aura of legitimacy which it was hoped it would, the United States then began to focus attention on a further invitation which the OECS was supposed to have received from the Governor-General of Grenada, Sir Paul Scoon. (Interestingly, this request was not mentioned in any of the administration's early statements about the invasion.) The circumstances surrounding this further invitation are, however, rather mysterious. Late in October when Sir Paul was first interviewed in Grenada, he claimed that he had sent a request for intervention by the OECS to the Prime Minister of Barbados (which is itself somewhat curious since Barbados is not a member of the OECS) on October 24, the day before the invasion.[48] This claim was, however, rather inconvenient, since according to Reagan's account the United States had by that time already received and accepted the OECS's invitation to conduct a "military operation" against Grenada. The claim is also difficult to reconcile with the fact that, while Sir Paul spoke with Buckingham Palace by telephone on October 22, had a long telephone conversation with the Commonwealth Secretariat on October 23, and met with a British diplomat on October 24, he never once mentioned the need for intervention.[49] When, later in October, Sir Paul was interviewed by the BBC, his story had changed, and he cited October 23 as the day when he had issued his request. This is also the date cited in the State Department's official version of the events.[50] On the other hand, a special adviser to Secretary of State Shultz has insisted that the request was received on October 21—the date which has also been cited by Eugenia Charles, the prime minister of Dominica.[51] To confuse matters even further, the Barbadian prime minister's press officer has told the *New Statesman* that letters dated October 24 and addressed to the various countries participating in the invasion were taken into Grenada by the invasion forces, where they were signed by Sir Paul on October 25, the first day of the invasion.[52] The fact that no document requesting intervention was made public when the invasion was announced lends plausibility to the press officer's claim.

It is not clear what one should make of these confused and conflicting stories. The fact that not even Sir Paul himself has been able to give a clear and consistent account of his request is enough to raise serious suspicions. What does seem clear, however, is that, even if Sir Paul did issue a request for help, that would not justify the U.S. action. First, there are doubts about the governor-general's authority in these matters. He is an official of the British Commonwealth, responsible to Buckingham Palace. He had access to Buckingham Palace but never sought assistance from the Commonwealth, nor authorization to request OECS or U.S. intervention. If he did request OECS or U.S. intervention, then, by bypassing those from whom he derived his powers and to whom he owed responsibility, he exceeded his authority.[53] Second, in the BBC interview referred to earlier, Sir Paul stated that what he had requested was simply "help from the outside," and that an invasion was the "last thing" he wanted.[54] Third, and finally, regardless of which account one chooses to accept of the origin of the request, it remains the case that, as in the case of the OECS request, the United States had already decided to invade before Sir Paul's request had been received. The request, even if genuine, in no way determined the U.S. decision to intervene.

Let us turn now to the last of the administration's four justifications. On the day after the invasion began, the *New York Times* editors wrote:

> If [the new regime in Grenada] was implanted by island hopping Cubans and with Soviet help, its overthrow may be worth the human and political cost. . . . If there were clear evidence of Cuban or Soviet intervention, there would be a case for United States intervention. . . . If President Reagan deserves the benefit of any doubt in Grenada, it is the possibility that Cuba and the Soviet Union had indeed moved, with only modest investments of men and weaponry, to establish a puppet regime that would give them bases for other operations. But if that were clear, why was it not proved, or even asserted?[55]

One can imagine the reaction of administration members, and especially those officials who drafted Reagan's speech announcing the invasion, when they read this. For the first time they completely forgot the standard formula for these occasions: to present U.S. action as a defensive reaction against external communist aggression. The administration moved quickly, however, to repair the omission. Reagan soon appeared on television to tell the American people that the invasion forces had discovered far more Cubans on the island than they had expected, and that the Cubans were not just workers but "were a military force":

> Six hundred have been taken prisoner and we have discovered a complete base with weapons and communications equipment which makes it clear a Cuban occupation of the country had been planned. . . [Grenada] was a Soviet-Cuban colony being readied as a

military bastion to export terror and undermine democracy. We got there just in time.[56]

The administration repeated its earlier charge that the new airport being constructed at Port Salines with Cuban assistance was intended for use by Soviet and Cuban military aircraft. As Reagan had earlier remarked, "The Cubans, with Soviet financing and backing, are in the process of building an airfield with a 10,000-foot runway. Grenada doesn't even have an air force. Who is it intended for?"[57] The administration even suggested that Cuba, and therefore ultimately the Soviet Union, had been behind the power struggle which led to the assassination of Maurice Bishop.[58]

The administration's claims were obediently accepted and repeated by the American media. *Time* reported that

> the administration was able to produce evidence that Grenada was becoming a Soviet-Cuban base that threatened U.S. strategic interests in the Caribbean. . . The Pentagon had expected to find about 500 Cubans on the island, including 350 workers and a small advisory group. Instead, they were facing more than 600 well-armed, professionally trained soldiers.[59]

The editors of the *Washington Post* wrote that "most will agree that events in once-tranquil Grenada would not have come to the point of a bloody coup without a Soviet role."[60] And *New York Times* columnist William Safire seized on and developed the new argument with evident enthusiasm: "The resistance put up by hundreds of Cuban soldiers shows that Grenada was already under the military domination of another country. The island had already been invaded; the US objective, as in Lebanon, is to get foreign forces out and leave."[61]

What are we to make of all this? The first and most important point is that this fourth "justification" is based on evidence which the United States supposedly discovered *after* the invasion had been launched. It could not, therefore, have been a *reason* for the invasion, and thus cannot justify the administration's decision to invade. Even if the claim that the island turned out to be controlled by Soviets and Cubans were true, and even if the United States had the right to expel the Cubans it found there, the most that that would entail is that the invasion had fortunate unforeseen consequences.

The next point to notice is that neither the administration's claims about the Cuban presence on the island nor the inferences it drew from these claims were correct. The administration never explained, for example, why Cuba should need Grenada as a base for "exporting terror." If Castro is anxious to export terror, he already has a base in the Caribbean. It is called Cuba. Nor has the administration been able to explain why Cuban workers and advisers, or even Cuban soldiers, who had been invited by the Bishop government, were not there on a legitimate basis, but were instead to be considered occupying forces which the United States had every right to evict. Does the presence of U.S. soldiers in Britain mean that Britain is the victim of military occupation, and that the Soviet Union has the right to "liberate" Great Britain from foreign occupation?

In order to bolster its claim that Grenada was under foreign domination, the Pentagon initially claimed that it had discovered 1,000 Cubans on the island. Soon the figure was increased to 1,600. Most of these were said to be "well-trained professional soldiers." In the end, however, when a few reporters were finally allowed on the island, the Pentagon had to concede that the figure which Cuba had been citing all along had been correct: there had been 784 Cubans on the island, most of whom were construction workers, doctors, teachers, and so on, and no more than 43 of whom could be classified as "military."[62] (The construction workers had no doubt had some militia training, but that hardly qualifies them as professional soldiers. Almost half of them were over 40 years old.[63])

The nature of the weapons caches which the invasion forces discovered was also exaggerated. As one commentator has noted:

> When journalists finally were permitted to visit the warehouses, they found them partially filled with small infantry arms, a few mortars and anti-aircraft weapons, many of them antiquated, of World War II vintage, and some Soviet made. These weapons are the type best suited for defense against an invasion.[64]

The very fact that Grenada *was* invaded by the United States—something about which Maurce Bishop had warned the Grenadians for years—demonstrates that the Grenadians' expectation that arms might be needed for defensive purposes was amply justified. There is now tremendous irony in the claim Reagan made in March 1983 that "the rapid build-up of Grenada's military potential is unrelated to any conceivable threat to this island country of under 110,000 people."[65] That the United States itself could threaten a tiny island is necessarily inconceivable. Even after the invasion had been completed, the editors of the *New York Times* wrote with unintended humor that "if the arms [the U.S. forces] now are uncrating turn out to be more than Grenadians could ever need, no such evidence was available when they stormed ashore."[66] If the arms which the U.S. forces were then uncrating had been more than the Grenadians could ever need, then the Americans would not have been there uncrating them. The Americans would instead have been massacred as they "stormed ashore."

As for the airport at Port Salines, it should have been perfectly obvious to anyone that it was intended to allow wide-bodied passenger jets to land in Grenada, thereby increasing the tourist trade there. Because increasing the tourist trade was seen as virtually the only way to boost Grenada's economy, even the most conservative businessmen were enthusiastic about the new airport. As one writer has pointed out:

> The case of St. Lucia shows what a new airport can do for an island in the Caribbean. In the early 1970s, when St. Lucia had a small airport, it received about the same number of tourists per year as Grenada—roughly 25,000. St. Lucia built a new airport with a 9,000-foot runway [which, contrary to Reagan's claim, is the length of the runway at Point Salines], and within three years the number of tourist arrivals almost tripled. The number in Grenada remained steady. The PRG projected an increase in arrivals to 40,000 in the first year after opening Point Salines.[67]

In addition to St. Lucia, other small islands in the area which have runways as long as or longer than that being built at Point Salines include Barbados, the Bahamas, Martinique, Guadeloupe, Jamaica, and Antigua—though Reagan never found it necessary to make speeches inquiring as to what or whom their runways were for. Plessey Airports, the British firm which was managing the construction of the new airport, noted that, if it were intended to be a military airport, it would require radar, underground fuel dumps, protected hangars, bomb shelters, and a number of other features, none of which were being incorporated in the facility at Point Salines. Point Salines, Plessey argued, "was being built to purely civilian specification."[68] After the invasion, however, the airport *was* used as a military facility—by the United States. Subsequently, when the public had had time to forget Reagan's earlier expressions of skepticism about the need for a larger civilian airport, Reagan officially conceded that the airport was necessary to boost tourism, and the United States itself completed the work which the Cubans had begun.

Finally, it is completely false to suggest that Cuba masterminded or even encouraged the overthrow of Bishop. Bishop and Castro were actually close friends, and the Cuban government outspokenly condemned Bishop's assassination several days before the invasion, and called for the punishment of those responsible.[69] (The British journalist Jonathan Steele has made the perceptive point that, if the island had really been controlled by the Cubans, as the administration alleged, then the Cubans would never had allowed Bishop to be killed.[70])

For the various reasons given above, the claim that Grenada was being transformed into a Soviet-Cuban base cannot possibly serve to justify the invasion. It is clear, therefore, that the administration has failed to provide any justification for its action that has even the least plausibility. Nor do any of its purported justifications provide any explanation of why the invasion was carried out.

Before going on to examine the real reasons for the invasion, it will be instructive to compare the Reagan administration's justifications for the Grenada invasion with those the Johnson administration offered for its invasion of the Dominican Republic almost twenty years earlier. This will not only illustrate the continuities in U.S. foreign policy, but will also show (if anyone needs convincing) that a lack of respect for the American people by the American government did not arise for the first time with the Reagan administration.

In 1963 Juan Bosch was elected president in the Dominican Republic, but after seven months he was overthrown in a coup led by the military. The coup provoked tremendous popular outrage which eventually found expression in a mass uprising by Dominican constitutionalists aimed at restoring the lawful government. Just as constitutionalist forces were on the verge of defeating the military conspirators, Lyndon Johnson dispatched nearly 22,000 Marines to put down the popular insurrection and occupy the island. Eventually, through carefully managed elections, a government more to the liking of the United States than that of Bosch was installed.[71]

While analysis of embassy cables and reports from correspondents who were there at the time shows that President Johnson's basic aim in invading the Dominican Republic was to prevent the reestablishment of a government which the United States found uncongenial—or, as the American ambassador put it in a cable to the president, to "prevent another Cuba"—the invasion was initially presented to the American public as a rescue operation. Johnson claimed that, unless the United States intervened, "American blood will run in the streets."[72] To make the threat more palpable Johnson treated the American public to various lurid tales of atrocities committed by the constitutionalists, all of which were subsequently proven to have been untrue. (In the case of Grenada, Reagan could appeal to a genuine atrocity: the murder of Bishop and his supporters.)

Soon, however, new elements of justification began to enter the president's speeches. In a television broadcast on April 30, 1965, Johnson stated that the invasion was intended "to preserve law and order."[73] By May 1 he was arguing that "our goal in the Dominican Republic . . . is that the people of that country must be permitted freely to choose the path of political democracy, social justice, and economic progress."[74] Just as a token OECS force provided diplomatic cover for the invasion of Grenada, so during the invasion of the Dominican Republic the United States organized an inter-American force under the supervision of the Organization of American States so that the invasion would not appear to be a unilateral U.S. action. OAS forces joined the U.S. occupation force to "facilitate the prompt restoration of democratic order in the Dominican Republic."[75]

From the outset Johnson emphasized that the United States was acting on the basis of a request from the Dominican Republic. As we noted earlier, however, this "request"—like the OECS's later "appeal" to Reagan—was actually drafted in Washington. Moreover, the request came not from a lawfully constituted government but from a faction in a civil war, and hence was in any case a very doubtful basis for intervention under international law.

The fourth and final element in Johnson's overall justification for the invasion was first suggested in his speech on May 1: "There are signs that people trained outside the Dominican Republic are seeking to gain control."[76] By May 2 this had become the major focus of justification for the invasion. In a television broadcast on that day, Johnson spoke of an "international conspiracy from which United States servicemen have rescued the [Dominican] people," claiming that "Communist leaders, many of them trained in Cuba, seeing a chance to increase disorder, to gain a foothold, joined the revolution. They took increasing control. And what began as a popular democratic revolution . . . very shortly moved and was taken over and really seized and placed into the hands of a band of Communist conspirators."[77] It was in this context that the Johnson Doctrine, to which we referred earlier, was announced: since communism is an *international* conspiracy, any attempt to establish communism (or, rather, anything identified by the United States as an attempt to establish communism) is to be regarded as external aggression to which the United States is entitled to respond. Hence "American nations cannot, must not, and will not permit the establishment of another Communist government in the Western Hemisphere."[78]

Here we have all the ingredients for a successful justification to the American public of a compaign of military aggression: a threat to American lives; the need, for humanitarian purposes, to restore order and democracy; a request from a beleaguered ally; and external communist aggression. According to one source, the invasion of the Dominican Republic aroused greater popular support in the United States than any of the many other American interventions over the past twenty-five years.[79] The lessons of that venture were apparently not lost on the Reagan administration, which, as we have seen, reproduced Johnson's tested formula with remarkable fidelity. It is noteworthy that, with the exception of the threat to American lives, all the elements of the formula are ripe for exploitation in the cases of El Salvador and Nicaragua.

Having now examined the administration's rationales for the invasion of Grenada, let us turn to the real reasons for its action. Perhaps the main aim of the invasion was, as we noted in Chapter 1, to restore the "credibility" of U.S. power at home by scoring a quick and relatively painless military victory. And indeed there were indications that many Americans were encouraged by the invasion to look favorably on the idea of using interventionist forces more readily as an instrument of foreign policy. As Reagan said when Jesse Jackson secured the freedom of an American airman in Syria, "It's hard to quarrel with success."[80]

As well as increasing the popularity of the military (Marine recruiting stations received applications for enlistment at two to three times the normal rate during ensuing weeks), the invasion also had the not unanticipated effect of increasing the popularity of the president. Public opinion polls taken in the United States soon after the invasion showed not only that between 68 and 71 percent of the people approved of the invasion, but also that support for the president had increased correspondingly—just as Margaret Thatcher's popularity had risen dramatically during and after the Falklands/Malvinas war, and as Prime Minister Begin's had done during the Israeli invasion of Lebanon.[81] One American patriot even telephoned the White House to express his satisfaction that "thank God, we finally have a real man in the White House."[82]

As we also noted in Chapter 1, another motivation behind the invasion was to restore American "credibility" abroad. As George Shultz exultantly proclaimed in a Cabinet meeting shortly after the invasion had commenced, "This may be a turning point in history. We've let the world know that we are going to protect our interests whatever it costs."[83] (This was intended to be a purely private outburst. In public it was necessary to maintain the official fictions. Hence Shultz's public assertion that "this was not taken as a signal about anything else. It was taken in the light of the threat to the lives and welfare of American citizens."[84]) It is significant that the invasion came only two days after the destruction of the Marines' quarters in Beirut. William Safire noted triumphantly that "the ability demonstrated by the United States [in Grenada] to react to provocation militarily will not be lost on the Syrians."[85] The administration was no doubt motivated by a desire to reassert U.S. power after the humiliation of Beirut (which savored too much of the Iranian hostage crisis of a few years earlier), but it would be a mistake to attribute too much significance to this. For, as we noted earlier, the invasion was being planned long before the attack in Beirut occurred. That attack merely served as a catalyst, an additional pressure, removing doubts and hesitations and perhaps affecting the timing of the invasion.

The United States certainly indulged in an orgy of self-congratulation over the military prowess it displayed in crushing this formidable enemy. The London *Times* reported that

> the United States Army is very pleased with the 7,000 officers and other ranks who invaded the British Commonwealth's spice island of Grenada. It has therefore awarded 8,612 medals. About fifty decorations have gone to personnel who got no closer to the fighting than the Pentagon. Staff and support troops who never actually left American soil have also been honoured.[86]

It is not clear, however, that the invasion of Grenada really was the military triumph it was advertised as being. In the end 6,000 U.S. troops were needed to subdue the resistance. As Jonathan Steele has pointed out, the official casualty figures "hardly bespeak a very glorious US military performance, but rather a series of engagements in which [Americans, Cubans, and Grenadians] suffered similarly."[87] Moreover, U.S. forces sometimes attacked the wrong targets, and as we noted earlier, on one occasion accidentally blew up a mental hospital. On another occasion U.S. jets strafed U.S. positions. Castro's jeers were not without some substance:

> Where is the glory, the grandeur and the victory in invading and defeating one of the tiniest countries in the world . . . ? Where is the heroism in fighting a handful of workers or other civilian cooperation personnel whose heroic resistance . . . against the air, sea and land forces of the most powerful Imperialist country in the world forced it to bring the 82nd Airborne Division when the last stronghold was being defended at dawn on October 26 by barely 50 fighters?[88]

It is difficult to avoid the suspicion that it was precisely to avoid humiliating charges such as these that the Pentagon attempted to suppress casualty figures and gave inflated accounts of the number and the status of the Cubans on the island.

A third reason for the invasion was obviously to destroy the Grenadian revolution, removing the left-wing pro-Cuban government and installing an ideologically acceptable pro-Western government. As in the case of El Salvador, however, the country iself was not the primary concern. Grenada is of considerably less strategic and economic importance even than El Salvador. Rather, the administration's concern was with the symbol, with the example that Grenada had set for other countries in the region. As one State Department official acknowledged, "Throughout the region, there are little-bitty leftist groups with power ambitions. If we [had] improved relations with Grenada at no cost to the government, imagine what it would have said to other putative authorities in the eastern Caribbean."[89]

Because the administration was concerned about the symbolic importance of the Grenadian revolution, it had been pressuring, harassing, and attempting to intimidate the Bishop government for years. As it has done to Nicaragua, the Reagan administration brought various economic pressures to bear on the revolutionary government in Grenada. It terminated U.S. aid programs, excluded Grenada from regional aid programs, including the Caribbean Basin Initiative, successfully blocked loans from the World Bank, and tried unsuccessfully both to block loans from the International Monetary Fund and to make its own contributions to the Caribbean Development Bank conditional on Grenada's being excluded as a beneficiary.[90] The United States also sought, with some success, to undermine Grenada's tourist industry. According to the London-based Latin America Bureau, "A sample poll of 40 travel agents in the Washington and New York areas revealed that 90 per cent of them advised that Grenada was an 'unsafe destination,' having been given this advice by the State Department."[91]

Diplomatic pressures were applied as well. In spite of Maurice Bishop's efforts to establish better relations with the United States, Reagan refused to accept Grenada's ambassador to the United States and instructed the American ambassador in Barbados not to present his letters of credence in Grenada.[92] Efforts at military intimidation were also made. On one occasion in 1981, while the United States was conducing the large "Ocean Venture '81" naval exercises in the Caribbean, U.S. forces staged a mock invasion of Vieques off the coast of Puerto Rico, an island roughly of the same size and shape as Grenada. The island's code name was "Amber and the Amberines," an obvious reference to Grenada and the nearby Grenadines. The exercise involved the rescue of American hostages and the occupation of the island in order to "install a regime favorable to the way of life we espouse." Similar operations were conducted again in 1982. The purpose, according to the commander-in-chief of the U.S. Caribbean Command, was "to send a signal to those who are friends and those who would oppose us in this part of the world that we can project military force."[93] Later, early in 1983, the United States staged more large-scale naval maneuvers in the Caribbean, this time assembling seventy-seven warships off the coast of Grenada, some within six miles of Point Salines. Around the same time it was revealed in congressional testimony that the CIA had proposed a plan for the "destabilization" of the Bishop government. The plan was rejected by Congress.[94]

The invasion finally brought to an end the Grenadian revolution which Reagan had tried for so long to destroy. The country has now been firmly returned to the U.S. sphere of influence. Soon after the invasion had ended and the occupation had begun, Grenada severed diplomatic relations with the Soviet Union, Cuba, and Libya, and diplomats from those countries were expelled.[95] Bernard Coard and the other conspirators involved in the murder of Bishop have been in detention since the invasion and are being tried under a law which carries a mandatory death penalty for those convicted. A British barrister who went to Grenada to observe the trial on behalf of the London-based Committee for Human Rights in Grenada was expelled from the country, as was an American reporter who was accused of "trying to incite dissent."[96] By contrast, Sir Eric Gairy has been readmitted to Grenada after five years of exile in the United States. Although, like Coard and Austin, he is known to have been responsible for the murders of a number of people, he is a right-wing murderer who enjoyed good relations with the United States, and hence is not facing prosecution.

In the immediate aftermath of the invasion the United States began to play a major role in running the country. Plans to install an interim government consisting of heavily financed right-wing exiles were apparently thwarted only by resistance from the Commonwealth.[97] About a month after the invasion, a European diplomat in Grenada was quoted as having said that "'the fact is the government here is still very much headed by Ambassador Charles Gillespie' of the U.S. Mission and Major General Jack Farris, the U.S. military commander. 'The sad fact is that they look like [they will be] the government behind the government here for a long, long time.'"[98] Scoon was known to have daily meetings with Farris and Gillespie, and the latter's power became so obvious in Grenada that he soon acquired the nickname "Sir Paul" Gillespie.[99] U.S. officials have considered the possibility of establishing a base on the island.

Even internal changes within the country have been profound. Under the Bishop government,

> secondary education was provided free, a literacy campaign was under way, and the number of university scholarships had greatly

> increased. Medical care, too, was free, and health clinics had been opened in the countryside (thanks largely to the Cubans). Free milk and other foodstuffs were being distributed to the public, as were materials for home improvement. Cultural and sports programs had been set up for young people.[100]

Now, however, free education is under threat, the distribution of free milk has stopped, youth programs have been suspended, and day-care centers have been closed.[101]

Other traces of communism are also being rapidly expunged. Schools named after heroes of the revolution have been renamed, and schoolchildren are taken to the U.S. Information Service's offices on the island to see a film entitled "Grenada: Return to Freedom."[102] In the economic sphere, U.S. officials have been pressing for the "privatization" of the economy, and the interim Grenadian government began accordingly to divest itself of businesses that had been nationalized by the previous two regimes. U.S. investment has also begun to pour in. Announcing plans to build a new luxury hotel in St. George's, the mayor of Fort Lauderdale, Florida, declared that Grenada "is going to provide a very stable environment for investment" in a "very pro-American political climate."[103] To ensure that this stable pro-Americanism persists, the United States is spending millions of dollars to build up a huge police force equipped with sophisticated computers for monitoring the activities of persons suspected of leftist sentiments.[104]

In the end, of course, the key to maintaining stability and, equally importantly, providing legitimacy for a U.S.-backed government was to hold elections under appropriate conditions. Hence on December 3, 1984, after thirteen months in which great efforts had been made to expunge the memory of Maurice Bishop—or, as the U.S. Information Service put it, to "re-educate people away from communism"—elections were held in Grenada. Fourteen of the fifteen seats in the Grenadian Parliament went to candidates of the New National Party (NNP), a coalition of three right-wing parties which was forged by the United States and backed by the conservative Grenadian business community. (Sir Eric Gairy, while obligingly pro-American, is regarded internationally as a bit of a lunatic, primarily because of his interest in UFOs, and hence, to avoid the embarrassment of having him returned to power, the United States pressured him not only not to run but also not to campaign for candidates from his party.) The United States openly subsidized the NNP's campaign, which was also assisted in various ways by the new American Embassy. According to the editors of the London *Guardian,* "Private American groups contributed more than $100,000 to encourage a high turnout in the polls, a subsidy of about three dollars for every vote cast"—an unnecessary expense, the editors note, since "every Grenadian knew that the only hope for investment in their impoverished island would be if they voted for the American candidate." As in other recent instances of U.S.-sponsored elections, the triumph of right-wing pro-American forces was guaranteed in advance.[105]

Two further reasons for the invasion remain to be mentioned. They are closely related. One was, as U.S. officials are fond of saying, "to send a signal" to the Sandinistas in Nicaragua. Thus one Pentagon official was quoted as saying that he hoped that the Nicaraguans would get "the message."[106] Whether or not the Sandinistas got the message, the contras certainly did. Edgar Chamorro, then a leader of the FDN, stated soon after the invasion that "the U.S. will let some time go by and then they'll do it again."[107] Yet whether Reagan would "do it again" depended on the character of the domestic and international reaction to the invasion. This was the other purpose of the invasion: to test the waters of public opinion to see what the likely response to an invasion of Nicaragua would be. The response to the Grenada invasion was mixed. Support was very strong in the United States, but there are doubts whether support for this relatively painless operation can be transferred to an inevitably much bloodier and more protracted campaign in Nicaragua—especially since many Americans supported the Grenada invasion at least in part because they bought the administration's story about the threat to American lives on the island. (The American community in Nicaragua has said very loudly that it does not wish to be used as a pretext for a repeat performance there.) So it is not entirely clear that the American public has been purged and cured of the Vietnam syndrome.

The international reaction was almost uniformly negative. A resolution condemning the invasion was passed in the U.N. General Assembly by a vote of 108 to 9. Besides the United States and the six Caribbean countries that participated in the invasion, the only countries which voted against the resolution were, predictably, Israel and El Salvador. Some U.S. allies, including Britain, abstained, but even they were critical of the invasion in speeches made by their representatives.[108] Reagan's comment on the United Nations vote typifies the arrogant vulgarity of this administration: "It didn't upset my breakfast at all."[109]

Richard Barnet has written that "just as the successful military interventions of the 1950s—Iran (1953), Guatemala (1954), and Lebanon (1958)—created the climate for the Vietnam catastrophe, Grenada may embolden the Administration to try again in Nicaragua."[110] One can, however, make a case for the contrary view that the invasion may have been rather good news for Nicaragua. While the implications of the domestic response are unclear, the international response was surprisingly harsh. And, perhaps equally important, the surprisingly stubborn resistance by the Cuban workers has made it quite clear to the administration that Latin Americans will not roll over and play dead in the face of U.S. power.

Was the invasion justified? The conclusion of this chapter is that it clearly was not. The administration's public rationales are all miserable failures, and its real reasons for invading are contemptibly self-serving, opportunist, and immoral. John Stuart Mill once wrote that "it is during an arduous struggle to become free by their own efforts" that people have the best chance of developing what he referred to as "the virtues needful for maintaining freedom." Hence, he argued, "the liberty which is bestowed on them by hands other than their own will have nothing real, nothing permanent."[111] As a general argument against intervention, Mill's reasoning is not very persuasive, since it is an objectionable form of paternalism to refuse people one's assistance on the ground that facing adversity by themselves will be good for them. But, in the case of Grenada, Mill's point has considerable force. The RMC was terribly isolated, both internationally and among its own people. As the British journalist Hugh O'Shaughnessy has argued, "It would have been only a matter of time before the Leninist aspirations of Coard and Austin were swept away by Grenadians themselves. By mounting the invasion the US robbed them of that opportunity."[112]

Perhaps in the end the Grenadian people will benefit from the invasion. It is doubtful whether they will. If they do that will be a happy accident. Their welfare was not among the administration's concerns when it invaded.

★8★

The New Cold War and the Prospects for Peace

The Manipulation of Cold War Tensions

Previous chapters have provided a wealth of examples of the way in which the administration attempts to justify virtually all aspects of its foreign policy in terms of the threat from the Soviet Union: its new nuclear weapons programs are all necessary to deter a Soviet nuclear attack or Soviet nuclear blackmail, and to force a reluctant Soviet Union to negotiate arms control agreements; arms control negotiations have so far failed either because the Soviet Union's determination to retain its "margin of superiority" has led it to reject reasonable U.S. proposals, or because it has been unwilling to accept verification techniques which would allow the United States to detect its efforts to cheat on its agreements; arms sales and military assistance are necessary in order to enable other countries to defend themselves against Soviet or Soviet-sponsored aggression; the defense of human rights is of necessity anti-Soviet, since serious violations of human rights are a feature primarily of communist societies, and thus are ultimately linked to the Soviet Union; in El Salvador the government is challenged by guerrillas armed and directed by the Soviet Union; while in Nicaragua the government itself is merely a Soviet puppet bent on exporting communist revolution throughout the hemisphere; and Grenada was also being transformed into a "Soviet-Cuban colony" whose function in the Soviet Union's global scheme was to be the same as that of Nicaragua. In each case U.S. policy is presented as a defensive effort to restrain the Soviet Union's relentless and aggressive expansion of its power and therefore of its totalitarian influence.

Yet the evidence presented in this book overwhelmingly suggests that these aspects of the Reagan administration's foreign policy have motivations which are largely if not entirely independent of Soviet provocations. The nuclear arms buildup, far from being merely a reaction to Soviet efforts, constitutes an attempt to win the arms race by achieving the ability to defeat the Soviet Union in a nuclear war. Arms control negotiations have been sabotaged because agreements would interfere with the arms buildup. And the policies on arms sales, human rights, and intervention in the third world are all aimed, directly or indirectly, at securing U.S. control over the natural and human resources of the third world. In each case the U.S. program is essentially autonomous rather than reactive. U.S. policies would of course be different if the Soviet Union did not exist, or if the Soviet Union had not deprived the United States of the nuclear superiority it enjoyed during the late 1940s, the 1950s, and the early 1960s. But the fact that the Soviet Union exists and has established itself as the military equal to the United States has relatively little value in explaining the details of U.S. foreign policy. (This is not to deny that the sharp rightward turn in U.S. politics generally, and the consequent triumph of Reaganism, are in part attributable to the impact on public opinion of the Soviet Union's military buildup, its interventions in Africa, Poland, and Afghanistan, and so on.)

It is because U.S. foreign policy under Reagan in general cannot be adequately explained as a reaction to specific actions of the Soviet Union that there is so little in this book on Soviet foreign policy. Critics may complain that this reflects a pro-Soviet bias, but the simple fact is that the book is concerned with U.S. rather than Soviet foreign policy, and hence Soviet foreign policy is relevant only to the extent that it helps to explain U.S. foreign policy, which is not very much.

Nevertheless the administration's efforts to portray its foreign policy as a defensive reaction to Soviet aggression requires that the Soviet Union should be portrayed in the blackest possible terms. Thus, even during the 1980 election campaign, Reagan asserted that "we have a different regard for human life than those monsters do. . . . [The Soviets] have no respect for human life."[1] Later, after taking office, he claimed that the Soviet leaders "reserve unto themselves the right to commit any crime, to lie, to cheat."[2] But the best-known instance of Reagan's abusive anti-Soviet rhetoric came during an address to a convention of the National Association of Evangelicals in Florida in 1983. In an oratorical style suited to the pulpit, Reagan proclaimed the Soviet Union "an evil empire," and denounced "all those who live in totalitarian darkness" as "the focus of evil in the modern world." The conflict between the United States and the Soviet Union, he asserted, embodies "the struggle between right and wrong, good and evil."[3] While these occasional vituperative assaults probably reflect Reagan's own cartoon vision of the world, they were also calculated to stimulate the fear and hatred of the Soviet Union which Reagan and his administration rightly deem necessary in order to gain public support for their policies.

The administration has seized greedily on every opportunity to vilify and condemn the Soviet Union. While rightly condemning the Soviet invasion and occupation of Afghanistan, administration officials have continued to lecture the world endlessly on the "lessons" which the Soviet action contained for the many countries, including the United States, which might be next on the Soviet Union's list. Moreover, during the period of Solidarity's emergence in Poland, the administration exhausted its diplomatic resources by making various menacing gestures at both the Polish and Soviet governments, and railing against them publicly at every opportunity. It is arguable that this behavior actually worsened Solidarity's prospects. First, just as disarmament movements in the West are not helped by expressions of support from the Soviet government, so Solidarity was not helped by being visibly linked to the West within the framework of the Cold War. And, second, the administration's public posturing undoubtedly led the Polish and Soviet governments to feel that taking a more permissive stance toward Solidarity would be seen as giving in to Western pressure. That gave them a reason to respond with defiance. Such a response may not have been unanticipated. Reading between the lines in the administration's pronouncements, one could detect a barely concealed yearning for a crackdown in Poland, or, better yet, direct Soviet intervention. This was also evident in the fact that, when the crackdown finally occurred, administration officials descended like vultures on the corpse of Solidarity in order to reap in propaganda the fruits of its suppression. (During the episode with Solidarity, the administration never tired of reminding the world that it is not the prerogative of the Soviet Union to determine events in Poland. Yet, in the midst of the Polish crisis, Reagan publicly held Jimmy Carter responsible for the war between Iran and Iraq on the ground that the war would never have occurred had Carter not allowed the Shah to be deposed. Thus, if anyone needed reminding, it *is* the United States's prerogative, which Carter irresponsibly failed to exercise, to determine events in Iran.)

While the tragedy in Poland provided a number of useful opportunities for scoring points against the Soviet Union, the administration's big moment did not arrive until September 1983. On the first day of that month, a Korean commercial 747 airliner strayed deep into Soviet airspace and was shot down by a Soviet fighter, killing all 269 people on board. For a number of days the Soviet Union obstinately refused to concede that the plane had been shot down. During that period Reagan launched his attack. It is worth quoting extensively from three public statements he made about the incident.

> What can we think of a regime that so broadly trumpets its vision of peace and global disarmament and yet so quickly and so callously commits a terrorist act to sacrifice the lives of innocent human beings?

> . . . What can be the scope of legitimate mutual discourse with a state whose values permit such atrocities? . . . This murder of innocent civilians is a serious international issue between the Soviet Union and civilized people everywhere who cherish individual rights and value human life. . . . The evidence is clear. It leaves no doubt. It is time for the Soviets to account. The Soviet Union owes the world the fullest possible explanation and apology for their inexcusable act of brutality. . . . They speak endlessly about their love of brotherhood, disarmament and peace. But they reserve the right to disregard aviation safety and to sacrifice human lives. . . . We and other civilized countries follow procedures to prevent a tragedy rather than to provoke one. But while the Soviets accuse others of wanting to return to the Cold War, it is they who have never left it behind. . . . Make no mistake about it, this attack was not just against ourselves or the Republic of Korea. This was the Soviet Union against the world and the moral precepts which guide human relations among people everywhere. It was an act of barbarism, born of a society which wantonly disregards individual rights and the value of human life and seeks constantly to expand to dominate other nations. . . . But we shouldn't be surprised by such inhuman brutality. Memories come back of Czechoslovakia, Hungary, Poland, the gassing of villages in Afghanistan. If the massacre and their subsequent conduct is intended to intimidate, they have failed in their purpose. . . . When John F. Kennedy was President, defense spending as a share of the Federal Budget was 70 percent greater than it is today. Since then, the Soviet Union has carried on the most massive military build-up the world has ever seen. Until they are willing to join the rest of the world community, we must maintain the strength to deter their aggression.[4]

These passages contain some fairly astounding charges: that the shooting was a calculated act of *terrorism,* a deliberate provocation, and an act of intimidation; that it was aimed primarily at the United States and hence that the United States is the principal victim; that the Soviet Union was deliberately flaunting internationally recognized moral standards; that the Soviet Union is neither a civilized nation nor a member of the world community; and that *Soviet society as a whole* neither believes in the value of human life nor has any regard for human rights. The level of cynicism in this torrent of invective is no less astounding. For Reagan was exploiting the incident to suggest that arms control negotiations with the Soviet Union are of dubious value, both because of the unseemliness of having any contact with such people, and because Soviet professions of a desire for mutual disarmament could now be seen as an obvious fraud. He also took the opportunity to put in a plug for his rearmament program. This latter theme was one which he continued to hammer away at in the ensuing weeks. Three weeks after the event he was pushing the

MX and various other programs with the argument that "we live in a dangerous world with cruel people who reject our ideals. . . . In dealing with adversaries as brutal as the Soviets, America must remain strong to preserve the peace."[5]

Where domestic politics was concerned, this was one of the most effective performances of Reagan's career. Less than three weeks after the shooting the House of Representatives voted by almost two to one to allocate funds both for the MX and for the production of binary nerve gas shells. About six weeks later it approved funds for the development of the B-1 bomber.[6] In both instances the destruction of the airliner was acknowledged to be an important factor in determining the vote. Opposition within the House to the administration's support for the contras also apparently declined, and polls showed a drop in support for the freeze movement among the general public.[7] A senior State Department official noted that "until the KAL [Korean Air Lines, a reference to the shooting], everyone remembered [Reagan] had called them 'liars and cheats.' But after the KAL shooting down, the President seemed to make sense to a lot of people."[8] Another official said: "I'd almost go so far as to say it created a consensus in this country about the Soviets. A basic kind of anti-Soviet mood was created that is fairly supportive of the President."[9]

Reagan's nonverbal reactions to the incident were fairly restrained, at least in contrast to what one might have expected them to be. He enacted a few minor sanctions, mainly consisting in the breaking off of contacts in various areas, but there was no major effort to punish the Soviet Union. (Since relations between the countries were already so minimal, there was not much that he could have done.) This combination of sanctimonious fulminations on radio and television and relative inaction at the prctical level earned him the deep admiration of the press. The *New York Times* described his response as "shrewd and moderate," and praised his "dignified, justified anger." The *Washington Post* found him "firm and restrained," while *Time* described his speech for television as "stirring and statesmanlike."[10] According to a poll taken about two weeks after the incident occurred, only 1 percent of the American people thought that Reagan had been "too tough" on the Soviet Union.[11]

The affair seemed to be developing into a dream-come-true for Reagan when suddenly some embarrassing information began to emerge. After having attended a special meeting between administration members and congressional leaders, the Democratic leader in the House of Representatives revealed to reporters that he had been played a tape of the Soviet pilots' conversations which showed that they had mistaken the Korean airliner for a U.S. RC-135 reconnaissance aircraft. White House officials denied that the tape showed this, but in trying to explain how the Congressman could have been misled they were forced to concede that an RC-135 had indeed been patroling in the area at the time that the Korean airliner strayed into Soviet airspace, and that Soviet air defense personnel had initially mistaken the Korean plane for an RC-135.[12] A few days later it emerged that an Orion antisubmarine aircraft was also in the area, and some observers have suggested that there may have been more than one RC-135 in the area at the time, and that at least one RC-135 may have violated Soviet airspace.[13] The reason for the heightened U.S. activity soon became clear as well. The area which the Korean airliner overflew (the Kamchatka Peninsula and the island of Sakhalin) is a sensitive area even in ordinary circumstances. There is a vast naval complex there, one component of which is the submarine base at Petropavlovsk. Also located in the region are concentrations of land-based nuclear missiles and a missile testing range. On September 1, however, the region would have been of particular interest to U.S. reconnaissance aircraft, since the Soviets were planning a test launch of a new missile that very night.

Even before the White House revealed that an RC-135 had been flying in the area, Soviet officials had suggested that the pilot who shot down the Korean airliner had mistaken it for an RC-135. Earlier on the same day that the presence of the U.S. plane was acknowledged, *Tass* quoted Soviet General Romanov as saying that the "outlines [of the Korean airliner] resembled those of the American reconnaissance plane RC-135."[14] Two days later, on September 6, a Soviet government statement on the nightly news claimed that "the Soviet pilots stopping the actions of the intruder plane couldn't know it was a civilian plane. The allegations of the US President that the Soviet pilots knew that it was a civilian plane do not correspond to reality."[15] Later, however, the official Soviet account rejected this version of the events in favor of a conflicting version which had also been appearing in certain Soviet statements. At a press conference on September 9 the Soviet chief of staff, Marshal Nikolai Ogarkov, asserted that there had been no mistake and that the Soviet air defense system had worked flawlessly. The Korean airliner, he claimed, was on an intelligence-gathering mission for the United States: "There was full conviction that we were dealing with an intelligence plane."[16] According to this story, the United States had deliberately jeopardized the lives of the passengers by sending the plane on a spy mission in the hope that the Soviet Union would not attack a civilian aircraft.

Even today the circumstances of this tragic incident are not clear, and many questions remain unanswered. That the airliner was indeed on an intelligence-gathering mission cannot be lightly dismissed, for there is considerable evidence which supports this hypothesis. The plane could have been on either of two possible missions. It could itself have been gathering data on the impending missile test, or it could have been a "probe" intended to activate the Soviet air defense system, whose responses could then be monitored by U.S. reconnaissance craft. Probing, or conducting "exciter flights," is indeed one of the functions of the RC-135s. By stimulating and then monitoring the Soviet air defense systems, the United States aims not only to gather information on Soviet communication channels but also to collect data on the radar network which U.S. cruise missiles would have to penetrate in the event of a war. Since the Korean airliner was shot down it has been revealed that the radar and electronic signals provoked by the intrusion were in fact monitored both by an orbiting Ferret reconnaissance satellite which happened conveniently to be over the area at the time and by the recently launched space shuttle Challenger.[17]

It is conceivable that the Korean airliner could have been on either of these missions. U.S. intelligence services could have reasoned that, if the plane were located, it would be identified as a civilian aircraft and hence would not be attacked. The suggestion is perhaps excessively cynical, but they may also have reasoned that, if the Soviets were unexpectedly to attack the aircraft, the result would be a propaganda windfall for the United States. Either way the United States would benefit.

Various theories have been proposed to explain how the airliner could have strayed so far off course without the pilots being aware of it, and they have not all been decisively refuted. But Major-General Richard Rohmer (Canadian Air Force, retired) has argued rigorously and convincingly that the accident theories are all utterly implausible.[18] It therefore seems overwhelmingly likely that the plane was deliberately flying in Soviet airspace. It is this fact, together with the fact that both the Korean airliner and a U.S. spy satellite happened to be passing over a highly sensitive area at a time when the Soviets were preparing to test launch a new missile, which constitutes the main evidence for the theory that the plane was actually on a spy mission. (Major-General Rohmer rejects this theory, and argues instead for the claim that the pilots were deliberately flying a great circle route from Anchorage to Seoul in order to reduce their flying time, thereby saving their company $2,600 in operating costs.[19])

Another curious fact which lends credibility to the espionage theory is that no effort was made to warn the airliner that it was off course. Most of the accident theories presuppose that the plane went off course from the start, but if this were true then the deviation would have been picked up by U.S. military radars and the plane could have been alerted to the fact that it was on a course which would soon take it into Soviet airspace. Moreover, two former Air Force officers who flew RC-135s have contended that the RC-135 that was in the area at the time would have been aware of the course of the Korean plane and could have contacted it to warn it that it was straying into Soviet airspace. Failing that, the RC-135 had the capacity to communicate almost instantaneously with persons at the highest levels of the U.S. government, and so could have warned the government of the problem so that the government could in turn have alerted the Soviets.[20]

More recently, former State Department intelligence analyst John Keppel has called attention to a discrepancy in the timing of the events associated with the shooting. Tokyo's Narita Airport has recorded receiving a perfectly ordinary communication from a source which identified itself as KAL 007 (the plane which was shot down) 38 seconds *after* the Soviet fighter radioed to ground control that "the target is destroyed." Keppel speculates that the communications received at Narita Airport were actually sent by KAL 015, which had left Anchorage shortly after KAL 007 and was traveling along the route which 007 should have taken. According to Keppel, 015 sent the "fake" messages in order to provide cover for 007 on its spy mission.[21]

Finally, there is extensive circumstantial evidence of a cover-up. For example, on the day after the shooting the Japanese Broadcasting Corporation announced that two and a half hours of conversation between Soviet fighters and the ground stations controlling them had been recorded. This was later confirmed both by Japan's chief cabinet secretary and by White House spokesman Larry Speakes. But the tapes were never released and the Japanese Defense Agency later denied that they ever existed.[22] (The only tape to be released was that of the Soviet pilot's reports to his ground controller.) Furthermore, the National Transportation Safety Board was ordered to halt an investigation it was conducting into the incident and to turn over all of its documents to the State Department. All Federal Aviation Authority employees, as well as the relatives of the flight passengers, have been served gag orders to prevent them from divulging any information they might have.[23] This behavior seems unaccountable if the United States has nothing to hide.

It is, however, not essential to the argument of this chapter to try to confirm the theory that the Korean airliner was actually on an intelligence-gathering mission—a theory for which the evidence is in any case far from conclusive. What is important is that the Soviets certainly *believed* that the plane they were dealing with was on such a mission. In fact, evidence has emerged which strongly suggests that the Soviets' initial account, according to which Soviet air defense personnel were unaware that the plane was a civilian airliner and instead mistook it for an military intelligence aircraft, is in fact correct. Much of this evidence became known when a report by U.S. intelligence analysts was leaked to the press in early October. Judging on the basis of the evidence presented in this report, together with other known facts, it would seem that the most plausible account of the Soviets' action on the night of September 1 is as follows.[24]

As U.S. officials have confirmed, Soviet radar operators initially misidentified the Korean airliner as an RC-135. As we have noted, one function the RC-135s perform is to test Soviet air defense systems by deliberately penetrating Soviet airspace and then recording the Soviet response. The fact that RC-135s regularly violate Soviet airspace for this purpose means that there may have already been a tendency in the minds of the Soviet air defense personnel to assume that the plane that was violating their airspace must be an RC-135, especially since special information might be obtained by a probe just at the time that a sensitive missile test was scheduled. (Some Soviet air defense personnel may have soon revised their initial identification of the plane as an RC-135, since RC-135s do not normally travel as fast as the 747 was going. But they could easily have mistaken the plane for an E4A or an E4B, both of which are 747s modified for military use. These planes, which would have been familiar to Soviet air defense personnel, both carry sophisticated electronics equipment and perform the same functions as the RC-135.) According to the U.S. intelligence analysts, the decision to shoot down the airliner was for all intents and purposes made as soon as it was misidentified as an RC-135. The idea that the plane was a military reconnaissance craft became fixed in the minds of the air defense officials, and the idea was apparently reinforced by the fact that Soviet interceptor aircraft were unable to locate the plane for two hours. After the plane had penetrated deep into Soviet territory, antiaircraft missile batteries on the island of Sakhalin were ordered to "stop the RC-135."

U.S. officials dismissed the claim that the Soviets had not been aware that the plane was a passenger plane on the ground that, even though the incident occurred at night, there was sufficient visibility to enable the Soviet pilot to recognize the distinctive shape of a 747, and so to distinguish the plane from an RC-135. But the intelligence analysts now claim that a close analysis of transcripts of Soviet radio transmissions, radar impulses, and other data shows that the Soviet fighter that destroyed the plane was below and behind it in the normal attack position rather than parallel to it, and so would have been unable to distinguish it from an RC-135. This, however, is difficult to square with the fact that the pilot reported to his ground controller that "I'm already abeam of the target"—that is, flying alongside it. On the other hand, even if the pilot was able to make out the contours of the 747, he could easily have assumed that the plane was an E4A or an E4B. Although the United States initially denied that the pilot had given any warning signals or attempted to establish contact with the plane, careful analysis of the tapes of the pilot's reports showed that at one point he had said "I am firing cannon bursts" (that is, streams of luminous tracer bullets), and at another point reported that "the target isn't responding to the call." (U.S. government officials claimed that, in an effort to prevent defections, the Soviets equip their military aircrafts with radios unable to reach the universal emergency channel—that is, the channel on which it would have been appropriate to try to contact the airliner. This claim was later demonstrated to be false.) So the pilot did, it seems, make at least cursory efforts to signal to the airliner, whose failure to respond may have confirmed the pilot's initial belief that he was dealing with a military reconnaissance aircraft.

In any case the important point is that the pilot never made any report of the aircraft's identity. Such was ground control's certainty about the nature of the aircraft that he was never even requested to do so. A later report of the International Civil Aviation Organization concluded that "the U.S.S.R. authorities assumed that KE [KAL] 007 was an intelligence aircraft and, therefore, did not make exhaustive efforts to identify the aircraft through inflight visual observation." And the U.S. intelligence analysts also concluded their report by noting that there is "no indication that the Soviet air defense personnel knew it was a commercial plane before the attack."

It may be argued that the Soviets should have taken care to determine the identity of the aircraft. Indeed, they should have: their failure to do so is inexcusable. But, bearing in mind that nothing can excuse their negligence in this case, it is nevertheless worth noting the pressures that they were under. Soviet law is explicit about the duties of the Air Defense Forces in dealing with intruding aircraft: "In cases where an end to a violation or the apprehension of violators cannot be achieved by other means, weapons must be used" (a thoroughly barbarous law, citation of which does not imply endorsement). Moreover, local and regional commanders are liable to extremely severe penalties, even death, if they allow intruding aircraft to escape. These pressures on the air defense personnel were compounded by the embarrassing fact that the airliner had been in Soviet airspace for a full two hours before it was finally intercepted. When the plane was shot down it was only one minute away from leaving Soviet airspace, and the pilot who was chasing it was rapidly running out of fuel. The choice with which the Air Defense Forces were faced was between shooting the aircraft down or facing the penalties of letting it escape.

Whatever else may be true, it is abundantly clear that the Soviets believed themselves to be dealing with a plane that was on a spy mission. *Time* observed that "what is most clear from the incident is that the Soviets did not seem to care that their target was merely an innocent commercial passenger plane."[25] But if they knew that the plane was an *innocent* civilian airliner, what reason would they have for shooting it down?

All of the information on which the foregoing reconstruction of events is based was accessible to the administration within two weeks of the time that the incident occurred. Moreover, it had been revealed on September 9 that the decision to shoot down "the intruder plane" had been taken by a local air defense commander, and that the political authorities in Moscow had not been consulted. Yet these revelations had no effect on the volume of the rhetoric emanating from Washington. Reagan carried on with his virulent harangues at the United Nations and elsewhere just as if no new evidence had come to light at all. But if this account is correct, as it seems to be, then virtually all of Reagan's abusive charges, which assume that the Soviets knowingly shot down a civilian plane containing hundreds of innocent people, become grossly unjust. Assuming that the account given above is correct, the Soviets can be charged with criminal negligence, monumental incompetence, and extreme callousness and mendacity after the fact. But, deplorable as their conduct was, it did not deserve the savage abuse which was heaped upon it by an opportunistic administration. Indeed it is highly likely that it was precisely because of Reagan's repeated sermons on their moral depravity that the Soviets responded to the incident with defiance, refusing to admit that they had made a mistake and instead locating moral responsibility for the whole affair with the United States. It should have been evident to anyone that there was no chance whatsoever for an apology once Reagan had sanctimoniously demanded one.

It is interesting to contrast this recent incident with a similar incident in 1973 when the Israelis shot down a Libyan airliner which had overflown Cairo airport during a sandstorm and strayed over Sinai, which, though then under Israeli occupation, was not even part of Israeli territory. The Libyan plane was shot down as it was attempting to return to unoccupied Egyptian territory, killing 110 people. In this case there was no question of mistaken identity: the Israelis knew they were shooting down a passenger plane. Moshe Dayan, then the Israeli Defense Minister, rejected the idea that Israel was guilty of any crime, and explained that the plane was clearly on a spy mission. He also noted that it had been feared that the plane was on a kamikaze mission aimed at the destruction of Tel Aviv airport, or perhaps even the Dimona nuclear reactor.[26] There seems to be little to distinguish this incident from the more recent one, except that the Soviets appear to have had a morally more plausible justification for their action, though in the end they chose not to avail themselves of it. Yet Reagan has so far declined to use his moral authority to excommunicate the Israelis from the "world community," or to banish them from civilization. (The hypocrisy of Reagan's fulminations is evident elsewhere as well. His "different regard for human life" has been well displayed in El Salvador and Nicaragua, where, as we have seen, his administration has been sponsoring the continuous mass killing of the innocent for several years.)

Reagan's exploitation of the airliner tragedy for Cold War purposes has had and will continue to have profound political consequences. East-West relations were already on the verge of complete collapse well before the incident occurred. In May of 1983, Marshall Shulman, the director of the Russian Research Center at Columbia University and former Soviet affairs specialist in the Carter administration, contended that "relations are on a low plateau—poor communications, tension, dismantling of cooperative activities, sharp rhetoric."[27] George Kennan, the distinguished historian and former American ambassador to the Soviet Union, took an even grimmer view. Soviet-American relations, he said, were in a "dreadful and dangerous" state which displayed the "unfailing characteristics of a march toward war."[28] In the aftermath of the airliner incident, relations between the two countries plummeted even further. Talks to modernize the "hot-line" were allowed to lapse, and the trading of insults continued to escalate. The Soviets suffered new indignities, as when the United States announced that Soviet Foreign Minister Gromyko's diplomatic plane, in which he was intending to fly to the United States in order to attend the opening of the thirty-eighth session of the U.N. General Assembly in New York, would not be allowed to land. In the end

Gromyko decided not to attend ("even though," *Time* remarked, "the U.S. offered the use of a military airfield near New York if the Soviet diplomat would arrive in a military aircraft."[29] This generosity, with which *Time* was obviously impressed, can be put into perspective if one asks whether the U.S. secretary of state would be willing to allow the Soviets to dictate the kind of aircraft he could fly in.)

The full extent of the breach between the two countries did not, however, become apparent in the West until President Andropov addressed his country on September 28. His statement was widely regarded as the strongest attack on the U.S. government made by a Soviet leader since the collapse of détente. An American correspondent in Moscow noted that "the format of Mr. Andropov's statement—issued as a declaration by the general secretary of the party—is significant, since it is a form previously used only at times of crisis."[30] The burden of the statement was that the Soviet government had concluded that it was not possible to do business with the Reagan administration. As Soviet officials pointed out, the crucial point in the statement was that, "if anyone had any illusions about the possibility of an evolution for the better in the policy of the present American administration, recent events have dispelled them once and for all."[31] The "recent events" were, of course, Reagan's attacks on the Soviet Union in the wake of the airliner disaster.

The Soviet leaders and the Soviet people had been wounded more deeply by Reagan's attacks than perhaps anyone in the U.S. government had suspected. Not long after Andropov's address, two distinguished American observers of the Soviet Union made separate visits to that country and, upon returning, reported their impressions and the results of their discussions with Soviet citizens and Soviet officials. Raymond Garthoff, a senior fellow at the Brookings Institution and a former American ambassador to Bulgaria, noted that the Soviets deeply resent Reagan's refusal to accord them the respect due to a great power. He also found that Soviet officials "point[ed] out . . . , and with pained expression, that they are careful only to criticize the U.S. government and its policies, not the American people or nation. They are hurt that American official practice is more broadly anti-Soviet and anti-Russian."[32]

The other American observer is Seweryn Bialer, the director of the Research Institute on International Change at Columbia University (and, by his own admission, not a person who could in any way be considered "soft on the Soviets"). His observations deserve to be quoted at length.

> President Reagan's rhetoric has badly shaken the self-esteem and patriotic pride of the Soviet political elites. The administration's self-righteous moralistic tone, its reduction of Soviet achievements to crimes by international outlaws from an "evil empire"—such language stunned and humiliated the Soviet leaders, especially since it followed so suddenly a decade of the greatest mutual civility in the history of Soviet-American relations. No one who seeks to understand the political culture of Soviet Russia, not to speak of its historical tradition, should underestimate the potency of words. Among the Soviet elites, who have spent much of their lives manipulating the nuances of ideology, words are taken very seriously. . . . [Reagan's] public disrespect toward the Soviet leaders affected them personally. His assault on the legitimacy of the Soviet system and the prestige of its leaders humiliated them before their domestic audience. His denunciation of Soviet international behavior diminished them before the world audience. The persistent rhetorical onslaught created for the Soviet leaders not only personal grievances but domestic and foreign problems. . . . The consequence for Soviet-American relations is a deeply rooted situation of confrontations exacerbated by personal grudges and high emotions.[33]

Once the extent of the damage had become apparent, various State Department officials began to worry out loud that Reagan had carried his crusade against the Soviet Union too far. Now, with hindsight, they can perhaps recognize what should have been evident along: that Reagan's continual taunts, his superior and patronizing attitudes, his gross insensitivity, his grandiose pose as champion of the forces of good, and his obstreperous and hypocritical moralizing—that all of these, while unavoidable in the schoolyard, are entirely out of place in relations between the leaders of nations. Perhaps no incident typifies Reagan's schoolboy mentality better than the occasion in West Berlin when, at Checkpoint Charlie, the crossing point in the Berlin Wall, he dangled his foot over the white line marking the perimeter in a puerile gesture of defiance.[34]

No one can say, however, that the Reagan administration had not been warned about the probable consequences of its treatment of the Soviets. In an important article published in January 1982, but which evidently fell on deaf ears, George Kennan wrote that

> the view of the Soviet Union that prevails today in large portions of our governmental and journalistic establishments [is] so extreme, so subjective, so far removed from what any sober scrutiny of external reality would reveal, that it is not only ineffective but dangerous as a guide to political action. This endless series of distortions and oversimplifications; this systematic dehumanization of the leadership of another great country; this routine exaggeration of Moscow's mili-

> tary capabilities and of the supposed iniquity of Soviet intentions; this monotonous misrepresentation of the nature and the attitudes of another great people—and a long-suffering people at that, sorely tried by the vicissitudes of this past century; this ignoring their pride, their hopes—yes, even their illusions (for they have their illusions, just as we have ours; and illusions too, deserve respect); this reckless application of the double standard to the judgment of Soviet conduct and our own; this failure to recognize, finally, the communality of many of their problems and ours as we both move inexorably into the modern technological age; and this corresponding tendency to view all aspects of the relationship in terms of a supposed total and irreconcilable conflict of concerns and of aims: these, believe me, are not the marks of the maturity and discrimination one expects in the diplomacy of a great power; they are the marks of an intellectual primitivism and naivete unpardonable in a great government. . . . Above all, we must learn to see the behavior of the leadership of [the Soviet Union] as partly the reflection of our own treatment of it. If we insist on demonizing these Soviet leaders—on viewing them as total and incorrigible enemies, consumed only with their fear or hatred of us and dedicated to nothing other than our destruction—that, in the end, is the way we shall assuredly have them—if for no other reason than that our view of them allows for nothing else—either for them or for us.[35]

The administration's failure to heed such warnings, and its consequent persistence in exacerbating East-West tensions, have brought the world closer to annihilation. Even more than the destabilizing trends in nuclear-weapons technology, the current mutual fears and animosities between the United States and the Soviet Union threaten at any moment to erupt into war. Not only is it now likely that there will be more occasions for crisis and confrontation, but also, in the absence of communication and mutual understanding, moments of crisis are likely to be far more dangerous than they have been even in the recent past. The situation is now such that neither side will be likely to yield. The Beirut débâcle notwithstanding, Reagan is not the sort of man who is likely to back down in a serious showdown with the evil empire—especially not now, when he has years of crusading rhetoric to live up to. Nor are the Soviets in any mood to suffer further humiliation. Bialer has remarked that, in the case of the Soviet Union, "a rekindled sense of insecurity fires an angry and defiant response, a desire to lash out, to reassert self-esteem, to restore the diminished respect of others."[36] The Soviets will not now retreat as they did during the Cuban missile crisis. Thus, as the editors of the London *Guardian* observed in the wake of Andropov's address, "the immediate outlook has seldom seemed so bleak."[37]

The Prospects for Peace

Since *The Guardian* published that somber assessment, there have been faint signs of improvement in the perilous state of Soviet-American relations. While the airliner incident helped to create a solid anti-Soviet consensus, there remained a countervailing consensus: that nuclear war would be a bad idea. Thus, despite their hostility to the Soviet Union, the American people became increasingly disturbed by the complete breakdown in relations between the two countries. When Reagan's pollsters and image engineers discovered that these fears were his greatest liability in the forthcoming election, they quickly converted him to the cause of international peace and reconciliation, whereupon he immediately began rehearsing for the dramatic new role of peacemaker. In January 1984, in a fulsome display of high statesmanship, he appeared on television shaking an olive branch at the Soviet Union: "1984 is a year of opportunities for peace. . . . Our commitment to dialogue is firm and unshakeable. . . . We will negotiate in good faith. Whenever the Soviet Union is ready to do likewise, we'll meet them halfway."[38] The performance ended with a poignant and edifying homily based on a little story about Jim and Sally who find themselves sharing a shelter in a storm with Ivan and Anya. These two charming fictitious couples immediately bridge the gulf of the Cold War and begin to discuss such things as "what they wanted for the children."[39] The moral of the story was that "above all they would have proven that people don't make wars. People want to raise their children in a world without fear and without war"—a moral which demonstrated beyond question that the President understood, sympathized with, and even shared the yearning for peace of all the Jims and Sallys who would be casting their votes in November.

Nine months later, with the election only a month away and with most of the year of opportunities for peace having passed without any appreciable change in the state of Soviet-American relations, Reagan pursued the same upbeat themes in a speech before the U.N. General Assembly. A few days later he received Soviet Foreign Minister Andrei Gromyko at the White House—his first meeting with a member of the Soviet Politburo since he had assumed office almost four years earlier.

All of this could be entirely dismissed as pre-election politicking were it not that there has been continued evidence of a slight thaw in relations since Reagan's reelection. While the thaw has been evident in small things, such as the resumption of agricultural cooperation, the most important sign of improvement was the announcement, soon after the election, that the Soviet and American foreign ministers would be meeting in Geneva on January 7–8, 1985, to discuss a broad range of issues including the resumption of arms control negotiations.

The prospect of high-level talks between the two countries following a full four years of estrangement and intense hostility has set off a wave of optimism in the United States. The optimism has been fueled by Reagan's decision to appoint Paul Nitze as a special adviser to Secretary of State Shultz. This is considered auspicious on the ground that, remarkable as it may seem, Nitze is a "moderate" among Reagan's arms control advisers—that is, he is not implacably opposed to any arms control agreement whatsoever. Shultz and Nitze together, it is thought, may carry enough weight to override the objections of the real hard-liners in the administration who want to abandon the arms control process altogether.[40]

Is there any real basis for optimism here? One encouraging fact is that the opening is occurring when Reagan no longer has to worry about reelection. So there is reason for thinking that this is more than just a public relations ploy—unless, of course, one extends the relevant public to include future generations. One plausible speculation is that the intended audience for Reagan's performance as the man of peace is none other than posterity, or history itself. If true, this is certainly encouraging.

On the other hand, there are reasons for doubting that much will come of this new initiative. There is, for one thing, considerable uncertainty on the Soviet side. The Soviet Union has recently passed through two succession crises, and yet another is likely to occur in the relatively near future. Until there is some stability in the leadership of the Soviet Union, the Soviet role in any process of mutual accommodation will remain unpredictable. On the U.S. side, there is continued factional strife within the administration on the question of relations with the Soviet Union and the value of arms control, and the hard-liners have by no means lost their clout. The tension was revealed rather vividly when, just three days before making the conciliatory address in January 1984 in which he affirmed the "unshakeable" commitment to negotiations, Reagan dispatched White House aides to the Congress to brief conservative senators on a recently completed report he had had prepared which alleged that the Soviets were cheating in a number of ways on previous arms control agreements. The report stated that "Soviet non-compliance is a serious matter. It calls into question important security benefits from arms control."[41] A short while later Assistant Defense Secretary Richard Perle presented further evidence to the Senate Armed Services Committee, saying that "at some point one has to ask the question whether the objective of arms control—which is to create stability and greater security—is best served by unverifiable arms control agreements or by the classical resort to self-defense measures."[42] Shortly after the announcement in November of the forthcoming talks between Shultz and Gromyko, hard-liners in the administration again sought to undermine the new conciliatory approach by sending the Congress a revised version of the original report.

Another worrying possibility is that, even if the hard-liners are unable to block a limited rapprochement with the Soviet Union, it may nevertheless be necessary to appease them by, for example, offering them Nicaragua or El Salvador as a sacrifice. In calling attention to this possibility, Richard Falk has pointed out that "Nixon extended the war in IndoChina in various ways on the eve of his 1972 'peacemaking' journey to Peking and Moscow, including the heavy and provocative bombing of Haiphong Harbor."[43]

A further ground for skepticism about the significance of the new opening is that popular pressure for improved relations and an end to the nuclear arms race appears to be subsiding. Americans seem to suffer from short-term political attention spans. For example, the evidence suggests that the nuclear-freeze movement, which in the summer of 1982 attracted three quarters of a million people to the streets of New York City, is now fading as an active force in American politics. Soon it may pass into oblivion along with the many other fads which have appeared and disappeared in the rapid succession of ephemera to which Americans have become addicted. Certainly the movement proved to be of little help to Mondale, whose own capitulation to the right on so many matters of foreign policy was itself an ominous portent for opposition politics in the coming years.

Perhaps as a result of people repressing anxieties which they find too disturbing to confront, concern about the precarious state of the world has for the moment been supplanted by a burst of carefree patriotic fervor. People have simply abandoned themselves to mindless flag-waving and largely groundless optimism about the future. As *Time* magazine put it, in phrases attuned to the national mood, "America feels fat and sassy, loose and sure-footed . . . for now it is as refreshing as a summer romance."[44] How refreshing this is is perhaps a matter of perspective. There is certainly an ugly, assertive side to the new mood. And the superior, aggressive attitudes to the outside world have been accompanied by a celebration of the pursuit of self-interest at home. Reagan has not only made people feel good about being Americans; he has also made them feel comfortable about being selfish.

With the American public so engrossed in the pleasures of self-appreciation, it is doubtful whether Reagan will be called upon to take radical action to reduce the threat of nuclear war with the Soviet Union. And, given his record, he is even more unlikely to seize the initiative himself. As various parts of the foregoing discussion have suggested, the Reagan administration's foreign policy has been astonishingly similar in most respects to those of his recent predecessors. He is by no means unique in his vigorous escalation of the arms race and his efforts to control the nations of the third world. (It is not the Reagan administration but the Carter administration which most deviated from the recurrent pattern which American foreign policy has followed since World War II.) The most striking difference between Reagan and his predecessors is that his enthusiasm for the Cold War and determination to win the arms race have prevented him from seriously pursuing even largely symbolic or cosmetic agreements with the Soviet Union on the control of nuclear arms. If we see a change in this respect during the second term—and Reagan really may wish to carry a peace treaty with him into the history books—the most that can be hoped for is a treaty which, like those his predecessors signed, keeps things from getting worse in certain respects but does nothing to *enhance* the security of the world by reversing the trends of the past four decades.

It would be a mistake to expect good things from Reagan's second term. Our hopes must focus on the future after Reagan—on the possibility, admittedly rather remote, that the American people will come to understand just how far the country has strayed from the moral and political ideals which they mistakenly believe it represents. For this to happen, people will have to be disabused of their patriotic delusions and recognize that, in addition to those aspects of the country of which they can be justifiably proud, the country has a darker side which the government tries to conceal but which is painfully evident to the victims of its aggression. These latter view the United States, not as the selfless protector and promoter of freedom, democracy, justice, and human rights that it is portrayed to be in domestic political propaganda, but as an acquisitive, bullying, exploiter of oppressed and impoverished peoples, a country whose continuous struggles with the Soviet Union recklessly put at risk the future of the whole of humanity.

Is there any real hope that the American people can be aroused from their complacent patriotic fantasies? One scenario suggests itself. If Central America were to explode, there would be an outbreak of Vietnam syndrome which could soon reach epidemic proportions. Even those young Americans whose sole concern at present is the advancement of their own careers might become less enthusiastic about Reagan's imperial policies if they were to be required to share in the killing and dying. Let us hope, however, that there is a way less costly in innocent blood to bring an arrogant "superpower" to its senses.

Appendix: The Report of the Kissinger Commission on Central America

The enthusiasm with which the report of the Scowcroft Commission on Strategic Forces was received confirmed the Reagan administration's estimation of the effectiveness of bipartisan commissions as instruments for the manipulation of public opinion. Hence, shortly after the Scowcroft commission delivered its report, the president established another bipartisan commission to do for the administration's policies in Central America what the Scowcroft Commission had done for the MX. The new commission's mandate was to "study the nature of United States interests in the Central American region and the threats now posed to those interests," to recommend a long-term policy toward the region, and to "provide advice on means of building a national consensus" in support of that policy.[1] In the end the commission had little to say about how a consensus could be engineered; for, as is evident from the report, the commission's real job was to present the essential elements of the administration's preexistent Central America policies as part of a larger package that would appeal to the American public. In short, the commission's primary function was to assist in the creation of the desired consensus in support of the administration's policies.

Henry Kissinger was chosen to chair the commission—perhaps in part because of his known tendency to ingratiate himself in the White House by adopting and aggressively defending the views of whatever president he happens to be serving. Unfortunately for the commission's credibility, however, Kissinger's appointment roughly coincided with the publication of Seymour Hersh's devastating critique of Kissinger's role in the White House during Nixon's first term in office.[2] Hersh's book revealed, among a great many other things, the contempt with which Kissinger had always regarded the whole of Latin America. The book relates an exchange between Kissinger and Gabriel Valdés, who was at the time the Chilean foreign minister. After Valdés had had the audacity to speak to Nixon in defense of Latin American interests, Kissinger addressed him as follows:

> "Mr. Minister, you made a strange speech. You come here speaking of Latin America, but this is not important. Nothing important can come from the South. History has never been produced in the South. The axis of history starts in Moscow, goes to Bonn, crosses over to Wash-

> ington, and then goes to Tokyo. What happens in the South is of no importance. You're wasting your time." "I said," Valdés recalls, "Mr. Kissinger, you know nothing of the South." "No," Kissinger answered, "and I don't care."[3]

On another occasion, Kissinger disparagingly referred to Latin America as "a dagger pointed at the heart of Antarctica."[4] These earlier performances make a mockery of Kissinger's pious expression, on behalf of the commission, of his "deep respect for the people" of Central America.

The report of Kissinger's harangue against "the South" occurs in the context of Hersh's exposure of the guiding role Kissinger played in the conspiracy against Allende—a conspiracy which involved the manipulation of elections and, ultimately, the subversion of Chilean democracy in order to remove an elected government which threatened U.S. business interests and challenged U.S. hegemony in the area. The sordid facts Hersh has assembled, including apparently reliable reports of a plan, produced at Kissinger's personal initiative, for the assassination of Allende, serve to cast some doubt on the sincerity of the commission's repeated encomiums to democracy, and its declaration that "the issue is not what particular system a nation might choose when it votes. The issue is rather that nations should choose for themselves, free of outside pressure, force or threat. There is room in the hemisphere for differing forms of governance and different political economies."[5]

In order to demonstrate the willingness of the United States to tolerate political and economic diversity in the hemisphere, and in order thereby to discredit the absurd "propaganda of the radical left, which has played upon the theme of economic hegemony and 'imperialism,'" the commission has produced a sanitized history according to which "the nations of the Western Hemisphere have been moved from the beginning of their histories by a common devotion to freedom from foreign domination, sovereign equality, and the right of people to determine the forms and methods of their own governance."[6] In pursuit of these high ideals, the United States in 1823 proclaimed the Monroe Doctrine, the purpose of which, according to the commission, was to keep "this hemisphere off limits to the territorial ambitions of European colonialism."[7] Though some Latin Americans have challenged some aspects of this doctrine, to this day "they have never questioned its central inspiration: the vision of a hemisphere united by a core of common commitment to independence and liberty."[8]

Moving along to the twentieth century, the commission notes that

> for the most part, U.S. policy toward Central America during the early part of this century focused primarily on promoting the stability and solvency of local governments so as to keep other nations out. This was reflected in Theodore Roosevelt's Corollary to the Monroe Doctrine, which held that the United States should take action to prevent situations from arising that might lead to interventions by extra-hemispheric powers. Theodore Roosevelt once defined the sole desire of the United States as being "to see all neighbouring countries stable, orderly and prosperous." This formulation reflects both a great-power interest in keeping the hemisphere insulated from European intrigue and the concern for others' well-being that has often animated our foreign policy.[9]

The commission concedes, however, that the pursuit of these disinterested and benevolent aims required "a high degree of intervention in Central America during the early 1900s." Nicaragua is cited by way of example: U.S. Marines invaded the country and deposed its president in 1909 "in an effort to restore stability." They soon returned to occupy the country from 1912 to 1925 and from 1926 to 1933, creating the notorious National Guard with Anastasio Somoza García as its commander before they left—all "to provide stability."[10]

In short, it is only the Europeans who have harbored colonialist "territorial ambitions" and have engaged in "intrigues" in Central America. (Even the acquisitive, scheming Europeans cannot be accused of "subversion" and "terrorism"—these labels being reserved for the actions of Cuba and the Soviet Union.) By contrast, the United States and its allies in the region have been motivated entirely by an altruistic concern for "stability" and "order." (Even the wave of fierce repression in Central America in the 1930s, which included the *matanza* in El Salvador, is referred to as "having restored order."[11]) In political discourse, however, "stability" and "order" are notoriously empty concepts which are in general used to designate states of affairs congenial to the speaker. In order to gain some insight into the reality which those terms mask, we may refer to several quotations from those responsible for U.S. policy during the relevant period—quotations the commission unaccountably fails to mention. Thus the transcendent moral purpose of the United States in Central America was eloquently articulated by Theodore Roosevelt's successor, William Howard Taft, in 1912—the year the Marines returned to Nicaragua: "The day is not far distant when three Stars and Stripes at three equidistant points will mark our territory: one at the North Pole, another at the Panama Canal, and the third at the South Pole. The whole hemisphere will be ours in fact as, by virtue of our superiority of race, it already is ours morally." According to the commission, "in Central America today, our strategic and moral interests coincide."[12] Happily, U.S. officials found this to be true earlier in the century as well. As Under Secretary of State Robert Olds noted in 1927, "We do control Central America and we do so for the simple reason that the national interest absolutely dictates such a course." In 1935 General Smedley D. Butler elaborated on the interests involved:

> I spent thirty-three years and four months in active service as a member of our country's most agile military force—the Marine Corps. . . . And during that period I spent most of my time being a high-class muscle man for Big Business, for Wall Street, and for the bankers. In short, I was a racketeer for capitalism. . . . Thus I helped make Mexico and especially Tampico safe for American oil interests in 1914. I helped make Haiti and Cuba a decent place for the National City Bank to collect revenues in. . . . I helped purify Nicaragua for the international banking house of Brown Brothers in 1909–1912. I brought light to the Dominican Republic for American sugar interests in 1916. I helped make Honduras "right" for American fruit companies in 1903.

These quotations, from people obviously deluded by "propaganda of the radical left," are taken from the admirable history by Jenny Pearce, *Under the Eagle.*[13] This and other histories which bear some relation to the facts (for example, Walter LaFeber's *Inevitable Revolutions*[14]) show a consistent pattern in which the countries of Central America and the Caribbean were regularly invaded, continuously controlled and directed (either under occupation or through the American Embassy), and rapaciously plundered by the United States. Pearce's chronology of events from 1900 to 1962 includes the following:[15]

1898–02	U.S. troops occupy Cuba
1901	U.S. acquires Puerto Rico
1905	U.S. marines land at Puerto Cortes, Honduras
1906–09	U.S. troops occupy Cuba
1908	U.S. troops sent to Panama
1909	U.S.-backed overthrow of Zelaya in Nicaragua
1910	U.S. troops land in Honduras
1912	U.S. troops sent to Panama
1912	U.S. troops occupy Cuba
1912	U.S. troops briefly occupy Puerto Cortes, Honduras
1912–25	U.S. marines occupy Nicaragua

1914–34	U.S. marines occupy Haiti
1916–24	U.S. marines occupy Dominican Republic
1917–23	U.S. marines occupy Cuba
1918	U.S. troops sent to Panama
1919	U.S. marines occupy Honduras' ports
1924	U.S. marines land in Honduras
1926–33	U.S. marines occupy Nicaragua and set up National Guard under Somoza; Sandino defeated and assassinated
1932	U.S. warships stand by during El Salvador *matanza*
1954	CIA-backed invasion of Guatemala
1961	Abortive CIA-backed Bay of Pigs invasion of Cuba

Unlike the Kissinger commission, the State Department was often candid in acknowledging the aims of these interventions. Thus what the commission refers to as efforts to "restore stability" in Nicaragua between 1912 and 1925 was actually intended, according to the State Department at the time, "to protect American interests during an attempted revolution," while the occupation from 1926 to 1933 was intended "to protect the interests of the United States."[16]

The commission has had to rewrite this inconvenient history, since it shows that there is some substance to the disagreeable "progaganda of the radical left," and also provides some foundation for the charge, which the commission dismisses, that "this nation's policies have been the principal cause of the region's afflictions."[17] At a minimum it raises the awkward question how the problems of poverty, inequality, illiteracy, repression, and so on, which the commission deplores, were allowed to develop when, as Robert Olds noted, "our ministers accredited to the five little republics . . . have been advisers whose advice has been accepted virtually as law in the capitals where they respectively reside. . . . Central America has always understood that governments which we recognize and support stay in power, while those we do not recognize and support fail."[18] The idea that previous American meddling in Central America is one of the primary causes of the region's problems would be difficult to reconcile with the commission's call for expanded American intervention. Therefore the evidence for this idea must be expunged from the historical record.

The commission's account of the current situation in Central America is similarly distorted. Thus, in discussing El Salvador, the commission rehearses the administration's myth of the beleaguered democratic center:

> In El Salvador two separate conflicts have raged since 1979. One conflict pits persons seeking democratic government and its associated rights and freedoms against those trying to maintain oligarchical rule and its associated privileges. A second conflict pits guerrillas seeking to establish a Marxist-Leninist state as part of a broader Central American revolution against those who oppose a Marxist-Leninist victory.[19]

The commission then naturally identifies the democratic center with the government, thereby neatly providing itself a way of making the politically necessary expressions of revulsion at the activities of the death squads without compromising its support for those whom, as we saw earlier, the death squads in fact serve—namely, the military, which was then and for the most part still is the de facto government. (There were of course divisions within the government—with Magaña, a piece of civilian window dressing, serving as the figurehead of one faction and D'Aubuisson leading the other—but these could hardly be characterized as a conflict between the democratic center and the oligarchy. Until Duarte reemerged as president in March 1984, after the commission had reported, nothing even remotely resembling the fabled democratic center had been involved in the power structure of the Salvadoran government since the civilian members of the 1979–80 junta resigned in despair over their impotence—some, including Ungo, in order to join the guerrillas.)

The government is depicted as striving against great odds to enact reforms. Thus on several occasions the commission speaks in glowing terms of the government's "sweeping program of land reform"[20]—ignoring the fact that the agrarian reform program had been completely subverted by D'Aubuisson and his supporters following his election to the presidency of the Constituent Assembly in the U.S.-staged elections of 1982, which the commission describes as "impressive."[21] The commission further asserts without elaboration that the Salvadoran government "allows debate, freedom of assembly, opposition and other aspects of democracy, however imperfect."[22] Nothing is said about what happens to those who are foolhardy enough to try to exercise these democratic freedoms.

By contrast with the government, the opposition guerrillas are consistently portrayed as brutal terrorists who "hide behind" the death squads.[23] In the passage quoted above, they are not even given credit for being involved with the Forces of Good in the struggle against the injustice of the oligarchical system: they are instead said to be obsessed solely with the establishment of tyranny throughout Central America. The commission also repeatedly claims that the guerrillas have attracted little popular support, though later it warns that the defeat of the government "is not inconceivable."[24] This leaves it with the job of explaining how the guerrillas are able to maintain their remarkable strength in the absence of a popular base. While the commission never addresses this problem directly, it asserts elsewhere that the guerrillas' strength derives from external support (from Cuba, Nicaragua, and the Soviet Union). To accept this explanation one would have to believe that the external assistance received by the guerrillas is many times greater than that which the United States has provided to the government—a claim the commission understandably fails to defend.

Similarly, in discussing the situation in Guatemala, the commission notes with enthusiasm that the coup which installed General Ríos Montt "broke the political pattern of the past": "Under Ríos Montt the Guatemalan army made significant progress against the guerrilla forces, combining civic action with aggressive military action into a strategy of 'beans and bullets.' "[25] As we saw earlier, this "progress" in counterinsurgency was the result of a campaign of mass murder aimed at destroying the guerrillas' base of support among the peasants. Ríos Montt explained the strategy as follows: "Look, the problem of the war is not just a question of who is shooting; for each one that is shooting there are ten working behind him." His press secretary then elaborated further: "The guerrillas won over many Indian collaborators. Therefore, the Indians were subversives, right? And how do you fight subversion? Clearly, you had to kill Indians because they were collaborating with subversion. And then they would say, you are massacring innocent people. But they weren't innocent. They had sold out to subversion."[26] In order to produce a "balanced" account, the commission notes the reports of genocide in the Guatemalan countryside, though with judicious skepticism: "Some rural areas were reportedly terrorized with killings designed to end local support for the guerrillas."[27]

The commission found it unnecessary, however, to qualify in a similar fashion its account of the brutality of the Sandinistas in Nicaragua. According to the commission, the Sandinistas are developing "sophisticated agencies of internal repression and external subversion," and thus, if there were to be "a proliferation of Marxist-Leninist states" (as Nicaragua is said to be), "that would *increase* violence, dislocation, and political repression in the region."[28] This of course implies that violence and repression are *already* greater in Nicaragua (and, by implication, in Cuba) than in El Salvador or Guatemala. Indeed, the commission asserts that the record of the Salvadoran government "compares very favourably

. . . with that of its neighbour, Nicaragua."[29] In its account of the Salvadoran government's glorious achievements—such as the 1982 elections and the land reform program—the commission points out that it is "only fair" to note that "all of this has been done in the midst of a bitter war."[30] By contrast, nothing is said of the effects on Sandinista policy of the war being waged against the Nicaraguan government by U.S. proxy forces. These forces, the contras, are led by men who, according to the commission, are among the "democratic opposition" whom the Sandinistas have excluded from power. There is no suggestion that these patriots could ever have been involved in the violation of human rights. Once again avoiding any rash speculation, the commission notes that the contras are only "reportedly" in receipt of U.S. aid, though a majority of the commissioners favor U.S. support for the contras on the ground that the war gives the Sandinistas an "incentive" to negotiate. There is no discussion of the repeated rejections of the Sandinistas' many offers to negotiate, or of the U.S. refusal to allow Tomás Borge Martínez, the Nicaraguan interior minister, to enter the United States for talks with government officials.

Neither is there any discussion of the contra war, the U.S. military exercises in the region, or the transformation of Honduras into an American forward base when the commission comes to consider Nicaragua's efforts to strengthen its military forces. Rather the commission is content to repeat Reagan's assertion that Nicaragua's arms programs threaten Honduras: Honduras is said to be gripped by "a deep anxiety over the extraordinary military buildup in Nicaragua."[31] With this claim the commission has reached the outer limits of cynical mendacity. With Nicaragua under attack by forces based in Honduras and supported by the Honduran government, and with the United States and Honduras doing their utmost, though without success, to provoke a Nicaraguan attack in order for Honduras to have a pretext for inviting direct U.S. intervention, it is little short of insulting to be told that it is Nicaragua that is the aggressor.

With this incredible fabricated history and distorted survey of recent events as background, the commission passes on to its recommendations for economic assistance, reforms, and military assistance. I shall not discuss in detail the program of economic aid, except to remark that, while it is superficially magnanimous, its likely upshot would be the strengthening of U.S. economic dominance in the region, along with a tremendous flow of U.S. dollars into the coffers of Central America's ruling elites, with little perceptible effect on the region's impoverished masses—as has happened before during periods of economic growth stimulated in part by similar programs of U.S. economic assistance (for example, in the 1960s during the days of the Alliance for Progress).

While the commission's economic recommendations might do very little to benefit the region's poor, the humanitarian programs and reforms which it proposes are directly intended to help relieve some of the most pressing problems which the mass of Central Americans face: poverty, hunger, high infant mortality, low life expectancy, the spread of preventable infectious diseases, illiteracy, inadequate housing, and so on. In various places throughout the report the commission reviews with apparent concern the appalling conditions in which most Central Americans live. It would have been interesting, however, had the commission compared conditions in Nicaragua and Cuba today with prerevolutionary conditions in those countries, and with conditions in El Salvador, Guatemala, and Honduras today. Such a comparison would have revealed that, despite the economic sanctions imposed by the United States, the revolutions in Cuba and Nicaragua resulted in a remarkable improvement in the lives of the poor, with reductions in both the infant mortality rate and the incidence of infectious disease, and increases in both life expectancy and the level of literacy. While at one point the commission grudgingly concedes that the Sandinistas have made "significant gains against illiteracy and disease," it goes on immediately to criticize them for economic mismanagement which, it is claimed, is responsible for the country's low per capita income, as well as the shortages of food and consumer goods.[32] No mention is made in this connection of the legacy of decades of mismanagement and corruption under the Somozas, the continuing effects of the civil war, U.S. economic sanctions, and the assaults mounted against the Nicaraguan economy by the contras. In general, while the commission eagerly clutches at straws—such as the bogus and moribund agrarian reform program in El Salvador and the genocidal "beans and bullets" campaign in Guatemala—in order to heap praise on U.S. allies in the region, it consistently plays down the achievements of the Sandinistas, as, for example, when it asserts that infant mortality "is" higher in Nicaragua than elsewhere in the region, while citing as evidence a statistic from 1980, before the Sandinista programs had had a chance to bring the infant imortality rate down.[33] According to State Department officials, Kissinger even went so far as to engineer the replacement of Anthony Quainton as U.S. ambassador to Nicaragua because Quainton had reported that the Sandinistas were making progress in the areas of education and health care, thereby supposedly damaging the credibility of the commission's report.[34]

These facts raise fundamental questions about the commission's priorities. Why are the commissioners so anxious to suppress in El Salvador, Guatamala, and Honduras a revolutionary process which in Nicaragua and Cuba has made dramatic progress in achieving the humanitarian aims which the commission claims to endorse? Why is it that the American elite have been undisturbed since the mid 1960s by the poverty and misery of most Central Americans, and have only now begun to evince concern for their well-being? What does it tell us about the commissioners' concern for human development that they recommend continued support for the contras, who specialize in slaughtering doctors, teachers, and persons involved in development projects in the Nicaraguan countryside?

The fact that the commissioners are anxious to preserve regimes which have repeatedly demonstrated their utter indifference to social justice and the plight of the region's impoverished majority, together with the fact that they support armed attacks by the remnants of one such regime against the government of Nicaragua, whose efforts on behalf of the poor are obscured or ignored in the commission's report, suggests that the commissioners' primary interest is in effective counterinsurgency rather than the well-being of the people of Central America. Just as in the case of the Alliance for Progress, which was a direct response to the Cuban revolution, with programs for reform and development aimed primarily at containing the spread of revolutionary sentiment, the Kissinger commission's recommendations come at a time when conditions in Central America have reached such an appalling state that the people, emboldened perhaps by the successful revolution in Nicaragua, are striving to overthrow by force the old order which has been responsible for the maintenance of those conditions. The commission recognizes (as some administration officials apparently have not) that these domestic conditions provide the impetus for revolt: "Discontents are real, and for much of the population conditions of life are miserable; just as Nicaragua was ripe for revolution, so the conditions that invite revolution are present elsewhere in the region as well."[35] Therefore counterinsurgency—the prevention or suppression of popular revolt—requires reforms which to some extent alleviate the sources of discontent.

The idea that reforms can serve as an instrument of counterinsurgency is an old one, but it has been well discussed in a recent book by Richard Alan White.[36] White writes that "certainly reforms are not inherently negative or implicitly a means of forestalling social change. But when used within the context of a counterinsurgency campaign [as the Kissinger commission recommends], their objective is not to improve the well-being of the people per se;

rather, it is to make relatively superficial changes which would undermine popular support of the rebels."[37] He cites the example of land reform in El Salvador to illustrate how the process works. He notes that, according to Thomas Enders, formerly the Reagan administration's assistant secretary of state for inter-American affairs,

> "for the United States it is vital to carry the agrarian reform through. Peasants who have become landowners will be a strong bulwark against the guerrillas." Granting peasants their own piece of land has an immediate, enduring, and conservative influence. The new landowners feel that they must protect their newly acquired possession of land, which by extension means preserving the existing social order. Their false sense of security, and insecurity, is exploited by the government through campaigns against the "communist subversives" who threaten the new status of the "peasant capitalist."[38]

These remarks explain how, as we saw earlier, land reform is supposed to "breed capitalists like rabbits."

There is considerable evidence in the report that the commission's primary aim in advocating reforms is to defeat the insurgents in Central America. At one point, for example, the commissioners note that the insurgencies in Central America have acquired "a momentum which reforms *alone* cannot stop"; hence "political, economic and social programs do not *by themselves* defeat these insurgencies, *though they address a central part of the problem.*"[39] The commissioners then go on to recommend an "enlightened counterinsurgency" strategy which requires "two forms of military action . . . *in addition to* continued action on the economic and social fronts."[40] Even the promotion of human rights has its function in the overall counterinsurgency strategy: "Respect for human rights is . . . of great importance to improved security in Central America."[41] Here, of course, the commissioners mean more than that people are unlikely to be "secure" when they are being tortured. "Security" in this context is shorthand for the absence of armed revolt. The commission's concern for human rights is further elucidated in its condemnation of the death squads: "Their violent attacks upon Salvadoran democrats handicap the struggle to resist the armed insurgency of the guerrillas."[42] In short, the activities of the death squads are counterproductive. (Apparently, however, they are counterproductive only when they are aimed at "democrats"—unless we are to believe that the death squads do not kill insurgents or their supporters.) Of course, the commissioners also express a moral concern for the protection of human rights, and for reforms generally, and no doubt they are sincere in this;

but, in the light of the rest of their report, it is unclear how far this moral concern would take them if reforms were not also relevant to the counterinsurgency effort.

Perhaps the most revealing passage in the chapter on reforms concerns the provision of scholarships for Central Americans to attend universities in the United States. The commission notes that the Soviet Union, Eastern European countries, and Cuba have recently been providing a very large number of scholarships for Central American students to attend their universities. The United States, by contrast, has provided far fewer scholarships, and those which it has given have generally gone to students from affluent families, while the efforts of the communist states have focused on students from low-income families. The commissioners find this alarming. Why? They provide the answer indirectly: "In all the Central American countries, political and academic leaders emphasized the long-run cost of having so many of Central America's potential future leaders—especially those from disadvantaged backgrounds—educated in Soviet bloc countries."[43] In short, if Central America's future leaders receive their higher education in communist states, they may become sympathetic to those countries and their values. This could ultimately lead to a loss of U.S. influence in the region. Thus, according to the commission, the United States must surpass the efforts of the communist states in order to ensure that the United States rather than its enemies wins the hearts and minds of future Central American leaders: "Because of the important implications which the training of a country's future leaders has on its political development, we believe this would represent a sound investment of U.S. assistance funds."[44] This is fairly typical of the way in which the commission treats the subject of reforms.

Reforms are, in effect, treated as an adjunct to the military efforts against insurgents in Central America. In support of these efforts, the commission recommends the provision of "significantly increased levels of military aid as quickly as possible" to the government of El Salvador, "increased U.S. military assistance to Honduras," and the authorization of renewed military aid and military sales to the government of Guatemala.[45] The commission stipulates, however, that aid should be provided to the governments of El Salvador and Guatemala only if they demonstrate progress toward satisfying "certain minimum standards of respect for human rights."[46] (Since the commission recommends an *immediate* increase in military aid to El Salvador, it is presumably only *subsequent* provisions of aid that are to be conditional on progress in respect for human rights.) On the other hand, the commission recommends no effective way of ensuring that this condition is met before aid is given. It proposes that there should be "legislation requiring periodic reports"—that is, a certification process which allows the executive itself to determine whether the condition has been met. As experience has shown, this arrangement cannot constrain an administration determined to get aid through to an ally. Before Reagan vetoed a previous certification requirement of exactly the sort the commission recommends, he had no qualms about asserting before Congress that the Salvadoran government was making progress in controlling the violation of human rights, even when it was evident that respect for human rights was deteriorating. (Even though the human rights condition is thus completely without teeth, Kissinger and two other commissioners filed a dissenting comment, asserting their "strong view that neither the Congress nor the Executive Branch [should] interpret conditionality in a manner that leads to a Marxist-Leninist victory in El Salvador, thereby damaging vital American interests and risking a larger war."[47] In short, "friendly" butchers, no matter how repressive they may be, are preferable to the guerrillas, regardless of how much popular support within the country the latter might have.)

The overriding aim of the commission's report, which underlies all of its more specific recommendations, is thus to ensure the defeat of the insurgent movements in Central America. Although the commissioners repeatedly assert that their recommendations are in the interests of North and Central Americans alike, the reasons which they give for assigning overriding priority to the defeat of the insurgents all appeal essentially to U.S. self-interest. The principal reason they cite is that the insurgents pose a threat to U.S. security. If the insurgents in either El Salvador or Guatemala were to succeed in seizing power, they would then pose a military threat to the southern borders of the United States to which the United States would be obliged to respond. Hence "we would either have to assume a permanently increased defense burden, or see our capacity to defend distant troublespots reduced, and as a result have to reduce important commitments elsewhere in the world."[48]

Why does the commission assume that victorious revolutionaries in Central America would be hostile to the United States and thus pose a threat to its security? The answer is that, according to the commission, the revolutionaries are sponsored by and aligned with the Soviet Union, so that their achieving control in their respective countries would constitute "a further projection of Soviet and Cuban power in the region."[49]

The commission cites several reasons for thinking that the insurgent movements in Central America are inspired and controlled by the Soviet Union. The main reason is that they depend on "imported arms and imported ideology."[50] The idea that an insurgent movement must be under foreign domination if it has a supposedly "imported ideology" is a curious one. The suggestion seems to be that the adoption by Central Americans of theories prominent in the East is somehow equivalent to ideological or philosophical *aggression* by the authors or other adherents of those ideas. Using this logic, one could cite the fact that the revolutions in Central America have been inspired to a considerable extent by Christian theology (a fact which the commission is careful to suppress) to prove that they are the products of a sinister plot hatched in the bowels of the Vatican.

On the question of imported arms, it is not clear what it would show if it were indeed true that the guerrillas in El Salvador were receiving significant supplies of arms from Cuba and the Soviet Union. As William LeoGrande has pointed out, "The American Revolution received substantial assistance from France, but one could hardly deny its indigenous character on these grounds alone."[51] And, in any case, the commission is unable to marshall any credible evidence that the Salvadoran guerrillas are in receipt of more than a minimal supply of arms from Cuba or the Soviet Union. The most impressive piece of evidence that the commission is able to muster is the claim of the chairman of the House Intelligence Oversight Committee in 1982 that there was "persuasive evidence that the Sandinista government is helping train [Salvadoran] insurgents and is transferring arms and support from and through Nicaragua to the insurgents. . . . Cuban involvement in providing arms—is also evident."[52] The commissioners have put aside the cautious skepticism with which they received reports of U.S. aid to the contras, and accept without question the congressman's assurance that compelling evidence of some sort or other does exist—perhaps on the ground that evidence which could be convincing to a congressman must be valid, since everyone knows how difficult it is to convince a member of Congress of the existence of external communist subversion in "America's backyard." But, even granting the known reluctance of members of Congress to give credence to tales of communist subversion, the congressman's statement gives no indication of the extent of the support which the Salvadoran rebels are said to receive, nor any reason to believe that the Soviet Union is involved in the transfer of arms. Later in the report the commission devotes a section entitled "The Cuban-Soviet Connection" to an examination of Cuba's military forces, noting the unsurprising fact that Cuba has received arms from the Soviet Union, including such dangerous offensive systems as minesweepers. The commission suggests that Cuba has expanded its armed forces in order to be better able to "export revolution," although with Cuba having suffered for two decades from covert terror operations conducted by its superpower neighbor, and with Reagan's repeated talk of blockading the island, other explanations for Cuba's action do suggest themselves.[53] In any case, the commission's catalog of Cuban jets, submarines, and so on seems at best doubtfully relevant as evidence for Soviet sponsorship of revolution in El Salvador.

Since the commission is unable to cite any direct empirical evidence of Soviet or Cuban aid to the Salvadoran guerrillas, it resorts in the end to a rather simple abstract argument. Appealing to the principle that "protracted guerrilla insurgencies require external assistance," the commission notes that the insurgency in El Salvador has been protracted, and concludes that it must be sustained by external support.[54] William LeoGrande comments that "the elegance of [this argument] has to be envied; if one takes [it] seriously, 'indigenous revolutionary movements' becomes a null set."[55] For the argument's major premise implies that there could never be a successful revolution that was not sustained externally. Thus, as LeoGrande rightly points out, the commission's claim that the United States can tolerate indigenous revolutions becomes "vacuous."

The commission attempts to defend the principle that protracted insurgencies require external support by arguing that "if wretched conditions were themselves enough to create such insurgencies we would see them in many more countries in the world."[56] This is surely right. But it is irrelevant. No one supposes that wretched conditions *alone* are always sufficient to provoke revolution. But from the fact that other factors are necessary it does not follow that among these other factors must be the external provision of arms and ideology.

The commission's comments on the insurgency in Guatemala are interesting in this connection. Nowhere is there any effort to adduce evidence showing that the Guatemalan guerrillas are sponsored by Cuba or the Soviet Union. Indeed, the commission concedes the obvious point that the guerrillas in Guatemala have "geographical" difficulties in obtaining arms from Nicaragua—an oblique way of registering the fact that Guatemala is separated from Nicaragua by Honduras and El Salvador.[57] Nor can the commission appeal to the claim that the insurgency has been protracted in order to prove that it is not indigenous: for, while the insurgency has survived some years, "the Guatemalan armed forces have been able so far to contain [it] without assistance from abroad"—indeed, using the techniques described earlier, they have nearly decimated it on more than one occasion. At the same time the commission recognizes the dreadful conditions in which the majority of Guatemalans have had to live, and acknowleges the exceptional brutality of the Guatemalan "security forces" (that is, of the government). Given the commissioners' repeated assertions that the United States is not threatened by and can therefore tolerate indigenous insurgencies in the hemisphere, one would suppose that they would go some way toward recognizing the legitimacy of the insurgency in Guatemala.[58] Instead, as we have seen, they applaud the government's "progress" in its counterinsurgency war, and recommend military assistance to the government if the insurgency begins to gain in strength. What this shows, I think, is that the commission is concerned to prevent, if necessary by military means, the establishment of *any* left-wing regimes in the hemisphere, regardless of how brutal the regimes they would replace might be. The scaremongering about the "projection" of Soviet power into the hemisphere may be sincere, but it is also exploited to mask a deeper hostility to movements which threaten the U.S. hegemony in its "backyard."

Even if the expressions of anxiety about the threat to the southern borders of the United States are sincere, they are nevertheless misplaced. Do the commissioners really suppose that Cuba and Nicaragua pose a military threat to the United States which can be met only if the United States is willing to shoulder "a permanently increased defense burden"? If not, how can they seriously suggest that such a threat would arise if El Salvador, or even Guatemala, were also to "fall to the communists"?

It is, however, not just the threat from Central American armies that worries the commission; it is also concerned about the establishment of Soviet bases in the region and, in particular, the threat which those bases would pose to US sea lanes through the Caribbean. But the commissioners apparently never asked themselves what incentives Central American countries would have to allow the Soviet Union to establish military bases on their territory. The risks involved in accepting Soviet bases would be high, as Cuba learned in the early 1960s. Surely these countries, whatever their ideological orientation, would rather have U.S. economic aid and freedom from U.S. harassment than a Soviet military base. There would, moreover, be little pressure from the Soviet Union for the establishment of bases, and not just because of the risks involved. LeoGrande has argued that, because the establishment of a Soviet base

> would effectively close off [to the host country] all normal economic relations with the United States and much of the West, the Central

> Americans would presumably demand an economic quid pro quo of the Soviet Union. Therefore, one must . . . assume that the Soviet Union would be prepared to take on the economic burden of "another Cuba"—no small matter given the state of the Soviet economy and Soviet commitments in Afghanistan, Poland, Vietnam, Africa, and Cuba. In exchange for this investment, the Kremlin would acquire military assets that would give it only a marginal strategic advantage over what it already has in Cuba.[59]

Given these facts, it should be a fairly easy matter for the United States to negotiate agreements with revolutionary Central American governments promising them both aid and security in exchange for neutrality. Such agreements have in fact been proposed, but to date the United States has shown no interest whatsoever in accepting them.

In addition to the threat to the U.S. borders and the threat of Soviet bases, there are two other threats to U.S. national security which the commission cites in justification for seeking the defeat of Central American insurgent movements. One is the threat of "foot people," which we discussed in Chapter 5. The commission, it will be recalled, is out to engineer a consensus, and it is no doubt aware that, in certain circles in the United States, nothing kindles the passions more effectively than the specter of teeming brown hordes spilling across the Rio Grande. Thus, taking care to ignore the facts, the commission speculates that further revolutionary advances in Central America would open the floodgates, producing "perhaps millions" of refugees, "many of whom would seek entry into the United States."[60]

The final threat is that to American "credibility." The commission argues, as we have seen, that "the triumph of hostile forces in what the Soviets call the 'strategic rear' of the United States would be read as a sign of U.S. impotence," and hence would erode "our power to influence events worldwide."[61] Of course, if, as I have argued, the insurgent movements in Central America do not in fact threaten U.S. security in other respects, then it may seem unclear why credibility should be at stake. In effect, it is at stake because the United States insists on being perceived as capable of maintaining its hegemony within its "sphere of influence" regardless of whether real interests are at issue. It is to preserve its credibility in this respect that the United States must prevent the people of Central America from working out their own destiny. As one rather more candid defender of U.S. hegemony in the region has argued,

> Central America bears geographical proximity to the United States, and historically it has long been regarded as falling within our sphere of influence. As such, we have long exercised the role great powers have traditionally exercised over small states which fall within their

> respective spheres of influence. We have regularly played a determining role in making and unmaking governments, and we have defined what we have considered to be the acceptable behavior of governments. In Central America our pride is engaged. . . . Reasons of pride and historic tradition apart, it is here, if anywhere, that we enjoy clear military superiority and may expect to retain such superiority in the future.[62]

In short, allowing the Central Americans to wrest control of their own destinies would be humiliating to the United States in its role as a great power. The United States wants Central America—in part for its natural and human resources, but more importantly for its symbolic value—and has the power to keep it. In this instance, therefore, the U.S. commitment to the ideals of "freedom from foreign domination, sovereign equality, and the right of people to determine the forms and methods of their own governance" must give way to weightier concerns.

Notes

1. The Quest for Global Control

1. Quoted in Ian Mather, "A Hawk Upsets NATO," *Observer* (London), 12 April 1981.
2. Dan Smith and Ron Smith, *The Economics of Militarism* (London: Pluto Press, 1983), pp. 45–50.
3. Michael T. Klare, *Beyond the "Vietnam Syndrome": US Interventionism in the 1980s* (Washington, D.C.: Institute for Policy Studies, 1981), esp. chaps. 3 and 4.
4. Quoted in Richard J. Barnet, *Roots of War: The Men and Institutions Behind U.S. Foreign Policy* (Harmondsworth: Penguin Books, 1973), p. 139. My account of why successive governments have thought it important to guarantee favorable conditions for U.S. foreign investment owes much to Barnet's analysis.
5. Ibid., p. 146.
6. See ibid., pp. 168–75.
7. Tom Barry, Beth Wood, and Deb Preusch, *Dollars and Dictators: A Guide to Central America* (Albuquerque: The Resource Center, 1982), p. 119.
8. Richard J. Barnet, *Intervention and Revolution: The United States in the Third World* (New York: Meridian, 1980), p. 275. Information on the intervention in Guatemala can also be found in Stephen Schlesinger and Stephen Kinzer, *Bitter Fruit: The Untold Story of the American Coup in Guatemala* (Garden City, N.Y.: Doubleday, 1982); Richard H. Immerman, *The CIA in Guatemala: The Foreign Policy of Intervention* (Austin: University of Texas Press, 1982); Walter LaFeber, *Inevitable Revolutions: The United States in Central America* (New York: Norton, 1983), pp. 111–26; and Max Gordon, "A Case History of U.S. Subversion in Guatemala, 1954," reprinted in *Guatemala in Rebellion: Unfinished History,* ed. Jonathan L. Fried et al., (New York: Grove Press, 1983).
9. Quoted in Barnet, *Roots of War,* p. 157.
10. Information on the intervention in Chile is from the following sources: James Petras and Morris Morley, *The United States and Chile: Imperialism and the Overthrow of Allende* (New York: Monthly Review Press, 1975); Morton H. Halperin et al., *The Lawless State: The Crimes of the US Intelligence Agencies* (New York: Penguin Books, 1976), chap. 1; and Seymour M. Hersh, *The Price of Power: Henry Kissinger in the Nixon White House* (New York: Summit Books, 1983), chaps. 21 and 22.
11. Quoted in Richard J. Barnet and Ronald E. Müller, *Global Reach: The Power of the Multinational Corporations* (New York: Simon & Schuster, 1974), p. 83.
12. Ronald Brownstein and Nina Easton, "The Culture of Reaganism," *New Republic,* October 25, 1982.
13. Quoted in Anthony Lewis, "Reagan Associating Himself with Nixonism," *Raleigh News and Observer* (North Carolina), 13 October 1981.
14. Halperin et al., *The Lawless State,* p. 17. Also see Noam Chomsky and Edward S. Herman, *After the Cataclysm: Postwar Indochina and the Reconstruction of Imperial Ideology* (Boston: South End Press, 1979), pp. 10–11.
15. Barnet, *Intervention and Revolution,* pp. 237 and 212–13, and, more generally, chaps. 6, 7, and 9.
16. Quoted in Roger Burbach and Marc Herold, "The U.S. Economic Stake in Central America and the Caribbean," in *The Politics of Intervention: The United*

States in Central America, ed. Roger Burbach and Patricia Flynn (New York: Monthly Review Press, 1984), p. 190.

17. William M. LeoGrande, "A Splendid Little War: Drawing the Line in El Salvador," *International Security* 6, no. 1 (Summer 1981): 27.
18. The full text of this amazingly mendacious speech is printed in the *New York Times,* 28 April 1983.
19. Quoted in PACCA (Policy Alternatives for the Caribbean and Central America), *Changing Course: Blueprint for Peace in Central America and the Caribbean* (Washington, D.C.: Institute for Policy Studies, 1984), p. 58, n. 21.
20. Quoted in Eldon Kenworthy, "Why the United States Is in Central America," *Bulletin of the Atomic Scientists* 39, no. 8 (October 1983): 15.
21. Tom Wicker, ". . . And 3 Dangerous Traps He Faces," *International Herald Tribune,* 31 October 1983.
22. George F. Will, "The Price of Power," *Newsweek,* November 7, 1983.
23. Robert W. Tucker, "The Purposes of American Power," *Foreign Affairs* 59, no. 2 (Winter 1980–81): 268–69.
24. "Green Grow the Green Berets," *Newsweek,* October 19, 1983.
25. Quoted in *U.S. News and World Report,* March 2, 1981.
26. Jeane Kirkpatrick, "U.S. Security and Latin America," *Commentary,* January 1981, p. 31.
27. "President's Address to Joint Session of Congress on Central America," *New York Times,* 28 April 1983.
28. Quoted in Robert G. Kaiser, "Carter, Reagan Work from Different Scripts on Role U.S. Should Play in the World," *International Herald Tribune,* 11–12 October 1980.
29. Quoted in Jenny Pearce, *Under the Eagle: U.S. Intervention in Central America and the Caribbean* (London: Latin America Bureau, 1982), p. 172.
30. Cf. Noam Chomsky's analysis of the Cold War in his *Towards a New Cold War: Essays on the Current Crisis and How We Got There* (New York: Pantheon, 1982).
31. Quoted in Robert G. Kaiser, "Reagan's Foreign Policy Is Missing That Certain Something—a Policy," *International Herald Tribune,* 7 May 1981.
32. Quoted in Barnet, *Intervention and Revolution,* p. 204.
33. Cf. Kenworthy, "Why the United States," p. 17.
34. Quoted in Petras and Morley, *The United States and Chile,* p. viii.
35. Barnet, *Intervention and Revolution,* p. 233.
36. Quoted in Harold Jackson, "George Bush—the Low-Key Troubleshooter," *Guardian* (London), 29 January 1983.
37. Quoted in "President May Boost Advisers," *Raleigh News and Observer* (North Carolina), 5 March 1983. Emphasis added.
38. For a careful analysis of the U.S. use of staged elections, see Edward S. Herman and Frank Brodhead, *Demonstration Elections: U.S.-Staged Elections in the Dominican Republic, Vietnam, and El Salvador* (Boston: South End Press, 1984).
39. Quoted in Greg Chamberlain, "Haiti Poll Seen as Masquerade to Gain U.S. Aid," *Guardian* (London), 13 February 1984.
40. Quoted in Greg Chamberlain, "Haiti Wave of Arrests Follows Outbreak of Riots," *Guardian* (London), 27 July 1984.
41. Quoted in Robert Chesshyre, "White House Pedlar of an Ageless Dream," *Observer* (London), 29 January 1984. Emphasis added.
42. Edward S. Herman, *The* Real *Terror Network: Terrorism in Fact and Propaganda* (Boston: South End Press, 1982), p. 9.
43. Quoted in Noam Chomsky and Edward S. Herman, *The Washington Connection and Third World Facism* (Boston: South End Press, 1979), p. 27.
44. Quoted in Harold Jackson, "Reagan Blames Appeasers," *Guardian* (London), 24 August 1983.

2. Nuclear Weapons as Instruments of Political Coercion

1. Harold Jackson, "Pentagon Blunder Reveals Secrets of Warhead Stockpile," *Guardian* (London), 27 August 1983.
2. Charles Mohr, "Atomic Arms: New Power," *New York Times,* 23 May 1983.
3. The information on military spending comes from Mohr, "Atomic Arms"; Robert Dallek, *Ronald Reagan: The Politics of Symbolism* (Cambridge: Harvard University Press, 1984), p. 157; "Pentagon Cannot Spend Quickly Enough to Balance its Budget," *Guardian* (London), 22 May 1984; Richard Halloran, "New Weinberger Directive Redefines Military Policy," *New York Times,* 22 March 1983; and Alex Brummer, "Big Spender Reagan Still Plumps for Arms," *Guardian* (London), 2 February 1984.
4. Quoted in Robert Scheer, *With Enough Shovels: Reagan, Bush, and Nuclear War* (New York: Random House, 1982), p. 89. Cf. the quotation from Rostow on p. 14. For more on the problem of nuclear blackmail, see Jeff McMahan, "Nuclear Blackmail," in *Dangers of Deterrence: Philosophers on Nuclear Strategy,* ed. Nigel Blake and Kay Pole (Boston: South End Press, 1983).
5. Bernard Rogers, "A Conventional Punch That Might Avert a Nuclear Knock-Out," *Guardian* (London), 26 September 1983. Emphasis added.
6. Quoted in John Palmer, "Reagan Sticks to Missile Base Plan Despite NATO Proposal," *Guardian* (London), 19 October 1982.
7. Details of the Defense Guidance Plan were first revealed in Richard Halloran, "Pentagon Draws Up First Strategy for Fighting a Long Nuclear War," *New York Times,* 30 May 1982. Weinberger's defense of the plan is in a letter he sent to newspaper editors in the fifteen NATO countries. See "US 'Not Planning to Wage Protracted Nuclear Warfare,'" *Guardian* (London), 25 August 1982.
8. See "Excerpts from Report of the Commission on Strategic Forces," *New York Times,* 12 April 1983; and Steven V. Roberts, "Schultz [*sic*], in MX Drive, Raises Specter of 'Nuclear Blackmail,'" *New York Times,* 21 April 1983.
9. Quoted in Bill Moyers, "Documentation: The New Cold War," *International Security* 6, no. 2 (Fall 1981): 200.
10. Richard Halloran, Leslie Gelb, and Howell Raines, "Weinberger Said to Offer Reagan Plan to Regain Atomic Superiority," *New York Times,* 14 August 1981.
11. Halloran, "Pentagon Draws Up Strategy."
12. "US 'Not Planning to Wage Protracted Nuclear Warfare'."
13. Quoted in Christopher Paine, "Nuclear Combat: The Five-Year Defense Plan," *Bulletin of the Atomic Scientists* 38, no. 9 (November 1982): 10.
14. Colin S. Gray and Keith Payne, "Victory Is Possible," *Foreign Policy* 39 (Summer 1980): 21.
15. "Excerpts from Report of the Commission on Strategic Forces."
16. See Daniel Ellsberg, "Call to Mutiny," in *The Deadly Connection: Nuclear War and U.S. Intervention,* ed. Joseph Gerson (Cambridge: American Friends Service Committee, 1983), pp. 17–18. This essay appeared originally in E. P. Thompson and Dan Smith, eds., *Protest and Survive* (New York: Monthly Review Press, 1981). Also see McGeorge Bundy, "The Unimpressive Record of Atomic Diplomacy," in *The Choice: Nuclear Weapons Versus Security,* ed. Gwyn Prins (London: Chatto & Windus, 1984), pp. 44–46.
17. Barry M. Blechman and Stephen S. Kaplan et al., *Force Without War: U.S. Armed Forces as a Political Instrument* (Washington, D.C.: The Brookings Institution, 1978), p. 47.
18. Ibid., p. 48.
19. Ibid., p. 47. Cf. Ellsberg, "Call to Mutiny," p. 20.
20. Blechman and Kaplan et al., *Force Without War,* pp. 47–48; Ellsberg, "Call to

Mutiny," p. 20; and Harry S. Truman, *Years of Trial and Hope, 1946–1953* (London: Hodder and Stoughton, 1956), pp. 419–20 and 435.

21. Quoted in Bernard Gwertzman, "Eisenhower Was Set to Use A-Bomb in Korea," *International Herald Tribune,* 9–10 June 1984. Also see Alexander L. George and Richard Smoke, *Deterrence in American Foreign Policy: Theory and Practice* (New York: Columbia University Press, 1974), pp. 237–41; Bundy, "The Unimpressive Record," pp. 46–47.
22. Blechman and Kaplan et al., *Force Without War,* p. 48.
23. Ibid., pp. 232, 238, and 256. Cf. Noam Chomsky, "What Directions for the Disarmament Movement? Interventionism and Nuclear War," in *Beyond Survival: New Directions for the Disarmament Movement,* ed. Michael Albert and David Dellinger (Boston: South End Press, 1983), pp. 251 and 298.
24. Blechman and Kaplan et al., *Force Without War,* p. 48; George and Smoke, *Deterrence,* p. 364; and Bundy, "The Unimpressive Record," p. 47.
25. Blechman and Kaplan et al., *Force Without War,* pp. 48 and 376–77.
26. There are a great many studies of the Cuban missile crisis. George and Smoke, *Deterrence,* pp. 447–99, provide a useful account.
27. Ellsberg, "Call to Mutiny," pp. 20 and 28, and references cited there. Also see Seymour M. Hersh, *The Price of Power: Henry Kissinger in the Nixon White House* (New York: Summit Books, 1983), pp. 51–53, 120, and 126–29.
28. See Barry M. Blechman and Douglas M. Hart, "The Political Utility of Nuclear Weapons: The 1973 Middle East Crisis," *International Security* 7, no. 1 (Summer 1982).
29. Ellsberg, "Call to Mutiny," pp. 18–19; and Barry M. Blechman and Douglas M. Hart, "Dangerous Shortcut," *New Republic,* July 26, 1980.
30. Blechman and Kaplan et al., *Force Without War,* pp. 47 and 48.
31. Ibid., p. 49.
32. Ibid.
33. Quoted in Jerry W. Sanders, *Peddlers of Crisis: The Committee on the Present Danger and the Politics of Containment* (Boston: South End Press, 1983), p. 257.
34. Quoted in Scheer, *With Enough Shovels,* p. 13.
35. Quoted in Christopher Paine, "On the Beach: The Rapid Deployment Force and the Nuclear Arms Race," *MERIP Reports* no. 111 (January 1983): 4.
36. Ibid., p. 7.
37. Quoted in Konrad Ege and Arjun Makhijani, "U.S. Nuclear Threats: A Documentary History," *CounterSpy* Magazine, Reprint No. 1, p. 3, citing Eugene V. Rostow, "The Case Against SALT II," *Commentary,* February 1979, p. 23.
38. Ibid., citing *Guardian* (New York), 17 February 1982.
39. Quoted in Paine, "On the Beach," p. 10.
40. Gray and Payne, "Victory Is Possible," pp. 14 and 20.
41. Ibid., p. 26.
42. See, for example, Richard Pipes, "Why the Soviet Union Thinks It Could Fight and Win a Nuclear War," *Commentary* 64, no. 1 (July 1977). Pipes was a member of Reagan's National Security Council. Also see Paul H. Nitze, "Deterring Our Deterrent," *Foreign Policy* 25 (Winter 1976–77): 196–97.
43. Bundy, "The Unimpressive Record," pp. 44–46.
44. Ibid., pp. 46–47.
45. Ibid., p. 47.
46. Ibid., p. 50. Cf. Blechman and Hart, "The Utility of Nuclear Weapons," p. 150.
47. Blechman and Kaplan et al., *Force Without War,* p. 128.
48. Ibid., pp. 128–29.
49. Quoted in Sidney Lens, *The Maginot Line Syndrome: America's Hopeless Foreign Policy* (Cambridge: Ballinger, 1982), p. 37.

50. Nitze, "Deterring Our Deterrent," pp. 197–98.
51. Ibid.
52. Ibid., p. 210.
53. Halloran, "Pentagon Draws Up Strategy for Long Nuclear War."
54. Gray and Payne, "Victory Is Possible," p. 25.
55. Richard Halloran, "Shift of Strategy on Missile Attack Hinted by Weinberger and Vessey," *New York Times,* 6 May 1983.
56. Robert C. Aldridge, *First Strike! The Pentagon's Strategy for Nuclear War* (London: Pluto Press, 1983), p. 118.
57. "MX: 'Missile Experimental,'" a reprint from *Nucleus* (Cambridge: Union of Concerned Scientists, 1980), p. 1.
58. Quoted in Steven V. Roberts, "Proposal to Put MX in Existing Silos," *New York Times,* 26 April 1983.
59. See, for example, James Fallows, *National Defense* (New York: Random House, 1981), pp. 144–64.
60. "Mr. Scowcroft's MX Mouse," *New York Times,* 7 April 1983.
61. "Excerpts from Report of the Commission on Strategic Forces." Subsequent quotations from the report are from this source.
62. For a proposal of this sort, see Herbert Scoville, Jr., *MX: Prescription for Disaster* (Cambridge: The MIT Press, 1981), pp. 195–218.
63. Tom Wicker, "And Still the MX," *New York Times,* 15 April 1983; and Tom Wicker, "MX and Arms Control," *New York Times,* 13 May 1983.
64. William M. Arkin, "Going with Small ICBMs," *Bulletin of the Atomic Scientists* 40, no. 5 (May 1984): 7.
65. Ibid., p. 8. Cf. "MX Bargain Is a Snare," *New York Times,* 17 May 1983.
66. Quoted in Harold Jackson, "President Prepared to Stop START talks in MX Budget Storm," *Guardian* (London), 18 January 1983. Emphasis added.
67. Harold Jackson, "Negotiator Held Third Party Talks with Soviet Delegate," *Guardian* (London), 19 January 1983.
68. Leslie H. Gelb, "As a Bargaining Chip, MX May Be No Bargain for the Soviets," *New York Times,* 24 April 1983.
69. Halloran, "Shift of Strategy Hinted by Weinberger and Vessey."
70. Hedrick Smith, "Colonel Stirs Questions on MX-Firing Doctrine," *New York Times,* 8 April 1983.
71. On the threat of accidental nuclear war, see Louis René Beres, *Apocalypse: Nuclear Catastrophe in World Politics* (Chicago: University of Chicago Press, 1980), pp. 34–52; and Arthur Macy Cox, *Russian Roulette: The Superpower Game* (New York: Times Books, 1982), pp. 3–28.
72. For an excellent study of the possibilities for nonnuclear defense in Europe, see the report of the Alternative Defense Commission, *Defence Without the Bomb* (London: Taylor and Francis, 1983).
73. See William R. Van Cleave and Samuel T. Cohen, *Tactical Nuclear Weapons: An Examination of the Issues* (New York: Crane, Russak, 1978), pp. 58–59.
74. Cf. Sverre Lodgaard, "Theatre Nuclear Weapons: The NATO Doctrine," in *Disarming Europe,* ed. Mary Kalder and Dan Smith (London: Merlin, 1982), pp. 69–76.
75. See the *Post*'s editorial, reprinted in the *International Herald Tribune,* 29 September 1983.
76. Strobe Talbott, *The Russians and Reagan* (New York: Random House, 1984), pp. 62–63.
77. Strobe Talbott, "Battling the Gods of War," *Time,* June 25, 1984, p. 22.
78. *International Herald Tribune,* 29 September 1983; and "More Britons Oppose Cruise," *International Herald Tribune,* 28 May 1984.
79. Halloran, "Pentagon Draws Up Strategy."

80. Quoted in Robert Chesshyre, "US Missile Offer Aimed at NATO," *Observer* (London), 3 April 1983.
81. Quoted in David S. Broder, "Where Does Reagan Get These Ideas?" *International Herald Tribune,* 29 October 1981.
82. Samuel Pisar, *Of Blood and Hope* (London: Cassell, 1980), p. 270. For a further defense of the claim that the Soviet system will not crumble under U.S. economic pressure, see Seweryn Bialer and Joan Afferica, "Reagan and Russia," *Foreign Affairs* 61, no. 2 (Winter 1982–83): 262–67.
83. See Stanley Hoffman, *Dead Ends: American Foreign Policy in the New Cold War* (Cambridge: Ballinger, 1983), p. 164.
84. Pisar, *Of Blood and Hope,* p. 273.
85. See the letter by Leonard S. Rodberg in *New York Times,* 10 June 1982.
86. Gwyn Prins, ed., *Defended to Death* (Harmondsworth: Penguin Books, 1983), p. 187.
87. Colin S. Gray, "Strategic Defense, Deterrence, and the Prospects for Peace," unpublished paper, August 1984, p. 33.
88. Quoted in Charles Mohr, "'Star Wars' Anti-Missile Systems: U.S. Scientists Tilt for and Against," *International Herald* Tribune, 9 November 1983.
89. See, for example, Ashton B. Carter, *Directed Energy Missile Defense in Space* (Washington, D.C.: U.S. Government Printing Office, 1984); Hans A. Bethe et al., "Reagan's Star Wars," *New York Review of Books,* 26 April 1984; Hans A. Bethe et al., "Space-based Ballistic-Missile Defense," *Scientific American* 251, no. 4 (October 1984); Sidney D. Drell, Philip J. Farley, and David Holloway, "Preserving the ABM Treaty: A Critique of the Reagan Strategic Defense Initiative," *International Security* 9, no. 2 (Fall 1984); and Richard Garwin and John Pike, "Space Weapons: History and Current Debate," *Bulletin of the Atomic Scientists* 40, no. 5 (May 1984).
90. See Bethe et al., "Reagan's Star Wars," p. 50.
91. Gray, "Strategic Defense," pp. 26–27.
92. Bethe et al., "Reagan's Star Wars," p. 50.
93. Quoted in Mohr, "'Star Wars' Anti-Missile Systems."
94. Bethe et al., "Space-based Defense," p. 46.
95. Cf. Drell, Farley, and Holloway, "Preserving the ABM Treaty," p. 81.
96. Charles L. Glaser, "Why Even Good Defenses May Be Bad," *International Security* 9, no. 2 (Fall 1984).
97. Union of Concerned Scientists, "Legislative Alert," 1 March 1984; and Harold Jackson, "Deficit and Derision for Star Wars Script," *Guardian* (London), 26 April 1984.
98. Noam Chomsky, "Strategic Arms, the Cold War, and the Third World," in Edward Thompson et al., *Exterminism and Cold War* (London: Verso, 1982), pp. 235–36.

3. Arms Control as an Exercise in Public Relations

1. "President's Speech on Military Spending and a New Defense," *New York Times,* 24 March 1983.
2. Robert Chesshyre, "Open Door Offers Boost for Reagan," *Observer* (London), 17 June 1984; and "Reagan: The Evidence," *Sanity,* July 1984, p. 19.
3. For the official statement of the administration's initial policy of linkage, see "Excerpts from Haig's Speech on U.S. Policy on Arms Control," *New York Times,* 15 July 1981.
4. Quoted in *International Herald Tribune,* 28 May 1981.
5. Quoted in Strobe Talbott, "Battling the Gods of War," *Time,* June 25, 1984, p. 16.

6. "US Seeks Revised Nuclear Test Ban," *Guardian* (London), 21 July 1982.
7. Joel Wit, "Verifying Weapons Accords," *New York Times,* 5 April 1983; and Hella Pick, "New Proposal Is Setback for Test Ban Treaty," *Guardian* (London), 24 July 1982.
8. Quoted in Jerry W. Sanders, *Peddlers of Crisis: The Committee on the Present Danger and the Politics of Containment* (Boston: South End Press, 1983), p. 335.
9. Harold Jackson, "US Buries Test Ban Negotiations," *Guardian* (London), 9 September 1983.
10. See his letter, "Ignored Prerequisite to Real Arms Control," in *New York Times,* 12 April 1983.
11. Tom Wicker, "Cheating on SALT," *New York Times,* 17 April 1983; and "US May Violate SALT Accords," *Guardian* (London), 31 March 1984.
12. Richard Halloran, "50 Lawmakers Assail U.S. War Plan," *New York Times,* 23 July 1982; and Hans A. Bethe and Kurt Gottfried, "The 5-year War Plan—A Loser 2 Ways," *New York Times,* 10 June 1982.
13. John Darnton, "Ultimate Treaty Change Is Seen by Weinberger," *New York Times,* 25 March 1983.
14. Quoted in Steven R. Weisman, "Reagan Says Plan on Missile Defense Will Prevent War," *New York Times,* 26 March 1983.
15. On the question of Soviet compliance with arms control treaties, see Colin S. Gray, "Moscow Is Cheating," and Michael Krepon, "Both Sides Are Hedging," both in *Foreign Policy* 56 (Fall 1984).
16. James Reston, "Six More Years?" *New York Times,* 17 April 1983.
17. The information on Adelman is from the following sources: Jane Rosen, "Arms Talks Chief Will Take Orders from Shultz," *Guardian* (London), 17 January 1983; Alex Brummer, "Confirmation Certain," *Guardian* (London), 3 February 1983; "Treaty Pledge Helps Adelman," *Guardian* (London), 4 February 1983; "Committee Refuses to Back Adelman as Arms Negotiator," *Raleigh News and Observer* (North Carolina), 25 February 1983. On the "bee-excrement hypothesis," see the relevant articles in the *New York Times,* 1, 2, and 3 June 1983.
18. "It's a START," *New Republic,* May 26, 1982, p. 9.
19. Ibid.
20. "Starting Over," *Times* (London), 11 May 1982.
21. "It's a START," p. 9. Emphasis added.
22. Robert C. Johansen, "How to START Ending the Arms Race," *World Policy Journal* 1, no. 1 (Fall 1983): 78.
23. "It's a START," p. 9.
24. See the *New York Times* editorial "Encumbered Build-Down," reprinted in the *International Herald Tribune,* 10 October 1983; Ian Mather, "How US Proposes 'to Go the Last Mile,'" *Observer* (London), 9 October 1983; and Strobe Talbott, "Battling the Gods of War," pp. 20–1.
25. François de Rose, "Euromissiles' Value," *New York Times,* 29 March 1983.
26. Simon Lunn, "Cruise Missiles and the Prospects for Arms Control," *ADIU Report* 3, no. 5 (September–October 1981): 3.
27. See Hella Pick, "Bush Insists Zero Option Is an Agreed Objective," *Guardian* (London), 11 February 1983; Hella Pick, "Andropov Missile Proposal Rejected," *Guardian* (London), 22 December 1982; and "Issues as Talks Resume on Nuclear Forces in Europe," *New York Times,* 18 May 1983.
28. The quotations from Thatcher and Bush are in the *Guardian* (London), 5 February and 10 February 1983. Emphasis added.
29. See Serge Schmemann, "Soviet Warns NATO Over Missile Plans," *New York Times,* 28 May 1983; and Richard Halloran, "U.S. Says Soviet Is Keeping A-Warheads in East Europe," *New York Times,* 5 June 1983.

30. Quoted in Jonathan Steele, "Reagan Offers Nuclear Summit," *Guardian* (London), 1 February 1983; and Hella Pick and Jonathan Steele, "Andropov Rejects Reagan Summit," *Guardian,* 2 February 1983.
31. Quoted in Jonathan Steele, "Russians Challenged to Produce Own Plan for Missile Ban," *Guardian* (London), 5 February 1983.
32. Leslie H. Gelb, "Missile Plan: Plea to Allies," *New York Times,* 31 March 1983.
33. Ibid.
34. "Moscow's Attractive Offer on Euromissiles," *New York Times,* 12 April 1983.
35. "Issues as Talks Resume on Nuclear Forces in Europe."
36. Gelb, "Missile Plan: Pleas to Allies."
37. "Reagan: The Evidence," p. 23.
38. Strobe Talbott, *The Russians and Reagan* (New York: Random House, 1984), p. 65.
39. "Transcript of the Reagan-Mondale Debate on Foreign Policy," *New York Times,* 22 October 1984.
40. Lawrence Freedman, "Limited War, Unlimited Protest," *Orbis* 26, no. 1 (Spring 1982): 91–92.
41. Quoted in Christopher Paine, "Nuclear Combat: The Five-Year Defense Plan," *Bulletin of the Atomic Scientists* 38, no. 9 (November 1982): 5.
42. Quoted in "Reagan: The Evidence," p. 23.
43. Quoted in *Campaign,* January 1984.
44. Compare Jonathan Steele, "Russia Edges Towards Vienna Space Talks," *Guardian* (London), 7 July 1984.
45. Hella Pick, "Reagan Bluff Called on Space Arms Ban," *Guardian* (London), 30 June 1984.
46. Leslie Gelb, "Reagan Aide Doubts Soviet Seriousness on Arms," *International Herald Tribune,* 3 August 1984; and Hella Pick, "Russia Spurns US but Arms Offer Stands," *Guardian* (London), 2 July 1984.
47. Dusko Doder, "Soviet Opposes U.S. Plan Linking Space Talks to Resumption at Geneva," *International Herald Tribune,* 2 July 1984.
48. Alex Brummer, "US Writes Off Star Wars Negotiations," *Guardian* (London), 2 August 1984.

4. Third World Interventionism

1. See Phillip Berryman, *What's Wrong in Central America and What to Do About It* (Philadelphia: American Friends Service Committee, 1984), pp. 4, 8, and 41–42; Richard Alan White, *The Morass: United States Intervention in Central America* (New York: Harper-Colophon Books, 1984), p. 201; and Wayne S. Smith, "Myopic Diplomacy," *Foreign Policy* 48 (Fall 1982).
2. "National Security Council Document on Policy in Central America and Cuba," *New York Times,* 7 April 1983.
3. Quoted in James F. Petras and Morris H. Morley, "The New Cold War: Reagan's Policy Towards Europe and the Third World," in *ENDpapers Four—The New Cold War,* ed. Ken Coates (Nottingham: Spokesman, 1983), p. 98.
4. Andrew J. Pierre, *The Global Politics of Arms Sales* (Princeton: Princeton University Press, 1982), pp. 64–65.
5. Harold Jackson, "US Tops Arms Sales to Third World," *Guardian* (London), 15 May 1984.
6. Pierre, *Global Politics,* pp. 53–54 and 64.
7. See Noam Chomsky's excellent book *The Fateful Triangle: The United States, Israel and the Palestinians* (Boston: South End Press, 1983), p. 6, citing *Time,* October 11, 1982.
8. Ibid., pp. 464–69.

9. Joseph Gerson, "The Middle East and the Deadly Connection," in *The Deadly Connection: Nuclear War and U.S. Intervention,* ed. Joseph Gerson (Cambridge: American Friends Service Committee, 1983), p. 60.
10. White, *The Morass,* p. 209; Phil Gunson, "Honduras Tired of Being America's Aircraft Carrier," *Guardian* (London), 21 May 1984; Edward Cody, "Hondurans Seek Lower Ratio of Salvadorans at a U.S. Base," *International Herald Tribune,* 28 May 1984; and Tom Wicker, "Irony and Danger," *Chattanooga Times* (Tennessee), 8 August 1983.
11. White, *The Morass,* p. 190.
12. Ibid., pp. 155 and 188–92.
13. Jonathan Evan Maslow, "Honduras: Regional Pawn," *Atlantic,* June 1984, p. 36; George Russell, "Making Themselves at Home," *Time,* September 19, 1983, p. 31; and Bernard Gwertzman, "Watchdog Agency Claims Pentagon Improperly Spent Funds in Honduras," *International Herald Tribune,* 26 June 1984.
14. White, *The Morass,* pp. 184–86; and Lucy Komisar, "Honduras, Too, Has Sensitive National Sentiment," *International Herald Tribune,* 12 October 1984.
15. Amnesty International, *Torture in the Eighties* (Oxford and London: Martin Robertson and Amnesty International, 1984), pp. 164–65; *Amnesty International Report 1984* (London: Amnesty International Publications, 1984), pp. 168–71; White, *The Morass,* pp. 209–11; Tony Jenkins, "Civilian Record on Human Rights 'Worse Than That of the Generals,'" *Guardian* (London), 16 July 1983; and Phil Gunson, "US Dismisses Protest," *Guardian* (London), 7 April 1984.
16. Quoted in Karl Grossman, *Nicaragua: America's New Vietnam?* (New York: The Permanent Press, 1984), p. 12.
17. Maslow, "Honduras," p. 40.
18. Russell, "Making Themselves at Home," pp. 30–31.
19. Quoted in Naseer Aruri, "The United States and Israel: That Very Special Relationship," in *Reagan and the Middle East,* ed. by Naseer Aruri, Fouad Moughrabi, and Joe Stork (Belmont, Mass.: Association of Arab-American University Graduates, 1983), p. 7.
20. Quoted in Bernard Reich, *The United States and Israel: Influence in the Special Relationship* (New York: Praeger, 1984), p. 88.
21. Quoted in Aruri, "The United States and Israel," p. 5.
22. Alan Dowty, "The Voice of the Turtle," *Times Literary Supplement* (London), 27 July 1984.
23. Cf. Aruri, "The United States and Israel," pp. 7–8.
24. Chomsky, *The Fateful Triangle,* p. 10.
25. Patrick Seale, "Israel's Ruthless Poker Game in West Beirut," *Observer* (London), 1 August 1982; and Ze'ev Schiff, "Green Light, Lebanon," *Foreign Policy* 50 (Spring 1983). On the invasion of Lebanon itself and its consequences, see Chomsky, *The Fateful Triangle,* pp. 181–430; Michael Jansen, *The Battle of Beirut: Why Israel Invaded Lebanon* (London: Zed Press, 1982); Sean MacBride et al., *Israel in Lebanon: The Report of the International Commission to Enquire into Reported Violations of International Law By Israel During Its Invasion of the Lebanon* (London: Ithaca Press, 1983); Dov Yermiya, *My War Diary: Israel in Lebanon* (London: Pluto Press, 1984); and Amnon Kapeliouk, *Sabra & Shatila: Inquiry Into a Massacre* (Belmont, Mass.: Association of Arab-American University Graduates, 1984).
26. Claudia Wright, "US Stepped Up Arms for Invasion," *New Statesman* (London), 20 August 1982.
27. Joe Stork, "Israel as a Strategic Asset," in Aruri, Moughrabi, and Stork, *Reagan and the Middle East,* p. 39.

28. Quoted in Harold Jackson, "Shamir's Chilly Welcome on Capital Hill," *Guardian* (London), 4 August 1982.
29. Pierre, *The Global Politics of Arms Sales,* p. 63.
30. See Michael T. Klare and Cynthia Arnson, *Supplying Repression: U.S. Support for Authoritarian Regimes Abroad* (Washington, D.C.: Institute for Policy Studies, 1981).
31. "US Charged with Violation of South Africa Arms Embargo," *Guardian* (London), 14 January 1984.
32. Harold Jackson and Patrick Keatley, "Guatemala Dodged US Embargo," *Guardian* (London), 10 January 1983.
33. Walter LaFeber, "Inevitable Revolutions," *Atlantic,* June 1982, p. 83.
34. See Eric Hooglund, "Israel's Arms Exports: Proxy Merchant for the U.S.," American-Arab Anti-Discrimination Committee Background Paper no. 8.
35. *Massive Extra-Judicial Executions in Rural Areas Under the Government of Efraín Ríos Montt* (London: Amnesty International Publications, 1982); *Amnesty International Report 1983* (London: Amnesty International Publications, 1983), p. 141; and Jonathan L. Fried et al., eds, *Guatemala in Rebellion: Unfinished History* (New York: Grove Press, 1983), p. 236.
36. Harold Jackson, "Montt Regime 'Kills 10,000,'" *Guardian* (London), 30 December 1982.
37. White, *The Morass,* p. 105.
38. Ibid., p. 97.
39. Ibid., p. 11; and Fried et al., *Guatemala in Rebellion,* p. 236.
40. Iain Guest, "Guatemala Coup Fails to End Murders," *Guardian* (London), 17 August 1982.
41. "Rights Group Asserts Guatemala Is Killing Indians," *New York Times,* 8 May 1983. Compare Anthony Lewis, "In America's Name," *Chattanooga Times* (Tennessee), 16 March 1983, and *Amnesty International Report 1983,* esp p. 142.
42. See, for example, pt. 4, chap. 1 in Fried et al., *Guatemala in Rebellion.*
43. Patrick Marnham, "Less Death in Guatemala," *Spectator* (London), 7 May 1983.
44. Harold Jackson, "Reagan Steps Up Central American Offensive," *Guardian* (London), 6 December 1982.
45. White, *The Morass,* p. 126; and the joint report of the Americas Watch Committee, the Helsinki Watch Committee, and the Lawyers Committee for International Human Rights, *Failure: The Reagan Administration's Human Rights Policy in 1983* (New York: Americans Watch Committee, 1984), p. 8.
46. Richard J. Meislin, "Guatemala and U.S.: Reagan Gaining Support for Policies from New Central American Leader," *New York Times,* 13 August 1983. Cf. White, *The Morass,*pp. 128–29.
47. See, for example, *Amnesty International Report 1984,* p. 159.
48. White, *The Morass,* p. 258.
49. Quoted in Klare and Arnson, *Supplying Repression,* p. 88.
50. Quoted in ibid., p. 2.
51. Quoted in Michael T. Klare, *Beyond the "Vietnam Syndrome": US Intervention in the 1980s* (Washington, D.C.: Institute for Policy Studies, 1981), p. 57.
52. Quoted in Petras and Morley, "The New Cold War," p. 96.
53. Ibid.
54. *Failure,* p. 22.
55. Charles Maechling, Jr., "Human Rights Dehumanized," *Foreign Policy* 52 (Fall 1982): 122.
56. Quoted in Alan Tonelson, "Human Rights: The Bias We Need," *Foreign Policy* 49 (Winter 1982–83): 58.
57. Jerry W. Sanders, *Peddlers of Crisis: The Committee on the Present Danger and the Politics of Containment* (Boston: South End Press, 1983), p. 293.

58. Hurst Hannum, "In Seoul, a Mixed Picture," *International Herald Tribune,* 15 November 1983; *Amnesty International Report 1983,* pp. 207–11; *Amnesty International Report 1984,* pp. 233 and 235; and Amnesty International, *Torture in the Eighties,* pp. 192–94.
59. Sanders, *Peddlers of Crisis,* p. 300.
60. Quoted in *Failure,* p. 67.
61. "Dissenters Face Death Penalty in Philippines," *Guardian* (London), 18 October 1983.
62. *Amnesty International Report 1983,* p. 224; and Robert Chesshyre, "What Reagan and Marcos Left Unsaid," *Observer* (London), 19 September 1982.
63. Paul Quinn-Judge, "Troubled Marcos Angling for Reagan's Seal of Approval," *Guardian* (London), 15 September 1982.
64. *Amnesty International Report 1984,* pp. 164–68; and Amnesty International, *Torture in the Eighties,* pp. 162–64.
65. Greg Chamberlain, "Reagan Reassures Duvalier," *Guardian* (London), 12 January 1983; and Greg Chamberlain, "Haiti Wave of Arrests Follows Outbreak of Riots," *Guardian* (London), 27 July 1984.
66. *Failure,* pp. 39–40.
67. "American Foreign Policy in a Cold Climate" (an interview with Jeane Kirkpatrick), *Encounter,* November 1983, p. 26.
68. Nicholas Ashford, "Propaganda War Rages over Nicaragua Tribe," *Times* (London), 3 March 1982.
69. Jean Furtado, *Turkey: Peace on Trial* (London: Merlin Press and European Nuclear Disarmament, 1983), p. 7; *Amnesty International Report 1984,* p. 306; "US Official to Assess Human Rights in Turkey," *Guardian* (London), 9 July 1984; and Jean Furtado, "Turkey: A Land Occupied by Its Own Army," *ADIU Report* 6, no. 1 (January–February 1984): 6.
70. Furtado, *Turkey: Peace on Trial;* "Turkey Tries 56 Defiant Intellectuals," *Guardian* (London), 16 August 1984; *Amnesty International Report 1984,* pp. 306–10; and David Barchard, "Peace Campaigners Gaoled for 8 Years," *Guardian* (London), 15 November 1983.
71. Amnesty International, *Torture in the Eighties,* p. 217; *Amnesty International Report 1984,* p. 309; "Turkish Death Fasts Likely to Continue," *Guardian* (London), 25 June 1984; "US Official to Assess Human Rights in Turkey;" and "Turkish Prison Protest at a Bitter Stalemate," *International Herald Tribune,* 26 June 1984.
72. Edward S. Herman, *The* Real *Terror Network: Terrorism in Fact and Propaganda* (Boston: South End Press, 1982), p. 209.
73. *Failure,* p. 18.
74. Furtado, *Turkey: Peace on Trial,* pp. 3 and 5; idem, "Turkey: A Land Occupied," pp. 6 and 8; and idem, "Turkey: Activists' Agony Prolonged," *END* 12 (October–November 1984): 6.
75. Quoted in Jenny Pearce, *Under the Eagle: U.S. Intervention in Central America and the Caribbean* (London: Latin American Bureau, 1982), p. 182.
76. Jeane Kirkpatrick, "Dictatorships and Double Standards," *Commentary* 68, no. 5 (November 1979), reprinted in *El Salvador: Central America in the New Cold War,* ed. Marvin E. Gettleman et al. (New York: Grove Press, 1981), pp. 36–37.
77. Quoted in Penny Lernoux, *Cry of the People: The Struggle for Human Rights in Latin America—The Catholic Church in Conflict with U.S. Policy* (New York: Penguin Books, 1982), p. 85.
78. Kirkpatrick's allegedly factual claims about totalitarian and authoritarian regimes have been systematically and decisively refuted in Herman, *The* Real *Terror Network,* pp. 25–33. Also see Tom J. Farer, "Reagan's Latin America,"

New York Review of Books 28, no. 4 (March 19, 1981), reprinted in Gettleman et al., *El Salvador.*

79. Lydia Chavez, "4,500 Salvadoran Troops Prepare for Major Fight," *New York Times,* 11 June 1983.
80. Quoted in Maechling, "Human Rights Dehumanized," p. 121. Compare Henry Shue, "Playing Hardball with Human Rights," *Report from the Center for Philosophy and Public Policy,* 1983.
81. Maechling, "Human Rights Dehumanized," p. 121.
82. Jeane Kirkpatrick, "Human Rights in Nicaragua," in *The Reagan Phenomenon and Other Speeches on Foreign Policy* (Washington, D.C.: American Enterprise Institute, 1983). p. 62.
83. La Feber, "Inevitable Revolutions," pp. 77–78; Pearce, *Under the Eagle,* pp. 122 and 126; and Noam Chomsky and Edward S. Herman, *The Washington Connection and Third World Fascism* (Boston: South End Press, 1979), pp. 14 and 292–93.
84. Quoted in an interview with García Márquez in *Playboy,* February 1983, p. 72.
85. Paul E. Sigmund, "Latin America: Change or Continuity?" *Foreign Affairs* 60, no. 3 (1981): 653; and Sanders, *Peddlers of Crisis,* p. 301.
86. Tonelson, "Human Rights," p. 66.
87. Quoted in Edward J. Markey, with Douglas Walker, *Nuclear Peril: The Politics of Proliferation* (Cambridge, Mass.: Ballinger, 1982), p. 117.
88. "Reagan's Statement on Nuclear Weapons," *New York Times,* 17 July 1981.
89. Nicholas Ashford, "Doubts Cast on Nuclear Safeguards," *Times* (London), 17 November 1981; Peter Pringle, "The Nuclear Reality US Refuses to Face," *Observer* (London), 6 December 1981.
90. Markey, *Nuclear Peril,* pp. 113–14.
91. Stockholm International Peace Research Institute, *The NPT: The Main Political Barrer to Nuclear Weapon Proliferation* (London: Taylor & Francis, 1980), p. 21.
92. Milton Benjamin, "Argentina's Nuclear Plans Aided by Sale of US Technology," *Guardian* (London), 20 July 1982.
93. Quoted in ibid.
94. Kenneth Freed, "N-Arms Capability Claimed by Junta," *Guardian* (London), 21 September 1983; and Milton R. Benjamin, "Argentina Could Produce A-Bomb by '85, U.S. Says," *International Herald Tribune,* 7 December 1983.
95. Nicholas Ashford, "US Eases Way to Sell Pretoria Nuclear Material," *Times* (London), 20 May 1982.
96. On South Africa's nuclear potential, see Richard K. Betts, "A Diplomatic Bomb? South Africa's Nuclear Potential," in *Nonproliferation and U.S. Foreign Policy,* ed. Joseph A. Yager (Washington, D.C.: The Brookings Institution, 1980).
97. Warren Hoge, "Bush Tells Brazil Atom Ban Is Eased,"*New York Times,* 16 October 1981.
98. "Safe Nuclear Trade," reprinted in the *International Herald Tribune,* 11 July 1984.
99. John Gittings, "Nuclear Deal Agreed on Reagan China Visit," *Guardian* (London), 27 April 1984; Harold Jackson, "Chinese Gave No Nuclear Pledge," *Guardian* (London), 9 May 1984; and Leslie H. Gelb, "U.S. Aides Suspect Continuing Chinese Nuclear Aid to Pakistan," *International Herald Tribune,* 23–24 June 1984.
100. Milton R. Benjamin, "Study Details U.S. Technology Sales to Nations that Bar Nuclear Checks," *International Herald Tribune,* 17 October 1983.
101. Harold Jackson, "Reagan Drops Zia a Nuclear Hint," *Guardian* (London), 8 December 1982.

102. Quoted in Shyam Bhatia, "Zia Forced to Put Off Nuclear Test," *Observer* (London), 2 January 1983.
103. Ibid.
104. "Pakistan Can Now Make Nuclear Arms Says Senator," *Guardian* (London), 22 June 1984; and Michael White, "Pakistan 'On Verge of Nuclear Status,'" *Guardian* (London), 31 October 1984.
105. Pierre, *The Global Politics of Arms Sales,* pp. 30–31.
106. Klare, *Beyond the "Vietnam Syndrome,"* p. 69.
107. James A. Nathan, "Defending the Gulf: Worth It?" *International Herald Tribune,* 2 December 1983.
108. See, for example, Klare, *Beyond the "Vietnam Syndrome,"* pp. 78 and 82.
109. See, for example, Robert W. Tucker, "Oil: The Issue of American Intervention," *Commentary,* January 1975.
110. Richard Halloran, "Pentagon Draws Up First Strategy for Fighting a Long Nuclear War," *New York Times,* 30 May 1982.
111. Klare, *Beyond the "Vietnam Syndrome,"* p. 78.
112. Quoted in Joshua M. Epstein, "Soviet Vulnerabilities in Iran and the RDF Deterrent," *International Security* 6, no. 2 (Fall 1981): 127.
113. Nathan, "Defending the Gulf." Some of the difficulties the Soviets would face in invading Iran are described in Epstein, "Soviet Vulnerabilities."
114. Klare, *Beyond the "Vietnam Syndrome,"* p. 46. Emphases in the original.
115. Ibid., pp. 47–48.
116. Nathan, "Defending the Gulf."
117. Quoted in Eleanor Randolph, "Reagan Seems Cool to Fuel Conservation," *International Herald Tribune,* 27 November 1980.
118. Nathan, "Defending the Gulf."
119. Klare, Beyond the "Vietnam Syndrome," p. 47.
120. *The Report of the President's National Bipartisan Commission on Central America* (New York: Macmillan, 1984), p. 111.
121. Quoted in "Arming for the '80s," *Time,* July 27, 1981, p. 9.
122. Harold Jackson, "Intelligence Test," *Guardian* (London), 11 February 1983.
123. "America's Secret Warriors," *Newsweek,* October 10, 1983.

5. Some Notable Victims: (1) El Salvador

1. Walter LaFeber, "Inevitable Revolutions," *Atlantic,* June 1982, p. 81.
2. See Raymond Bonner's detailed and comprehensive account of recent events in El Salvador, *Weakness and Deceit: U.S. Policy and El Salvador* (New York: Times Books, 1984), p. 12. I have relied extensively on this excellent source in revising this chapter for American publication.
3. Quoted in the *Times* (London), 25 February 1982.
4. Jeane Kirkpatrick, "Human Rights in El Salvador," in *The Reagan Phenomenon and Other Speeches on Foreign Policy* (Washington, D.C.: American Enterprise Institute, 1983), p. 56.
5. Quoted in Lydia Chavez, "A Reporter's Notebook: Salvador's Death Squads," *New York Times,* 16 May 1983.
6. Kirkpatrick, "Human Rights in El Salvador," p. 57.
7. Quoted in Paul Ellman, "Salvador Killers 'Shielded by Left,'" *Guardian* (London), 10 November 1983. Cf. the comment by Elliot Abrams cited in the joint report of the Americas Watch Committee, the Helsinki Watch Committee, and the Lawyers Committee for International Human Rights, *Failure: The Reagan Administration's Human Rights Policy in 1983* (New York: America's Watch Committee, 1984), pp. 16–17.

8. Quoted in Juan Williams, "Reagan Links El Salvador's Left to Deaths," *International Herald Tribune,* 5 December 1983.
9. Kirkpatrick, "Human Rights in El Salvador," pp. 56–57. Emphasis in original.
10. Edward S. Herman and Frank Brodhead, *Demonstration Elections: U.S.-Staged Elections in the Dominican Republic, Vietnam, and El Salvador* (Boston: South End Press, 1984), p. 95.
11. Tom Barry, Beth Wood, and Deb Preusch, *Dollars and Dictators: A Guide to Central America* (Albuquerque: The Resource Center, 1982), p. 188, citing *New York Times,* 22 November 1981.
12. Ibid., p. 183.
13. Quoted in Bonner, *Weakness and Deceit,* p. 112. Cf. Bonner's own account on the preceding page.
14. Kirkpatrick quotation is from Charles Maechling, Jr., "Human Rights Dehumanized," *Foreign Policy* 52 (Fall 1983): 122.
15. Quoted in "American Foreign Policy in a Cold Climate," *Encounter* (November 1983): 28.
16. Robert Leiken, quoted in Bonner, *Weakness and Deceit,* pp. 91–92.
17. Jeane Kirkpatrick, "The Superpowers: Is There a Moral Difference?" *The World Today* 40, no. 5 (May 1984): 184.
18. "Communist Interference in El Salvador," reprinted in *El Salvador: Central America in the New Cold War,* ed. Marvin E. Gettleman et al. (New York: Grove Press, 1981), pp. 230–42.
19. On the White Paper, see, for example, James Petras, "Blots on the White Paper: The Reinvention of the 'Red Menace' "; and Robert G. Kaiser, "Further Blots on the White Paper: Doubts About Evidence and Conclusions," both reprinted in Gettleman et al., *El Salvador.* Extracts from the *Wall Street Journal* piece are reprinted in Jenny Pearce, *Under the Eagle: U.S. Intervention in Central America and the Caribbean* (London: Latin America Bureau, 1982), pp. 242–44. Also see Bonner, *Weakness and Deceit,* pp. 255–61.
20. Timothy Garton Ash, "Back Yards," *New York Review of Books,* 22 November 1984, p. 8.
21. See Bonner, *Weakness and Deceit,* p. 121, and Drew Middleton, "Salvador Army's Troubles," *New York Times,* 5 March 1983.
22. See Wayne S. Smith, "Myopic Diplomacy," *Foreign Policy* 48 (Fall 1982): 161, 166, 169; and the account of an interview with Smith in Bonner, *Weakness and Deceit,* pp. 264–65.
23. Quoted in Harold Jackson, "Former CIA Man Says Nicaraguan Arms for Salvador Ceased Three Years Ago," *Guardian* (London), 12 June 1984.
24. "Playboy Interview: José Napoleón Duarte," *Playboy,* November 1984, p. 74.
25. Ibid.
26. Edward S. Herman, *The* Real *Terror Network: Terrorism in Fact and Propaganda* (Boston: South End Press, 1982), p. 167.
27. Eldon Kenworthy, "Why the United States Is in Central America," *Bulletin of the Atomic Scientists* 39, no. 8 (October 1983): 16.
28. Flora Lewis, "The China Syndrome," *New York Times,* 27 May 1983; Guillermo Ungo, "The People's Struggle," *Foreign Policy* 52 (Fall 1983): 54; and Bonner, *Weakness and Deceit,* p. 268.
29. Kenworthy, "Why the United States Is in Central America," p. 20. n. 11.
30. Barry Cohen, "Front Line View," *New Statesman* (London), 6 May 1983, p. 15; and Morris Thompson, "Salvador Guerrillas Plan Widespread Disruption of Voting," *Guardian* (London), 25 April 1984.
31. Anthony Lewis, "Can it Work" *New York Times,* 28 April 1983, says there are 30,000 men in the Salvadoran "security forces," and 5,000 guerrillas. Figures are now higher for both sides.

32. Paul Ellman, "US Aims to Double Size of Salvadoran Armed Forces," *Guardian* (London), 19 January 1984; Paul Ellman, "Salvador Recruits with an Eye to the Future," *Guardian* (London), 1 February 1984; and "America Trains Rebels by Mistake," *Guardian* (London), 19 July 1984.
33. Richard J. Barnet, *Intervention and Revolution: The United States in the Third World* (New York: Meridian, 1980), p. 327.
34. Drew Middleton, "Trying New Tactics in Search of Salvadoran Military Gains," *New York Times,* 5 June 1983.
35. Barry, Wood, and Preusch, *Dollars and Dictators,* p. 185. (Since going to press I have learned that White neither said this nor believes it.)
36. Pearce, *Under the Eagle,* p. 226.
37. Quoted in Bonner, *Weakness and Deceit,* p. 203.
38. Walden Bello and Edward S. Herman, "U.S.-Sponsored Elections in El Salvador and the Philippines," *World Policy Journal* 1, no. 4 (Summer 1984); 856; and "Playboy Interview: Duarte," pp. 70 and 71.
39. Quoted in Bonner, *Weakness and Deceit,* p. 230–31.
40. Quoted in ibid., p. 168.
41. Quoted in ibid., p. 230.
42. Ibid., p. 156.
43. Ibid., p. 64.
44. Ibid., p. 312.
45. Guy Guliotta, "Duarte's Second Chance," *New Republic,* August 13 and 20, 1984, p. 18; and Leslie H. Gelb, "U.S. Debate on Salvador Raised Deeper Issue of Policy on Third World," *International Herald Tribune,* 14 May 1984.
46. John McAward, "Duarte Must Gain Control of the Military," reprinted in the *International Herald Tribune,* 7 June 1984; and Lydia Chavez, "The Testing of Jose Napoleon Duarte," *New York Times Magazine,* 2 September 1984, p. 45.
47. Chavez, "The Testing of Duarte," pp. 16 and 19.
48. Lydia Chavez, "Duarte Vows to Crush Death Squads," *New York Times,* 11 May 1984, cited in Bello and Herman, "U.S.-Sponsored Elections," p. 856.
49. Paul Ellman, "Duarte Caught in a Strait-Jacket," *Observer* (London), 13 May 1984.
50. Quoted in Bonner, *Weakness and Deceit,* p. 160.
51. Quoted in ibid., p. 162.
52. "New Choice in Salvador Likes Role of Mediator," *New York Times,* 19 April 1983.
53. Raymond Bonner, "Cover-Up Charged in Death of Nuns," *New York Times,* 16 February 1984.
54. "New Choice in Salvador."
55. Bonner, *Weakness and Deceit,* pp. 153–56.
56. Paul Ellman and Jonathan Steele,"Salvador Guerrillas Maintain the Pressure in Run-Up to Election," *Guardian* (London), 24 March 1984; and McAward, "Duarte Must Gain Control."
57. Enrique Baloyra, *El Salvador in Transition* (Chapel Hill, N.C.: The University of North Carolina Press, 1982), p. 164, citing Alma Guillermoprieto, "Business Wars on Government in El Salvador," *Washington Post,* 27 June 1981.
58. Quoted in Bonner, *Weakness and Deceit,* p. 223.
59. Bello and Herman, "U.S.-Sponsored Elections," p. 858.
60. See James Dunkerley, *The Long War: Dictatorship and Revolution in El Salvador* (London: Junction Books, 1982), p. 169.
61. The Americas Watch Committee and the American Civil Liberties Union, *Report on Human Rights in El Salvador* (New York: Vintage Books, 1982), p. 169.
62. Joanne Omang and Lydia Chavez,"Duarte Presents Condition for Talks," *International Herald Tribune,* 5 June 1984.

63. Bonner, *Weakness and Deceit,* pp. 324–25.
64. "Playboy Interview: Duarte," p. 66.
65. "Death Squads Inquiry Set Up," *Guardian* (London), 27 August 1984; and "Massacre Inquiry," *Guardian* (London), 29 August 1984.
66. Balorya, *El Salvador in Transition,* p. 151; and "Playboy Interview: Duarte," p. 66.
67. Quoted in Bonner, *Weakness and Deceit,* p. 218.
68. Dunkerley, *The Long War,* p. 172.
69. Bonner, *Weakness and Deceit,* pp. 188 and 238–39; and Baloyra, *El Salvador in Transition,* p. 139.
70. Quoted in Cynthia Arnson, "Update #8: Background Information on U.S. Policy and U.S. Military Assistance to Central America," *Institute for Policy Studies Resource,* March 1983, p. 3.
71. Baloyra, *El Salvador in Transition,* p. 133; citing Robert E. White, "The U.S. and El Salvador," *New York Times,* 2 October 1981.
72. Quoted in Tom Wicker, "Such Good Guys," *New York Times,* 26 April 1983.
73. Quoted in Bonner, *Weakness and Deceit,* p. 326. See also *Extrajudicial Executions in Él Salvador: Report of an Amnesty International Mission to Examine Post-Mortem and Investigative Procedures in Political Killings, 1–6 July 1983* (London: Amnesty International Publications, 1984), pp. 3–9; Edward Cody, "D'Aubuisson Said to Tie Army to Death Squads," *International Herald Tribune,* 19 October 1983; and Captain Ricardo Alejandro Fiallos, "The Death Squads Do Not Operate Independent of the Security Forces," in Gettleman et al., *El Salvador,* pp. 146–48.
74. *Report on Human Rights in El Salvador,* p. 44. Cf. Herman, *The* Real *Terror Network,* p. 117.
75. Kenneth E. Sharpe and Martin Diskin, "Facing Facts in El Salvador: Reconciliation or War," *World Policy Journal* 1, no. 3 (Spring 1984): 535.
76. "Salvador Observers 'Aghast,'" *Guardian* (London), 20 October 1983.
77. Phillip Berryman, *What's Wrong in Central America and What to Do About It* (Philadelphia: American Friends Service Committee, 1984), p. 19.
78. George Gelder, "Backyard Bias," *Amnesty!* (Journal of the British Section of Amnesty International) 8 (April/May 1984): 12.
79. See, for example, Harold Jackson and Paul Ellman, "Reagan Tacks Salvador Aid on to African Food Package," *Guardian,* (London), 9 March 1984; and Paul Ellman, "Salvador Rebels Press-Gang Young Boys," *Guardian* (London), 13 March 1983.
80. *Amnesty International Report 1981* (London: Amnesty International Publications, 1981), p. 140.
81. Bonner, *Weakness and Deceit,* p. 112.
82. Herman and Brodhead, *Demonstration Elections,* p. 151, citing Christopher Dickey, "U.S. Tactics Fail to Prevent Salvadoran Civilian Deaths," *Washington Post,* 10 June 1982.
83. Quoted in Bonner, *Weakness and Deceit,* p. 336.
84. Quoted in Berryman, *What's Wrong in Central America,* p. 72, n. 4. For a fuller account of Bourgois's observations, see Philippe Bourgois, "Rural El Salvador: An Eyewitness Account," *Monthly Review,* May 1982, pp. 14–32.
85. Bonner, *Weakness and Deceit,* pp. 112–13 and 337–43; and Berryman, *What's Wrong in Central America,* p. 72, n. 4.
86. Bonner, *Weakness and Deceit,* p. 335; Richard Alan White, *The Morass: United States Intervention in Central America* (New York: Harper-Colophon Books, 1984), p. 173; "Death Squads Inquiry Set Up"; and "Massacre Inquiry."
87. Quoted in Paul Ellman, "Long Gone . . . The Last of the Summer Optimism," *Guardian* (London), 22 November 1983.

88. "President Reagan's Address to Joint Session of Congress on Central America," *New York Times,* 28 April 1983.
89. *Report on Human Rights in El Salvador,* p. 196; and "Conversations with Salvadoran Refugees," p. 150.
90. *Report on Human Rights in El Salvador,* pp. 68 and 73.
91. Quoted in Allan Nairn, "Behind the Death Squads," *Progressive,* May 1984, p. 22.
92. Quoted in Bonner, *Weakness and Deceit,* p. 329.
93. Iain Guest, "Salvadoran Army 'Bombs Civilians,'" *Guardian* (London), 11 April 1984; idem, "Salvador's Peasants Turned 'Land Owners,'" *Guardian* (London), 24 August 1984; and Michael Simmons, "Doctor's Agony at 'Impending Salvador Invasion,'" *Guardian* (London), 27 April 1984.
94. Quoted in White, *The Morass,* p. 252.
95. PACCA (Policy Alternatives for the Caribbean and Central America), *Changing Course: Blueprint for Peace in Central America and the Caribbean* (Washington, D.C.: The Institute for Policy Studies, 1984), p. 99; and Herman and Brodhead, p. 124.
96. Quoted in *Failure,* pp. 35 and 88.
97. Herman and Brodhead, *Demonstration Elections,* p. 124.
98. Quoted in Harold Jackson, "Congressmen Move to Reverse Salvador Backing," *Guardian* (London), 29 July 1982.
99. Quoted in Pearce, *Under the Eagle,* p. 244.
100. Nairn, "Behind the Death Squads," p. 20.
101. Quoted in Berryman, *What's Wrong in Central America,* p. 5.
102. Quoted in Lydia Chavez, "G.I.'s in Salvador: Busy Behind Battle Scenes," *New York Times,* 26 May 1983.
103. Quoted in Bonner, *Weakness and Deceit,* p. 367.
104. Ibid., p. 197.
105. Baloyra, *El Salvador in Transition,* p. 138.
106. Carmen Diana Deere, "Agrarian Reform as Revolution and Counter-Revolution: Nicaragua and El Salvador," in *The Politics of Intervention: The United States in Central America,* ed. Roger Burbach and Patricia Flynn (New York: Monthly Review Press, 1984), pp. 174–75.
107. Herman and Brodhead, *Demonstration Elections,* p. 143.
108. Quoted in Deere, "Agrarian Reform," p. 173; and Bonner, *Weakness and Deceit,* p. 196.
109. See Philip Wheaton, "Agrarian Reform in El Salvador: A Program of Rural Pacification," in *Revolution in Central America,* ed. The Stanford Central America Action Network (Boulder, Colo.: Westview Press, 1983).
110. "Reagan's Address to Congress."
111. Jeane Kirkpatrick, "The Superpowers," p. 185.
112. Bonner, *Weakness and Deceit,* p. 302; Herman and Brodhead, *Demonstration Elections,* pp. 130–33; and Cynthia Arnson, *El Salvador: A Revolution Confronts the United States* (Washington, D.C.: Institute for Policy Studies, 1982), p. 115.
113. Quoted in Herman and Brodhead, *Demonstration Elections,* p. 128.
114. Walter LaFeber, *Inevitable Revolutions: The United States in Central America* (New York: Norton, 1983), p. 287.
115. Arnson, *El Salvador,* p. 86.
116. Ibid., p. 116; and Ungo, "The People's Struggle," p. 55.
117. Lydia Chavez, "Salvadoran Chief Says Main Task Is to Bring Leftist into Elections," *New York Times,* 28 March 1983. The quotation from *Time* is cited in Tom J. Farer, "Manage the Revolution?" *Foreign Policy* 52 (Fall 1983): 102.
118. Quoted in Timothy Garton Ash, "Whose Salvador?" *New Republic,* April 16, 1984, p. 9.

119. Ash, "Back Yards," p. 3.
120. "A Hail of Ballots: Elections and Democracy," *Central America Report* 17 (May/June 1984): 2.
121. Philip Taubman, "CIA Said to Give $1.4 Million to 2 Salvador Parties," *International Herald Tribune,* 14 May 1984.
122. Frank Hammer, "El Salvador: You Call This Justice?" *International Herald Tribune,* 12 December 1984.
123. The case for a similar settlement is well made in Piero Gleijeses, "The Case for Power Sharing in El Salvador," *Foreign Affairs* 61, no. 5 (Summer 1983): 1048–63.
124. Kirkpatrick, "The Superpowers," p. 185.
125. Fred C. Iklé, "US Policy for Central America—Can We Succeed?" in *The Nicaraguan Reader: Documents of a Revolution Under Fire,* ed. Peter Rosset and John Vandermeer (New York: Grove Press, 1983), p. 23.
126. Paul Glickman, "Americans Return to Honduras," *Guardian* (London), 10 August 1984; Paul Ellman, "Reagan Bases Spy Copter in Salvador," *Guardian* (London), 6 April 1984; and Doyle McManus, "US Plan for Air Strikes in Salvador," *Guardian* (London), 14 July 1984.
127. Bonner, *Weakness and Deceit,* p. 11.
128. Quoted in William M. LeoGrande, "A Splendid Little War: Drawing the Line in El Salvador," *International Security* 6, no. 1 (Summer 1981): 27.
129. Robert W. Tucker, "Their Wars, Our Choices," *New Republic,* October 24, 1983, p. 26.

6. Some Notable Victims: (2) Nicaragua

1. Jonathan Steele and Tony Jenkins, "The Slaughter at the Cooperatives," *Guardian* (London), 15 November 1984.
2. Information on U.S. support for the contras is from the following sources: Christopher Thomas, "No Place for Sissies at Camp Nicaragua," *Times* (London), 22 March 1982; "US 'Plot' Against the Sandinistas," *Guardian* (London), 1 November 1982; Paul Ellman, "Argentine Advisers Still Help Honduras," *Observer* (London), 6 March 1983; Alan Riding, "Nicaragua Says Honduran Troops Moved In but Were Driven Back," *New York Times,* 26 March 1983; idem, "A Reporter's Notebook: Nicaraguans Read All About How to Use Grenades," *New York Times,* 31 March 1983; Raymond Bonner and Philip Taubman, "U.S. Ties to Anti-Sandinists Are Reported to Be Extensive," *New York Times,* 3 April 1983; Alex Brummer, "White House Defends Decision on Task Force," *Guardian* (London), 22 July 1983; Jeff Gerth and Philip Taubman, "U.S. Network Arms Rebels in Nicaragua," *International Herald Tribune,* 9 September 1983; Tony Jenkins, "US Rebuff Angers Managua," *Guardian* (London), 1 December 1983; and Richard Alan White, *The Morass: United States Intervention in Central America* (New York: Harper-Colophon Books, 1984), p. 67.
3. Robert Parry, "Nicaragua Rebels Given Warfare Manual by CIA," *International Herald Tribune,* 16 October 1984; and Joel Brinkley, "Nicaragua Rebel Disputes U.S. Aide," *New York Times,* 20 October 1984.
4. Quoted in Joel Brinkley, "Legislators Ask If Reagan Knew of CIA's Role," *New York Times,* 21 October 1984.
5. Christopher Dickey, "Author of Hit Manual Named," *Guardian* (London), 22 October 1984.
6. "Transcript of the Reagan-Mondale Debate on Foreign Policy," *New York Times,* 22 October 1984.

7. Quoted in Brinkley, "Rebel Disputes U.S. Aide."
8. Harold Jackson, "CIA Contradicts Reagan over Nicaragua Contras' Manual," *Guardian* (London), 24 October 1984.
9. Information on the Big Pine exercises is drawn from the following sources: Jonathan Steele, "The Fears Tying Cuba and the Sandinistas," *Guardian* (London), 21 July 1983; Paul Ellman, "Nicaragua Relents Too Late," *Observer* (London), 24 July 1983; Richard Halloran, "Pentagon Reports Encounter at Sea with Soviet Ship," *New York Times,* 4 August 1983; Harold Jackson, "Confusion as Troops Are Detailed for Costa Rica," *Guardian* (London), 15 November 1983; Tony Jenkins, "Nicaraguans Dig In and Prepare for US Invasion," *Guardian* (London), 19 November 1983; Fred Hiatt, "Pentagon Extends Honduras Exercise," *Guardian* (London), 12 January 1984; and Nicholas Ashford, "Hawks Press Reagan to Take Tough Action Against Managua," *Times* (London), 13 November 1984.
10. Quoted in Robert Chesshyre, "How Non-Stick Reagan Frustrates His Critics," *Observer* (London), 15 April 1984.
11. Alex Brummer, "US 'Must Halt Mining,'" *Guardian* (London), 11 May 1984.
12. "CIA 'Confirms It Backs Raids,'" *Guardian* (London), 11 January 1983; "National Security Council Document on Policy in Central America and Cuba," *New York Times,* 7 April 1983.
13. Bernard Gwertzman, "U.S. Refusing to Dispel Impression It Is Helping Anti-Sandinist Forces," *New York Times,* 29 March 1983.
14. Stephen Kinzer, "Honduras Denies Sandinist Charges," *New York Times,* 26 March 1983.
15. "President Reagan's Address to Joint Session of Congress on Central America," *New York Times,* 28 April 1983. Emphasis added.
16. Martin Tolchin, "Report of U.S. Aid for Anti-Sandinist Guerrillas Worrying Senators," *New York Times,* 6 April 1983.
17. Quoted in Francis X. Clines, "Reagan Says U.S. Is Acting Legally over Nicaraguans," *New York Times,* 15 April 1983. Emphasis added.
18. Alex Brummer, "US 'Is Prepared to Remain in Central America,'" *Guardian* (London), 8 August 1983.
19. Joanne Omang, "New U.S. Justification of Covert Role in Nicaragua Set Out by Shultz, Casey," *International Herald Tribune,* 22 September 1983.
20. Quoted in "Panel Cites Fears on Role of Nicaragua," *International Herald Tribune,* 15–16 October 1983.
21. Quoted in Lance Morgan, "US Steps Up Diplomatic Offensive," *Guardian* (London), 1 August 1983.
22. "Transcript of President's News Conference on Foreign and Domestic Matters," *New York Times,* 5 May 1983; and Philip Taubman, "Sandinist Factions at Issue in Hostilities, Reagan Says," *New York Times,* 30 March 1983.
23. "President's News Conference."
24. Ibid.; and Alex Brummer, "Kissinger Takes Top Post for Reagan," *Guardian* (London), 19 July 1983.
25. Tom Wicker, "Shame in Nicaragua," *New York Times,* 1 March 1983; and "A Bad War in Nicaragua," *New York Times,* 30 March 1983.
26. Bernard Gwertzman, "Shultz Buttresses Plea on Salvador," *New York Times,* 16 April 1983; and Paul Ellman, "Contras Respond to Taunts with New Offensive," *Guardian* (London), 22 August 1983.
27. Morton Kondracke, "Nicaraguan 'Freedom Fighter' Pleads for Help," *Chicago Sun-Times,* 9 May 1983.
28. "No to Reagan's War," reprinted in *International Herald Tribune,* 21 October 1983; Bernard Weinraub, "'Many-Sided Dialogue' Asked on Latin Fighting," *New York Times,* 6 April 1983.

29. "The Issue Is Salvador, Not the Alamo," *New York Times,* 29 April 1983.
30. Quoted in Harold Jackson, "Arms Cargo War of Words Rumbles On," *Guardian* (London), 15 November 1984.
31. See "Managua 'Planning Guerrilla Invasion,'" *Guardian* (London), 4 October 1983; and Tony Jenkins, "Managua Fears New Attacks," *Guardian* (London), 26 July 1983.
32. Eldon Kenworthy, "Central America: Beyond the Credibility Trap," *World Policy Journal* 1, no. 1 (Fall 1983): 188.
33. Lieutenant-Colonel John H. Buchanan, "Honduras/Nicaragua: War Without Winners," in *The Nicaragua Reader: Documents of a Revolution Under Fire,* ed. Peter Rosset and John Vandermeer (New York: Grove Press, 1983), pp. 48–57; and Jackson, "Arms Cargo."
34. Walter LaFeber, "Inevitable Revolutions," *Atlantic,* June 1982, p. 78; and Arturo José Cruz, "Nicaragua's Imperiled Revolution," *Foreign Affairs* 61, no. 5 (Summer 1983): 1035.
35. Phillip Berryman, *What's Wrong in Central America and What to Do About It* (Philadelphia: American Friends Service Committee, 1984), p. 36.
36. "Reagan's Address to Congress"; and Marlise Simons, "Sandinist Assails Reagan on Speech," *New York Times,* 29 April 1983.
37. Quoted in Karl Grossman, *Nicaragua: America's New Vietnam?* (New York: The Permanent Press, 1984), pp. 102–3.
38. Richard Fagen, "Revolution and Crisis in Nicaragua," in *Trouble in Our Backyard: Central America and the United States in the Eighties,* ed. Martin Diskin (New York: Pantheon Books, 1983), pp. 136–37 and 145.
39. Stuart Holland, MP, and Donald Anderson, MP, *Kissinger's Kingdom? A Counter-Report on Central America* (Nottingham: Spokesman, 1984), p. 12; and Cruz, "Nicaragua's Imperiled Revolution," p. 1036. Cf. Fagen, "Revolution and Crisis," p. 131.
40. Jonathan Power, *Against Oblivion: Amnesty International's Fight for Human Rights* (Glasgow: Fontana, 1981), p. 122.
41. Ibid.
42. Günter Grass, "America's Backyard," in Diskin, *Trouble in Our Backyard,* p. 247.
43. Ronald Radosh, "Darkening Nicaragua," *New Republic,* October 24, 1983, p. 12.
44. Grossman, *Nicaragua,* p. 104.
45. Quoted in ibid., pp. 106 and 108.
46. Quoted in "Playboy Interview: The Sandinistas," *Playboy,* September 1983, p. 140.
47. See, for example, Grossman, *Nicaragua,* p. 97. Cf. "Atlantic Coast: Miskitu Crisis and Counterrevolution," and Katherine Yih, "Inside a Miskitu Resettlement Camp," both in Rosset and Vandermeer, *The Nicaragua Reader.*
48. Jonathan Steele, "Building National Consciousness in Nicaragua," *Guardian* (London), 15 August 1983.
49. "Nicaragua Expels 10 Foreign Priests After Archbishop Leads Protest March" *International Herald Tribune,* 11 July 1984.
50. Quoted in Grossman, *Nicaragua,* p. 105.
51. Ibid., p. 119. Cf. John Rettie, "Stormy Times for a Revolution Under Seige," *Guardian* (London), 28 October 1982.
52. Rettie, "Stormy Times."
53. See Philip Berryman, "Christians in Sandinista Nicaragua," in *The Religious Roots of Rebellion* (Maryknoll, N.Y.: Orbis, 1984), pp. 273–85; Grossman, *Nicaragua,* pp. 121–22; David Lehmann, "Thanks Be to God and to the Revolution," *London Review of Books,* September 1–14, 1983; "Playboy Interview: The Sandinistas," pp. 140–41; and Robert Leiken, "Nicaragua's Untold Stories," *New Republic,* October 8, 1984, p. 19.

54. John Spicer Nichols, “The Nicaraguan Media: Revolution and Beyond,” in Rosset and Vandermeer, *The Nicaragua Reader,* p. 77.
55. Ibid., p. 78.
56. Ibid., pp. 72–73.
57. Jonathan Steele, “A Revolution That Proved Itself at the Poll,” *Guardian* (London), 7 November 1984.
58. Nichols, “The Nicaraguan Media,” pp. 76 and 79.
59. Holland and Anderson, *Kissinger's Kingdom,* pp. 55.
60. Ibid., p. 10; and Tony Jenkins, “Concern at Nicaragua Opposition Election Pullout,” *Guardian* (London), 31 July 1984.
61. Edward S. Herman and Frank Brodhead, *Demonstration Elections: U.S. Staged Elections in the Dominican Republic, Vietnam, and El Salvador* (Boston: South End Press, 1984), p. 12; and Raymond Bonner, *Weakness and Deceit: U.S. Policy and El Salvador* (New York: Times Books, 1984), pp. 82 and 206.
62. John Pilger, “Butterfly on a Wheel,” *New Statesman* (London), November 11, 1983, p. 16. Robert Leiken's criticisms appeared in the *New Republic,* October 8, 1984. A reply, by Peter Marchetti, can be found in *In These Times,* March 13–19, 1985.
63. Duane Shank, “Nicaragua: The Struggle for Peace,” *Sane World,* November 1982.
64. Fagen, “Revolution and Crisis,” p. 154.
65. Roy Gutman, “Nicaragua: America's Diplomatic Charade,” *Foreign Policy* 56 (Fall 1984): 16.
66. Harold Jackson, “US ‘Plot to Decry’ Nicaraguan Poll,” *Guardian* (London), 7 November 1983.
67. Jonathan Steele, “Conservatives Committed to Contest Nicaraguan Election,” *Guardian* (London), 30 July 1984.
68. Philip Taubman, “Key Aides Dispute U.S. Role in Nicaraguan Vote,” *New York Times,* 21 October 1984.
69. Jenkins, “Concern at Opposition Pullout.”
70. Tony Jenkins, “Political Violence Breaks Out Between Nicaraguan Groups,” *Guardian* (London), 6 August 1984; and idem, “Managua Opposition Out of Poll,” *Guardian* (London), 7 August 1984.
71. Tony Jenkins, “Three Conservative Parties in Nicaragua Lose Political Rights,” *Guardian* (London), 24 August 1984.
72. Tony Jenkins, “Managua Opposition May Join Contras,” *Guardian* (London), 1 October 1984.
73. Quoted in Jenkins, “Concern at Opposition Pullout.”
74. Jonathan Steele and Tony Jenkins, “Nicaraguans Pack the Polling Stations,” *Guardian* (London), 5 November 1984.
75. Steele, “Conservatives Committed to Election.”
76. Ibid.; and Steele and Jenkins, “Nicaraguans Pack the Polling Stations.”
77. Tony Jenkins, “Sandinistas Shadow Box in the No-Contest Ring,” *Guardian* (London), 26 October 1984; Jenkins, “Political Violence Breaks Out”; and Steele and Jenkins, “Nicaraguans Pack the Polling Stations.”
78. Alan Tomlinson, “Nicaragua Party Refused Leave to Quit Election,” *Times* (London), 2 November 1984.
79. “U.S. Panel Calls Nicaraguan Vote Fair,” *International Herald Tribune,* 13 December 1984; Jonathan Steele and Tony Jenkins, “Huge Vote of Confidence for Sandinistas but Conservative Showing a Surprise,” *Guardian* (London), 6 November 1984; and Steele, “A Revolution That Proved Itself.”
80. Quoted in Steele, “A Revolution That Proved Itself.”
81. Tony Jenkins, “Managua Declares Maximum Alert,” *Guardian* (London), 13 November 1984.
82. Steele and Jenkins, “Vote of Confidence for Sandinistas.”

83. Cf. White, *The Morass,* p. 67.
84. Berryman, *What's Wrong,* p. 27.
85. Jonathan Steele, "Ortega Ready for Indefinite Alert," *Guardian* (London), 14 November 1984.
86. White, *The Morass,* p. 57.
87. Jonathan Evan Maslow, "Regional Pawn," *Atlantic,* June 1984, p. 40.
88. Steele and Jenkins, "The Slaughter at the Cooperatives."
89. See, for example, Grossman, *Nicaragua,* pp. 108, 191, and 204–5; Tony Jenkins, "Nicaraguan Peasants 'Massacred,'" *Guardian* (London), 12 August 1983; and idem, "Terror Band Blows Up Bridge," *Guardian* (London), 13 August 1983.
90. "Sorting Out a High-Stakes Game," *Time,* April 23, 1984, p. 15.
91. Quoted in Tony Jenkins, "Honduran Vessels Skirmish in Nicaraguan Waters," *Guardian* (London), 22 July 1983.
92. Fred C. Iklé, "US Policy for Central America—Can We Succeed?" in Rosset and Vandermeer, *The Nicaragua Reader,* p. 25.
93. See "Stage Is Set for Contras' Big Attack," *Guardian Weekly,* 14 August 1983; and Bonner and Taubman, "U.S. Ties to Anti-Sandinists."
94. Gutman, "Nicaragua," p. 12.
95. Kenworthy, "Central America," p. 191, citing "In Search of Results," *Washington Report on the Hemisphere,* 23 August 1983.
96. Kenneth E. Sharpe and Martin Diskin, "Facing Facts in El Salvador: Reconciliation or War," *World Policy Journal* 1, no. 3 (Spring 1984): 542–3; and Tony Jenkins, "Nicaragua Winning Support as US Policy Founders," *Guardian* (London), 20 December 1983.
97. Tony Jenkins, "Nicaraguans Thrown Off Balance," *Guardian* (London), 12 December 1983; and Grossman, *Nicaragua,* pp. 108–11.
98. Harold Jackson, "Nicaraguan Envoy Refused Visa for Washington Talks," *Guardian* (London), 30 November 1983.
99. See Berryman, *What's Wrong,* pp. 4 and 42.
100. Quoted in Gutman, "Nicaragua," p. 22.
101. Paul Ellman, "Europe Backs Contadora Plan," *Guardian* (London), 1 October 1984; and Jonathan Steele, "Salvador Echoes US Refusal to Sign Contadora Treaty," *Guardian* (London), 5 October 1984.
102. Quoted in Jackson, "US 'Plot to Decry' Nicaragua Poll."
103. "Heavy Shelling Marks Debate on Central America," *The New York Times,* 17 April 1983; and "Reagan's Address to Congress."
104. Gutman, "Nicaragua," pp. 7–8.
105. Ibid., pp. 3–4.
106. "Shultz, Initiating Talks in Nicaragua, Outlines Concern Over Policies," *International Herald Tribune,* 4 June 1984; Gutman, "Nicaragua," p. 20; Philip Geyelin, "Take-Your-Pick Policy on Central America," *International Herald Tribune,* 9–10 June 1984; and John M. Goshko and Joanne Omang, "U.S. Officials Said to Be Split on Nicaragua Policy," *International Herald Tribune,* 9 July 1984.
107. Doyle McManus and Don Shannon, "Ortega Says U.S. Talks Hit Snag but Could Still Forestall a War," *International Herald Tribune,* 5 October 1984.
108. Jeane Kirkpatrick, "Human Rights in El Salvador," in *The Reagan Phenomenon and Other Speeches on Foreign Policy* (Washington D.C.: American Enterprise Institute, 1983), pp. 58–59. Cf. *The Report of the President's National Bipartisan Commission on Central America* (New York: Macmillan, 1984), p. 104.
109. Jeane Kirkpatrick, "Nicaragua and Her Neighbors," in *The Reagan Phenomenon,* p. 184.
110. "Nicaraguan Oil Port Wrecked in Rebel Raid," *Guardian* (London), 13 October 1983.

111. Paul Ellman and Alex Brummer, "CIA 'Aids Saboteurs to Cripple Managua Economy,'" *Guardian* (London), 17 October 1983; "House Rejects Aid to Rebels in Nicaragua," *International Herald Tribune,* 21 October 1983.
112. Jenkins, "Honduran Vessels Skirmish in Nicaraguan Waters."
113. Tony Jenkins, "Port Peril May Hit Nicaragua Economy," *Guardian* (London), 5 March 1984.
114. See Harold Jackson, "US and Mexico Clash on Cause of Region's Crisis," *Guardian* (London), 16 August 1983; Jonathan Steele, "Contra Contra Moves," *Guardian* (London), 21 February 1984; and Tony Jenkins, "War Damage Forces Nicaraguan Price Explosion," *Guardian* (London), 30 May 1984.
115. Walter LaFeber, *Inevitable Revolutions: The United States in Central America* (New York: Norton, 1983), p. 294.
116. Holland and Anderson, *Kissinger's Kingdom,* pp. 62–63; White, *The Morass,* p. 194; and Jenkins, "War Damage Forces Price Explosion."
117. See Piero Gleijeses, "Nicaragua: Resist Romanticism," *Foreign Policy* 54 (Spring 1984).
118. Quoted in R. Gregory Nokes, "Shultz Says America Will Not Send Troops to Topple Sandinistas," *Chattanooga Times* (Tennessee), 8 August 1983.
119. Geoffrey Lean, "Britain and US Blocked Famine Aid," *Observer* (London), 28 October 1984.
120. See Bonner and Taubman, "U.S. Ties to Anti-Sandinists."
121. Alex Brummer, "Reagan Goes on TV to Justify Task Force," *Guardian* (London), 27 July 1983.
122. Ibid.
123. Robert E. White, "Perilous Latin Policy," *New York Times,* 2 May 1983.
124. Phil Gunson, "US Military 'Is Planning to Stay' in Honduras," *Guardian* (London), 7 February 1984; and Fred Hiatt, "Pentagon Extends Honduras Exercise," *Guardian* (London), 12 January 1984.
125. "American 'Secret Plan of Attack' Leaked," *Guardian* (London), 19 November 1983.
126. Quoted in Harold Jackson, "US Says Mines Operation Goes On," *Guardian* (London), 9 April 1984.
127. Fred Hiatt, "U.S. Conservatives Increase Aid to Nicaragua Rebels," *International Herald Tribune,* 11 December 1984; and Philip Taubman, "Nicaragua Victims Tied to Recruiting," *New York Times,* 4 September 1984.
128. Quoted in Grossman, *Nicaragua,* p. 179.
129. Stansfield Turner, "Why the CIA Should Pull Out of Nicaragua," *Manchester Guardian Weekly,* 1 May 1983.
130. "Remember the Mine," *New Republic,* May 7, 1984, p. 7.
131. Turner, "Why the CIA Should Pull Out," Emphasis added.
132. Alex Brummer, "Reagan's Covert CIA Support for Contras Wins First Test," *Guardian* (London), 29 July 1983.

7. Some Notable Victims: (3) Grenada

1. See "Thatcher Snubbed over Grenada," *Guardian* (London), 26 October 1983; and Harold Jackson, "Gunboat Diplomacy Attack on Reagan Opens Rift in US," *Guardian* (London), 29 October 1983.
2. Quoted in Harold Jackson, "Shultz Promises US Troops Will Pull Out Promptly, but Caribbean Units to Stay On," *Guardian* (London), 26 October 1983.
3. Victoria Brittain and Dan Sewell, "Cubans Fall Back After a Fight," *Guardian* (London), 26 October 1983; and Eldon Kenworthy, "Grenada as Theater," *World Policy Journal* 1, no. 3 (Spring 1984): 637.

4. Quoted in Don Bonker, "Fact-Finding in Grenada: The Misgivings Persist," *International Herald Tribune,* 14 November 1983; Hugh O'Shaughnessy, *Grenada: Revolution, Invasion and Aftermath* (London: Sphere Books, 1984), p. 165; and Anthony Payne, Paul Sutton, and Tony Thorndike, *Grenada: Revolution and Invasion* (London: Croom Helm, 1984), p. 155.
5. Quoted in Robert Pastor, "When the Most Powerful Nation Attacks One of the Weakest," *International Herald Tribune,* 28 October 1983.
6. O'Shaughnessy, *Grenada,* p. 165.
7. Quoted in Harold Jackson, "Shift of Ground on Motive for Attack," *Guardian* (London), 28 October, 1983.
8. Duane Shank, "'Operation Urgent Fury'—The Empire Strikes Back," *Sane World,* December 1983; and "D-Day in Grenada," *Time,* November 7, 1983, p. 20.
9. Brittain and Sewell, "Cubans Fall Back"; Shank, "'Operation Urgent Fury'"; and Claudia Wright, "Tell That to the Marines," *New Statesman* (London), November 4, 1983, p. 12.
10. The quotations from Reagan and *Newsweek* are both in O'Shaughnessy, *Grenada,* pp. 174 and 213.
11. See Shank, "'Operation Urgent Fury;'" Richard J. Barnet, "The Empire Strikes Back," *Progressive,* January 1984; O'Shaughnessy, *Grenada,* p. 168; and Fitzroy Ambursley and James Dunkerley, *Grenada: Whose Freedom?* (London: Latin America Bureau, 1984), p. 84.
12. Bonker, "Fact-finding in Grenada."
13. Ibid.
14. Quoted in "US Admits Bombing Grenadian Mental Hospital in Error," *Guardian* (London), 1 November 1983.
15. "D-Day in Grenada," p. 20.
16. Jonathan Steele, "The Corrosive Effect of the Cuban Obsession," *Guardian* (London), 25 November 1983; and Ambursley and Dunkerley, *Grenada,* p. 92.
17. Alex Brummer, "High Grenada Toll May Embarrass Reagan," *Guardian* (London), 10 November 1983.
18. Victoria Brittain, "Deaths in Grenada 'May Reach 1,000,'" *Guardian* (London), 8 November 1983; and Tony Benn, *Guardian* (London), 7 November 1983.
19. Jackson, "Shultz Promises US Troops Will Pull Out Promptly."
20. Ambursley and Dunkerley, *Grenada,* p. 83; O'Shaughnessy, *Grenada,* p. 159; and Payne, Sutton, and Thorndike, *Grenada,*p. 156.
21. Quoted in Payne, Sutton, and Thorndike, *Grenada,* p. 64.
22. Andrew A. Reding, "Backing Democracy and Development," *World Policy Journal* 1, no. 3 (Spring 1984): 660.
23. Quoted in "Weighing the Proper Role," *Time,* November 7, 1983, p. 38.
24. O'Shaughnessy, *Grenada,* p. 203.
25. Kenworthy, "Grenada as Theater," p. 636.
26. Lou Cannon, "Cubans Were Told More," *International Herald Tribune,* 9 January 1984.
27. I. F. Stone, "Whose Side Is the General On?" *International Herald Tribune,* 9 January 1984.
28. Quoted in Colin Brown, "Howe Refuses to Condemn US for Breach of the Law," *Guardian* (London), 27 October 1983. Also see Jonathan Rosenblum, "Grenadian Dilemmas," *New Republic,* January 9 and 16, 1984; "Tight Security Measures, Ban on Public Meetings Is Imposed," *International Herald Tribune,* 11 November 1983; Victoria Brittain, "US Occupation Force Will Stay at Least Six Months," *Guardian* (London), 5 November 1983; and Jonathan Steele, "Grenada Captives Held in 'Crates,'" *Guardian* (London), 14 November 1983.
29. Jonathan Steele, "US Broadcasts Told Grenadians Britain Backed the Invasion," *Guardian* (London), 16 November 1983.

30. Rosenblum, "Grenadian Dilemmas," p. 15.
31. Steele, "The Cuban Obsession."
32. Rosenblum, "Grenadian Dilemmas," p. 15.
33. Quoted in "Reagan Says Action in Grenada Is Over, Withdrawal Will Begin," *International Herald Tribune,* 4 November 1983.
34. Quoted in "Trouble Spots 'Linked,'" *Guardian* (London), 29 October 1983.
35. Jonathan Steele, "US Planned Action When Bishop Died," *Guardian* (London), 25 January 1984; and O'Shaughnessy,*Grenada,* pp. 8, 153, and 207.
36. Kenworthy, "Grenada as Theater," p. 644; and Tony Gilbert and Chris Searle, *Global Aggression: The Consistent Pattern of United States Foreign Policy* (London: Liberation, 1984), p. 47.
37. Nigel Hawkes et al., "Why Washington Lied," *Observer* (London), 30 October 1983. Cf. Shank, "'Operation Urgent Fury'"; Kenworthy, "Grenada as Theater," p. 639; and Ambursley and Dunkerley, *Grenada,* p. 81.
38. Richard J. Barnet, *Intervention and Revolution: The United States in the Third World* (New York: Meridian, 1980), pp. 140–41.
39. Hawkes et al., "Why Washington Lied."
40. On the illegality of the invasion under international law, see the letter "The Way to Control Reagan's Outlaw Leanings," by Professor Francis A. Boyle et al., *Guardian* (London), 29 November 1983.
41. "Weighing the Proper Role," p. 30.
42. Quoted in Robert Chesshyre, "Reagan's Final Screen Test," *Observer* (London), 21 October 1984.
43. Quoted in Bernard D. Nossiter, "Nicaragua and U.S. Disagree at U.N.," *New York Times,* 10 May 1983.
44. Anthony Lewis, "In Grenada, U.S. Sullied Its Character, Legitimacy," *International Herald Tribune,* 28 October 1983.
45. Jeane Kirkpatrick, "Central America: Sandino Betrayed I," in *The Reagan Phenomenon and Other Speeches on Foreign Policy* (Washington, D.C.: American Enterprise Institute, 1983), p. 194.
46. Quoted in Jane Rosen, "Governor General 'In Aid Appeal,'" *Guardian* (London), 27 October 1983.
47. "American Foreign Policy in a Cold Climate," *Encounter,* November 1983, pp. 10, 25, and 32.
48. Alex Brummer, "Scoon Tells of Rescue by Paras," *Guardian* (London), 1 November 1983.
49. Ian Aitken and Martin Wainwright, "Hurt Thatcher Widens Breach with Reagan," *Guardian* (London), 31 October 1983; and Ambursley and Dunkerley, *Grenada,* p. 87.
50. Alan George, "Did Washington Ghost-Write Scoon's Appeal?" *New Statesman* (London), November 11, 1983.
51. Ibid.
52. Ibid. Cf. Patrick Keatley, "Governor Had Right to Call in Troops, Britain Concedes," *Guardian* (London), 28 October 1983.
53. Payne, Sutton, and Thorndike, *Grenada,* pp. 181–82; and Kenworthy, "Grenada as Theater," p. 646.
54. "Washington Seeks Talks with Scoon on Peace Force," *Guardian* (London), 1 November 1983.
55. Quoted in "Operation Grenada: How the World's Press Reacted," *Guardian* (London), 27 October 1983.
56. Quoted in "Trouble Spots 'Linked'"; and Jackson, "Gunboat Diplomacy."
57. "President's Speech on Military Spending and a New Defense," *New York Times,* 24 March 1983.
58. "Trouble Spots 'Linked'"; and "D-Day in Grenada," p. 19.
59. "D-Day in Grenada," p. 13.

60. "A Scalpel, Not a Club," reprinted in the *International Herald Tribune,* 31 October 1983.
61. William Safire, "A Well-Conceived Operation in Response to a Real Threat," *International Herald Tribune,* 28 October 1983.
62. Shank, "'Operation Urgent Fury'"; Fred Hiatt and David Hoffman, "U.S. Military Reduces Estimate of Cubans on Grenada to About 750," *International Herald Tribune,* 31 October 1983; Noll Scott, "Wounded Cubans Delayed," *Guardian* (London), 1 November 1983; and Philip Taubman, "Broad Charges, Lack of Documentation on Grenada Raise Doubts on U.S. Credibility," *International Herald Tribune,* 3 November 1983.
63. Payne, Sutton, and Thorndike, *Grenada,* p. 162.
64. Shank, "'Operation Urgent Fury.'"
65. "President's Speech on Military Spending."
66. "A Pathetic Little War," reprinted in the *International Herald Tribune,* 3 November 1983.
67. Michael Massing, "Grenada Before and After," *Atlantic,* February 1984, p. 82.
68. "Plessey to Stay at New Airport," *Guardian* (London), 31 October 1983; and Anne McHardy, "Airport 'Only for Civil Use,'" *Guardian* (London), 2 November 1983.
69. Greg Chamberlain, "Army Killing Goes On in Grenada," *Guardian* (London), 22 October 1983; and Keatley, "Governor Had Right to Call Troops."
70. Jonathan Steele, "The Key Questions About the Cuban Presence," *Guardian* (London), 29 October 1983.
71. On the 1966 Dominican election, see Edward S. Herman and Frank Brodhead, *Demonstration Elections: U.S.-Staged Elections in The Dominican Republic, Vietnam, and El Salvador* (Boston: South End Press, 1984), chap. 2.
72. Quoted in Barnet, *Intervention and Revolution,* pp. 200, 202. Cf. Thomas M. Franck and Edward Weisband, *Word Politics: Verbal Strategy Among the Superpowers* (New York: Oxford University Press, 1972), p. 74.
73. Quoted in Franck and Weisband, *Word Politics,* p. 76.
74. Ibid.
75. Ibid., p. 93.
76. Ibid., p. 76.
77. Ibid., p. 79.
78. Ibid.
79. Quoted in Wright, "Tell That to the Marines," p. 12.
80. Harold Jackson, "Jackson Gets a Pat on the Back," *Guardian* (London), 5 January 1984.
81. Harold Jackson, "Polls Show Leap Forward in Reagan's Popularity" *Guardian* (London), 10 November 1983.
82. Quoted in Robert Chesshyre, "America Revels in Hour of Glory," *Observer* (London), 30 October 1983.
83. "Weighing the Proper Role," p. 30.
84. Ibid., p. 34.
85. Safire, "A Well-Conceived Operation."
86. *Times* (London), 31 March 1984.
87. Steele, "The Cuban Obsession."
88. Quoted in "President Castro Bitterly Mourns Cuban Workers Killed in Grenada," *Guardian* (London), 19 November 1983.
89. Quoted in Massing, "Grenada," p. 87.
90. Ibid., p. 81; Greg Chamberlain, "Bishop: A Salesman for New Socialism," *Guardian* (London), 21 November 1983; and Jeremy Taylor, "Grenada: Defiance After US Snub," *Times* (London), 13 March 1982.
91. Ambursley and Dunkerley, *Grenada,* p. 47.

92. Taylor, "Grenada."
93. Quoted in Michael Klare, "The Reagan Doctrine," *New Statesman* (London), November 4, 1983; see also Massing, "Grenada," pp. 81–82; Taylor, "Grenada"; Payne, Sutton, and Thorndike, *Grenada,* pp. 65–66; and Kenworthy, "Grenada as Theater," pp. 644–45.
94. Massing, "Grenada," p. 83; Chamberlain, "Bishop"; Payne, Sutton, and Thorndike, *Grenada,*p. 67; and Ambursley and Dunkerley, *Grenada,* pp. 51–52.
95. "Grenada Expels Cuban, Libyan, Soviet Envoys," *International Herald Tribune,* 3 November 1983; Loren Jenkins, "Grenada Grinds to Near Standstill," *Guardian* (London), 21 November 1983.
96. Alex Brummer, "Grenadian Refugee Detained in US," *Guardian* (London), 27 October 1984; and Greg Chamberlain, "Gairy Believes He May Face Murder Trial," *Guardian* (London), 24 April 1984.
97. Richard Hall et al., "Queen's Man Asks for Help in Grenada," *Observer* (London), 30 October 1983.
98. Loren Jenkins, "New Regime in Grenada Seen to Have Little Power," *International Herald Tribune,* 22 November 1983.
99. Payne, Sutton, and Thorndike, *Grenada,* p. 186.
100. Massing, "Grenada," pp. 79–80.
101. Hugh O'Shaughnessy, "Grenadians Have Second Thoughts About 'Rescuers,'" *Observer* (London), 18 December 1983.
102. Greg Chamberlain, "Grenada's Love-Hate Affair with the US," *Guardian* (London), 12 June 1984.
103. Quoted in Ambursley and Dunkerley, *Grenada,* p. 102; see also Joseph B. Treaster, "Grenada Interim Regime Is Returning Businesses, Land to Private Ownership," *International Herald Tribune,* 30 July 1984.
104. Reding, "Backing Democracy and Development," p. 656.
105. Greg Chamberlain, "Grenada Poll Haunted By Ghosts of Violent Past," *Guardian* (London), 3 December 1984; idem, "Reagan Favourite Sweeps Grenada," *Guardian* (London), 5 December 1984; and "Blaize the American Way," *Guardian* (London), 5 December 1984. The quotation from the U.S. Information Service is from Payne, Sutton, and Thorndike, *Grenada,* p. 188.
106. Bernard Gwertzman, "Aides Say Reagan Feared Potential Soviet Outpost in Grenada," *International Herald Tribune,* 27 October 1983.
107. Quoted in "Weighing the Proper Role," p. 35.
108. Jane Rosen, "Big Majority to Condemn Invasion," *Guardian* (London), 4 November 1983; and Jonathan Steele, "Latin America Unites in Hostility," *Guardian* (London), 31 October 1983.
109. Jackson, "Reagan Declares Hostilities Over."
110. Barnet, "The Empire Strikes Back."
111. John Stuart Mill, "A Few Words on Non-Intervention," in *Dissertations and Discussions: Political, Philosophical, and Historical,* vol. 3 (London, 1875), pp. 153–78.
112. O'Shaughnessy, *Grenada,* p. 220.

8. The New Cold War and the Prospects for Peace

1. Quoted in Robert Scheer, *With Enough Shovels: Reagan, Bush, and Nuclear War* (New York: Random House, 1982), pp. 241 and 254.
2. Quoted in Murray Marder, "Maybe Andropov, Too, Believes His Own Rhetoric," *International Herald Tribune,* 4 October 1983.
3. Quoted in David Shears, "Communism 'Focus of Evil in the World,' Says Reagan," *Daily Telegraph* (London), 9 March 1983.

4. Quoted in Harold Jackson, "Kremlin Has Twisted Facts—Reagan," *Guardian* (London), 3 September 1983; "Reagan Says Moscow Committed 'Act of Brutality,'" *Guardian* (London), 5 September 1983; and "Reagan: Crime Against Humanity Must Never Be Forgotten," *Guardian* (London), 7 September 1983.
5. Quoted in Francis X. Clines, "Reagan Cites KAL Jet in Arguing for Buildup," *International Herald Tribune,* 22 September 1983.
6. Alex Brummer, "Outrage Over Jet Propels Arms Bill," *Guardian* (London), 17 September 1983; and Harold Jackson, "House Gives Reagan MX Go-Ahead," *Guardian* (London), 3 November 1983.
7. Paul Ellman, "Reagan Steps Up the Pressure," *Guardian* (London), 3 October 1983; Adam Clymer, "Doubts Seen in U.S. over Facts on 747," *International Herald Tribune,* 17–18 September 1983; and Hella Pick, "Mr. Reagan's Cold Front," *Guardian* (London), 20 September 1983.
8. Quoted in Bernard Gwertzman, "Downing of Jet a Year Ago Said to Lead to U.S. Gains," *New York Times,* 31 August 1984.
9. Quoted in ibid.
10. Reported in Robert Chesshyre, "Reagan Roars Like a Lion but Keeps His Cool," *Observer* (London), 11 September 1983; "Anger Is Not a Policy," *International Herald Tribune,* 24 September 1983; and "Turning On the Heat," *Time,* September 19, 1983, p. 8.
11. Clymer, "Doubts Seen in U.S."
12. Harold Jackson, "US Spy Plane Was Near Area of Jet Attack," *Guardian* (London), 5 September 1983.
13. Robert Chesshyre et al., "Why West Failed to Warn Korean Jumbo of Danger," *Observer* (London), 11 September 1983; and Stephen F. Cohen, "Once Again, a Lethal Coup de Théatre," *International Herald Tribune,* 11 October 1983.
14. Quoted in Jackson, "US Spy Plane Was Near Area of Attack."
15. Quoted in "Kremlin Confirms Shooting Down Jet," *Guardian* (London), 7 September 1983.
16. Quoted in David Fairhall et al., "Kremlin Not Told Before Attack on Airliner," *Guardian* (London), 10 September 1983.
17. Andrew Wilson, "British Experts Radar Clue to Flight 007 Riddle," *Observer* (London), 17 June 1984; and William J. Broad and Philip Taubman, "Flight 007: Many Questions Remain a Year After the Incident," *New York Times,* 1 September 1984.
18. Richard Rohmer, *Massacre 007: The Story of the Korean Air Lines Disaster* (London: Coronet Books, 1984), pp. 60, 62–63, and 193–201.
19. Rohmer's theory has been effectively criticized in R. W. Johnson, "Licensed to Kill," *New Society* (London), August 23, 1984, p. 172.
20. "US 'Could Have Averted' Korean Tragedy," *Guardian* (London), 15 September 1983.
21. Keppel's Theories are discussed in Peter McGill, "Messages from Korean Jumbo 'Were Fakes,'" *Observer* (London), 5 August 1984.
22. Rohmer, *Massacre 007,* pp. 130 and 135.
23. Johnson, "Licensed to Kill," p. 172.
24. The reconstruction of events on September 1 is based on the following sources: "US 'Could Have Averted' Tragedy"; Chesshyre et al., "Why West Failed"; Alexander Brummer, "'Pilot Didn't Know Jet Was Civilian,'" *Guardian* (London), 8 October 1983; David Shribman, "U.S. Experts Now Say Russians Misidentified Korean Jetliner," *International Herald Tribune,* 8–9 October 1983; William Pfaff, "A Propaganda War That Both Sides Lose," *International Herald Tribune,* 13 October 1983; Cohen, "Once Again"; Stephen S. Rosenfeld, "Foreign Policy in an Abusive Debate Mode," *International Herald Tribune,* 25 October 1983; Murray Sayle, "The Inevitable Shootdown," *Sunday Times* (London), 27 May 1984; and Rohmer, *Massacre 007*.

25. "Explaining the Inexplicable," *Time,* September 19, 1983.
26. On the destruction of the Libyan airliner, see Noam Chomsky, *Towards a New Cold War: Essays on the Current Crisis and How We Got There* (New York: Pantheon, 1982), p. 48; Robert Scheer, "How a Democratic Society Handled it," *International Herald Tribune,* 19 September 1983; and "Murder in the Sky," *Observer* (London), 4 September 1983.
27. Quoted in Hedrick Smith, "Ties Between U.S. and Soviet Viewed as at Low Point," *New York Times,* 24 May 1983.
28. "Kennan Questions U.S. View of Soviet," *New York Times,* 18 May 1983.
29. "Moscow's Hard Line," *Time,* June 25, 1984, p. 10.
30. Dusko Doder, "Dark Clouds Mushroom over Moscow," *Guardian* (London), 20 October 1983.
31. See Leslie H. Gelb, "Soviet Stance Raises Concern," *International Herald Tribune,* 30 September 1983; Raymond L. Garthoff, "The Dangerous Tension Between U.S. and Russia," *International Herald Tribune,* 8 November 1983.
32. Garthoff, "The Dangerous Tension."
33. Seweryn Bialer, "Danger in Moscow, *New York Review of Books,* February 16, 1984, pp. 6 and 7.
34. Patricia Clough, "Street Battles Rage as Reagan Speaks," *Times* (London), 12 June 1982.
35. George Kennan, "On Nuclear War," *New York Review of Books,* January 21, 1982, p. 10.
36. Bialer, "Danger in Moscow," p. 6.
37. "On the Edge of a New Cold War," *Guardian* (London), 30 September 1983.
38. Quoted in Strobe Talbott, *The Russians and Reagan* (New York: Vintage Books, 1984), pp. 131 and 136. The full text of Reagan's speech is reprinted as an appendix.
39. Ibid., p. 140.
40. See the *New York Times* editorial, "Upstairs to Arms Control," reprinted in the *International Herald Tribune,* 14 December 1984.
41. Quoted in Harold Jackson, "Congress to Hear List of Soviet Arms Violations," *Guardian* (London), 30 November 1984.
42. Quoted in ibid.
43. Richard Falk, "After the Reagan Landslide," *END* 13 (December 1984–January 1985): 9.
44. Quoted in Alex Brummer, "America Basks in Superdollar Glory," *Guardian* (London), 19 September 1984.

Appendix

1. *The Report of the President's National Bipartisan Commission on Central America* (New York: Macmillan, 1984), p. vii.
2. Seymour M. Hersh, *The Price of Power: Henry Kissinger in the Nixon White House* (New York: Summit Books, 1983).
3. Ibid., p. 263.
4. Quoted in Richard Alan White, *The Morass: United States Intervention in Central America* (New York: Harper-Colophon Books, 1984), p. 251.
5. *Report of the President's Commission,* p. 14.
6. Ibid., p. 10.
7. Ibid., pp. 10–11.
8. Ibid., p. 15.
9. Ibid., p. 41.
10. Ibid.
11. Ibid., p. 24.

12. Ibid., pp. 44–45.
13. Jenny Pearce, *Under the Eagle: U.S. Intervention in Central America and the Caribbean* (London: Latin America Bureau, 1982). The quotations from Taft, Olds, and Butler are on pages 17, 19, and 20, respectively.
14. Walter LaFeber, *Inevitable Revolutions: The United States in Central America* (New York: Norton, 1983).
15. Pearce, *Under the Eagle,* pp. 6–7.
16. PACCA (Policy Alternatives for the Caribbean and Central America), *Changing Course: Blueprint for Peace in Central America and the Caribbean* (Washington, D.C.: Institute for Policy Studies, 1984), p. 19, citing Dean Rusk, "Instances of the Use of United States Armed Forces Abroad, 1798–1945," Hearing before the Committee on Foreign Relations and the Committee on Armed Services, 87th Congress, 2nd Session, September 17, 1962.
17. *Report of the President's Commission,* p. 44.
18. Quoted in Pearce, *Under the Eagle,* p. 19.
19. *Report of the President's Commission,* p. 101.
20. Ibid., p. 34, Cf. p. 113.
21. Ibid., p. 113.
22. Ibid.
23. Ibid., pp. 34 and 101–2.
24. Ibid., pp. 34, 116, and 120.
25. Ibid., p. 35.
26. Quoted in White, *The Morass,* p. 105.
27. *Report of the President's Commission,* p. 35.
28. Ibid., p. 111. Emphasis added.
29. Ibid., p. 113.
30. Ibid.
31. Ibid., p. 119. Cf. p. 37.
32. Ibid., pp. 36–37.
33. Ibid., p. 90.
34. Karl Grossman, *Nicaragua: America's New Vietnam?* (New York: The Permanent Press, 1984), p. 106; and *Changing Course,* p. 16, n. 2.
35. *Report of the President's Commission,* p. 5.
36. White, *The Morass,* pp. 16–39.
37. Ibid., p. 16.
38. Ibid., p. 17.
39. *Report of the President's Commission,* pp. 104 and 105. Emphasis added. Cf. pp. 99 and 100.
40. Ibid., pp. 113–14. Emphasis added. Cf. p. 121.
41. Ibid., p. 123.
42. Ibid., p. 102.
43. Ibid., p. 86.
44. Ibid., p. 87.
45. Ibid., p. 122.
46. Ibid., p. 124.
47. Ibid., p. 156.
48. Ibid., p. 110.
49. Ibid., p. 109.
50. Ibid., p. 16.
51. William M. LeoGrande, "Through the Looking Glass: The Kissinger Report on Central America," *World Policy Journal* 1, no. 2 (Winter 1984): 259.
52. *Report of the President's Commission,* p. 32.
53. For a review of U.S.-sponsored terrorist attacks against Cuba, see Noam Chomsky, *Towards a New Cold War: Essays on the Current Crisis and How We Got*

There (New York: Pantheon, 1982), pp. 48–50; and Edward S. Herman, *The* Real *Terror Network* (Boston: South End Press, 1982), pp. 65–69.

54. *Report of the President's Commission,* p. 104.
55. LeoGrande, "Through the Looking Glass," p. 259.
56. *Report of the President's Commission,* p. 104.
57. Ibid., p. 119.
58. Ibid., pp. 14, 100, and 127–28.
59. LeoGrande, "Through the Looking Glass," p. 268.
60. *Report of the President's Commission,* p. 111.
61 Ibid.
62. Robert W. Tucker, "The Purposes of American Power," *Foreign Affairs* 59, no. 2 (Winter 1980/81): 270–1.

Index